THE PLAYFUL REVOLUTION

Drama and Performance Studies

Timothy Wiles, general editor

THE
PLAYFUL
REVOLUTION

Theatre and Liberation in Asia

EUGÈNE VAN ERVEN

INDIANA UNIVERSITY PRESS

Bloomington and Indianapolis

Library of Congress Cataloging-in-Publication Data
Van Erven, Eugène.
The playful revolution / theatre and liberation in Asia / Eugène
van Erven.
p.   cm.—(Drama and performance studies)
Includes bibliographical references and index.
ISBN 0-253-36204-0 (alk. paper) ; ISBN 0-253-20729-0 (pbk.)
1. Theater—Political aspects—Asia, Southeastern.   2. Theater—
Political aspects—South Asia.   I. Title.   II. Series.
PN2860.V36   1992
792'.095—dc20   91-23369
1 2 3 4 5 96 95 94 93 92

To Safdar Hashmi and all the other Asian artists who were killed in action on the stages of the theatre of liberation

The great leaders of the human race are those who have awakened man from his half slumber. The great enemies of humanity are those who put it to sleep, and it does not matter whether their sleeping potion is the worship of God or that of the Golden Calf.

Erich Fromm, *Beyond the Chains of Illusion*

Song of the night, War of the Flea,
Deep inside the jungle you will find me.
War of the small, War of the Flea,
Where the strongest bomb is human,
Who is bursting to be free.

Anonymous, Amerasian liberation song

CONTENTS

LIST OF ILLUSTRATIONS

PREFACE

This book is somewhat of a hybrid, just like its subject and its author. It aspires to operate on several different levels. It pretends to be a serious and informative book on a hitherto relatively unexplored subject: the contemporary political theatre in Asia. As such it is interdisciplinary: it crosses freely between politics, popular culture, and high art which themselves, in their Asian manifestations, have not been immune to manifold extra-Asian influences, both before and after the official colonization period ended. But the following pages are far from being mere neutral analyses of so-called objectively gathered data. As my investigations evolved from tentative, curious letters written in 1985 to full-fledged research "in the field" by January 1986, I suddenly found myself in the middle of an enormous adventure, with no idea where or when it would end. I opted not to exclude that more personal dimension from this book, not because I think my experiences were so unusual but because I wanted my eyes to become the reader's in an attempt to convey as many aspects of this fascinating Asian phenomenon as possible.

The contemporary Asian political theatre resists dry, analytical observation because it is the people, their passions, their deaths, their hopes, their anger, their fears, and their aspirations that make it tick. It varies from place to place, from region to region, and from country to country, blending with ocher and incense here and blood-curdling screams in the middle of the night there. Physically speaking, it is nothing more than humans in motion on a bamboo stage, vibrating vocal chords, a few tunes on a tabla or a stringed instrument, and papier-mâché props. Yet its impact is so powerful that fascist soldiers and their superiors regularly feel obliged to silence its practitioners with guns, machetes, and boots. Hence this book is the account of a personal journey through Asia; a written documentary of a quest to find political theatre that really works and which possesses a vitality and passion that the contemporary Western theatre seems to have lost somewhere between the Delano grapefields of California and the newly retiled toilet of the Cartoucherie in Paris. It is a tribute to the work of thousands of Asian theatre practitioners even if it does not shy away from criticizing them on occasion.

This book can be regarded as a sequel to my *Radical People's Theatre* (Indiana University Press, 1988), in which I attempted to trace the roots and the rise and fall of the popular political theatre movement in the West in the period from 1965 to 1985. In its conclusion, written upon my return from my second trip to Asia, I argued that radical theatre in the West had gone into an unstoppable decline because it had been affected by subtle, irreversible cooptation mechanisms, but that it could possibly derive renewed inspiration from an exciting new political theatre movement that was beginning to develop in several Asian countries. I also claimed that Western political theatre practitioners had failed to incorporate two life-saving ingredients into their work: international networking and the emphasis on theatre as a socio-political and creative process rather than as an aesthetic product. Now, five years after my first visit to Asia and almost four years after writing that conclusion to *Radical People's Theatre,* the time has come to present and evaluate the achievements of twenty-five years of Asian political theatre in the hope that it may benefit both people in Asia and readers elsewhere in the world.

In the midst of widespread euphoria about the defeat of Eastblock Communism and the imminent dismantling of Apartheid, it is high time to redirect our attention to the third world, where greedy power wielders—with the conscious financial and military support of the first and second world—still force three quarters of the world's population to "live" in abject poverty. It is all too easily forgotten that Westerners continue to derive much of their wealth from their former colonies in Africa, Latin America, and Asia. Multimillion-dollar development aid and spectacularly televised fund-raisers for starving children in Ethiopia only cover up continuing unfair North-South trade practices and oppressive social and political structures in the third world. The political theatre in Asia—as well as in Africa and Latin America—has been developing an impressive methodology for tackling this unjust status quo.

If anything, the Western theatre seems to have lost even more of its passion and concern with contemporary reality since 1986. Big business dominates the theatre more than ever, and corporate sponsorship is replacing state subsidy in alarming proportions. Audience attendance figures and box office revenues have hence become the main standard by which to judge the success of a show. Visual spectacle and big-name screen stars have become indispensable ingredients for attracting the well-to-do and assuring a production's profitability. For the less fortunate there is an ever-expanding package of mind-narrowing television.

Beckett is dead and Shepard is attempting, through trial and error, to write his elusive masterpiece in the nineties but unsure whether to do it for the cinema or the stage. The same can be said of the French hope Jean-Claude Carrière. Vaclav Havel turned president of Czechoslovakia after oscillating for two decades between the theatre and jail. Harold Pinter's pen is becoming increasingly political and passionate, but thus far his attempts to reveal the lies intrinsic to all forms of public language remain without echo. In the absence of new voices, the strength of the contemporary Western theatre continues to lie with innovative directors like Mnouchkine, Barba, and Brook, whose interests during the last decade have increasingly turned to the traditional forms and folk stories of the classical Asian theatre.[1] But there is far more to Asian theatre than epic traditions, colorful shapes, stylized motions, and theatrical deconstructions of ritual. There is a powerful contemporary

theatre movement in Asia that Brook, Mnouchkine, and Barba wittingly ignore. This contemporary Asian theatre, which for lack of a better term I have
labeled "theatre of liberation," both embraces and rejects traditional Asian
theatre forms. In the final analysis, however, it is a theatre that, unlike its
Western counterpart, is not ashamed to call itself political.

The Playful Revolution is, of course, not the first book to deal with Asian
theatre—the pioneering work done in this field by James R. Brandon is well
known—but it attempts to fill a gap where its contemporary, politically oriented manifestations are concerned.[2] Some of this gap was recently filled by
Kees Epskamp's *Theatre in Search of Social Change,* but he only pays limited
attention to some Asian examples of theatre for development.[3] As the title of
my book indicates, many contemporary Asian theatre practitioners regard
theatre as a very attractive and effective means to attain indispensable social
and political changes in their often undemocratic, corruption-ridden countries. In these efforts, they collaborate with other, more purely politically
oriented organizations like unions, women's groups, churches, and educational institutions. Side by side, they fight in a symphonic struggle to attain
sociopolitical change. But if my main aim in this book is to show the social
and political effectiveness of the Asian theatre of liberation process, I will
certainly not ignore the aesthetic significance of the impressive corpus of new
plays it has already generated. If it has failed to create genuine comprehensive
sociopolitical reforms, without a doubt the "playful revolution" has contributed to a great number of small-scale social changes and has succeeded in
developing a number of important playwrights, directors, and actors who
deserve to be pulled from the shadows of that cultural wall that we in the
West still continue to erect between North and South, notwithstanding the
prestige of a few writers like Wole Soyinka and Salman Rushdie, who, after
all, now live and work in the West. Their plays and novels have assumed
universal dimensions and seem no longer rooted in the struggle of their destitute compatriots. The same must be said, I am afraid, of the creators of
contemporary Asian theatre with literary pretensions. Catering predominantly to a limited target group from the affluent and educated middle class
and supported by an in-crowd of intellectual critics from university circles,
they are not part of what I would call the playful revolution of the theatre of
liberation. Not surprisingly, most of the award-winning playwrights from
the Asian countries I discuss either ignore the theatre of liberation or reject it
as politically radical and technically and aesthetically weak. By dismissing it
on these grounds the mainstream political playwrights only emphasize their
own broader social irrelevance in favor of a dubious place among their country's artistic and intellectual élite. Instead, I argue that the Asian theatre of
liberation which they dismiss constitutes an international cultural movement
of unprecedented importance and scale.

The contemporary Asian theatre of liberation can be said to have started
in the late sixties and early seventies and, just like radical people's theatre in

the West, originated in student circles and anti-Vietnam demonstrations. But unlike Western radical theatre, which never really amounted to a full-fledged, self-conscious international movement, the Asian theatre of liberation is alive today with greater vigor than ever in cities and villages alike. For approximately ten years, regular pan-Asian contacts have been fostered in the form of international theatre workshops and coproductions. The Asian theatre of liberation is therefore likely to expand rather than decline in the decades to come. *The Playful Revolution* attempts to chart its philosophical dimensions, historical path, current state, and future direction.

Chapter 1 is a long theoretical essay, "Revolution, Freedom, and Theatre." In it, I explore the concept of freedom from a psychological, pedagogical, economic, political, and cultural angle, and the various ways (including the theatrical) in which people in Asia are attempting to achieve their liberation. It should be clear that the Asian theatre of liberation cannot be analyzed in isolation from its sociopolitical and economic context, let alone from its traditional cultural roots. All of these aspects will receive attention in the subsequent chapters, which deal with the national contemporary political theatre movements in different Asian countries.

The second chapter, called "Building Stages of People Power: The Philippines Educational Theater Association," describes and analyzes the development of political theatre in this extensive Asian archipelago. If it seems disproportionately long, this is justified, I think, because the Philippine network is already far advanced in its use of theatre for purposes of liberation and can serve as a reference for the development of the theatre of liberation in the other countries I discuss. To illustrate its extraordinary potential I wanted to paint as complete a picture as possible of the Philippine network, its activities, and achievements by focusing first on the extraordinary repertory and training activities of the Philippines Educational Theater Association, one of the undisputed pioneers of theatre of liberation in Asia. In chapter 3 I then enter the impressive cultural action network artists have built in virtually every island of the Philippines. This view from the provinces will be compounded by personal impressions and interviews with key theatre artists from the islands of Cebu, Samar, Panay, Bohol, Negros, and Mindanao.

Chapter 4 deals with the explosive situation in South Korea, where theatre has played (and continues to play) an important role in mobilizing the masses against the authoritarian régime, the continued presence of nuclear arms, a powerful U.S. military, and the artificial separation from North Korea. As in Spain under Franco, theatre in South Korea is instrumental in creating local pockets of resistance and freedom throughout this divided country.

In chapter 5 I try to sketch the enormous diversity and territoriality of the Indian political theatre landscape. I discuss the work of some of India's most important theatre of liberation activists who are responsible for the emerging networks in the states of Orissa, Tamil Nadu, Karnataka, and Kerala. In the subsequent chapter, entitled "Killed in Action: Safdar Hashmi's Street Theatre in Delhi," I give an in-depth account of the development of one of India's most important theatre of liberation companies, Janam. Most of the material from this chapter comes from lengthy interviews I conducted in April and May of 1988 with Safdar Hashmi, the founder of Janam, who was later kicked to death during a performance of one of his plays by a group of thugs hired by a right-wing politician.

Chapters 7, 8, and 9 deal with the perhaps less advanced but no less interesting theatre of liberation initiatives in Pakistan, Indonesia, and Thailand respectively. In chapter 10, I sum up the general trends I perceive in the different Asian manifestations of the theatre of liberation. In this concluding chapter, I also discuss recent attempts to unite theatre of liberation practitioners from different countries into an Asia-Pacific theatre of liberation movement, and speculate on possible ways of applying the Asian methodology in the West, which, to use Erich Fromm's words, continues to be caught in the chains of an illusionary freedom created by a deceptive material comfort and a heavily commodified escapist culture that only serves to hide an increasing spiritual poverty.

China, Vietnam, Cambodia, Laos, North Korea, Mongolia, and the Muslim nations of Asia Minor are conspicuously absent from this book. These countries were virtually inaccessible for the type of politically sensitive fieldwork I needed to do. Besides, to the best of my knowledge, theatre artists from these countries have little or no contact with their colleagues in the rest of Asia and do not do much in the way of theatre of liberation. In Japan, radical people's theatre is gaining ground, thanks largely to the effort of companies like the Black Tent Theatre and Minoru Satomi's company in Tokyo, but given the first-world status of this country I have opted to exclude the Japanese theatre of liberation from this book as well.

A book like this does not get written without the support of a great many organizations and individuals. I thank Edwin Gentzler for pointing me East and providing me with my first contacts in Asian literary circles. Without his help I would still be orbiting around Calcutta in a dilapidated rickshaw. Jenny Spencer I thank for her continuous reminders that publishing is not necessarily synonymous with inflating one's ego. I am grateful to the University Grants Committee of the Victoria University of Wellington, Aotearoa (New Zealand), for providing me with a postdoctoral research fellowship from March 1986 through June 1987. I thank Phil Mann and David Carnegie of the Drama Studies program at that same university for first recognizing the importance of my work and then providing me with all the stimulation and facilities I required in the first phase of this project. Roma Potiki I thank for being such a tough guide to Aotearoa. Tough guides are the best. Bong Ramilo, Jules Holledge, Venetia Gillot, Brian Crow, Susan Melrose, Diana Palaversic, Jim George, Dave Watt, Gordon Beattie, Daze Williams, Gaby Hyslop, Geoffrey Borney, Veronica Kelly, Adrian Kiernander, John Garcia, Alaide and Gamsyra Maciel, and the incomparable Madeleine Blackwell I thank for helping me find my way through Australia and for providing me with enough speaking engagements to finance part of my third trip through Asia. In Indonesia, Linus Suryadi, Fred Wibowo, Emha Ainun Nadjib, Rendra, Simon Hate and Michael Bodden proved invaluable sources of information and good companions. In Korea I received the help of many visible and even more invisible friends. Of those I remember by name and face I wish to express my gratitude to Jung Kisub, Kim Sok-man, Kim Myung Gon, and Hwang Sok-yong in particular. I hope they will excuse my spelling of their names. I am grateful to Keith Rodabaugh, my favorite carpenter, for taking some marvelous pictures. In the Philippines, the list of helpful people is endless but I must single out Jack Yabut, Beth Mondragon, Dessa Quesada, Alan Glinoga, Nestor Horfilla, Marili Fernandez, Mimi Villareal, Gardy Labad, Jess Santiago, Joel Arbolario, Babie Delmoro, Hansel Alviola, Don-Don, Bubu Alora, Aster Tecson, Sally Minoza, Bundo Dedma, Dolor Mercadez, Father Larry Helar, Father Eli Balboa, Jojo Noval, Julius Valmores, Greg Tabañag, Eva Confesor, Lando Arban, Samo Balt, Bet-Bet and Rita Palo, Jojo Sanchez, Chris Millado, Evelyn Vargas, Weni Gamboa, Mary Joan and Brenda Fajardo, Nanding Josef, Manny Pambid, Nicanor Tiongson, and Behn Cervantes. I thank some of them for their unfaltering friendship and the others for their time and patience, even if they may disagree with some of the things that are written here.

From the Philippines my odyssey took me via Hong Kong (thanks, Manny Calonzo, Samidorai, and Boonthan Verawongse) to Thailand, where the help of Busaba Baratacharya, Santi Chitrachinda, Somsak Kanha, Sam Kalayanee, and Orn-anong Vong-asavathepchai proved invaluable. From there, I journeyed to Pakistan where I was graciously hosted by Adnan Qadir Khan, Nisar Moyud-Din, Muhammad Wasim, Sohail Akbarwarraich, and Imtiaz Ahmed Khan in Lahore, and by Nadeem Khalid and Hoori Noorani Malik in Karachi. Aslam Azhar, of the Dastak theatre company and Pakistan Television, proved an eloquent interviewee. From Pakistan, before finally returning to Europe, I traveled on to India. In that vast country, I received generous help from Arun Mukherjee, Badal Sircar, Utpal Dutt, and Sanjib Sarcar in Calcutta; from Jos Chiramel in Trichur (Kerala); from Subodh Patnayk of Orissa; from Shashi Adapa and Gladius of MESCA in Bangalore; from the people of the Association of the Rural Poor in Tamil Nadu; from Father Amal in Madras; and from Moloyashree and Safdar Hashmi, my wonderful hosts in Delhi. I dedicate this book to Safdar, who was killed on the streets of a Delhi industrial suburb while performing his last play *Halla Bol!* [Attack] for a large group of workers on January 2, 1989.

I wish to thank Professor Hans Bertens of the American Studies Program at the University of Utrecht for granting me the necessary time and intellectual support to finish this book. I also thank the participants of the *Cry of Asia!* project for their courage in sticking it out till the end, for a most difficult but worthwhile and exciting adventure, and for providing me with the latest updates on the theatre of liberation in their countries. A special thank-you goes to Nung, Orn, Shashi, Nathan, Kim, Musadiq, Putu, May Lyn, Archie, Uchazi, Ed, Hemi, and my Dutch *Cry of Asia!* associates G.J., Francine, Bas, Petra, Erika, and Mariëtta. Michael Kooren made some of the best photographs in this book. *Masha danki* to Ria Green for fixing the printer and my *curason*.

Parts of this book have been published in *The Drama Review, Minnesota Review, New Theatre Quarterly, Illusions, CESO Monographs, Australasian Drama Studies, Research in African Literatures,* and *New Theatre Australia.* I am grateful to the publishers and editors of these publications for permitting me to reprint some of these materials here and for indirectly encouraging me to go on. I particularly thank Mariellen Sandford of *The Drama Review* for helping me find a suitable style.

Finally, for a white European there is always a certain risk in commenting on a cultural phenomenon from the developing world. Charges of eurocentricity will be unavoidable, I am afraid. Some of those I criticize may even deny me the right to be critical *because* I am white and European or not wedded to any particular dogma. Undoubtedly, this book contains mistakes and misjudgments, for which I, of course, am solely responsible, not the hundreds of people I interviewed. Despite my undeniable linguistic, cultural, and social handicaps, this is a book I simply could not *not* have written. I hope people in the Western and the developing world find some good use for it.

I

REVOLUTION, FREEDOM, AND THEATRE

Cultural awakening is arguably a crucial stage in the development of a people. There is little point in introducing high technology to improve the efficiency of developing economies if one does not also stimulate the minds of the people to take creative control of their own destinies. For once in modern history, this is not yet another progressive idea developed by Western intellectuals and subsequently imposed on the developing world along with so many other material and immaterial products. It is genuinely homegrown and deduced from local and authentic third world experience.

For approximately twenty-five years—and more systematically since the early eighties—a new type of pragmatically oriented political theatre has been emerging in the developing world. Some observers refer to it as People's Theatre, others label it Popular Theatre for Social Change. Both terms, unfortunately, evoke previous, unsuccessful Western attempts at making political theatre for the underprivileged. I therefore prefer to call this new type of political theatre from the developing world "theatre of liberation" instead. The associations of that name with Liberation Theology and Pedagogy of the Oppressed are quite deliberate, since the activities and methods of the theatre of liberation are inspired by similarly oriented activities in the religious and educational sectors of developing societies. As such, it differs fundamentally from most Western political theatre practice, for it is process–oriented and does not focus on the performance as the sole purpose of theatre.

Liberation and the "Third World" Predicament

Liberation as a political idea became popular in the late sixties, when a worldwide solidarity movement took shape in support of the plight of all oppressed and exploited peoples of the world, ranging from women in the West to Vietnamese peasants in the Far East, from Bolivian *campesinos* in South America to Blacks in southern Africa and in the United States of America.

1

The impetus toward liberation in the developing world is intricately linked to the colonial past and the neocolonial present.

In most Latin American, African, and Asian countries, white rulers dressed in khaki were only nominally replaced by a small local élite who, for their own material benefit, facilitated the economic penetration of their newly "independent" countries for Western transnational corporations. Thus, one type of domination was substituted for another, and the great majority of the third-world peoples were effectively imprisoned in a "culture of silence." Through military intimidation and continuing illiteracy, they were manipulated to serve the interests of others as inexpensive industrial or agricultural laborers, and, later, as consumers. This deplorable situation was only aggravated by the effects of modernization and industrialization—euphemistically termed "development"—which, from the fifties onwards, caused many people to flock to the urban centers in search of employment.

In the sixties, the economies of the developing world were dominated by the flawed idea that if the Western model of industrialization and expansion were simply transposed to the African, Asian, and Latin American context, market growth—and therefore development—would automatically follow. Meanwhile, in the cultural domain, television, films, and advertisements presented United States society as the ideal to which the developing countries should aspire. The fallacy of this scheme lay, of course, in the mistaken assumption that social welfare and liberal democracy are the natural corollaries of economic growth. It severely underestimated the effects of power and greed on the new rulers, who often managed to manipulate the hierarchical structures of their countries and the remnants of feudal thinking in the masses to serve their own interests. What happened further was that the new industries in the developing world were largely designed to serve Western economy. They were (and continue to be) controlled by transnational companies, which, instead of improving the overall distribution of wealth, made the developing countries only more dependent on the West. This deplorable situation was only compounded by the the so-called Green Revolution.

The detrimental economical and ecological effects of the Green Revolution for the peasant and small farmer of the developing world have been convincingly presented by Susan George in her book *How the Other Half Dies: The Real Reasons for World Hunger*. According to George, the Green Revolution involved cultivation of "plants that will bear more edible grain—the 'two ears where only one grew before'—and thus increase yields without increasing cultivated crop areas."[1] Despite the apparent economic attractions of this genetic and agricultural scheme, there are many indirect drawbacks: the genetically manipulated plants are highly susceptible to diseases and therefore require heavy protective doses of chemical pesticides and fungicides, and large quantities of additional nutrition in the form of fertilizers and water, the high monetary and ecological expenses of which have to be borne by the farmers themselves. The Green Revolution is, in other words, capital intensive, even more so because the chemicals required can only be obtained from Western chemical companies with hard Western currency. As a result, only large-scale plantations run by big landowners or Western multinationals benefit fully from the Green Revolution. Because small farmers have to make the required technological and chemical investments with money borrowed at usurious rates from loan sharks, they frequently lose their small plots of land when unfavorable conditions force them to default on their loans. One season of drought, one tidal wave, or one hurricane can bring about a disastrous harvest, which invariably results in bankruptcy. Those who are evicted from their lands then either have to resort to underpaid farm labor jobs or join the ranks of the underemployed in the city. Susan George's statistics speak for themselves: "Land prices in areas of Pakistan where the Green Revolution has been introduced have increased 500 per cent as landlords compete for land from which tenants have been removed. In 1969, there were 40,000 eviction suits against sharecroppers in Bihar state; 80,000 in Mysore state, India" (p. 129). The situation in many other Asian countries is not essentially different, and the prospects of improved agricultural policies in Asia are not bright when one considers that many local, regional, and national politicians are large landowners themselves.[2]

Politics and Economics in the Asian Context

In the early seventies, the Asian skyline continued to be dominated by the Vietnam War, a bloody struggle for decolonization that has often been misrepresented as a benevolent effort by the Americans to fight Communism. This book is not concerned with that war nor really with how it affected the surrounding Asian continent. Japan and China are also beyond my immediate scope, although the influence of their external industrial and military policies, like the Vietnam traumas, have been considerable in the countries that I do discuss.

Of more direct concern to the theatre of liberation is the complex sociopolitical and cultural makeup of the Asian countries under consideration. It is well-nigh impossible to generalize about "the Asian situation," although, of course, common traits of underdevelopment can readily be found everywhere in the region: lopsided, dependent economies; cash crop agriculture geared for export; undernourishment; oppressive social and political structures; continuing feudalism in the countryside; explosive population growth; authoritarian government structures; censorship; lack of efficient social and educational services; a "synthetic culture" of government-controlled media and commercial advertisements that control popular taste, consumption patterns, and public opinion;[3] and heavy militarization accompanied by frequent human rights abuses. On the other hand, Asia is a continent of huge cultural contrasts between Pakistan in the West and Korea in the East, between Hindus, Buddhists, and Muslims, and between the educated middle class in the cities and tribal minorities in the mountains and rain forests.

Despite the mushrooming of metropoles like Bangkok, Calcutta, and Manila, and the ever-growing quantities of high-tech products from South Korea, Taiwan, Malaysia, Singapore, and Thailand appearing on Western markets, Asian societies have remained predominantly rural and hierarchical. Although urban slum dwellers are often employed in factories, usually they started leaving the countryside not much more than twenty years ago. Even in the cities, first generation industrial workers remain peasants at heart and often maintain close emotional and economic ties with their relatives in the countryside. Nevertheless, their children have begun to adopt increasingly Western lifestyles as the result of having been exposed to television, consumer goods, and European and American-style schooling.

Notwithstanding the rapidly expanding slums in the major cities, the vast majority of Asians continue to be small farmers or landless plantation laborers. Their economic existence is, at best, subsistence level, and not a few live in conditions of virtual slavery. Life for small Asian fisherman is not significantly better.

The politics and economics of the countryside are usually totally controlled by a small number of powerful families who own large tracts of land and can often trace the roots of their ownership back through several centuries. In many cases, they have direct family links to powerful politicians and military leaders in the capital, and not rarely do they uphold their private feudal domains with private security forces that can sometimes number into the hundreds.

The position of women is deplorable in all but the upper classes. Although many carry an equal burden in the economic support of the family—often working in fields and factories—they also have to do a disportionate amount of work in the household, and, in addition, are expected to be faithful lovers as well as loving mothers.

Birthrates and child mortality are high, life expectancy low, educational opportunities minimal, and hence social mobility extremely restricted. Religion continues to have a predominantly conservative influence on the mass of people and is sometimes blatantly manipulated by high priests of all sorts—be they Hindu, Muslim, or Christian—who often have lucrative political and economic stakes of their own to protect.

It is clear that, in numerical and moral terms, the status quo in most Asian countries is unfair to the large majority of the population. Many commentators have identified potential sociopolitical and historical causes for this current Asian condition.[4] Unquestioningly, this status quo is a function of the peculiar way in which most of the countries in question emerged from French, British, Dutch, Portuguese, Spanish, American, and Japanese colonial rule. After nominal independence was granted, these countries were immediately hijacked by a local élite of former colonial collaborators, who, educated in

Western ways, continued to be almost totally dependent on Western transnational corporations, Western foreign aid, and military training. In exchange for the right to dine at glamorous Western tables, ski in Saint Moritz,
and send their offspring to Oxford and Harvard, Asia's military and civil
millionaires allow emergent middle classes to enjoy a modicum of material
comfort and hold out promises of greater wealth in the future. Yet because
their wealth depends upon the continued exploitation of peasants and workers, the rulers of these Asian countries find it necessary to silence dissidents
and to control social unrest by creating an extensive, corrupt, and brutal
(para)military apparatus.

With increasing—rather than decreasing—social polarization, and revolutionary radicalism slowly taking root among the impoverished masses, the
prevailing political tendency of most Asian governments has been more toward
military dictatorships than toward free democracies. The idea of liberation
grows, then, almost naturally out of unbearable socioeconomic predica-
ments. This grassroots discontent is further conceptualized and directed by
progressive intellectuals and pragmatic local leaders in an attempt to provide
a sorely needed alternative to the suffocating constriction in which the proletarian and peasant majority are being held by a small upper class minority.

Reasons for the current status quo are complex, then, but it is more important for our purposes to turn to the many different kinds of activities that
are undertaken to combat this clearly unjust situation. Although resistance to
oppression has existed since colonial times, the current movement to liberate
Asia is only about thirty years old. It started more or less simultaneously
among middle class, intellectual, union, and religious circles. The inspiration
for these liberation activities came, surprisingly enough, not from the West
but from Latin America, although progressive European development workers and Christian priests often served as intermediaries in this fascinating example of third-world-to-third-world grassroots cultural cross-fertilization.

There is no point in arguing whether radical Latin American priests, Che
Guevara, Ho Chi Minh, or Paulo Freire actually first formulated the current
idea of liberation. By all accounts, however, 1968 always appears as a magical year, both for the radical movements in the West and for the developing
world. In May of that year, radical students erected barricades in the Parisian
Latin Quarter and fought Molotov cocktail battles with the riot police. It
was also the year of the "Prague spring" that was so rudely and violently
disturbed by Russian army tanks. Che Guevara and the Bolivian revolution
had just died and Vietnam was a red-hot issue. Another significant event in
that year was the second general conference of the Latin American Episcopal
Council held in the Colombian city of Medellín.

Starting in the late sixties, a growing awareness of the neocolonial exploitation of many Asian countries resulted in a wide range of overt and covert
activities of students, teachers, industrial and peasant union organizers, wom-
en's groups, priests, intellectuals, guerrilla fighters, and, not least, artists.[5]

Freedom

Before discussing the different types of Asian liberation initiatives (of which the theatre of liberation is an integral part), I want to dwell for a moment on the philosophical and psychological ramifications of freedom. The psychological dimensions of liberation are too often ignored in the ongoing debate on causes and effects of underdevelopment. Freedom thus remains a conveniently vague and abstract concept in the discourses of Western and third world ideologues, sociologists, anthropologists, and welfare workers alike. For a better understanding of theatre of liberation, which operates, after all, in the hearts and minds of the people, a more concrete insight into the psychological aspects of liberation is indispensable.

Freedom in the "third world" context involves more than freedom from hunger, thirst, political violence, homelessness, and physical abuse. It also involves the liberty to create and enjoy the economic, political, educational, social, psychological, and cultural conditions that would assure the maximum realization of the human potential. Gustavo Gutierrez, one of the leading liberation theologians, defines liberation as the expression of the oppressed people's aspirations, "emphasizing the conflictual aspects of the economic, social and political process which puts them at odds with wealthy nations and oppressive classes."[6] He qualifies this definition by adding that "the gradual conquest of true freedom leads to the creation of a new man and a qualitatively different society" (pp. 36–37). Similarly, Brazilian educator Paulo Freire agrees with Erich Fromm, who claimed that people need "not merely freedom from hunger, but also freedom to create and to construct, to wonder and to venture."[7]

Although he was a Western psychologist and not specifically concerned with third world issues, Fromm's *Fear of Freedom* (1942) and *Beyond the Chains of Illusion* (1962) provide a useful starting point for a psychology of liberation applicable to the developing world as well. Fromm's main importance for the third world lies in his very thorough political and psychological analysis of the rise of the bourgeois mentality and its links with the conservative ethics of Catholicism, Calvinism, and Lutheranism. Fromm irrefutably showed how these three Christian doctrines were indispensable for the efficient functioning of the capitalist system and how, pushed to their ideological extremes, they led to the excesses of European fascism in the 1930s. Moreover, Fromm was keenly aware that Western psychotherapeutic practice is predominantly conservative in its strivings to reintegrate derailed individuals ("neurotics") into the economic and social mainstream and thereby essentially serves the capitalist status quo. "Most psychiatrists," Fromm claims, "take the structure of their own society so much for granted that to them the person who is not well adapted assumes the stigma of being less valuable."[8] Psychologists, he continues, have become "the priests of the industrial society."[9] According to Fromm, the term mental health can therefore be defined in two ways:

> Firstly, from the standpoint of a functioning society, one can call a person normal or healthy if he is able to fulfill the social rôle he is to take in that given society. More concretely, this means that he is able to work in the fashion which is required in that particular society, and furthermore that he is able to participate in the reproduction of society, that is, that he can raise a family. Secondly, from the standpoint of the individual, we look upon health or normalcy as the optimum of growth and happiness of the individual.
>
> If the structure of a given society were such that it offered the optimum possibility for individual happiness, both viewpoints would coincide. However, this is not the case in most societies we know, including our own.[10]

Fromm then proceeds to argue that most people who are well adapted to capitalist society have all lost essential aspects of their "genuine individuality and spontaneity" (p. 119). Instead of calling the individuals neurotic, Fromm reserves that term for the type of society that cripples its members "in the growth of their personality" and "in terms of its being adverse to human happiness and self-realization" (p. 120).

Given the fact that most societies that we know are "neurotic" in Fromm's sense, the individual has two options: he can either escape in some form of "negative freedom" or progress to "positive freedom." Negative freedom is constituted by the various mechanisms by which one tries to escape unbearable feelings of aloneness and powerlessness that are the natural consequence of the alienating industrial system. Psychologically, negative freedom manifests itself in a desire to get rid of the "burden of freedom" by submitting oneself to a person or power that is overwhelmingly strong. Fromm contrasts negative freedom with positive freedom, which he defines as the condition in which man "can relate himself spontaneously to the world in love and work, in the genuine expression of his emotional, sensuous, and intellectual capacities; he can thus become one again with man, nature, and himself, without giving up the independence and integrity of his individual self" (p. 120).

In Fromm's view, spontaneity is one of the key ingredients of freedom, but, unfortunately, this essential source of liberation is systematically suppressed by traditional education. Emotion, the other indispensable vehicle for liberation, is all but eliminated:

> To be "emotional" has become synonymous with being unsound or unbalanced. By the acceptance of this standard the individual has become greatly weakened; his thinking is impoverished and flattened. On the other hand, since emotions cannot be completely killed, they must have their existence totally apart from the intellectual side of the personality; the result is the cheap and insincere sentimentality with which movies and popular songs feed millions of emotion-starved customers. (p. 211)

The state of negative freedom is further enhanced by all kinds of illusions from which virtually no individual is free. Fromm here refers in particular to the deceptive freedom of thought and speech: "We feel that freedom of speech is the last step in the march of victory of freedom. We forget that, although freedom of speech constitutes an important victory in the battle against *old* restraints, modern man is in a position where much of what 'he' thinks and says are the things that everybody else thinks and says; that he has not acquired the ability to think originally—that is, for himself—which alone can give meaning to his claim that nobody can interfere with the expression of his thoughts" (pp. 90–91). In addition to external repressive agents, then, people must resist the pressures of public opinion and the desire to conform, for these restraints have been deposited in their consciousness by the media, the church, the school, and the family.[11] If we accept Fromm's suggestions, the liberation process must include a reappropriation of man's spontaneity and emotions, "for only if man does not repress essential parts of his self, only if he has become transparent to himself, and only if the different spheres of life have reached a fundamental integration, is spontaneous activity possible" (p. 223).

Fromm sees an important task for artists in the liberation process because they are "individuals who are spontaneous, whose thinking, feeling, and acting [are] the expression of their selves and not an automaton" (p. 223). In this sense, artists are like revolutionaries, because just as successful rebels become respected statesmen and unsuccessful ones are thrown in jail as criminals, successful artists sell their art and become famous, whereas unsuccessful ones are labeled eccentrics or neurotics. In the developing world, progressive artists have recognized the power of art to stimulate the spontaneous creativity and emotional expression of the oppressed, and some of them have developed effective workshop methods at the grassroots level with the explicit aim of breaking through the "culture of silence" and promoting freedom in the broadest sense of the term.

Fromm's identification of freedom with spontaneous creative activity is a crucial step in the establishment of a theoretical foundation for the theatre of liberation. His emphasis on process as opposed to product is also important because the capitalist mode of production, which is a primary cause of oppression in the third world, has produced societies in which the product (i.e., commodity) is regarded as paramount.

The Liberation Psychology of Frantz Fanon

The pioneer of the psychology of the oppressed as it applies to the colonial and neocolonial world is Frantz Fanon, a black psychiatrist from Martinique who worked for the Algerian indépendistes in the fifties. In *Peau noire, masques blancs* [Black Skin, White Masks] (1952) and *Les Damnés de la terre*

[The Wretched of the Earth] (1961) he brilliantly dissected the colonial mentalities of settlers, slaves, and the neocolonial bourgeoisie, and thus undeniably enriched Fromm's ideas on freedom by placing them in a third world framework.

Fanon shared Fromm's view that human relationships have become stained by materialistic opportunism: "Brother, sister, friend—these are words outlawed by the colonial bourgeoisie, because for them my brother is my purse, my friend is part of my scheme for getting on." [12] Fanon heavily criticized the indigenous neocolonial middle class whom he accused of intellectual laziness and greed. Instead of sharing its intelligence and technical know-how acquired at Western universities with their own people, the neocolonial bourgeois continue to sell their country as a cheap source for raw materials to the West; they erect luxury resorts for the entertainment of Westerners and "in practice set up [the developing country] as the brothel of Europe" (p. 154). According to Fanon, no good can be expected from this get-rich-quick middle class, whom he considers considerably more backwards than its European counterpart. The European bourgeois had, at least, the audacity to invent new machines and the courage to discover new worlds. The third world bourgeois, on the other hand, "literally . . . is good for nothing [and] tries to hide [his] mediocrity by buildings which have prestige value at the individual level, by chromium-plating on big American cars, by holidays on the Riviera and weekends in neon-lit nightclubs" (p. 176).

As a psychiatrist, it is hardly surprising that Fanon saw the liberation of the (neo)colonial *mind* as one of the main priorities of the struggle for freedom. Political education and the stimulation of creativity should be implemented in all sectors of society but particularly among the young who, "Idle and illiterate, are a prey to all sorts of disintegrating influences" (p. 195). Thus, Fanon also argued for the building of an alternative nationalist culture to counteract the "various assaults made upon [the people] by the very nature of Western culture" (p. 196). In this process, he predicted an important role for the progressive middle class intellectual and artist.

According to Fanon, the new national culture should incorporate the cultural traditions of the particular country or region to which it belongs because colonialism has devalued and distorted them in order to convince the local peoples of their cultural inferiority vis-à-vis the West. But Fanon warned intellectuals not to become obsessed with the glory of the past while ignoring contemporary realities. Furthermore, they must be thoroughly aware that their ideas and their words are profoundly Western and tend to estrange them from their own people: "We have taken everything from the other side. . . . It is not enough to try to get back to the people in that past from which they have already emerged; rather we must join them in that fluctuating movement which they are just giving shape to" (p. 227).

To Fanon, then, the construction of a new national culture was an essential component of the overall struggle for liberation: "A national culture is the whole body of efforts made by a people in the sphere of thought to describe, justify, and praise the action through which that people has created itself and keeps itself in existence. A national culture in underdeveloped countries should therefore take its place at the very heart of the struggle for freedom which these countries are carrying on" (p. 233).

Liberating Minds

Fanon stopped short of formulating practical guidelines for the liberation of the colonial mind. But in *Frantz Fanon and the Psychology of Oppression* (1985), Hussein Abdilahi Bulhan proposes a very useful outline of what should eventually become a full-fledged psychology of liberation based on Fanon's ideas.

Bulhan suggests that a psychology of liberation should first of all rid itself of the flawed notion of individual liberty which, in the third world context, only benefits the "haves" at the expense of the "have-nots," who are only reduced to "socially defenseless individuals who privatize their collective victimization." [13] Bulhan argues that collective freedom should take precedence over individual freedom and that a psychology of liberation should "emphasize how best to further the consciousness and organized action of the collective" (p. 259).

In all discussions about freedom, satisfaction of basic human needs is taken for granted, but Bulhan correctly stresses that in the developing world the psychological impact of worrying about food should not be underestimated; relatively speaking, the average third world citizen has to spend a great deal of time and energy to satisfy this basic human need. Bulhan therefore places the satisfaction of biological needs at the top of his list of prerequisites for freedom. It is followed by the necessity to feel one with a community and a culture for which, in turn, self-consciousness is a primary necessity. Finally, Bulhan finds the ultimate state of freedom in what he calls maximum self-determination: "Self-determination refers to the process and capacity to choose among alternatives, to determine one's behavior, and to affect one's destiny. As such, self-determination assumes a consciousness of human possibilities, an awareness of necessary constraints, and a willed, self-motivated engagement with one's world. . . . Without the right of self-determination, we are reduced to rigid and automatic behaviors, to a life and destiny shorn of human will and freedom" (pp. 265–66). Long-term frustration of the basic human needs described above leads to an intolerable condition of oppression that sooner or later will have to be resisted in one form or another, Bulhan claims.

The oppressive condition, or the condition of "un-freedom," can and should be treated in the psychological domain, but obviously mainstream methods of psychotherapy are inappropriate and in any case inacessible to the poor from developing countries. Bulhan convincingly points out that psychotherapy only aims at changing symptoms, behavior, and personality, not oppressive institutions and social structures. He therefore recommends a kind of psychologically based social intervention that aims at empowering victims to solve their own problems instead of "keeping them dependent and powerless" and that stimulates "collective action and not a self-defeating privatization of difficulties" (p. 268). Bulhan believes that such psychosocial interventions should avoid: (1) "bandaging" the immediate, private psychological distress of oppressed individuals only to send them back to a condition of oppression; and (2) conceiving of social change only in abstract terms, forgetting that it is only meaningful in terms of its impact on living people. Rather than paternalism, true liberation requires the *simultaneous* transformation of the oppressed individual *within* an oppressed group and of the social conditions that caused the individual's distress in the first place. Bulhan realizes that these transformations should take place without help from external sources, but he acknowledges that some intermediary may be indispensable in the initial stages of the psychosocial liberation process: "One critical focus of intervention has to do with unraveling, through active involvement and demonstrations in the social world, the self-defeating patterns of relating, the tendency toward betrayal of the self and/or others, the internalized script for failure and disaster, as well as the conditioned fear of taking a stand or even fear of freedom—all of which derive from a contrived system of socialization, an elaborate formula to produce willing victims" (p. 276).

The sad fact is, of course, that freedom from oppression is not readily granted by those who benefit from its perpetuation and that, even if the oppressed were not violently prevented from organizing themselves and from initiating social action (which they are), the Church, the official and commercial media, and the educational system would not immediately give way to friendlier structures. What is required, then, is a well-orchestrated struggle for liberation that takes place on several fronts at one and the same time. We shall see that the theatre of liberation is conspicuously present on almost all frontlines of the battle for freedom. Apart from metropolitan theatre buildings, it erects its stages in rural areas, slums, schools, guerrilla-controlled territories, places of worship, psychological clinics, and even television studios.

Liberating Temples, Mosques, and Churches

Religious liberation with a progressive sociopolitical orientation is still hardly noticeable in Hinduism and Islam, which remain hotbeds of conservatism as recent communal riots in the southern USSR, Pakistan, and Kashmir well illustrate. Whatever religious liberation activities exist are channeled primarily through the various pockets of Catholicism that are spread throughout the region. The Philippines is by far the most catholicized country in Asia, but important Catholic regions can also be found in India (Kerala, Tamil Nadu), South Korea, and former French Indochina. Smaller but still significant groups of Catholics exist, finally, in Indonesia, Thailand, Sri Lanka, Singapore, and Bangladesh.

Confronted with abject poverty and frequent human rights abuses against inhabitants of slum areas and the countryside, an increasing number of Asian parish priests are turning to Latin American liberation theology for theoretical and practical guidance in their struggle against injustice. The works of the Brazilian liberation theologian Leonardo Boff and the radical Guatemalan priest Gustavo Gutierrez are now also studied in many Asian seminaries.[14]

The Medellín Bishops' Conference of 1968 is usually regarded as the official starting point of liberation theology, for it was on that occasion that the Latin American Church took a radical stance in solidarity with the poor and explicitly identified colonialism and neocolonialism as the causes of the widespread poverty in the developing world. Short of accepting armed revolution as the sole alternative to the oppressive system, the Church recommended the spiritual development of so-called *Basic Christian Communities* (BCs), grassroots people's organizations whose activities range from enlightened Bible study to social action and community organizing:

> BC's are made up of small groups of an average of ten people; it is most usually a number of these groups—generally ten, usually one parish, that is known as a BC. A large parish may encompass more than one BC—five, six or more. . . . normally the structure goes from small group to BC to parish. . . . The overwhelming majority of members of the BC's are poor people. They come from the lowest strata of society, the peasants and the workers— those who suffer. This is not principally a religious but a social fact: evidence shows it to be so. In fact, the BC's have till now only flourished in the two areas where the poor live: the country districts and the peripheries of the big cities.[15]

According to Clodovis Boff, Basic Christian Communities come into existence either for religious reasons—to keep the faith alive in the absence of a priest—or for social reasons—the threat of slum demolition, eviction or strikes, or the need to brainstorm about technological improvements of the community: "The basic group usually meets once a week, in a set place, usually a family house, but it might be any room available, in a chapel or simply the shade of a tree. And what do they do? They pray, they listen to the word of God, and they discuss problems affecting their lives. . . . The atmosphere in a BC is full of human worth and greatness of heart, but never the ingenuous happiness of those who know nothing of the contradictions and hardships of life. No, it goes with a fairly critical outlook on reality, a very sharp class feeling, and an extremely committed and dangerous struggle. . . . This is a real exercise in participatory democracy" (p. 55).

In Asia, fascist-leaning local authorities often regard BCs as potential Communist cells and take action to intimidate or sometimes even liquidate their members or leaders. It is noteworthy that particularly in the Philippines many BCs have been formed by means of grassroots theatre of liberation workshops.[16]

Liberating Schools, Teachers, and Students

Apart from theatre techniques, the pedagogical methods of the Brazilian educator Paulo Freire also figure prominently in the actual formative process of Asian Basic Christian Communities. Furthermore, Freire's pedagogy is used in a multitude of adult education projects in many Asian countries. Most Asian initiatives for radical changes in existing educational systems have been inspired by Freire's writings.

Freire's pedagogy is specifically designed for the benefit of illiterate or semiliterate adults in the developing world and is radically opposed to Western concepts of education, which cast the teacher in the untenable role of omniscient narrator and are designed to develop students into productive elements of capitalist economy. Freire calls the traditional Western pedagogical principle "The Banking Concept of Education," in which "knowledge is a gift bestowed by those who consider themselves knowledgeable upon those whom they consider to know nothing":[17]

> Education thus becomes an act of depositing, in which the students are the depositories and the teacher the depositor. Instead of communicating, the teacher issues communiqués and makes deposits which the students patiently receive, memorize and repeat . . . but true knowledge emerges only through invention and reinvention, through the restless, impatient, continuing, hopeful inquiry men pursue in the world, with the world and with each other. (p. 56)

Most educational systems in the developing world are, in fact, instruments of the status quo. They project a mystifying picture of present and past reality and confirm the negative self-image of the working classes. Through education and the mass media, the poor are inculcated with a belief in a fixed, unchangeable world that they cannot hope to influence. The predicament in which they find themselves is exacerbated by the diffusion of several myths that serve as control mechanisms: "the myth that anyone who is industrious can become an entrepreneur . . . the myth of the universal right of education . . . the myth of the industriousness of the oppressors and the laziness and dishonesty of the oppressed, as well as the myth of the natural inferiority of the latter and the superiority of the former" (p. 135). To counteract the oppressive effects of traditional educational methods, Freire's education for liberation requires a new kind of teacher, one who fundamentally believes in the innate creativity, wisdom, and knowledge of the people with whom he or she works: "The view that educators are benevolent counselors scouring the slums for potential students to whom they can give the gift of the word

. . . such attempts at literacy can never be efforts toward liberation, for they will never question the very reality which prevent men of the right to speak up. In reality they are not marginal to society; they are oppressed within it."[18]

Freire, who has links with the progressive Catholic Church and currently works for the World Council of Churches in Geneva, started developing grassroots adult education workshops in the sixties. The methods of these nonhierarchical, often informal encounters soon spread to Africa and Asia as well. However, it is a mistake to attach a foolproof warranty label to Freirian pedagogy of the oppressed. Education, like freedom itself, is a lifelong process. Complacently applying it like a magic formula will lead to disastrous results. Pedagogy of the oppressed requires a thorough understanding of the society on the local, national, and international level. It also requires a very well trained, gregarious, and sensitive instructor preferably born and raised in the target community itself. In an article entitled "Co-opting Freire: A Critical Analysis of Pseudo-Freirian Adult Education," Ross Kidd and Krishna Kumar convincingly point out that since the seventies conservative Western development agencies have increasingly made use of Freirian methodology in peasant communities to introduce technological skills crucial to the promotion of the Green Revolution.[19] Reports of similar undesirable pseudo-Freirian adult education practices have come from all over the developing world.

Even well-intentioned Freirian initiatives are not always foolproof either. Often they are facilitated by grassroots social action units which are funded by Western development agencies. Over the years, the instructors become economically and psychologically dependent on this type of funding. A certain routine develops and the need for success stories becomes as important for the indigenous adult educator as for the Western funding agent. Cooptation of Freirian methodology develops, then, not infrequently along this less conspicuous avenue as well.[20]

We shall see that theatre of liberation workshops start from the same basic premise as the pedagogy of the oppressed. Theatre of liberation also requires a new kind of actor who, like the Freirian teacher, activates the inherent creativity of his oppressed target group. What is more, in his earliest adult education experiments in Brazil and Peru, Freire successfully collaborated with Augusto Boal, a theatre practitioner from Sao Paulo, who, on the basis of his Freirian experiences, developed his own concept of the theatre of the oppressed.

Theatre of Liberation

Ostensibly, Bertolt Brecht's plays or those created by the radical people's theatre that developed in the West after 1968 aim at a liberation similar to that described by Gutierrez, Freire, and Fromm. John McGrath, the leader of the 7:84 Theatre Company from Britain, for example, explicitly stated his objective: to create a theatre "which is searching, through the experience and forms of the working class, for those elements which point forward in the direction of a future rational, non-exploitative, classless society, in which all struggle together to resolve humanity's conflict with nature, and to allow all to grow to the fullest experience of life on earth."[21] But just like the Western teacher with a banking orientation, the actors of Western types of political theatre unwittingly adopted a top-down attitude. In their shows, they processed elements from the traditional proletarian cultural partrimony and proceeded to perform *for* farmers and factory workers. Never mind the token post-performance discussions that were added on for good form. Their involvement with the oppressed was limited to a few interviews during the creative phase of the play and the approximately two hours that the show itself lasted. Despite their progressive analyses and objectives, they remained essentially "cultural invaders," to use Freire's term; they came as skillful artists to interpret the predicament of their target group essentially from their own middle class educated perspectives and system of values. They failed to revive cultural activities as a regular practice among their target groups. Freire proposed, instead, "cultural synthesis" in which the actors do not come "to teach or to transmit or to give anything, but rather to learn, with the people, about the people's world . . . [and become] integrated with the people, who are co-authors of the action that both perform upon the world . . . in cultural synthesis, there are no spectators."[22] By extension, in genuine theatre of liberation, the spectators become the protagonist in their own play.

Freire endorses both liberation theology and theatre of liberation as valid and useful practices in the general process of what he calls "cultural action for freedom". Moreover, theatre of liberation frequently collaborates with social workers in literacy campaigns and also with progressive priests in Basic Christian Communities to help celebrate events on the liturgical calendar or to help found new grassroots communities.

One of the first extensively documented theatre of liberation experiments was conducted by Augusto Boal in Peru in August 1973.[23] Prior to this date, Boal had been creating performance-oriented political theatre with his Arena theatre company in Sao Paulo, Brazil, for over a decade. Moving from productions of Western classics to adaptations of Brecht, he finally arrived at the inescapable conclusion that it is not the plotline, the dialogue, or the epic acting of a committed actor that should be the focal point of effective political theatre, but the operations in the spectator's mind. The most effective way of making political theatre, Boal found, was to involve the spectator in the creation and performance of a play:

Aristotle proposes a poetics in which the spectator delegates power to the dramatic character so that the latter may act and think for him. Brecht proposes

Nestor Horfilla from Mindanao leads a warm-up session at a workshop in
Hokianga, a Maori tribal area in New Zealand.

a poetics in which the spectator delegates power to the character who thus acts
in his place but the spectator reserves the right to think for himself, often in
opposition to the character. In the first case, a "catharsis" occurs; in the second, an awakening of critical consciousness. But the *poetics of the oppressed* focuses on the action itself: the spectator delegates no power to the character (or
actor) either to act or to think in his place; on the contrary, he himself assumes
the protagonic role, changes the dramatic action, tries out solutions, discusses
plans for change—in short, trains himself for real action. In this case, perhaps
the theater is not revolutionary in itself, but it is surely a rehearsal for the
revolution. (p. 122)

This discovery and his later association with Paulo Freire prompted Boal to
develop the now legendary methods of what he called "the theatre of the
oppressed," which he started implementing in Latin American slums and
rural communities from the late sixties onwards, until he was first imprisoned and finally forced into exile by the Brazilian authorities.[24]

Boal distinguishes two kinds of theatre of the oppressed. The first kind is
made by professional actors who polish the results of the grassroot processes
into high-quality theatre performances. The second kind is the grassroots
theatre of the oppressed workshop itself. This process is composed of four
phases. The first phase contains

five categories of exercises that try to develop the capacity of the body. Now, in everyday life we are obliged to do lots of movements that are always repetitive; these mechanized body movements reduce the capacity of the body to feel what we touch. So we have 20 or more exercises to help us diminish the gap between feeling and touching; even the air we touch with our skin we don't feel; so we try to develop the feeling of touch. Similarly there is a difference between seeing and looking: sometimes we look at things, we don't see them. And we still have another exercise which helps us to listen to what we hear. To listen is an act of the conscience; we have to be conscious of what we are hearing, sometimes we are not conscious of most of the things we hear. Fourthly, we have an exercise in which we try to develop multiple senses at the same time. And we have a last category which works with the memory of the senses—we try to develop the memory of the senses.[25]

In the second phase, the physical discoveries of the first phase are intellectualized and subsequently politicized through advanced theatre communication methods and games that first teach participants to express themselves through their bodies and finally result in different kinds of informal performances. In other words, the participants learn a theatre language. The applicability of this process for literacy practices is obvious.

In the third phase, the participants explore the practical conventions of theatre as a medium for communication: "one begins to practice theatre as a language that is living and *present,* not as a finished product displaying images from the past."[26] The workshop participants begin to write their own scenarios that are instantaneously performed by trained actors. Another option is to create "Image Theatre": participants instruct the actors to compose a human sculpture that expresses an idea or an emotion and subsequently suggest they bring the sculpture to life in an improvised scene, guiding them constantly as the action progresses. The third type of performance that can result from the theatre of the oppressed workshop is called "Forum Theatre." It involves a realistically performed scene of some form of oppression from the experience of the participants. Just the slice of life is performed, not the resolution. The participants are given time to think and react, and the scene is then replayed with the suggestions from the participants. If they have the confidence, participants can even take over the part of an actor and show how they think it should be done.

In the fourth phase of the workshop, participants actually become playwrights, directors, and actors themselves to communicate a certain issue or to rehearse a particular action. One of the examples of this kind of theatre of the oppressed is called "newspaper theatre." As the name suggests, it is based on newspaper reports. It is related to the "Living Newspapers" developed by the Federal Theatre Project in the United States during the Great Depression.[27] Boal's version contrasts two opposing news items: for example, the report of a lavish reception for a foreign dignitary in the Rio de Janeiro city hall with the announcement of widespread famine in the Brazilian north east.

Theatre of liberation workshop in Mindanao.

Relaxation exercise, theatre of liberation workshop.

"invisible theatre," another example from the fourth phase, is an ultra-realistic scene acted out in a public place to provoke reactions from passers-by. Invisible theatre could depict, for example, a slightly exaggerated instance of police brutality or an incident of racism.

In addition to the more or less finished public performances, the fourth phase of the theatre of the oppressed can also contain simple in-house skits for social analysis, to stimulate discussion in a community, or to prepare citizens for social action. For instance, a scene from a cheap soap opera can be reenacted and subsequently analyzed to point out the undesirable domestic man-woman relations it portrays. Alternatively, participants can reconstruct an incident of oppression and, secondly, experiment with new versions of the same scene in which the victim actually stands up to the oppressor. Other theatrical practices that can be introduced in this phase of the process include analyses of traditional myths and behavioral patterns.[28]

Theatre of Liberation in Asia

In the late sixties and early seventies, variations on the theatre of the oppressed were also introduced to several African and Asian communities, often by theatre practitioners who had reached the same conclusions as Boal, even though they had never been directly exposed to his theories or his methods.[29] Two Third World Theatre Conferences organized by UNESCO—one in Manila (1971), the other in Shiraz, Iran (1973)—were instrumental in developing the concept of theatre for social change in the third world.

In Asia, theatre had been used as an alternative to the colonial media from the forties into the sixties, but, as Ross Kidd rightly points out, it had been primarily a performance-oriented theatre *for* the people:

> It often failed to achieve its educational and organizing goals. As an externally induced theatre it reinforced dependence on creative resources outside the community and failed to recognize the cultural strengths of the community which had not only survived colonialism but stiffened resistance against the colonial occupation. . . . Another problem was the lack of an organizational base. Many of the groups had no links to a movement or organizing process. They came into the community, put on their play, held a discussion and hit the road.[30]

Fully aware of the shortcomings of these earlier attempts, middle-class Filipino and Indian artists, who had become politicized by the authoritarian repression that reigned in their countries, began developing the first theatre of liberation workshops in the early seventies. Dissatisfied with performing Western classics or their own intellectual creations for the urban bourgeoisie, they wanted these grassroots workshops to serve as training sessions for the creation of self-reliant, small-scale theatrical media that could be completely controlled by local residents. Independently of Boal,[31] these Asian artists had concluded that a phased cumulative workshop structure would be most effective for their purpose: (1) a "get-to-know-you" group integration phase; (2) a structural analysis phase in which local stories and social problems are extracted from the participants; and (3) basic theatre training, followed by the production of a script written by the workshop participants and performed by local actors for a local audience.

The major innovation of the Asian theatre of liberation was the attention that its practitioners paid to the pre-workshop and post-workshop periods. They discovered the importance of investigating the social, political, economic, and cultural conditions of a community before exposing it to a theatre of liberation workshop. They also realized that follow-up activities such as monitoring, refresher courses, advanced leadership and theatre training (the so-called "trainer's training"), and the integration of the community in a regional or national network were crucial to the long-term survival of the theatre of liberation.[32] In other words, they regarded the theatre of liberation workshop as a vehicle for establishing community theatre groups that would eventually merge into a nationwide (or even an international) cultural movement.

The main pioneer of Asian theatre of liberation is the Philippines Educational Theater Association (PETA) from Manila, originally a mainstream performance-oriented theatre company founded in 1967. Politicized by the atrocites committed by the Marcos dictatorship, the company developed an increasingly progressive political orientation in the course of the 1970s. After successfully organizing the UNESCO Third World Theatre Festival in 1971, the company received a grant to internationalize its grassroots theatre training activities. For this purpose, the Philippines Educational Theater Association adopted a new workshop model designed by Lutgardo Labad, a young composer and director and one of the leaders of the company. According to Labad, the four-week workshop schedule was designed to first expose participants to a variety of theatre forms: movement theatre, bread and puppet theatre, realistic theatre, and expressionism: "During the day there will be different exercises to explore these forms. Then, in the fourth week, there is outreach. We divide the participants into teams and conduct workshops in the communities. That is always a high for the participants because they get to see the value of theatrical work in a social context. Then they come back and do a two-week production."[33] All of PETA's training activities, which range from grassroots theatre of liberation workshops to advanced courses for professional performers, adopt the same three-phase cumulative strategy.

Although PETA conducts community theatre workshops throughout the year, its main training activities are concentrated in six-week courses during the summer, with an average annual participation of two to three hundred people. This summer theatre school is also used to screen prospective new core members for the various collectives that exist within PETA, but the majority of the participants return to their homes to found theatre groups that service their own communities. PETA's training program does not produce actors for the classical stage; rather, it trains a new breed of all-round committed artist called ATOR, an acronym of *Actor-Trainer-Organizer-Researcher*: "We may not provide you with the best possible training for you to act in Ibsen or Chekhov," says Lutgardo Labad, "although some of our actors and actresses are of international calibre. We offer the best training for you to put up a community theatre group, a self-reliant nucleus in a school or a rural or urban community, because that's the kind of theatre we want to develop. One of the significant objectives of the workshop is to rekindle in the community an appreciation and love for local culture to express local issues."[34]

At the end of a workshop, the musical, visual, and theatrical art works are presented to the community at large in a mini-culture of liberation festival that is sometimes also taken to neighboring communities. Following such a performance, "audience feedback is gathered in an impromptu sharing of ideas, problems, and insights with the community [. . .] all for the purpose of *dialogue, reflection,* and hopefully, when the discussion is spontaneously threaded into the activities of other [grassroots] organizations: *action.*"[35]

One of the more spectacular "actions" took place in Davao City in the southern Philippine island of Mindanao at the end of 1985. Artist-trainers from a local theatre of liberation collective had gathered close to one hundred men and women in a gymnasium for a three-day live-in workshop. Professional dancers introduced the participants to creative and martial arts movements and to symbolic choreography. Visual artists taught them how to make masks and costumes from materials like branches, leaves, and junk found nearby. Under the guidance of professional actors, the workshop participants—recruited from the urban poor—collectively composed a drama that told the story of their exploitation and oppression on the local level. The final day of the theatre of liberation workshop was filled with the excitement of having found a powerful new means of expression. Participants began to compose their own songs, they painted murals and banners, and fleshed out the dramatic scenes they had improvised on the previous day. At the end of the day, they spontaneously marched out of the gymnasium, waving their banners, singing their songs, and performing their skits on street corners; they attracted a crowd of several thousand that followed them to several government offices, which were subsequently picketed for an entire week.[36]

Hundreds upon hundreds of talented and committed youngsters from all over the Philippines and neighboring countries have already undergone the theatre of liberation process. They have gone back to their respective places, founded community theatre groups of their own, and conducted duplicate workshops in impoverished townships, rural settlements, and tribal areas. They communicate regularly with other groups in their region and beyond. As a result, today there is a well-organized theatre of liberation network in the Philippines that unites over four hundred groups and represents a very powerful popular force that is constantly generating alternative emancipatory culture. Through their participation in the Philippines Educational Theatre Association's summer courses, theatre artists from Indonesia, Thailand, Pakistan, South Korea, India, and Japan have been importing the Philippine theatre of liberation model into their own countries. PETA has also exported its methods by sending teams of instructors abroad to conduct workshops in countries like Bangladesh, Papua New Guinea, Malaysia, Singapore, Hong Kong, Aotearoa [New Zealand], and Australia.

Typically, a theatre of liberation training team gets invited to do its outreach work by local organizations like progressive parishes, student groups, teachers, chapters of labor unions, or cooperatives of plantation workers. Although the dynamics, strategies, and exercises of the theatre of liberation workshop have evolved considerably over the years and vary from country to country and from culture to culture, its basic process can be divided into three phases: (1) the pre-workshop period; (2) the workshop proper; and (3) the post-workshop period.

The Pre-Workshop Period

Before entering a specific area or community, the workshop trainers conduct extensive investigation into its social, political, economic, and cultural conditions. During several consultations, the local organizers furnish the necessary information to the actor-trainers in the form of a "situationer," a written or oral analysis of local conditions. The trainers also get acquainted with the environment and the local populace, with whom they sometimes conduct informal interviews. The best workshop results are obtained if participants can work and live together for several days at a stretch. The workshops are therefore usually planned in a natural (or unnatural) break from work like a strike, a holiday, or the off-season for fishermen and plantation workers. The training team arrives a few days prior to the official beginning of the workshop in order to familiarize the community and the participants with their presence. It is crucial that they live and eat with the target group and adapt themselves as much as possible to the local conditions. This is particularly important for workshops held with peasants or tribal minorities in remote rural settings where feudal attitudes can still be deeply entrenched. The rural population often still looks up to educated middle-class people from the big city, an attitude which can obstruct the creative liberation process.

The Workshop Proper

The theatre of liberation workshop begins with the get-to-know-you phase in which games and exercises are used to break the ice. In the "name chain,"

"Give me a shape." Theatre of liberation workshop in Mindanao.

for example, one of the actor-trainers says his or her first name with a creative sound or movement and asks the participants, who stand in a circle, to
imitate the name, the sound, and the movement. All participants subsequently get a chance to introduce themselves and then see themselves mim-
icked by the others. The game efficiently breaks initial inhibitions and helps
people to memorize the names of their fellow participants if they don't yet
know them. Various other games of this kind enhance the get-to-know-you
process and serve to establish mutual trust and sensitivity. In this phase, variations on the children's game blind-man's buff can be used to explore and
creatively manipulate space as well as build up trust in one's fellow participants.

A cartoon-drawing exercise provides the playful framework for the "expectation check" with which the actor-trainers find out what exactly the participants intend to learn from the workshop. The game proceeds as follows:
pairs of participants sit down opposite each other. They look each other straight
in the eyes and, without looking down, begin to draw the contours of their
partner's face with a pencil on a sheet of paper placed before them on the
floor. The result is invariably a caricature. Next, the two partners interview
each other rapidly for two minutes. They exchange information on names,
residence, age, background, and reasons for attending the workshop. The
two partners then change identity by attaching the drawing they made of
their partner to their own chest with a piece of scotch tape or a safety pin.

Subsequently, they share the information (in first person singular) with the rest of the group while the actor-trainers take notes. Apart from an extension of the get-to-know-you process, this exercise also provides an initial exposure to acting in that, during their presentations, participants can be encouraged to imitate gestures, intonation, and other characteristics of their partners without, of course, ridiculing them.

The theatre of liberation workshop is structured cumulatively and hence new participants should not be allowed in once the process has been set in motion. Relationships and collective working attitudes have already begun to gel to such a degree that the introduction of a newcomer would only disrupt the process. By the same token, the effectiveness of the second phase depends on the success of the first. If inhibitions have not been sufficiently broken and a healthy collaboration does not exist, the results of the second phase—in which private experiences are shared with the group—will be proportionally meager.

One of the aims of the theatre of liberation workshop is to be nonthreatening and transparent. Upon completion of a certain phase or after major exercises, the whole group sits down in the round for feedback. The actor-trainers explain the purpose and the method of a completed phase or a particular exercise and ask for the participants' reactions. Ideally, the actor-trainers evaluate the workshop's progress at the end of each day and make adjustments wherever necessary. If the sessions are too long, they will incorporate more action songs and other "ice-breakers." If particular participants are withdrawn or recalcitrant, they will get special attention the following day.

The second phase opens with a creative version of the structural social analysis of the community. The participants are requested to make a "social map," in which they indicate what they consider to be the most prominent landmarks in their community by means of symbols which they can either draw, paint, or cut from a magazine. They can select, for example, symbols of people or institutions who hold the political or economic power in their community. The collages that are thus created are exhibited in an improvised "art gallery." The participants study each other's maps and select four or five that they find the most intriguing or feel a certain affinity with. In groups of five or six, the participants then proceed to interview each other as to the significance of certain symbols and eventually produce a collective map that represents the group's consensus view of the structural analysis of their community. They finally present their collective map in a short showcase in which they can use songs or skits.

"Social map making" requires a relatively high level of literacy and ability to think in abstract terms. Simpler exercises utilizing the same kind of creative participation—albeit with more guidance—can produce similar results with less advanced target groups. One relatively expensive alternative is to give the participants two or three simple cameras loaded with slide film and instruct them to take photographs of things, people, and activities which they find essential to the life in their community. The subsequent slide show can lead to an animated debate. A less expensive medium that has been used in the Philippines, Thailand, and Indonesia is the "Flexaflan," a flannel board with cardboard puppets and objects that can be moved around to help the participants to tell their stories. In this way, the participants can be brought into discussions, arguing over what puppets in what place and in what relation to each other best represent the social structure in their community. Through all these methods, people's stories can be extracted that are processed (in phase three) in the form of original scripts.

Structural analysis is always followed by a round-table session in which participants tell stories from their own lives or from their community. These stories, which are often moving, form the basis for the drama pieces that will evolve later on. At this stage, the actor-trainers may elect to introduce basic acting techniques, or exercises in plot construction and storytelling. Alternatively, they may introduce some more exercises to stimulate the imagination, creativity, and spontaneity, or they can organize additional activities to enhance trust and sensitivity between participants. Simple exercises serve to explore the creative potential of the human body. In "Give me a shape" the participants, individually or alone, imitate the shape of an object chosen by the actor-trainer or by themselves: e.g., a bowl of rice, a fish, or a church. In "A day in the life of . . ." the participants lie on the floor, close their eyes, and mime the actions to a story narrated by the actor-trainer. If they have to imitate a character, they are told to pay careful attention to facial expressions and gestures. In an exercise called "Creative sounds" the participants learn to turn found objects like tin cans and coconut shells into musical instruments. Furthermore, they are made aware that sensitivity and cooperation are crucial requirements for collective creation. When performing together, they realize that they should not dominate with their "instrument," as it can disturb the harmony.

In phase three, one or more original people's plays are created and produced by the participants themselves, who by now have virtually taken full control of the workshop process. Divided into groups of five or six, they work out scenarios based on one or more of the stories told by the participants. They compose songs, rehearse, and finally mount their plays, which they can perform for the community at large or for the rest of the group, depending on their level of confidence. The participants are encouraged to utilize performing art forms indigenous to their culture. In any event, closed or public performances invariably result in an open forum of sorts in which the issues raised by the plays are discussed. In this sense, theatre of liberation can be regarded as a grassroots exercise in people's democracy. On a different level, it can be a powerful instrument for communal therapy and it can assist a community in creatively expressing its defeats or in celebrating its victories.

A People's Play from Negros: *Sakada*

In 1983, a group of sugar workers from the island of Negros in the central
Philippines came up with the following skit in a theatre of liberation workshop. It was their own creative expression of a massacre that had occurred in
the town of Escalante earlier that same year. Their short play is a powerful
example of a people's story becoming theatre of liberation. It starts with a
joyful children's story about an old, toothless water buffalo, called *carabao* in
the local language, whereupon one of the *sakadas* (or sugar workers) steps
forward to explain that Negros is not the happy, beautiful island people think
it is.

(SAKADAS line up to get their pay.)
SAKADA I: We work under the sun the entire day. I feel I'm falling apart. What sin
have we committed to deserve this kind of punishment? Sometimes I can't help
calling out to God, "You better kill us all so we can finally rest in peace!" The
tractors of the landlords are far better off than we. When the tractors break down
they get fixed right away, but if we sugarworkers get sick, they leave us to die.
*(SAKADAS move together to cut imaginary sugarcane. SAKADA I moves around the stage trying
to catch a field rat.)*
SAKADA I: One day, I caught a rat in the sugarcane fields. It was huge. I called my
son, Nonoy. "Noy! Noy! Come over here! Quick! Bring this home and boil it!
Add a little salt and soy sauce and we'll have a delicious dinner tonight." When
I came home the children were already eating. They were laughing and laughing
while eating the rat. But I felt bad. *(Pause.)* That is why, when I heard about a
meeting that was going to be held in the neighboring town, I agreed to join at
once. *(To SAKADA II.)* Are you joining us?
SAKADA II: Of course, we have to find a way to let our landlords know of our prob-
lems.
SAKADA I: What are we waiting for?
SAKADA II: Wait, you forgot something!
SAKADA I: Ah, yes!
*(They quickly put together some placards to take to the rally. The SAKADAS begin their march
to the tune of the Carabao song.)*
SAKADA I: When we reached the town, we saw six trucks full of military men. They
had automatic rifles.
SAKADA II: *(To SAKADA III, worried.)* We're not doing anything wrong, are we?
SAKADA III: The central labor contracting agency has closed down. Where are we
going to work?
SAKADA IV: We don't have anything to eat.
SAKADA V: Our pockets are empty. Our stomachs are empty.
SAKADA VI: We're asking for rice, not bullets!
ALL: Rice, not bullets! Rice, not bullets!
SAKADA I: Suddenly they threw tear gas at us.
SAKADA II: Everybody down on the pavement!
SAKADA I: I looked for my son, Nonoy . . . "Noy! Noy! Where are you, Noy?!"

Sakada.

Then they started shooting at us. I could see the smoke on the road while they were firing at us. *(Pause.)* When they stopped shooting, I looked for my son. "Noy! Noy! Where are you, Noy?!" *(He spots Nonoy on the ground.)* I saw Nonoy face down on the pavement. He was lying in a pool of blood. They had shot him while he was taking cover from the tear gas. *(Pause.)* I remember how I used to sing lullabies to Nonoy on the days that we didn't have anything to eat. I sang to make him forget his hunger.

(SAKADA I mimes picking up his son's body and sings "Ili-Ili," a traditional Ilongo lullaby from Negros. As he walks off stage, the other SAKADAS resume the Carabao song.)[37]

At the end of *Sakada* one of the sugar workers addresses the audience, saying that Negros is indeed known for its sugar and its sweet, smiling people. But they can only take so much. If nothing is done to prevent their starvation, they have no choice but to organize themselves and take up arms.

After the Workshop

Sakada is just one of the hundreds of original plays that have been created throughout Asia by means of theatre of liberation workshops. But the process does not end with the performance. After the final showcase and the community forum, participants and instructors evaluate the entire workshop.

They match results with the initial expectations and discuss follow-up possibilities. Demystification of the workshop process is essential. Throughout the workshop, the participants have been informed all along where they were headed and what phase of the workshop they were in at any given time. The instructors try to convince the participants that with a minimum of training and practice they could conduct their own workshops for other members of their community or for neighboring villages and towns. The workshop participants then frequently decided to form their own community theatre group.

The new grassroots theatre of liberation company can be regarded as a micromedia unit. From the start, its activities are divided into training and performing. As a performing unit, the group creates its own original plays for important social, political, or religious occasions. As a training unit, the group develops its own instructors capable of conducting outreach workshops in other communities. A snowball effect can be created when one theatre of liberation unit founds another, and so forth.

Community theatre of liberation groups can be regarded as small-scale experiments in community building. By promoting interpersonal sensitivity and methods of communal communication, the theatre of liberation workshop contributes to the establishment of healthy, democratic, equitable, creative, and self-reliant grassroots communities. For that reason, the security of theatre of liberation activists has come under increasing threat from authorities in repressive countries, who often regard them as subversives. As the following pages hope to illustrate, the grassroots theatre of liberation groups and their performance-oriented semiprofessional allies in the cities succeed in creating ever-larger spaces of liberty in their countries. The theatre of liberation workshop helps to release spontaneity, the fundamental ingredient of freedom and artistic creation. Through its networks, its workshops, and its repertory, the theatre of liberation is able, like a mobile culture of liberation factory as it were, to create an alternative nationalist and people-oriented culture that can successfully compete with the status quo—oriented commercial and government-controlled culture. For middle-class actors, finally, the workshop experience is infinitely more rewarding than a ten-minute standing ovation after a performance in an urban theatre, for in a relatively short period of time they can see the direct sociopolitical impact of their creative input in the participants' newly gained self-respect and the discovery of an empowering creativity they did not know they possessed.

II

BUILDING STAGES OF
PEOPLE POWER
THE PHILIPPINES EDUCATIONAL THEATER
ASSOCIATION

I arrived in the Philippines the day before the anxiously awaited presidential elections of 7 February 1986 and encountered an incredible array of dramatic activities and an extensive theatre of liberation network that was fully mobilized and bubbling over with energy. Throughout this island-nation of 60 million inhabitants—from the Cordillera mountain region of Luzon in the north to the Muslim provinces of Mindanao in the south—community-based and repertory troupes incorporated in the network were involved in the election campaign, siding either with Corazon Aquino's Laban coalition movement or the more radical Bayan boycott faction.[1] The plays that were created during this turbulent period from December 1985 (when the elections were first announced) to late February (when Marcos finally escaped) ranged from satirical agitprop pieces performed in urban slum areas to sophisticated, realistic three-act dramas and multimedia rock musicals presented in fully equipped playhouses or university gymnasiums. It was clear to me that I was right in the middle of an exciting political theatre movement that really worked (for a change). But where did it come from and where was it headed?

A Brief Look at History

The Philippines offers an almost perfect model of the neocolonial situation described in the previous chapter. Four hundred years of Spanish colonial rule (still evident in the country's name, which honors the Spanish imperialist King Philip II) were followed, in 1899, by half a century of undisguised American occupation. The Japanese put in five imperialistic years of their own and, following the Second World War, a nominally independent Philippines saw the arrival of a new breed of colonizer: the foreign investor. Dressed in business suits instead of uniforms and with the help of local upper class strawmen, they proceeded to exploit the country's abundant natural resources more subtly but no less profitably than their predecessors. The situation was further aggravated when American military strategists started seeing the advantages of having a permanent foothold in the South Pacific basin and selected the Philippines as the ideal spot for that purpose. Hence, during the Vietnam War, the Subic Bay naval facility and Clark air force base were drastically expanded to form the largest American military installations outside the continental United States. Along with the weapons and soldiers came a cultural entourage of a U.S. military television and radio station. In no time, adjacent cities like Olongapo and Angeles had spawned all-night discos, bars, and brothels. The extensive American economic and military interests in the Philippines created the need for a firm and stable government as well as a subtle, indirect influence over Philippine culture through media and education, which even today continue to be clones of their American counterparts. Results have been disastrous. The hand-me-down official culture instilled the worst kind of consumerism and escapism in the Filipino people. It was further fed by ever-expanding American hamburger and pizza chains, omnipresent American sportswear, American rock and disco music and their Filipino imitations blaring from portable stereos in the slums, increasingly popular video rental services, and soap-opera emotions on Hallmark greeting cards. The Filipino mind continued to be colonized even if the country itself had officially become a sovereign state. Behind the scenes, meanwhile, Western industrial opportunists, sex tour operators, and the American military contributed to the development of a ruling class of ruthlessly corrupt political and military leaders. Enter the glib orator and brilliant dictator Senator Ferdinand Marcos in the late sixties.

It has by now been sufficiently well documented how, until 1986, Marcos and his cronies systematically amassed enormous fortunes from the Filipino people and invested their booty in Swiss banks and lucrative foreign real estate projects. The former First Lady of the Philippines—once a close friend of Nancy Reagan's—was recently acquitted of criminal charges for large-scale real estate fraud in the state of New York. Ferdinand Marcos has died and rumors have it that he is still waiting, embalmed in a glass coffin in Hawaii, to be flown to his native territory in Ilocos Norte for a stateman's funeral. The corpse of his dead mother has been paraded around villages there in a similar transparent case for several years now, a feudal queen waiting for her son's return.

Under Marcos, the ruling élite lived in extravagant luxury while many Filipinos literally starved and increasingly vocal political opponents were brutally silenced through torture and murders euphemistically labeled "accidental deaths." From 21 September 1972 until effectively 25 February 1986, the U.S.-backed Marcos government held its own population at gunpoint through the terrorizing instrument of martial law. In the face of such gross abuses of power, how could the sensitive actor continue to play Hamlet for the Makati bourgeoisie on the posh, multimillion-dollar stage of the Cultural Center of the Philippines?[2]

In the shadow of the wasteful and megalomaniacal exploits of the former First Family, since the beginning of the seventies an effective theatre of liberation network has been operating in the Philippines with the express objective of counteracting the products of the government-controlled culture and information channels. The political activities of this movement were manifested in many different ways during the climactic days between the rigged presidential elections of 7 February 1986 and the ailing dictator's escape to Guam on 26 February of that same year. Actors and actresses were conspicuously present during marches and mass rallies, performing street plays for crowds numbering more than a million. They also hosted talk shows at the occupied television studios of Channels Four and Nine, and entertained and encouraged the human barricades in front of the military headquarters of Camp Aguinaldo at EDSA Avenue in Quezon City during the three-day uprising before the fall of Marcos. Before those events, theatre had already been intricately involved in the political dynamics of the Philippines for over two decades. The struggle for liberation was (and continues to be) very much fought on the cultural front.

The First Filipino Theatre

The present wave of theatre of liberation in the Philippines began in the early seventies, but the real roots of Filipino political theatre go back much further. Theatrical activities in this Asian country are closely interwoven with the colonial past and the consequent domination of its culture by foreign rulers. Only in the last decade or so have scholars like Nicanor Tiongson, Doreen Fernandez, and Isagani Cruz started investigating indigenous forms of Filipino drama and made Filipino cultural studies a legitimate academic discipline.[3] They have traced the origins of Filipino drama back to the rituals, songs, and dances of the tribal cultures from before the Spanish conquest. They argue that modern Philippine drama should be as popular and as firmly rooted in contemporary society as were these primitive forms of dramatic expression.

During the first period of colonial rule (1521–1898), the Spanish *conquistadores* introduced a range of play types to the Philippine archipelago that were Iberian in origin and often Catholic evangelical in intention. Many of these plays were directly occasioned by the Church calendar. The *panunuluyan,* for example, presented every year during Advent, dramatized Joseph and Mary's search for lodging on Christmas Eve. But the semi-religious *komedya* (also called *moro-moro*), the *sarswela,* and the *sinakulo* became the true hallmarks of the Hispanic-Filipino theatre.

The *komedya* was a kind of verse drama based on Spanish tales about heroic battles between Christian knights and Muslim Moors, who occupied the southern regions of the Iberian peninsula in the eighth century. These action-filled plays, which also contained a forceful dose of romance, invariably ended in the defeat and subsequent baptism of the Moors. Needless to say, *komedyas* served the strategic purposes of the colonial forces in the Philippines by portraying them as benevolent Christian warriors defending God's heavenly interests by fighting the heathenish Muslims of the southern Philippine island of Mindanao. Likewise, the *sinakulos,* dramatizations of Christ's crucifixion, taught the Filipinos to resign themselves to their earthly poverty and oppression as a trial of God for which they would reap their rewards in the Hereafter.

The *sarswelas* were musical slices of life with romantic happy endings.[4] They were introduced by the Spanish rulers as *zarzuelas* at the end of the nineteenth century but rapidly took on a vernacular life of their own as they became favorite vehicles for the first native Filipino playwrights to practice covert social criticism. The typical *sarswela* dramatizes a love story between two members of the upper class while at the same time cautiously satirizing the social vices of macho Filipino collaborationists.

Severino Reyes, Juan Abad, and Aurelio Tolentino were best known for their controversial political dramas in the first decades of the twentieth century. Tolentino's *Kahapon, Ngayon, at Bukas* [Yesterday, Today, and Tomorrow], for example, depicts a popular uprising which results in the Filipino people kicking the Americans out of their country. The plays of these three nationalist playwrights were extremely popular, and the American authorities, fearing their subversive impact, raided performances and regularly arrested authors, directors, and actors.

The period of indigenous revolutionary drama was not to last long. Even more effectively than military intimidation, American motion pictures drew the audiences away from playhouses and into movie houses. From then on, the native Filipino theatre fought a losing battle against American-dominated mass media and educational institutions, which succeeded in diffusing Western cultural standards throughout the country. Primary and secondary schools throughout the Philippines used American textbooks and English as the official language of instruction until well into the sixties. Concurrently, Philippine drama remained largely an imitation of Western theatre with hardly any original Filipino plays written in the vernacular.[5]

The Formation of PETA

The decisive event that made Filipino theatre the force it is today was the foundation in 1967 of the Philippines Educational Theater Association. PETA was the brainchild of Cecilia Reyes Guidote, an enterprising young woman who had received her first exposure to Western drama while in high school, and had gone on to write a "Prospectus for the National Theatre of the Philippines" as her M.A. Thesis for Trinity University in Dallas, Texas.

When she returned from the United States to Manila she was ready to implement her ideas of what a Philippine national theatre should look like. She founded a new institution which she called PETA: "The national theatre of the Philippines should embrace the capital, the cities, the towns, and barrios of the islands. It should be primarily devoted to the quest for a dramaturgy truly expressive of the Filipino's national culture."[6]

Guidote's grandiose concept—clearly inspired by Jean Vilar and other such Western advocates of a popular theatre catering to all sectors of society—comprised a professional performing arm (called the Kalinangan Ensemble); branches reaching out to the communities and the educational and industrial sectors; an experimental theatre; an international exchange program; a touring company; a television and cinema unit; and a performing arts academy which she baptized the Central Institute of Theatre Arts in the Philippines (CITAP). Guidote managed to lay the groundwork for all these activities and invited several foreign directors, including Brooks Jones of the Cincinnati Playhouse and Fritz Bennewitz, the director of the East German National Theatre in Weimar, to conduct workshops and direct productions. Thus the technical skills of the young company improved by leaps and bounds. Guidote subsequently succeeded in attracting financial support from UNESCO and arranged for PETA to become the Philippine Center of the International Theatre Institute. In 1971 she organized the Third World Theatre Festival in Manila.

It was not long before Imelda Marcos discovered Cecile Guidote's visionary qualities and organizational talents and tried to engage her for one of her own élitist cultural projects, inviting her to become artistic director of the projected multimillion-dollar Cultural Center of the Philippines, a luxurious structure located on reclaimed land in Manila Bay that was intended to be a venue for expensive foreign shows catering to wealthy Filipinos. Guidote rejected the offer and soon thereafter went into exile in the United States with her husband, a prominent political enemy of the Marcoses.

With Guidote gone, a group of young CITAP graduates were more or less forced to take over PETA's leadership. Among them were Cecilia ("CB") Garrucho, Lino Brocka (who later became the first Filipino cinema director to win prestigeous awards at both the Cannes and London international film festivals), Lutgardo ("Gardy") Labad, and Socrates ("Soxy") Topacio. They were largely responsible for introducing a more democratic decision-making process, which had been lacking under Guidote's rather autocratic rule. More importantly, with the new collective organizational structure, PETA developed a progressive orientation that manifested itself in a diminished top-down attitude, a new concept of a socially committed artist-teacher, a method of collective creation, and a genuine commitment to help build a counterculture for liberation through an extensive nationwide theatre of liberation network.

The smoothly operating theatre of liberation network of today is the fruit of a carefully planned strategy that was initiated more or less simultaneously by PETA and a Mindanao-based organization in the mid seventies. That is not to say that there was no political theatre before that time, but earlier political theatre had been more incidental than consciously part of a progressive nationwide cultural movement.

The idea of theatre as a weapon for liberation had been born in the late sixties, inspired by the cultural analyses of such Filipino political philosophers as Claro M. Recto, José-Maria Sison, and Renato Constantino.[7] During this period, the radical student union, Kabataang Makabayan, also formed its cultural arm, called Panday Sining, which performed political theatre in the style of the Chinese Cultural Revolution. Nicanor Tiongson, the current artistic director of the Cultural Center of the Philippines, recalls:

> It turned a lot of people off: clenched fists and all that. Films like *Taking Tiger Mountain by Strategy* and *The East Is Red* from China and the Peking Opera influenced us enormously. That's why there was a predominance of tableaux, red flags, marching, and the usual chanting. But just as we were beginning to realize what we were doing wrong, Martial Law was declared. Actually, this was beneficial in a sense, because we had to find a new way to tell the truth and thus Martial Law contributed to the maturation of our political theatre.[8]

Before Martial Law, in the optimistic period of militant student protest (1969–1972) that is now commonly referred to as "The First Quarter Storm," theatre was considered a secondary activity at best; a useful means to attract and entertain an audience between speeches at political rallies, but not a political weapon in its own right. This perception did not fundamentally change until the mid seventies.

Creating an Alternative Force

After the declaration of Martial Law on 21 September 1972, many radical students and artists took to the countryside, either to join the guerrillas of the New People's Army or to engage in community organizing. Other previously militant actors like Tony Espejo joined the establishment theatre of the Cultural Center of the Philippines. The group *Babaylan,* founded by Nicanor Tiongson and Doreen Fernandez, started experimenting with traditional theatre forms like the *sarswela,* while PETA, still recovering from the shock of Guidote's departure, was taking its first hesitant steps on the slippery surface of political culture with some socially critical plays of its own.

Meanwhile, the most fearless attempt at political theatre was being made by the repertory company of the University of the Philippines at Diliman, a continuation of *Kabataang Makabayan's* cultural arm. Under the direction of

Behn Cervantes, a graduate of New York's Columbia University and an accomplished theatre artist in his own right, U.P.-Rep, as it was called, became for a while the most potent voice of cultural protest in the capital. U.P.-Rep was well-known for satirical plays that ridiculed Imelda and Ferdinand Marcos. Their theatre became an alternative medium presenting facts about human rights abuses that were routinely ignored by the government-controlled media. One of the most effective forms developed by U.P.-Rep during this period was the *Pagsambang Bayan,* or "People's Mass," a liturgical theatre that fused theatre of liberation and liberation theology.[9]

Playwright Bonifacio Ilagan and direction Behn Cervantes came up with this concept while discussing the parallel architectural development of churches and playhouses—both luxuriously ornamented edifices in which metaphysical concepts rather than the down-to-earth problems of daily life were celebrated. The *Pagsambang Bayan* set out to expose the contrast between the rich architecture of the church and the poverty and the cruelty of the adjacent slums. Apart from choruses representing the oppressed workers, the peasants, and the tribal minorities, Cervantes used slides to depict the political violence and the abject poverty of Manila's shanty towns:

> One day we were invited to perform the play in Tondo, one of the most depressed areas of Manila. Children helped us to set up the stage. The military couldn't get to us because Tondo was already a very organized slum community. But two thirds of the way through the play they shut down the generator and we lost our lights. It was amazing to see how fast the people ran to their houses to get their gas lamps, and before we knew it the stage was lit up with the eerie light from these *gazeras*. We couldn't show any slides but that didn't really matter because these people knew all about poverty and cruelty. At the university we had to explain and show slides, but not in Tondo. And in the end they were not just shouting "Down with Marcos!" but "Long live the Revolution!"[10]

Nine days after the Tondo performance, Behn Cervantes was arrested in his Quezon City home and imprisoned for six months.[11]

U.P.-Rep has done four subsequent versions of *Pagsambang Bayan,* but from 1976 onward its new productions became repetitive and, as a result, less effective politically. Meanwhile, PETA was rapidly expanding after a three-year period of low political profile.

Immediately following the declaration of Martial Law, the military stepped up its intimidation campaign and Ferdinand Marcos took almost full control of the cultural media. The First Lady opened her Cultural Center of the Philippines in 1973 and her husband began to systematically reinforce censorship of opposition newspapers and to place the directorship of the most popular television and radio stations in the hands of close friends and relatives, who were selected not for their competence but for their loyalty.

In the face of these repressive measures, PETA's young, inexperienced leadership opted for a careful repertory of historical and allegorical plays. Thus *Nasa Puso Ang Amerika* [America Is in the Heart], for example, was based on Carlos Bulosan's novel of the same title about Filipino immigrant workers in the United States. Another play, *Cabesang Tales,* a period piece set in the nineteenth century, was about the rise and fall in the fortunes of a Mr. C. Tales, a tax collector who becomes bankrupt after failing to collect sufficient taxes. In this period, PETA was very much influenced by the Brechtian concept of historicity: theatre should show that economic and political structures are transient rather than permanent and that they are determined by people's actions instead of by universal laws.

Until 1974, PETA's repertory consisted mainly of adaptations, imitations, and translations of Western plays, in which Brecht in particular figured prominently. Realizing the limitations of secondhand work, the company began to stimulate the writing of original plays, developing a scriptwriting course for its summer theatre school. This initiative quickly bore fruit when a particularly talented batch of prospective playwrights emerged that included Alfredo Santos, Alan Glinoga, Malu Jacob, and Rody Vera. In 1975, no less than eight original plays were created, and from that moment on PETA has been making a concerted effort to develop excellence in playwriting through the formation of so-called writers' pools and laboratory production schemes for its new dramas. This strategy has resulted in some fine plays, among which *Si Tatang At Ibapang Mga Tauhan ng Aming Dula* [The Old Man and Other Characters in Our Play—1979], *Juan Tamban* [1979], *Panunuluyan* [The Search for an Inn—1979], *Pilipinas Circa 1907* [The Philippines around 1907—1982], *Oratoryo ng Bayan* [Oratorio of the People—1983], and *Buwan At Baril Sa E Major* [Moon and Gun in E Major—1984], stand out.

Si Tatang At Ibapang Mga Tauhan ng Aming Dula, written by the young playwright Alfredo Santos, was based on the true story of Valentín de los Santos, the founder of the *Lapiang Malaya* or Freedom Party, who died in 1967 at the age of 85. He had participated in all the major revolutions in the Philippines, and so had fought against the Spanish, the Americans, the Japanese, and Marcos. The ideology of the Freedom Party was highly influenced by spiritualism; all party members wore amulets around their necks that were supposed to make them invulnerable. The play traces the deeds of de los Santos in chronological order in an attempt to cleanse the old man's tarnished reputation. Prior to the play, most Filipino historians and political scientists had dismissed Valentín de los Santos as an obsessed lunatic, whereas the PETA play instead revealed him to be a well-read antibureaucratic, antibourgeois, humanitarian socialist.

The piece skillfully builds up to the climactic event in 1967 when de los Santos and five hundred knife-wielding followers were massacred in the Manila suburb of Pasay by Marcos's military guard. Valentín de los Santos himself died a few months later in a mental institution under mysterious circumstances that were never fully investigated. But the play suggests a political assassination and an official cover-up. Immediately following the old man's final speech ("In a crazy society, those in their right minds are treated as lunatics"), a jacket with the conspicuous sign "Media" is placed over his body.

Si Tatang At Ibapang Mga Tauhan Ng Aming Dula is a historical documentary play that uses slides, newspaper clippings, and radio excerpts to convey its information. It succeeded in overcoming public bias during a time when the Marcos régime was making an all-out effort to mystify historical facts. Indeed, demystifying government-controlled media items and cultural products subsequently became one of PETA's primary tasks.

Although the company gradually developed a more radical political outlook, which manifested itself most sharply in the discrete development of its grassroots theatre of liberation workshops, PETA's repertory could hardly be labeled agitational. The company did not yet have a tradition of performing in the streets—partly because of Cecile Guidote's Western mainstream theatre legacy, but also because of its own lack of genuine political consciousness, explains Lutgardo Labad:

> PETA became more socially relevant (we don't want to call it "radical" or "revolutionary") through a historical process. In 1975, most of our writers came from the student movement and carried over the concerns that lived in the universities. But we had to be protective; that's why we were doing mostly psychological plays and artistic experiments. It was the workshop programs that really politicized our people; they went into the provinces and learned of the atrocities being committed there.[12]

In the mid seventies, then, the development of PETA's theatre of liberation workshop method, not its repertory work, constituted its most radical activity. Given the repressive circumstances, the company had to go very quietly about its training activities, giving workshops at the request of church parishes, elementary schools, factory workers, and university students. Meanwhile, PETA's performing ensemble continued to become increasingly popular in Manila's middle class circles with sophisticated plays produced with limited means.

The Aesthetics of Poverty

Artistically, a typical PETA style was beginning to emerge which came to be known as the Aesthetics of Poverty, the fruit of artistic inventiveness forced upon the company by its chronic lack of finances. PETA's chief designer Brenda Fajardo rightly wondered, "How can an artist claim to be socially responsible when he mounts high-cost productions during times of deprivation?"[13] She continued,

> What is initially a by-product of material poverty becomes an expression which results from [the artist's] sensitivity to the world around him. The artist begins deliberately to choose particular nuances and tones of color and texture that would express the qualities that he perceives around him—economic deprivation, cultural pollution, senseless violence. He evolves a new art which is authentic because it expresses life which happens to be poor; thus "the aesthetics of poverty" . . . implies that there is a sense of beauty which belongs to people who live in a condition of material deprivation.[14]

Even today, PETA struggles to get by with little or no funding and, as a result, its designer pool still continues to work with found materials and junk.

The production of *Juan Tamban* well illustrates the lavish use of imagination and thrifty use of materials that have become typical of PETA's creative method. The direct inspiration for the play came from an article, "Meet Estong, a Child of the Slums," which appeared in the weekly *Philippine Panorama* magazine of 16 July 1978. It is the story of a street kid who makes a living by eating live lizards. Lutgardo Labad had read the piece and passed it on to Malu Jacob of the PETA writers' pool. Malu went in search of the boy, befriended him, talked to his relatives, and immersed herself for a considerable time in Manila slum life. She based her play on these experiences and created it in close consultation with the director, Joel Lamangan, who reconstructed the collaboration as follows: "I like her style. She's good. We communicate. I tell her, one rehearsal night: 'Malu, we need some revisions here.' We talk. She goes home and delivers the following day."[15] The cast too had a say in the creative process, although not always with the author's immediate consent:

> I wanted it to end with Marina's walkout, her speech at the international Conference on Children (Scene 25). I wanted it open-ended. The audience draw their own conclusions. Will Marina go to the slums? But Joel and the cast wanted a song instead, and with bravura. I allowed them to improvise. So Juan goes back home while the people are rebuilding their shanties. And Marina joins them . . . I kind of gave in. And during performances it worked very well.[16]

The set of *Juan Tamban* was designed collectively according to Aesthetics of Poverty principles. Brenda Fajardo took her designers' pool on several fact-finding missions to Manila's shanty towns. They chose the play's set pieces for their capacity to evoke meaningful and functional images, not for ornamentation or local color. Hence the play's identifying set piece: empty plastic pails lined up in rows suggest the chronic water shortages in many urban communities.[17]

The play itself dramatizes the encounter between Estong, renamed Juan

Tamban, and an upper-class sociology student called Marina. It is made up of two acts containing twelve scenes each. It opens with a child announcing the "lizard eater from Santa Ana," upon which a crowd gathers and Juan does his "act." They are dispersed by two policemen who try to grab little Juan. Marina arrives. She has read a newspaper article about the kid and wants to check him out. He is quite hostile to her but then collapses suddenly from the effects of eating the lizard. A doctor arrives and attends to Juan while the chorus, serving as an omniscient narrator and clearly intended as a Brechtian distancing device, recites the facts of Juan's case. In some of the subsequent scenes, the chorus also provides insights into Marina's thoughts and feelings. Through this clever theatrical tool, we witness her growth from an opportunistic student, who considers Juan merely a convenient subject for an academic case study, to Juan's loving friend, who gradually and painfully wakens to the miserable social realities that cause his predicament. To emphasize this point, scenes depicting the lifestyles of the well-to-do upper middle class are juxtaposed with scenes that show the stark, unhygienic realities of slum life. The scenes set in Marina's social habitat introduce a subplot involving her engagement to Mike, a fellow student, and nights of dancing, drinking, and smoking. The slum scenes show the struggles of Mang Tino, Juan's father, who makes a meager living as a garbage collector.

Many times Marina is on the verge of giving up as she encounters aggressive resistance from the kid. Her social background has not prepared her for persevering and roughing it. However, challenged by her academic advisor, Dr. de Leon, who offers her the chance to present a paper on Juan at an upcoming conference sponsored by the UNESCO International Year of the Child, she decides to immerse herself in the life of the Santa Ana shanty town to investigate the social context of her subject. Through flashbacks, Juan's turbulent experiences with his parents are revealed. Meanwhile, Marina manages to keep Juan, who is wanted for purse snatching, out of the hands of the police by officially taking him into the custody of the university's social science research center where she is employed. By the end of Act One, her scientific objectivity has ceded to a deeper emotional involvement with Juan.

In the first scene of Act Two, Marina visits the slums to tell Mang Tino of his son's illness. In the background, a government demolition team, assisted by riot police, moves in to tear down the improvised dwellings of the squatters. Mang Tino accompanies Marina to the hospital to make peace with his estranged son. Their reconciliation is contrasted with the increasing distance between Marina and Mike, who is jealous of what he sees as his girlfriend's exaggerated concern for a street urchin. As Juan begins to recover, fears about his imminent trial grow. Scenes 19 through 21 bring the trial, in which the plaintiff, a rich woman from the exclusive Dasmariñas subdivision, is confronted with the young purse snatcher. It soon becomes evident that the Philippine legal system is set up to protect the haves from the have-

nots, thereby perpetuating the sociopolitical status quo: Juan is found to be a
menace to society rather than the other way around, and Mang Tino is re-
primanded for not taking better care of his child. The father explodes:

> You have confiscated my garbage cart because I had no license, you have de-
> molished my house because it didn't look pretty enough for the tourists, now
> you want my son! Do you always have to take decisions for us? I have no job.
> *Basurero* [garbage collector] is the only job you can offer me. Do this! Do that!
> Don't do this! Don't do that! I am sick and tired of being told what to do and
> what not. I am taking my son with me. I have a right to take him with me![18]

Juan's father is cited for contempt of court and dragged out of the room. The
boy is returned to the juvenile detention center and the chorus quotes an
appropriate passage from the universal declaration of human rights.

The enforcers of the legal system have placed Marina back to square one
in her attempt to communicate with Juan. In Scene 22 she visits him at the
detention center. He is sullen and refuses to respond. This time, however,
the roles are reversed and Marina reveals to the young boy that, in fact, she
had been the patient and he the doctor, and she has learned more from his
street wisdom than from Dr. de Leon's lectures. Finally, Marina apologizes
for the police, for the judge, for the rich woman, and for the cruel and unjust
system they uphold. Ultimately, for having believed in the system so long,
she realizes she herself is also guilty of the crime perpetrated on Juan. In a
brief, expressionistic scene Juan is assaulted by a swarm of oversized in-
sects—imaginary versions of society's monsters that populate the nightmare
of his life: the judge, the police, and even Marina are among the hairy-legged
creatures that the young boy finally manages to crush and kick off stage. The
play concludes with a documentary scene in which Marina appears at the
conference, where she presents a radical paper highly critical of pretentious
antisocial social scientists and the inhuman rulers of Philippine society.

Juan Tamban received general praise from the press and the public and has
been performed in many subsequent productions throughout the country,
reaching many thousands of people. It was even televised and in 1984 the
published version of the play received the Philippine National Book Award,
confirming its reputation as a modern classic of modern Philippine liberation
drama and a landmark in the already respectable career of the Philippines
Educational Theatre Association.

A Political Version of the Nativity

Apart from developing an Aesthetics of Poverty, historical documentary dramas, and socialist-realist plays, in the late seventies PETA also started to con-
temporize traditional theatre forms for its repertory. *Panunuluyan* and *Pilipi-*

nas Circa 1907 are among the most successful examples of this trend. PETA modernized the *Panunuluyan* Christmas play for the first time in December 1979, and has performed it in updated versions every Advent season since then. In addition, the PETA *Panunuluyan* has been adapted into many of the other dialects spoken in the Philippines and around Christmas it is now often simultaneously performed by many different groups elsewhere in the country as well.

The creative process that generated *Panunuluyan* is typical of PETA's collective methodology. The three authors—Al Santos, Alan Glinoga, and Rody Vera—each assumed the role of one of the characters and started improvising, placing Mary and Joseph in a contemporary Filipino setting. Meanwhile, the cast went to live for several days with the urban and rural poor, conducting workshops and collecting valuable social data. The play that resulted from this collaboration is an amusing yet effective indictment of modern Philippine society, using the framework of a traditional Filipino theatre form.

Alan Glinoga informed me that *Panunuluyan* is usually performed around Manila by different church and school-based theatre of liberation groups throughout the month of December. PETA's performing arm, the Kalinangan Ensemble, normally presents the play in its homeground, the cozy Dulaang Raha Sulayman open-air theatre located, ironically, in the middle of historic Fort Santiago, the former stronghold of the Spanish colonizers. One of the board members of the National Parks Commission happens to be a patron of PETA; thus the company has been reluctantly permitted to use the facility since 1971. The ruined walls and starry night provide a spectacular backdrop for its performances and are particularly appropriate for *Panunuluyan*, which opens with Joseph and Mary wandering through the empty streets of Manila on Christmas Eve, looking for a place to spend the night. Haphazardly, they walk into an upper-class Christmas Ball in the posh Manila Hotel, where the high and mighty celebrate the imminent birth of Christ with champagne and caviar. Joseph and Mary are thrown out because they cannot show an official invitation and lack the appropriate attire. Next, they enter an American-style shopping mall where they are shocked to see their images displayed in advertisements. Everywhere they go, well-to-do Filipinos refuse to accommodate them, but in Tondo, one of Manila's poorest slums, they are received with open arms despite the lack of space and food. Touched by the generosity of the destitute, Joseph and Mary become politicized. Joseph even decides to join a strike of carpenters because, like him, they sell their labor to build houses but have no proper lodging of their own. The end of the performance features Mary in labor in the warm and supportive environment of the slum dwellers. On the stroke of midnight, archangel Gabriel appears amidst a spectacular display of thunder and lightning and guides the couple back to heaven. The epilogue shows Joseph and Mary commenting bitterly from up high on the hypocrisy of the rich, who are praying devoutly at midnight mass.

Exposing American Exploitation

Pilipinas Circa 1907 is rapidly gaining a popularity as great as that of *Panun-uluyan* and *Juan Tamban*. First performed in 1982, it has already been produced in Davao City on the island of Mindanao in the south and in Cebu City, the capital of the Visayas archipelago in the middle of the country, and has known several revivals in the Metro Manila area. It is a delightful political melodrama set around the turn of the century, complete with catchy songs, dances, boorish Americans, ugly Filipino opportunists, violent labor repression, murders, and blocked love affairs. The Filipino audiences both are entertained and learn a thing or two about the historical involvement of American big business in Philippine economy.

The play is based on Severino Reyes' *sarswela, Filipinas para los Filipinos*, an ambiguous title which can mean either "Philippine Women for Philippine Men" or "The Philippines Belong to the Filipinos." In the PETA version, written by Professor Nicanor Tiongson, *Pilipinas* refers to everything unalienably Filipino—from women to culture and from natural resources to indigenous control of national industries. The *sarswela* form itself becomes a cultural political statement in an attempt to reappropriate and revalidate a once extremely popular type of theatre that has all but died out under the corrupting influence of American mass culture. Even the play's musical score, composed by Lutgardo Labad, reveals political intentions: the militant nationalists sing Filipino–Hispanic songs, while the pro-American federalists sing to Broadway-type tunes.

The cast is divided into pro-and anti-Americans. The nationalists are led by Doña Nora Pilar, majority stockholder of the Germinal tobacco factory and a widow of a prominent revolutionary general who was tortured and then killed in the Filipino-American War. She has a politically naive daughter named Leonor, who is in love with a revolutionary poet named Emilio but who is also being courted by Robert, an opportunistic American navy officer. Pura, Leonor's cousin, is as culturally pure as her name indicates and is by far the most militantly anti-American of the three women. Pura's lover, Andrés, is the proletarian foreman of the factory. The greatest villain of the play is Don Pardo, Nora Pilar's brother, who is helping the Americans to get complete monopoly of the Philippine tobacco industry by both legal and illegal means.

The play's dramatic conflict revolves around the romantic rivalry between Leonor's two suitors. Don Pardo has asked his niece Leonor to escort the handsome American around town—a request which she cannot possibly deny, given the family status of her domineering uncle. The outings of Leonor and Robert give rise to rumors, which incite Emilio's jealousy. He publishes a cryptic announcement in the nationalist newspaper of his imminent marriage to a woman named Patria Gatlaya. To make matters even worse, on Leonor's birthday he offers her a package containing what she thinks are her old love letters and a picture of her she had once sent him. Robert, capitalizing on this crisis, makes her a symbolic gift of a precious pendant in the shape of the American Eagle, the U.S. national emblem.

Emilio explicates the symbolism of his deeds in the second scene of Act Two after he finally manages to convince Leonor to open the package he had given her. To her surprise, it does not contain the letters, but a box of Germinal cigars—"the symbol of Filipino capital which we must prevent from falling into the American hands."[19] Similarly, the picture Emilio had given to Leonor turns out not to be a photograph of her at all but an image of the Motherland, a woman who resembles Leonor "framed by the dawn, her upraised hands with broken chains" (p. 198). Suddenly, Leonor grasps the meaning of the newspaper announcement as well: *Patria* is the Pilipino (and Spanish) word for "homeland" and *Gatlaya* means "independence."

Pilipinas Circa 1907 does not end with this emotional and politically charged reconciliation of the two lovers. Don Pardo complicates matters by ordering the closure of the Germinal plant because of alleged subversive activities of its workers. Furthermore, he sends out a warrant for the arrest of Emilio and Andrés. The latter eludes the clutches of the military and joins the guerrillas in the mountains, but Emilio is less fortunate. He is captured and severely tortured. In order to save her lover, Leonor consents to marry Robert. Fortunately, a certain Dorothy appears in the nick of time, and, like a *deus ex machina,* reveals herself to be Robert's legal wife whom he had scandalously abandoned in California before departing to seek his fortune in the Philippines.

After Dorothy's climactic exposure, even Don Pardo feels ashamed of his actions, and the play's finale witnesses Pura, in peasant dress, departing to join her injured lover in the countryside, while Emilio, Leonor, Pilar, and the factory workers solemnly swear to cooperate to keep the Americans out of Germinal and to use the profits to support the rebel fighters.

The plot, structure, and dialogue of *Pilipinas Circa 1907* may seem somewhat simplistic by Western standards, but the live band under Gardy Labad's direction, the songs, dances, acting, period costumes, and set, and the clear political analysis all combine to make this one of the most effective stage shows in Philippine theatre history. It has subsequently been put on the repertoire of many theatre companies elsewhere in the country.

With *Buwan At Baril Sa E Major,* PETA showed that it could also create sophisticated theatre pieces. Written by Chris Millado, one of the most gifted playwrights ever to come out of the PETA summer theatre school, the play explores the form of a classical music concert. Accompanied by a string and wind quartet, five individuals from different social sectors relate in powerful monologues why they have joined the struggle for national liberation. Thus, Handel's "Messiah," Bach's "St. Matthew Passion" and Mozart's "Eine Kleine Nachtmusik" punctuate the personal tales of a peasant, a striking worker, an upper middle class lady politicized by the recent slaying of Senator Benigno Aquino, a tribal woman married to a New People's Army guerrilla fighter, and a student leader who is persecuted by the secret police.

The Makiisa Festivals

There was a noticeable increase in the militancy of PETA's plays in the eighties, partly as a result of an ideological clash after which the group adopted a more radical stance. Gardy Labad recalls:

> PETA as PETA did not go out into the streets until 1982 when we first performed at a political rally. We did a play to commemorate the assassination of Dr. de la Paz. After the Benigno Aquino murder, on 21 August 1983, we decided to come out in open solidarity. The rally on 21 September 1983 was a crucial moment: it was the anniversary of the Martial Law declaration and all the opposition groups had organized an illegal national day of mourning. We also did a play there. Another important point is that we have been consistently giving service to workers' cultural groups since the mid-seventies as well.[20]

The murder of opposition leader Benigno Aquino at Manila International Airport upon his return from exile was, in more ways than one, the key event for the Filipino opposition movement in general and the theatre of liberation in particular. Until that time, Ferdinand Marcos had been able to get away with gross abuses of power through his skillful manipulation of the media and the unwavering military and political support of the United States. But the blatant murder of the dictator's most popular political opponent created widespread outrage and subsequently became the catalyst for a fearless offensive by all anti-Marcos factions. The theatre of liberation network and the workshop methodology, which had by now been spread through the entire archipelago, proved crucial vehicles to politicize and mobilize the masses.

The extent and strength of their network did not become clear to the artists themselves until PETA, in collaboration with the Concerned Artists of the Philippines, organized *Makiisa-I,* a national festival of people's culture. This massive event took place at PETA's Dulaang Raha Sulayman open-air theatre from 28 through 30 December 1983.

Makiisa, the Tagalog word meaning "unite," had been conceived with two objectives. First, the organizers wanted to use the occasion to consolidate the commitment of all progressive artists in the country, so that they might be more effective in combating the excesses of the régime. Second, *Makiisa* was to promote "nationalist and mass culture among other artists and among the Filipino audiences in general."[21] There were workshops, discussion groups, expositions, and nightly theatre of liberation performances in which companies from all over the archipelago were able to show the best plays they had developed over the years. In his opening address, Nicanor Tiongson, one of the festival organizers, emphasized the crucial role theatre had played in the struggle against the Marcos dictatorship:

> It was the only medium that could not be captured permanently on film or print. Like the anti-American plays of the 1900s, these dramas could only speak of the régime tangentially—first by recreating historical episodes parallel to the present . . . through allegories using folklore . . . through revitalized traditional folkforms (e.g., the *panunuluyan, sarswela* and *bodabil,* which were infused with modern liberative messages); through foreign plays translated or adapted into Filipino (e.g., Brecht's *Galileo Galilei,* which shows science can be the most effective weapon to demolish the feudal world view and system of values); through realism (e.g., the realistic study of a middle-class social worker in the process of conscientization in *Juan Tamban*). . . . Drama groups from Davao, Lanao, Samar, Negros, Navotas, Parañaque and Metro Manila . . . [showed] how the present socio-politico-economic conditions affect students, workers, peasants, the national minorities, and other sectors; how the régime derives its power from U.S. support; and how the present régime violates the most fundamental rights of all human beings, as defined by the U.N. Charter of Human Rights, to which the Philippines is a signatory.[22]

Makiisa was, then, very much a public display of the best Filipino culture of liberation had to offer at that time. The festival was followed by a *Makiisa-II* festival in December 1984 and by several regional celebrations of culture of liberation in the islands of Negros, Mindanao, and Cebu. They constituted a concrete yardstick with which to measure the strength and extensiveness of the Philippine theatre of liberation network and the momentum that it was beginning to gain.

Theatre during the 1986 Election Campaign

In November 1985, President Marcos, wishing to reaffirm his loosening grip over his rebelling population, announced presidential elections which would be held in February 1986. Radicals called for a boycott of the elections because they expected widespread rigging of the vote, as had always happened in the past. The moderate middle class, meanwhile, hoping that election fraud would this time be kept to a minimum by the presence of a high-powered team of international observers led by American congressmen, pushed for the candidacy of Corazon Aquino, the widow of the assassinated opposition leader. Dividing their sympathies between these two camps, Philippine theatre of liberation practitioners mobilized their network on an unprecedented scale. Most existing theatre of liberation groups were performing almost daily in three to four hundred communities in the Philippines. Apart from real theatres and open-air spaces, they played in churches, schools, gymnasiums, basketball courts, and virtually any other suitable public arena. Most often, the performances were crude satires directed against Marcos, but some productions were sophisticated, like PETA's *Sigwa* and *Nukleyar*.

During this hectic and unpredictable period, security was even more of a problem than normal. Over the years, some groups had made a virtue out of such difficulties, developing ingenious strategies to minimize the risks for their performers. *U.P.-Peryante,* for instance, a street theatre group based at the University of the Philippines in Diliman, specialized in so-called hit-and-run performances.[23] The actors used light masks, throw-away props, and little or no costuming so as to avoid easy identification by the police.

One of Peryante's greatest coups was to penetrate, unnoticed, the Bicutan Prison for Political Detainees in July 1984. Using fake identity papers and posing as inmates' relatives, the performers arrived separately on a Sunday afternoon, when they knew security control would be more lenient. When all had gotten their makeshift costumes and props ready, Peryante performed a biting satire of the Marcos régime in the prison dining hall. Thereupon the prisoners, who had formed a theatre of liberation group after one of them had conducted a workshop, performed a short piece of their own. Before the prison wardens found out what was going on, the performances were finished and the actors had escaped the same way they had entered, leaving encouraged inmates behind.

In the days leading up to the February 1986 elections, Peryante and many other political theatre groups performed topical plays on a daily basis. Chris Millado, cofounder of U.P-Peryante, remembers the incredible intensity of theatre work in the streets:

> We participated in rallies and performed songs and skits on the sidewalks, explaining the political issues and trying to incite the pedestrians to join in with the marchers. After we had done this at one point, we would quickly run ahead of the march and perform again further up along the route. If we were informed of a rally at seven o'clock in the evening, we would brainstorm and write all night and have a street play ready the next day. We would rehearse in the morning and in the afternoon it would be ready to go. If we were given three days' notice, we were able to come up with a complete vaudeville show.[24]

Under this kind of pressure, Peryante created *Ilocula,* a political satire they performed throughout 1983 and, once again, in September 1984 during the mass celebration of Aquino's birthday, one year after his death.

Before the show started, the actors taught the crowd—reported to be as large as 500,000—to imitate the sounds of howling winds, barking dogs, heartbeats, and noise barrages whenever they were shown certain cue cards.[25] The sound of a heavy storm set the atmosphere for the beginning of the play, which was conceived in the tradition of the horror story, featuring vampires, monsters, and witches taken from old Filipino folk tales. These creatures entered one by one and introduced themselves. Doctor Maxima Bareta, the monster minister of finance, entered first and sang about her "development" plans for the Philippines with limitless foreign loans. Next, Drs. Varrile and Rebolber [Barrel and Revolver], monster ministers of Defense and Armed Forces, sang a song in which they threatened to shoot all subversives. Finally, a barker announced the arrival of the monster queen: "Our Lady of the supernatural center of the Philippines, the Philippine International Voodoo Center. The wife of Ilocula, better known as Madame Cula; i.e., Madame Asshole." An obvious caricature of Imelda Marcos, Madame Cula arrived late on a delayed KLM flight from Geneva. In a romantic song, the First Lady explained the gathering of her fellow monsters as a joint attempt to revive her vampire husband, Ilocula, the dracula from the province of Ilocos Norte, Marcos's home province.[26] After her solo, doctors wheeled in Ilocula, dressed like a horror movie vampire, while the audience produced the sound of a heartbeat. The medical team then informed Madame Cula that Ilocula's heart was in perfect condition, well supplied because the chambers of Finance, Defense, Agriculture, and Natural Resources were continuously fed with the blood of the people. His intestines were also revealed to be in good order. Ilocula's problem turned out to be in his stomach, which had finally given out under the strain of years of gluttony. Dr. Bareta, however, suggested that a total transfusion with the help of the "international blood-lending institution ng Star Spangled Mumu"and the "international Mumu Fund and World Blood" might save the vampire's life. The other doctors agreed, adding a prolonged treatment with "US AID medication at CIA injection" for good form.[27]

After the oversize pills and the huge, plastic syringe were administered, Ilocula was operated on. From his stomach, the surgeons extracted the fist of a worker, the back of a farmer, the legs of a student, followed by "a professor's brain, an artist's tongue, the hearts and livers of the many who were martyred for the country."[28] But even after removing all these alien, undigested elements and throwing them on a pile in the corner, Ilocula still did not wake up. Having no better alternative, the Filipino doctors called in an American physician for consultation. His CIA injection supplemented with IMF dextrose finally did the trick, and the barker announced that on 21 September 1983, the eleventh anniversary of the declaration of Martial Law, the vampire woke up and declared the perpetuation of his dynasty. But while the monsters celebrated with champagne, the barker showed the "noise barrage" cue card, encouraging the audience to create an enormous cacophony of sounds. The rejected limbs of the Filipino people were reanimated, and a strong, new, united body emerged. This liberated Filipino found the courage to attack the monsters. As he raised his fist to crush Ilocula and his cronies, he froze and the performance ended.

Peryante assumed a radical pro-boycott stance for the 1986 elections, as did many other community-based groups throughout the Philippines. Teatro Umalohokan [Towncrier Theatre], another student group based on the Los Baños campus of the University of the Philippines, toured the region of southern Tagalog with the play *Kontradiksyon* [Contradiction]. As the title indicates, the piece dealt with the basic contradiction between the political interests of the ruling classes and those of the workers. It attempted to explain how the imminent presidential election was more than a mere confrontation between the benevolent Cory Aquino and the evil dictator. The plot focuses on a poor peasant family evicted from its own land for the benefit of a large coconut plantation owned by a multinational corporation. The old peasant woman wants to go to Manila to complain, but her son, who left several years earlier to look for work in the city, returns as a community organizer and convinces his parents and the other villagers to join the national protest movement instead.

PETA, whose membership was divided over the election boycott issue, performed René Villanueva's *Sigwa* [Storm] from 30 January through 16 February 1986.[29] This realistic play provided food for thought for the thousands of middle class students and professionals who flocked to see it at Fort Santiago. Thematically, *Sigwa* resembled the American film *The Big Chill*. I saw the play on Thursday night, 13 February, one week after the rigged elections. All week long the Manila newspapers had been filled with reports of political murders and ballot snatching. The slides of assassinated dissidents and radio excerpts of Marcos and Nixon speeches that formed the beginning and end of each of *Sigwa*'s three acts provided a useful documentary frame for the fictional action and reminded the spectators that nothing had really changed since the declaration of Martial Law in September 1971. The characters— three former radical student leaders at the University of the Philippines, now comfortably settled, politically apathetic professionals in their mid thirties— were obviously intended to make the capacity crowd of 1,000 spectators question their own current ideological and material positions. Judging by the reactions from spectators during the post-performance discussion with the actors and the director, the play achieved this objective.

The title of the play refers to the so-called First Quarter Storm, the two-year period of sustained student protests against the Marcos dictatorship that was brutally ended by Martial Law. Del, a political science professor at the University of the Philippines, Ritchie, a journalist, and Mol, a government town planner, all used to be Marxist activists during the Storm. On the 1982 night that the play depicts, the three gather in Del's apartment on campus following the funeral of Nick, a former university comrade who had joined the guerrillas. He had died a few days earlier in a military torture chamber. This sad occasion gives the three friends, who have not seen each other for ten years, a reason to look at old pictures and talk nostalgically about their old political ideals and why they abandoned them. The emotionally charged, realistic dialogue reveals that Ritchie gave up her radicalism because she got married and found that her political activities were unacceptable to her banker husband Carlos. Their two children were a further reason to stay quiet. Only once did she break her silence—when she wrote an article to criticize the

Manny Pambid and Ellen Ongkeko of PETA perform in René Villanueva's *Sigwa*.

Chico River Dam project.[30] After the article was published, Ritchie was "invited" to the military headquarters in Manila for an "informal dialogue over lunch," which turned out to be a rather violent interrogation session. This experience taught her to refrain from writing further articles critical of the Marcos régime.

Mol was a political detainee from 1972 to 1976 and came out of prison a disillusioned man who saw material success as the only thing worth fighting for. In an attempt to hide her own cooptation, Ritchie attacks him: "He used to be our political leader and so strict, so dogmatic that he called you bourgeois if you washed your face in the morning; he called a woman feudalistic if she held a guy by the arm; and if you spoke English, you were a neocolonial. And now he goes in and out of the presidential palace and has his picture taken with the First Lady."[31] Del is the only one who realizes that they have all been intimidated. He himself backed out at the last moment after initially promising Nick that he would join the guerrillas with him:

DEL: I didn't go because of my poor health.
RITCHIE AND MOL: *(Together.)* Bullshit!

MOL: You were a coward! A bloody coward!
DEL: *(Softly.)* Maybe you're right . . . but . . . at least I didn't sell my principles for
  money, like you.

At this moment, Ritchie takes her last letter from Nick out of her pocket and
reads: "Not everybody can go to the mountains; there is a lot of work to be
done in the cities as well." This statement calms Mol down. He sinks to the
ground, buries his head in his hands, and says: "There is so much I could
have done and failed to do." Sadly, he follows up his speech with a moving
song about all the slain comrades: "Luksang Parangal" [Mourning in Deep
Veneration]. At the end of this requiem, he breaks down and exits in tears.
A little later, he returns for his jacket and whispers: "It will be very hard to
go back now." As he walks out of Del's apartment, slides of 1985–86 political assassinations and mass rallies are projected, while a recorded voice states:
"In a time of repression, we can still make songs and sing them so that
people can be united." It was an appeal to all the Dels, Mols, and Ritchies in
the audience to do what they could; perhaps not everyone has the guts to
join the guerrillas, but each can make contributions to the culture of liberation.

Sigwa's final performance was on 16 February 1986, immediately after a
huge Cory Aquino rally at the Luneta Grandstand in downtown Manila attended by two million people. The *Sigwa* cast and crew had been rehearsing
all morning with twenty other PETA members to perform at the mass gathering. Then they marched through the city with hundreds of other Filipino
artists. There was considerable tension because a young man had been killed
by snipers only a few days earlier at a similar pro-Cory rally. More worried
for me than for themselves, the performers, holding hands, took their guitars
and masks and sang revolutionary and nationalist songs to the multitudes for
whom the name PETA had long been synonymous with quality performances
created in solidarity with the people.

Two days later, on Tuesday 18 February, the Philippines Educational Theatre Association was again present at a Bayan rally in Plaza Bonifacio, in
front of Manila's central post office, performing an excerpt from its rock
musical *Nukleyar*. Before the crowd of 50,000 (many of whom had come
marching from the U.S. Embassy, waving red flags), PETA presented the
"*Prosesyon ng Bayan*" [The Procession of the People]. The procession is of
those killed or tortured by the Marcos régime. While the musical group sang
the incantatory verses of the litany set to the music of an indigenous funeral
march, a string of dancers, wearing masks depicting suffering and agonized
faces, emerged from either side of the makeshift stage, slowly swaying their
heads in perfect synchrony. This was more than an abstract aesthetic statement; almost everyone in the crowd and cast personally knew activists who
had been killed or tortured by the régime. Accompanied by the persistent
beat of a drum and two guitars, the performers sang of militarization, illegal

detention, torture, and the killing of intellectuals, artists, community organizers, and politicians while the People's Procession was crushed by a destructive monster wearing a dragon's mask. But suddenly the mythical bird of freedom rises from among the people, teaching them how, with courage and collective power, they can defeat the monster. Under her guidance, the masses free themselves from their oppression.

As we crossed "Welcome Rotunda" in a jeepney—a kind of converted, stretched, open army jeep that is Manila's chief means of public transportation—on our way back from the Bayan rally, two PETA performers told me about the many times they and others had run for their lives as riot police there had closed in on them from all sides and had started shooting randomly into the crowd. In their mid twenties, they were already hardened veterans of a decade-long physical and cultural battle with the authorities.

During the rest of that third week in February, theatre people were frantically speculating on events. As American advisers and special emissaries like Stephen Solarz and Philip Habib flew in and out of Manila, all kinds of scenarios were circulating. The Concerned Artists of the Philippines (CAP), presided over by theatre director Behn Cervantes and filmmaker Lino Brocka,[32] were on full alert; meetings were held around the clock with Bayan and Cory representatives. U.P.-Peryante was conducting theatrical sit-ins and Boal Forum Theatre sessions on the Diliman campus, and Teatro Umalohokan performed a revised version of *Kontradiksyon* during a three-day cultural festival on neoimperialism in Los Baños. There was a sense of expectation in the air. Some people talked about the possibility of a military coup, while others spoke of a new declaration of Martial Law.

On Saturday, 22 February 1986, General Fidel Ramos and Minister of Defense Juan Ponce Enrile, barricaded in the military headquarters of Camp Aguinaldo and Camp Crame in the Manila suburb of Quezon City, announced their defection from Marcos. They called on the anti-Marcos citizenry to come to the barracks and form a human buffer against the oncoming tanks of the loyalist troops. The people came in droves from all over the Metro Manila Region. Years of grassroots community organizing made such a mobilization a relatively easy operation. Hundreds of thousands of Filipinos remained in front of the military camps and the liberated television studios of Channels Four and Nine for three days, defying sniper bullets and armored pro-Marcos military vehicles. They upturned enormous trailers and burned truck tires on street corners to obstruct the passage of the Marcos forces. All the while, PETA and Peryante were with them, performing at regular intervals day and night and making appearances during the impromptu talk shows being broadcast from the newly liberated television studios.[33]

The battle between culture of liberation on the one side and government-controlled mass media on the other clearly came to the fore during that eventful weekend in February. While the Catholic Radio Veritas and the occupied Channels Four and Nine exhorted the masses to erect human barricades all over the city, PETA's "ATORS" were encouraging them with nationalist songs, flag and banner routines, and political skits.

I was in Cebu City, capital of the Visayan islands, when Ramos and Enrile announced their rebellion. PETA leaders Lutgardo Labad, Manny Pambid, Alan Glinoga, and I were participating in a four-day live-in seminar and street theatre workshop for leaders of community theatre groups from all over the Visayan islands. The conference was adjourned on Sunday, 23 February, because the performers felt they were needed in their groups. We flew back to Manila on the last plane before Philippine Airlines suspended all domestic flights. At midnight, I rode across a deserted Manila in a jeepney to PETA House in Quezon City. I did not realize yet that hundreds of thousands of people were holding a mass vigil in front of the military headquarters and the TV stations, less than a mile down the road.

On the morning of Tuesday, 25 February, I woke up to the sound of gunfire that came from the Channel Nine studio facilities, two blocks away from PETA's headquarters, where I was staying. We all rushed into the garden to watch what was going on. The gunshots sounded like innocent firecrackers to my naive ears, unaccustomed as I was to real political violence. That impression quickly changed when I saw the body of a sniper fall from the red and white broadcast tower and when, a little later, I saw a rebel soldier with a gaping chest wound being rushed into the emergency ward of the nearby Capitol Medical Center. At two in the afternoon, after the rebels had fended off the attack by the Marcos forces, I joined a group of PETA actors on their way to perform for the crowds in front of Channel Four. Another group went to the presidential palace, where other pro-Marcos snipers were trying to disperse the crowd. Everywhere the artists went, they were welcomed with a roaring cheer as the thousands spontaneously made space for performing.

Already at this early stage, the Concerned Artists of the Philippines were voicing words of caution in a circular that was being distributed all around town:

> We call on the new government and the Filipino people to defend the people's gains and not to relax their vigilance until the structures of dictatorship established under twenty years of Marcos rule have been completely dismantled. We pledge our support for and solidarity with all the initiatives of the new government that will lead to full freedom of expression, return to civil liberties and respect for human rights. [. . .] As artists and cultural workers, we urge the new government, as soon as it has consolidated power, to facilitate the creation of a separate Ministry of Culture which shall be mandated to ensure freedom of expression and at the same time promote Philippine art and culture committed to truth, justice, freedom, democracy and the interests of the Filipino people.[34]

That night, when the news of Marcos's escape to Guam was broken, millions of Filipinos rejoiced and danced in the streets. It reminded me of stories my

Jack Yabut of PETA performs a flag dance for a human barricade in front of a television studio during the "People Power" revolution.

parents had told me about Dutch liberation celebrations in our village in May 1945. Meanwhile, a group of PETA actors went to perform for Bayan supporters who had risked their lives all Tuesday afternoon at the presidential palace in an effort to prevent the Marcoses from escaping with the country's wealth. They were suspicious of Cory Aquino and her new government. It was made up of conservative, former Marcos ministers and a few liberal bourgeois; no progressive Bayan politicians, who had been so instrumental in mobilizing the basic masses, were represented in the cabinet.

PETA's Al Santos, author and director of *Nukleyar,* immediately went to work to update his rock musical, which he had created with composer Joey Ayala and choreographer Maribel Legarda. On Thursday, 27 February, their show opened with an ominous statement that was clearly intended to shock the predominantly student audience in the gymnasium of Gregorio Araneta University in Manila out of their post-Marcos euphoria: "The dictatorship was abolished by the power of the people. But do not forget the martyrs who died so you could be free! It doesn't mean that this is the real victory. The people who are in power now are still the same old politicians who may oppress us some day if we give them the opportunity."[35] Santos also added a new character, Mr. Habahabahabibi, a thinly veiled caricature of Philip Habib, who was widely thought to have orchestrated the overthrow with

West Point graduate General Ramos. "I added him and several new pieces of text," explained Al Santos, "to indicate that we should remain vigilant because the institutions of oppression still surround us: the Bataan nuclear power plant, the military, the political prisoners."[36]

Nukleyar is a fast-paced, satirical rock musical that had been performed for over two years in village squares, outdoor basketball courts, and gymnasiums throughout the Philippines. The original *Nukleyar* was the product of a 1983 interaction workshop with the Black Tent Theatre, a radical troupe from Japan, whose contribution is particularly evident in a chilling scene graphically depicting the effects of the nuclear explosion in Hiroshima. But *Nukleyar* is more than a theatrical demonstration of the horrors of the atomic age; it is a powerful indictment of the transnational capitalist forces at work behind the seemingly peaceful construction of a nuclear power plant. The plant in question is the incompetently designed $2.5 billion Westinghouse facility set in a highly active volcanic region near Morong in Bataan province. A building contractor with family links to the Marcoses raked in a fortune from the project, which also required the eviction of hundreds of tribal fishermen. It is now doubtful whether the flawed plant will ever become operational, although Westinghouse, the IMF, and several American banks are demanding that it be opened so that the Filipino government can start paying back the huge loans and accumulated interest.

Nukleyar was first performed right after Aquino's assassination in August 1983 and has been continuously updated ever since; almost daily, new names are added to the list of the victims of the Marcos régime. PETA also performed it in a public park of Morong with evicted fishermen, as the mayor and several American soldiers from the nearby military installation looked on. To many people, the Bataan power plant has become a symbol of exploitation and repression by Marcos and the American-based multinationals. Several people were killed during marches protesting the plant's construction.

The central scene of *Nukleyar* is a satirical investigation into the power plant's safety. Miss Liberty—her torch no longer a symbol of freedom but of nuclear energy—enters, surrounded by three skinny guardian angels and some boot-licking Filipino businessmen with enormous red lips (emphasizing the lip service paid by the country's leaders to American interests). Liberty and the Marcos cronies want the plant declared safe. For that purpose they have formed an investigative commission chaired by Mr. Habahabahabibi, who has brought along the Westinghouse dancers—"direct from Three Mile Island"—to state that "nuclear plants are safe, cheap, and clean." At the same time, excerpts from the TV movie *The Day After* are projected on the screen.

The finale of *Nukleyar* brings the *"Prosesyon ng Bayan"* back on stage. They tear off their masks and become a powerful people's collective led by the Bird of Freedom. The Bird helps the oppressed to generate the courage to attack and ultimately destroy Miss Liberty and her evil associates. In an ethnic war dance, the Filipino populace, wielding bamboo sticks, menacingly

The battle of the superpowers from PETA's rock musical *Nukleyar.*

close in on the imperialist invaders led by Miss Liberty and finally bring them to their knees. During the 27 February performance, the audience was invited to come on stage to celebrate this people's victory with the performers. While the band continued playing catchy rock tunes, the performers danced with members of the audience for at least half an hour following the conclusion of the actual show.

PETA's Present and Future

Cory Aquino's "People Power" revolution was punctuated by hundreds of theatre performances. When the Marcoses fled, everyone breathed a sigh of relief. Many theatre of liberation activists, particularly those from the middle class, thought that a genuine victory had been won and turned their attention to careers and families. Some former dissident artists even accepted positions in government jobs or the media. Right-wing and left-wing terrorism, four coups, lack of land reforms, and continuing poverty, however, have been enough to shatter any remaining illusions about the new Aquino government. The yellow paint is slowly peeling off the pro-Cory Aquino billboards. Behind it, grinning generals are still as firmly in power as during Marcos.

Although a considerable number of people left the theatre of liberation following the installation of the Aquino government, the strategists of the movement realized soon enough where things were headed. Subsequently, some artists in Luzon and Mindanao organized two large-scale cultural festivals with which they traveled from village to village for several months. Confronted with an essentially unchanged situation, the theatre of liberation eventually had to start up its regular activities again.

After the initial euphoria over Cory Aquino's victory in February 1986, PETA produced some outstanding plays and entered the field of mass media with the reactivation of its Film and Television Unit. The company has also been engaged in a thorough evaluation process of its training program and methods, which had come under increasing criticism from its own members and from groups in the provinces. But the single most important event of PETA in the immediate post-Marcos period was undoubtedly the daring and sometimes grueling performance tour it undertook to North America and Europe from September 1986 through August 1987.

The idea for the international tour was launched as far back as 1972 but it never became concrete until early February 1986. Its objectives were to showcase the variety of contemporary Filipino theatre to as broad an international audience as possible. Secondary objectives were to celebrate with the global community the victory of the Filipino people over a hated dictator and to raise sorely needed funds for the establishment of PETA's projected full-fledged training and research center, the Institute for People's Culture. In hindsight, the tour can be considered to have been moderately successful in all three areas.

The play that PETA took on tour was developed over a five-month period by a writers' collective composed of Al Santos, Alan Glinoga, Rody Vera, and Chris Millado. Its title, *Panata sa Kalayaan* [Oath to Freedom], refers to the pledge made by half a million people on 21 September 1983, the anniversary of the declaration of Martial Law, and less than a month after the killing of Benigno Aquino. Back then, these words had been solemnly proclaimed in solidarity with Cory Aquino, but as the tour progressed they came to be increasingly aimed at the human rights abuses that continued even under her presidency. Cory Aquino had originally endorsed the PETA actors as her "international ambassadors of goodwill," but the company did not take this as an executive command to propagate official Philippine policies to foreign audiences. On the contrary, *Panata sa Kalayaan* severely criticizes the Aquino government for its continuing tolerance of the presence of American military bases in the Philippines, its deference to IMF and World Bank dictates, its failure to implement genuine land reforms, and its dismal human rights record. In the fifth scene of Part Two, for example Sister Sol, a progressive nun, presents the audience with the following unambiguous statistics: "In the first seven months of the Aquino government, 603 persons had been arrested. A total of 239 torture cases have been reported, including 215 victims detained and 24 salvaged. There were 36 incidents of mass evacuation and 7 incidents of 'hamletting,' in which peasant communities suspected of assisting rebels were isolated behind barbed wire fences. In the massacres, 138 persons were killed and 35 others wounded. There have been 36 cases of disappearances reported."[37] Thus, one of the chief aims of the play was to dispel the view widely held in the West that all the country's problems had been instantaneously removed with Cory Aquino's fairy-tale rise to power.

PETA's *Panata sa Kalayaan* tour may well have been one of the largest and most complex tours by any theatre company in world history. It certainly is the boldest international projection on record by any third world theatre company. The tour premiered at the Cultural Center of the Philippines, Imelda Marcos's previous bastion of élitist performing art, on 19 September 1986. No admission was charged, and for the first time in its thirteen-year existence the plush seats of the auditorium were filled with workers and students. After Manila, the company of twenty-seven artists presented *Panata sa Kalayaan* all over the United States, Canada, Britain, France, West Germany, the Netherlands, Italy, Greece, Switzerland, Austria, Denmark, Sweden, and Eastblock countries like Czechoslovakia and East Germany. Simultaneously, a group of twenty other PETA artists performed a slightly different version of *Panata sa Kalayaan* in Hong Kong and Japan.

Although financially PETA barely broke even and critics did not always receive the play favorably—some Western reviewers found it simplistic and sloganeering—the tour was generally evaluated positively. "Our first and foremost message was to communicate that there was a cultural movement in the Philippines," Alan Glinoga explains.

> We wanted to show the world that we have come a long way as well as tell them about the political realities in our country. But the tour also served as an exposure for us because there is always the danger of inbreeding when you're just limited to your own environment. In our case it was valid to go because we know what we want and we're proud of what we have. We were not searching for an identity or anything. We were therefore not so vulnerable to confusions from outside influences like a new group might have been. It is also incredible that these twenty-seven people never had any serious conflicts. We were never really on the verge of breaking down. As a result, we came out as a much, much stronger group.[38]

During the tour, PETA was able to compare its work to the standards of the contemporary theatre practice in the West. In addition, there was also a cultural confrontation of sorts, ranging from personal experiences of subtle racism toward Asians in Europe to resistance to Filipino humor and emotions, which some Western spectators found corny and sentimental. "We were curious to try our skills and aesthetics on other audiences," comments Glinoga. "Most of the things that we used in *Panata sa Kalayaan* were actually not very sophisticated forms. It was a conscious choice to take simple

Panata sa Kalayaan, Tokyo, 1986.

theatre pieces. We could have presented a more sophisticated type of theatre but that was not our point. To present something in sophisticated Western dramaturgy would not be appreciated we thought. So we opted for simple improvisations, stage poetry. Even in terms of acting it was almost raw."[39]

In order to get the tour organized, PETA needed to set up an ad-hoc world-wide network. Funding for the project was problematic from the start. But when a Dutch third world funding agency agreed to provide a significant chunk of the required sum, the PETA leadership decided to go ahead with the tour. "It was a very bold decision," grins Glinoga. "When we decided to push through with it we realized it was now or never, even though we didn't have all the resources at hand yet. To give you an idea: when we flew over to Canada on the first leg of our trip we didn't even have enough money for our return flight to the Philippines. We raised the money from city to city until we were in the United States. As late as December 1986 we didn't even have enough for our airfare to Europe. The whole tour was a bit like crisis management. That may be exactly why Western theatre companies would never have been able to pull off a tour like ours."[40]

Although *Panata sa Kalayaan* exposed Western audiences to Filipino theatre of liberation, it was a pale reflection of PETA's true artistic potential. Its aesthetic ambitions were made subservient to pressing sociopolitical needs. PETA had wanted to give foreign audiences an impression of what the Marcos dictatorship and the People Power Revolution had really been like. It can be argued, however, that the show would have been more effective if a greater effort had been made to investigate current cultural and above all theatrical codes in the West, where forms of overt agitprop, facile audience participation, and other popular theatre elements reeking of the sixties are all too easily dismissed.

During the *Panata sa Kalayaan* tour, PETA artists often interacted with large contingents of Filipino maids and factory workers in foreign countries. These encounters formed the initial inspiration for a series of one-act plays on migrant workers' issues which PETA presented in Fort Santiago, Manila, at the celebration of its twentieth anniversary in December 1987, a few months after their return from the West. The most interesting of these one-acters was a play about Filipina striptease dancers in Japan, entitled *Konichiwa Piripin* [Hello, Philippines].

Working closely together and processing documented case studies as they went along, the playwrights, Phil Noble and Glecy Arellano, the cast, and the director developed five fictional characters and put them in motion. Virginia was already a striptease dancer in the Philippines before she went to Japan on a tourist visa. Agnes went to Japan to seek her fortune and perhaps marry a wealthy Japanese businessman. Fourteen-year-old Janina lied about her age to pass the audition; she ends up getting gang raped by four Japanese customers in a backroom of the bar where she dances. Socorro, the oldest of the group, was a qualified elementary school teacher in the Philippines but

Scenes from PETA's *Konichiwa Piri-pin*, a play about Filipina sex club entertainers in Japan.

could make three times as much as an entertainer in Japan. Kristine completes the cast. She is a typical young Filipina who dotes on her macho boyfriend, David, who only wanted her to go to Japan to make money for him.

Konichiwa Piripin is presented in the format of an erotic dance show interjected with realistic flashbacks and scenes from the one-room Tokyo apartment where the girls live. This effective formula makes for an entertaining as well as a meaningful and informative theatre event. By the rather prudish Philippine standards, it is one of the most explicit treatments of sex in the country's theatre history. The play includes a striptease with flesh-colored tights, an expressionistically rendered rape scene (using dolls), and some explicit dialogue.[41]

Plays like *Konichiwa Piripin* also reflect PETA's growing emphasis on women's issues, which has already led to the formation of an experimental women's theatre collective within the company. Apart from doing an adaptation of *Trojan Women* and original scripts based on the lives of heroic women in the Philippine struggle for liberation, the new collective has also started to conduct theatre of liberation workshops in collaboration with the progressive Philippine women's organization GABRIELA.

PETA's New Broadcast and Film Unit

It is PETA's ultimate ambition to develop activities along the entire spectrum of the cultural domain, ranging from performing arts like drama, dance, and music to training, publication, and cultural research. In the middle of 1988, the company boldly entered the field of television.

Back in the early seventies PETA already had a multi-award-winning weekly television drama series called *Balintataw* in which Lino Brocka got his first experience directing for the screen. Since then, many PETA artists have found employment in film and television. PETA's present executive director, Socrates Topacio, is a prominent television personality in his own right and makes a living as a professional television director. With this kind of expertise in its own ranks, PETA decided to take another shot at breaking into the heavily commercialized Philippine mass media market.

"We are entering television," Alan Glinoga comments, "because we recognize the effectiveness of mass media and also because we want to inject it with the discipline and the vision of theatre of liberation as it develops in the grassroots."[42] In March 1988, PETA started taping an original twenty-four-part television series. The first twelve episodes were television adaptations of existing PETA plays like *Juan Tamban* and *Pilipinas Circa 1907*. The other twelve episodes dealt with sectoral themes like the contemporary realities of sugar workers in Negros, fishermen in Mindanao, tribal minorities in the highlands, and women. This second series of programs was shot on location in the provinces in close collaboration with local grassroots theatre of liberation collectives, who acted, wrote scripts, and sometimes even directed complete episodes. For this purpose, PETA designed a special crash course in television drama for its less experienced partners.

Alan Glinoga sees PETA's television activities as complementary to its theatre and training activities. Television is widespread in the main cities and towns of the archipelago. Its importance in terms of numbers of viewers only continues to increase. In the rural areas, where television is not so readily available, PETA plans to distribute its TV serials through a grassroots video exchange network. "But," warns Glinoga pragmatically, "in the long run, given the fluid and unpredictable realities of the Philippines, the only reliable and ultimate venue for our work remains the grassroots live performance and the workshop."[43]

Criticisms and Self-Criticisms

Although there is little doubt that PETA has by far the best track record in terms of acting, directing, playwriting, training, research, documentation, and publication of any theatre group in the Philippines, it has not been immune to criticism.[44] PETA's continuing search for international exposure and success in attracting foreign funding in particular has caused irritation among groups in the provinces. Also, PETA's predominantly middle class identity and its rather intellectual profile have been at the basis of dissenting and critical voices from the grassroots, who question the company's efficacy in communicating with the masses. Part of the criticism sounds like the often justified impatience of provincials with the alleged arrogance of residents of the capital. There are, of course, the basic differences between big city and countryside, and between highly educated middle class artists on the one hand and simple peasants and workers on the other. To be truthful, only a handful of PETA artists have experienced long-term immersion in the cultural grassroots of regions outside Manila. Others in the provinces question PETA's right to present itself abroad as sole representatives of the Philippine cultural movement.

Relations between PETA and groups in the region seem to have improved considerably with the official launching of the national network, in which PETA has assumed a relatively low profile. Also the inclusion of regional artists in the recent PETA television productions has been generally appreciated as a step in the right direction. PETA's *Makiisa* magazine now also regularly features articles on cultural activities outside Manila, written by regional correspondents.

As for the effectiveness of middle class artists and workshop facilitators in non-middle class environments, Alan Glinoga offers the following comment:

> The issue is, of course, how far can we go? I mean, how long can you as a
> middle-class person sustain yourself physically and psychologically in the

provinces. In the upper, middle, or even the lower middle classes, you get used to a certain lifestyle and you need resources to support yourself and that lifestyle. You cannot get that in cultural work. There lies the contradiction. You have to get that from other sources. That already divides your time right away. At the same time I should underline the tremendous efforts and successes of the PETA members to overcome these obstacles. We try to counteract all this also by recruiting members from the lower classes—although we haven't been too successful yet—and through a very aggressive exposure program, working with the people, sending them out.[45]

One of the main criticisms directed at PETA concerns its grassroots workshops. At first it was assumed that the workshop method was so foolproof that every participant could successfully apply it simply by duplicating the process. That proved to be a fallacy. Later, it was discovered that the success of a workshop depends a great deal on the caliber of the artist-trainer. Not everybody has the temperament and skills to be a good workshop instructor. By the same token, an excellent middle class actor from Manila is not necessarily the ideal facilitator in a workshop for peasants. No matter how intelligent, energetic, and sensitive he or she may be, the undereducated rural Filipino will usually regard the city-bred artist with a mixture of awe and suspicion. But according to Alan Glinoga that is no longer a severe problem, "because now we know the groups that we are going to work with much better than before. Regional extension officers in cooperation with local organizers already build the necessary trust before the actual entry of our facilitators."[46]

There is no doubt that the Philippines Educational Theater Association is of extreme importance to the cultural movement in the Philippines and to the progressive arts movement in Asia and the South Pacific at large. Also, Western theatre practitioners have begun to draw from PETA's experiences and experiments. Most Western attempts at creating effective political theatre were purely performance-oriented, lacked solid networking, and were therefore short-lived. PETA's efforts in the field have been ongoing for nearly twenty-five years, partly because the company never ceases to question the validity of its own aesthetics and pedagogy. Its major contribution to world theatre has been the development of a total political theatre package that includes performance, training, and long-term interaction with target groups. Finally, it must be credited with emphasizing the necessity for networking on the local, regional, national, and international level as the one and only key to sustaining a genuinely effective theatre of liberation movement.

III

INSIDE THE PHILIPPINE THEATRE
OF LIBERATION NETWORK

I had heard a lot about the extensive network of the Philippine cultural movement. While staying in the basement of PETA House in the Manila suburb of Quezon City, I had met many (mostly young) men and women who had introduced themselves as cultural workers from the outlying provinces. On the National Bookstore map of the Philippines the network looked impressive enough. On paper, the theatre of liberation workshop concept, the sum total of original theatre productions generated by the network (hundreds), and the sheer number of artists involved (thousands), sounded more than formidable. But the Philippine theatre of liberation network only really came to life for me after several months of hard traveling through the vast archipelago.

From mere dots on a map and names of institutions and individuals, the network first became a hair-raising Philippines Airlines flight from Manila to Cebu in February 1986. Cynical Filipinos jokingly but not inaccurately turn the PAL acronym of the national Philippine airline company into "Plane Always Late." Flights with the small Sunriser planes the company uses for short interisland flights are no joke, however, but veritable Russian roulette. During several subsequent trips, the network became bumpy busrides; incessant "Hey Joe!" catcalls with which Filipino street kids greet all foreigners; a colorful ferry ride with a narrow escape from a pirate attack; bloodcurdling trips in jeepneys; and tons of dust, gallons of exhaust fumes (the blacker the better), and many blow-outs on muddy, winding mountain roads.

You finally reach a stage at which you learn to convert the body into a sack of rice and suspend it, like the locals, with one hand as a meathook from the bar attached to the jeepney roof, which is already threatening to cave in under the unreasonable load of produce, screaming slaughter-bound pigs, and spitting farmers. Traveling in the Filipino countryside then suddenly becomes a perverse delight and you giggle stupidly with your fellow passengers whenever the driver, who imagines he is competing in the Paris-Dakar Rally in a Range Rover, hits yet another pothole and the roof creaks ominously once more. I now know what metal fatigue really means. I have had several cases of it myself. But eventually the most amazing people and theatre groups emerged from the haze left by hours of discomfort, dust, and *Lambanok* coconut wine. I met them in churches, on top of roofs, in bars, on street corners, in bamboo huts, and—yes, even in actual theatre buildings.

In fact, the Philippine theatre of liberation is not as invisible as the preceding description may suggest. The national network is divided into five regional networks: one in central and northern Luzon, the large island in the north of the country; one in the metro Manila region, located in the southern part of Luzon; one in southern Tagalog, the peninsula immediately south of Manila; one in the Visayas, the central archipelago of the nation that encompasses the islands of Samar, Leyte, Bohol, Cebu, Negros, and Panay; and one in Mindanao, the second largest island of the country (after Luzon) in the deep south. All of these regional networks are administered by institutions that usually receive some funding from abroad and are structurally akin to PETA; i.e., they have a repertory ensemble, a research and documentary outfit, a networking officer, and a training team for theatre of liberation workshops. The main aim of these regional institutions is to provide training and follow-up services to affiliated subregional networks. In several provinces of Mindanao and on the islands of Negros, Cebu, and Samar, these subregional networks are already quite consolidated and, in some cases, even boast well-established service centers of their own.

Newsletters and magazines help maintain the necessary communication between all the intricate layers and branches of the network. Periodically conferences, workshops, and performing arts festivals take place on the subregional, regional, and national level. On these occasions, theatre of liberation practitioners exchange their latest strategies to circumvent military harassment, discuss the newest workshop methods, and showcase their most recent plays, dance dramas, or songs. Recently, the cultural movement has begun to expand into other fields of performing arts as well. Painters, sculptors, photographers, and filmmakers are joining the ranks in increasing numbers.

The Philippines Educational Theater Association recently moved its headquarters, called PETA House, to Cubao, a subdivision of Quezon City in greater Manila. PETA House is the nerve center of the regional theatre of liberation network of metro Manila. From this central location, PETA maintains close ties with university-based groups like U.P.-Peryante and Teatro Umalohokan and provides structural support to children's theatre groups, troupes composed of factory workers, women's groups, and groups of young professionals. Service centers in the other regions of of the Philippines carry out similar tasks.

The Visayas Archipelago

Banaag, the service center for the regional network of the Visayas, has its offices in a spacious house in the Lahug subdivision of Cebu City. Like PETA House, it is a place of bustling activity, although the atmosphere at Banaag is considerably more relaxed than in Manila. Typically a group of dancers or musicians rehearses in the main lounge, while at a desk near the window a staff researcher completes a paper on an age-old religious drama form that still survives in some remote Cebuano village. In another room, the workshop coordinator briefs a team of actor-trainers on an upcoming workshop for women workers at the nearby Tresco fish canning factory in the Cebu City suburb of Mandaue. The island coordinators from Bohol and Northern Samar, in town for network consultations, sleep on the floor of the guestroom, exhausted from their long ferry ride.

Mimi Villareal, a dancer and PETA member dispatched to Banaag to help coordinate interregional network activities, explains that the groups in the Visayan theatre of liberation network were either founded following PETA outreach workshops, formed spontaneously to animate demonstrations and mass gatherings during the height of the Marcos dictatorship, or developed from church choirs wishing to incorporate drama during special church services or religious processions. She specifies further: "There are 170 groups in the Visayas. Fifty-eight of these are off-shoots from political campaigns. Twenty-five were the result of community theatre workshops. There are fifteen church-based groups. Three groups were formed spontaneously by fine arts students who wished to create murals, plays, and songs for human rights groups, unions, etc. The rest of the groups are affiliated with trade unions or farm workers unions. On the island of Negros, for example, there are no less than forty-three groups based on sugarcane plantations."[1]

Most of the groups in the Visayas have participated in three- or five-day intensive community theatre workshops. A smaller number of artists have also participated in extensive summer theatre schools. The groups regularly perform their own original plays during public and church holidays and political occasions like elections or mass demonstrations. "They function like amateur community theatre groups," says Villareal. "They meet once or twice a week for rehearsals. Given the high frequency of human rights abuses, there are plenty of burning issues. Some of them also conduct their own outreach workshops in neighboring communities." Particularly in the outlying rural areas there is great interest in drama performances because, apart from radio and cassette music, pick-up basketball, and cock fights, there is no entertainment. Television and video are still scarce.

The Visayas have a rich performing arts tradition, but unfortunately most of the theatre of liberation groups in the region are still quite weak, artistically speaking. Villareal says: "Most of the plays they produce are quite stereotypical in content. Clenched fists and all that. That's because the workshops they attended were too short or conducted by inexperienced trainers. They all tended to generate *dula-tula,* political narrative poems read by one actor and illustrated with movements and mimed scenes by two or three other actors."[2]

The Visayan regional network is called Dungog, which stands for "dignity." It was formally launched in 1986, but its origins date back to 1983 when PETA first started its extension services in the central Philippines. "Back then there were already a lot of scattered groups that didn't know each other," comments Villareal. "We established contact between them. They discussed their situations and their common problems and then the idea of an alliance was born. They also wanted to establish an institute because they all felt the need to upgrade their writing, directing, and performing skills."[3] Nene Pacilan, an actress from a rural group, Bubu Alorro, a schoolteacher working in a working-class area, and Beth Mondragon, a former PETA member and cofounder of Cebu Repertory, asthetically the most advanced repertory company in the region, then joined forces to establish the Banaag service center, which officially opened its doors at the end of 1985.

The Local Network in Cebu City

One of the first activities of Banaag was to coordinate the participation of all Cebu-based theatre of liberation groups in the 1986 Good Friday Procession. They took turns performing appropriate short street theatre pieces at the different stations of the Cross. Explains Beth Mondragon: "a different actor played Christ at each new station. First a worker, then a slum dweller, a student, and a woman. One of the occasions when Christ falls, for example, was represented as the disintegration of the local trade union chapter after a series of military intimidations. The people in the street loudly encouraged him to keep going and several of them finally spontaneously helped the dejected union leader, who was carrying the cross, to get up again."[4]

The Good Friday processions, called *Prosesyon ng Cristo,* last two to three hours and have since become an annual event of the local network in Cebu City. In this alliance, the semiprofessional middle class company Cebu Repertory works side by side with slum-based amateur groups like Dulaang Katilingban sa Redemptorista (DKR), the Balitaw vocal ensemble, a church-based group called Prayer, a dance group called The Movers, and an as yet unnamed new women's theatre group, the result of a workshop at the Tresco fish canning factory.

DKR creates plays on issues that affect the urban poor community. The slum residents are very supportive of the group. "They give us money and manpower," says Angela de la Cruz, a seventy-year-old member of DKR. "If we have workshops, they help us with food. Many of the people here are vegetable vendors, fishermen, and factory workers, you see."[5] Angela became a member after attending a community theatre workshop in 1983, which, she claims, made her feel good about herself and more confident. Over the years, DKR has done several plays that deal with local government efforts to demolish the slum dwellings while providing no viable alternative lodging for the residents. More recent plays dealt with unsolved disappearances of radical community leaders and the abominable conditions of peasants and workers. "I helped write the script," says Angela. "It's about our own lives. We really felt something when we played it. It was the truth." The group meets every Sunday, although lately some members have stopped coming because of threats from right-wing vigilante groups. Commonly, vigilantes are trigger-happy locals armed by the police and licensed to kill alleged subversives. According to progressive analysts, vigilantism is a component of the so-called Low Intensity Conflict (LIC), a strategy Americans designed after the disastrous Vietnam War to destroy the radical left-wing opposition of a country by means of infiltration and intimidation from within local communities instead of by the high intensity conflict of an all-out war. Despite this campaign, which has affected many theatre of liberation groups since 1986, Angela de la Cruz feels her theatre group has brought the community closer together: "We help each other more. Sometimes when someone needs to buy medicine, we all pitch in one or two pesos."

Prayer operates a church choir and performs dramatized scenes from the gospel during Sunday services, but the group also tries to respond to the latest political developments with satirical street pieces. One of their "newspaper" plays exposed the structure behind the growing vigilante problem but proved flexible enough to also incorporate a scene about renegade army colonel "Gringo" Honasan the day after one of his abortive coup attempts. The LIC was represented by three businessmen wearing the letters, L, I, and C on their backs. Immediately after they enter, they kill three young street sweepers who are discussing an imminent strike. L, I, and C reason, "They are wondering why they are poor. Therefore they must be Communists!" L, I, and C subsequently convince the bereft parents that their sons were killed by guerrillas and urge them to join a vigilante group to combat Communism.

In a performance that took place in the gymnasium of the University of San Carlos in Cebu City, Prayer integrated the Honasan incident as follows. First, a group of evacuees arrives on the otherwise empty stage with all their belongings. Then a vigilante group enters, wielding guns and yelling anti-Communist slogans. They all freeze. A church worker comes in and tries to organize the community with a progressive interpretation of the Bible. She is shot by a vigilante. Once the scenes are finished, the characters freeze; thus a complex tableau is constructed. Finally, a newspaper reporter arrives with the latest edition of a national newspaper in his hand. He starts reading an announcement of Honasan's latest coup attempt. Government soldiers then come in on one side of the stage and rebel soldiers take their position opposite them. Then L, I, and C enter. They first walk to the side of the rebels but when the reporter cites a news update and states that the government forces have regained control, L, I, and C opportunistically walk over to the other side, flashing the L-sign of Cory Aquino's Laban party with their thumb and index finger.[6]

Since late 1986 Cebu has its own small-scale local service center as well. It is called LOTUS and mostly conducts workshops for the urban poor. On 28 January 1988, I traveled with three LOTUS instructors to the Cebu City suburb of Mandaue to participate in a theatre of liberation workshop at the Tresco fish canning factory. Sixteen female and four male workers had signed up. They had contacted LOTUS because they were interested in forming a theatre group to air their labor problems with fellow workers and the surrounding community. The three workshop trainers had carefully prepared the project for several months, visiting Mandaue more than once. They learned that the factory had a history of exploitation until the workers decided to go on strike in 1985 to protest against starvation wages and intimidations by members of the factory's security guard. The striking workers succeeded in keeping the very profitable factory closed down until March of the following year when the management finally gave in to their main demands. On the request of the strikers, one extremely conservative stockholder was removed from the board of directors and twenty particularly brutal security guards were fired. Since then, the management has become much more worker-friendly. During the strike, the union had come in to conduct leadership seminars. In the absence of a relief fund, the strikers survived by selling self-made necklaces. But in the course of the strike, half of the 300 workers had to resign because they were unable to support their families without income. Now, two years after the industrial action, the management had given permission for the theatre workshop and had even offered the use of one of the factory halls as a venue.

The place did not exactly smell of roses but at least it was spacious and after a day we got used to the stench. In the first few hours of the workshop, Hanzel and Don-Don, two young working-class actors, loosened up the group both physically and mentally with a number of theatre-related games. The following day, the social map exercise succeeded in getting the participants to talk about their lives. Many of the workers said they had come to Mandaue from remote rural areas to find a job. Most of them lived in bamboo huts they had built in the coconut grove across the street from the factory. Thanks to the closeness of the community, vigilantes had not been able to do any harm there yet. We could peacefully spend our nights on the floor of Sally Minoza's elevated bamboo hut.

The third day of the workshop was taken up by teaching basic acting skills and story telling. The "Travelog" exercise brought out innate acting talents. While the participants lay on their backs with their eyes closed, one of the trainers started telling a story about a factory worker going on a trip. Keeping their eyes closed, the participants were asked to imagine being the protagonist of the story and mime the movements. Thus the twenty workers mimed climbing stairs, exploring the jungle, being bitten by 1,000 ants, diving into a river, floating, being hungry, eating an open can of sardines, being attacked by a crazy dog, kicking the dog, and finally lying down to rest again. After ten counts the participants were allowed to "wake up" and the actors took them through all the motions they had mimed, step by step.

After thus exploring body movement and acting, participants were asked to compose some original poems, which they presented using creative sounds they had learned in a previous exercise. Inspired by the sounds and rhythms they heard around them in the work place, and using their bodies and found objects like empty cans, spoons, packing boxes, and broomsticks, the participants created an imaginary machine. Its hissing and pumping sounds turned into the collectively composed words of a poem about the victorious 1985 strike.

Although some of the participants continued to be shy, most of them were quite loose by now. Strangers before, they now leaned comfortably against one another. They felt proud of their machine poem. Said Teresita Palang: "It's not hard to make in a collective, but alone I'm sure I could never have done it."[7] The group felt confident they could produce a small performance. They decided to use their poems as the basis of the entire presentation. Two musically inclined workers composed a few songs; three others made masks; the rest of the group started improvising, writing, and rehearsing. The LOTUS facilitators offered their advice only when asked.

Excitement rose as curtain time drew nearer. The group picked a space in front of the factory gate as their venue, hoping to recruit an audience from among the clients of the adjacent corner grocery store and residents from their community across the street. It was five o'clock on a Sunday afternoon when the show began.

While LOTUS trainer Hanzel Alviola strummed the guitar, the workshop participants came marching out of the factory gate singing "Berto Makina" [Bert, the Machine Operator], a well-known political song by a musician from Cebu. They began to mime their regular work motions—skinning and cooking fish, sealing cans—and added appropriate sounds and rhythms. They then greeted the audience in chorus: "We are workers from the Tresco Canning Corporation. We want to tell you about this factory and what happened to the workers when there was no union."

The first scene of the play features Goryo, a fellow who has to work from 7 a.m. until 5 p.m. for 10 pesos [US$ 0.50] per day. He goes to work without breakfast and often has to work overtime. The second scene introduces Karya, a woman who has to carry cans all day. If she drops a small can, the manager fines her 20 pesos; dropping a big can costs 50 pesos. In the third scene, Ligaya, a pregnant worker, suffers from labor pains. Not entitled to maternity leave or medicare benefits, she continues working until she literally drops. Sally, who served as the narrator of the show, then steps forward: "The scenes you just saw are based on actual facts. So we decided to join a union because we couldn't stand the pain and the blatant exploitation anymore. On 23 March 1985, our strike exploded at Tresco."

Scene 4 depicts the strike. Workers express their frustrations and apprehen-

Theatre of liberation workshop performance at the Tresco fish canning factory in Mandaue, Cebu, Philippines.

Mandaue workshop performance in front of Tresco factory gates.

sions about the imminent arrival of the military dispersal squad, which, in the Philippines, often shoots to kill. "We will have to scramble and run," says one worker. "You kidding?" responds another, "We got to link arms and form a barricade!" Sally comments: "Because of our organized action we succeeded in obtaining higher wages and overtime benefits. The management now recognizes our union and we even get maternity leave."

In the final scene, Rosa becomes a tuna that is processed by the workers. The chorus yells the instructions and makes appropriate sounds ("cook the fish—psshh, psshh, psshh; skin the fish— swish, swish, swish; seal the cans— clong, clong, clong"), while others mime the motions. Finally, Rosa is put in a huge can as Sally delivers the epilogue: "We won the strike but our salaries have not yet reached minimum wage levels. We only have six free days per year, from which sick leave is deducted." The audience of fifty applauds. Suddenly a heavy gun-blast resounds from inside the factory complex. Momentary panic. Later, a guard explained nonchalantly that the assistant manager had only been practicing firing his .38 caliber pistol.

The participants evaluated during a final meal. Some of them admitted they had not been all that interested in the process and sometimes had not bothered to concentrate. Although most had felt rather uncomfortable performing, they recognized the tremendous potential of theatre. Said one woman: "It can help us a great deal with our union. We can show our problems, celebrate events, and remember our past." They all agreed to perform their show again the next day for their colleagues. All agreed that the biggest gain of the workshop was that they had been able to break through the daily routine. Sally: "We are much closer to each other now. Before we only said 'hi' and then went our own ways. Now we share food and we touch and hug. We have become friends. Also, before we thought of the factory as a hell. Now we have learned it can also be a place of fun and creativity."[8]

Bohol

Not all theatre of liberation workshops operate as smoothly as the one in the fish canning factory. The island of Bohol, for example, has eight theatre groups but only two are active because of harassment by the military and vigilantes. Says Toto Cuhit, the island coordinator: "Security is a big problem. Our groups have already been branded as Communist fronts. We also have difficulty facilitating workshops in rural communities. We lack competence in that area. We are from the city and their culture is very different from ours. On the other hand, we are workers and the middle classes look down on us. And because of our progressive public image, people are scared to join us."[9]

For a while, even unions and other progressive political organizations were skeptical of the theatre of liberation, whose activities they considered frivolous compared to strikes and mass demonstrations. Says Cuhit: "That was silly, of course. For many years now our minds have been colonized. We were taught to be submissive and passive. So art plays a crucial role in our emancipation process. Now the unions and other groups are beginning to invite us to conduct workshops with their members and help them form their own theatre companies. Finally they realize that cultural groups can be very effective in communicating issues to the people; much more so than boring speeches and lectures."

Panay

The island of Panay has problems similar to Bohol's. Although the island had a great deal of activity during the First Quarter Storm in the early seventies, many progressive artists were arrested during Martial Law. The others went up to the hills to join the guerrillas. PETA conducted theatre of liberation workshops in Panay in 1982 and again in 1984. This resulted in the formation of some groups. The present island coordinator, playwright Julian Jagudilla, was one of the first participants. During the election campaign of February 1986 he helped a group from the Panay capital of Iloilo City create a street theatre piece called *Sabungan ng Bayan* [Cockfight].

> We had developed the play from improvisations with peasants and urban poor. Drawing on the format of the cockfight, one of the most popular pastimes in the Philippines, the human cockfight of the play became a metaphor for the February elections: a proud, young cock, dressed in bright yellow feathers and a healthy red comb on his head, represented the Aquino candidacy; a weak, old, multicolored, sickly cock stood for Marcos. The Marcos cock was constantly doped with amphetamines and steroids symbolized by oversized pills and syringes. He also had spurs shaped like submachine guns on his skinny legs, which assisted him in his dirty fight.[10]

For the audience, there could be no mistaking the identity of the two cocks: during the election campaign, the entire country was awash in yellow carnations, T-shirts, bumper stickers, and Aquino banners. During *Sabungan ng Bayan,* the actors encouraged spectators to cheer for their favorite candidates, turning the performance into a people's forum on the question, "Who do you want to win the elections?" The play also featured a supposedly neutral referee who wore a gigantic cowboy hat and spoke with a Ronald Reagan accent. Jagudilla: "He clearly favored the drugged old cock. After several below-the-belt assaults with his gunspurs, the audience started loudly criticizing the referee's refusal to penalize the old cock. The American ignored all appeals for justice and declared the Marcos cock the winner." Thus, *Sabungan ng Bayan* made the audience in Iloilo City aware of the long-standing friendship of the Marcoses and the Reagans, dating back to Marcos's sizeable financial contributions to the Reagan-for-Governor-of-California fund. The truth of the intimidation tactics applied by the dictator was emphatically underlined when, during a performance at a huge Bayan rally on 5 January 1986, the actors were prevented from finishing their play by a truncheon-wielding battalion of riot police.

In 1986 and 1987, theatre of liberation activities in Panay diminished considerably due to lack of finances and the resignation of key organizers. Julian Jagudilla, absent for two years himself, has been busy trying to revive the network since the beginning of 1988.

Trouble in Samar

Dolor Mercadez is artist-organizer with the MAKATAO cultural center in Catbalogan City, western Samar. This institution coordinates seventeen theatre groups spread throughout the province. The repertory arm of MAKATAO, called Makabugwas, was founded after a PETA workshop in 1975. According to Mercadez, the seventeen groups vary considerably in artistry and orientation: "Groups in the rural areas tend to be much more progressive than in the city. They suffer more and consequently have less to lose." [11]

In both western and northern Samar, military intimidation is an even greater obstacle than in Bohol and Panay. Mercadez: "Our former training officer was arrested. Luckily he was able to get out alive. We had to ask him to resign because we had heard rumors that in exchange for his release he had promised the military to do intelligence work for them. We interrogated him about it, but he denied it. One day three military officers came to his house. He wasn't there. They asked the other residents why he was still doing theatre work even though they had asked him to stop."

To prepare for eventualities, theatre of liberation artists attend seminars that help them prepare for arrests. They learn how to behave when they are interrogated and what their legal rights are. Yet, on a psychological level, the fear is constantly there. Mercadez: "I was shot over the head once during a performance in 1979. It is very scary when they do that to you. We had to stop the play and the audience scattered in a panic. It was a play about the woes of the educational system, the continuing feudal mentality, and militarization. We were performing in a church hall near the Bagakay mines in the eastern part of the province. The parish priest had invited us to come perform at a *fiesta*. The soldiers had caught wind of it." [12]

Theatre of liberation activists continue risking their lives because they firmly believe in the necessity of their work. Babie Delmoro, one of the founders of the Northern Samar Theatre Arts Organisation (NSTAO), was arrested in 1984 and 1987. Delmoro: "In 1984 we were brought to the Military Intelligence Group after performing at a demonstration. In 1987 they arrested us when we returned home from a workshop in a village. We were all girls.

Negros Theater League on the way to a performance in rural Negros.

They questioned us for nine hours. They know that the work we do is effective and that it makes people understand what is really going on."[13]

Since 1987, NSTAO, which coordinates a subregional network of twelve groups, has been forced to lie low due to a smear campaign against them. The harassment continues. "They cut off the electricity when we're rehearsing," says Delmoro. "We are always playing a cat and mouse game with the military and therefore we can't really fix our headquarters in any particular location. We are continually watched. I have to move around all the time. Likewise, we never formally announce the formation of a new community theatre group, because if we did, they would immediately get harassed. So we just keep a low profile and rely on word of mouth for our publicity."[14]

In 1988, NSTAO changed its name to Arts Center Northern Samar and in 1989 was able to carefully go public again with some performances. Since then, the provincial network has been expanded with a dance company and a music group.

Negros: Theatre in the Sugarcane Fields

Negros is by far the most advanced island of the Visayas in terms of its number of theatre of liberation groups. At the beginning of 1988, the island counted seventy-five groups, forty-three of which were based in the countryside and belonged to a subnetwork of sugarcane workers called Teatro Obrero. The remaining thirty-two groups are associated with the Negros Theater League and are serviced by NAC, the Negros Arts Center, which is based in the capital city of Bacolod.

The roots of the Negros theatre of liberation go back to 1971. As elsewhere in the Philippines, students in Bacolod had started their own street theatre groups in the wake of the First Quarter Storm movement. Joel Arbolario, one of the founders of the Negros Theater League and current chairman of the Visayan-wide network Dungog, was first exposed to theatre during that hectic period: "I was in a group called Gintong Silahis, which means Golden Rays. It was the cultural arm of a student organization called Samahang Demokratiko ng Kabataan or Democratic Youth League. The forms we used were very Chinese. All our songs and scripts came from Manila. We performed mostly in the streets during rallies, but we also went to rural areas and to Panay."[15]

When Martial Law was declared, most Gintong Silahis members were arrested, along with more than one hundred student leaders. Other members went underground. Arbolario spent six months in prison. After his release he returned to college, joined a drama club, and started writing songs and plays. Meanwhile, unbeknownst to Arbolario, PETA had come to Negros in 1975 to conduct a workshop for Teatro Pangkatilingban [Community Theatre], a church-based troupe run by Father Alan Abadesco. Duplicating the theatre of liberation method, Abadesco eventually managed to establish drama groups in thirty-three parishes all over the island. They mostly produced liturgical plays with a political content. Soon, however, some of the more radical chapters of Abadesco's network also began to do realistic plays about the conditions in their communities.

In 1982, following a dramatic collapse of sugar prices on the world market, a wildcat strike broke out at the Negros-based la Carlota plant, the world's largest sugar mill. Teatro Pangkatilingban went to the factory to perform a play on the picket line to express solidarity with the striking workers. These responded so enthusiastically that the company decided to return every week to la Carlota to perform newspaper theatre with the latest updates on what was happening in the factory. Father Abadesco also held a workshop with striking workers who eventually started their own theatre group. It became the first chapter of Teatro Obrero. Supported by the Negros Federation of Sugar Workers (NFSW), Teatro Obrero began to perform at *haciendas* and during strikes. Within eight months, 120 new chapters of Teatro Obrero representing 5,000 community actors had been established throughout the island. Says Bundo Dedma, the present coordinator of Teatro Obrero: "The basic dynamic was that workers saw us perform during rallies and strikes. After the show, one of us told them, 'If you want to, we can come next week to perform at your *hacienda*.' Of course the workers said 'yes.' They gave us food and shelter and on the plantations the children of the sugar workers would ask us if they could join. It was as easy as water flowing from the river to the ocean."[16]

In 1983, PETA returned to Bacolod for an advanced trainer's training workshop. The diocese financed the session and Father Abadesco invited Joel Arbolario, who was employed by an insurance company and, in his free time, had built a reputation for his work with a local amateur theatre group, to join in. Arbolario: "I was impressed with PETA's methodology and after the workshop we put up an alliance. They elected me chairman. Bundo also became one of the officers. That's how the Negros Theater League was formed. We started doing productions and workshops and gradually new groups were born."[17]

In December 1983, members of the Negros Theater League went to the *Makiisa-I* Festival in Manila to perform a controversial version of the grassroots play *Sakada* [Sugar Worker]. (An excerpt is in chapter 1.) Arbolario explains:

> We improvised it together. It is basically a collage of scenes from the daily life of sugar cane workers here in Negros. Most of them were based on actual facts. We connected them with a traditional folksong about a water buffalo. One of the scenes depicts a progressive church service. Afterwards the military arrests several people and buries them alive. We mime the incident, which really happened in a town called Kabangkalan, 97 kilometers from here. In the final scene we show a people's organizer covering his face and taking up arms. He takes a position behind a group of government soldiers. He cocks his rifle and one by one the soldiers fall. The Manila audience went wild. It was the first time that the armed struggle was ever projected on a Filipino stage. Later, we also performed the play at a *hacienda*. The workers were very moved. But they didn't cheer during the guerrilla scene. They remained very quiet because they knew all about it.

Many theatre of liberation activists in the Philippines have no difficulty with the term "cultural revolution," although most of them do not want to be associated with the armed activities of the underground movement. Says one Negros community actor: "In essence what we're trying to do is get the rotten, colonial culture out of people's heads. Fight the enemy from within, you know. Ours is a crucial instrument for the creation of a new mentality and a more just society. We show the true issues that affect our people. We promote traditional and indigenous cultural forms. We teach the people to make their own dramas and songs with whatever means are available to them. We form groups that become, in fact, small, alternative, democratic, creative communities. All of that is, of course, part of the revolutionary process towards attaining change in society." Although there are no direct links with the guerrillas, indirect connections occur sporadically. Says the same actor-organizer, who preferred to stay anonymous: "Sometimes we conduct work-

shops in the rural countryside and we don't know where some of the participants take off to afterwards."

The New People's Army (NPA), the most powerful guerrilla force in the
Philippines, has also recognized the power of theatre. For many years the
NPA has operated so-called Armed Propaganda Units (Sandatahang Yunit
Pampsapaganda) in areas that are more or less under their control. This organization is involved in a very wide field of work, including education,
mobilization, and art. The units help set up cultural groups and sometimes
participate themselves in performances. These performances take place under
makeshift conditions, in village squares or in an open space in the countryside. The NPA plays provide the guerrillas with an opportunity to befriend
the local populations and explain their revolutionary ideology. They also explain to the peasants the economic causes of their poverty and, through theatre of liberation workshops, help them prepare for the verbal confrontations
with landlords or officials. The shy and submissive Filipino peasants gain
confidence through these rehearsals of public speeches and official com-
plaints, which they normally would never have the courage to deliver.

Theatre also serves to strengthen the feelings of community and commitment among the guerrilla fighters themselves. Cultural evenings of songs and
drama help boost the morale of the revolutionaries. Plays performed on such
occasions range from satires to emotional pieces dealing with the loss of a
close friend in an ambush, the pain of being separated from loved ones, or
the fears and frustrations of being constantly on the run.

Like their colleagues elsewhere in the Philippines, progressive actors from
Negros are frequently intimidated by police and military. Over the past fifteen years many have been randomly arrested and subjected to torture. A
few years back, Father Abadesco had to go underground after receiving re-
peated death threats. During my stay in Bacolod, news reached us that Peter
Alderete, a community theatre worker from Mindanao, had been hacked to
death by machete-wielding vigilantes. In the volatile political climate of the
Philippines that is the ultimate price for making theatre of liberation. "We
are scared but we accept it," says Eman Carmona, a choreographer working
with the Negros Theater League. "Last night Jordi, one of our members,
was branded as a Communist by someone in his community. He lives in a
fishing village nearby. He has received threats to his life. We take precautions if we can. We move around a lot. It affects us also in our private lives,
of course. I have broken completely with my family. I had to leave my
previous girlfriend because we didn't share the same views. Our commitments go beyond the mere lengths of our lives, you see."[18] Teatro Obrero
suffers similar setbacks. Says Bundo Dedma, "One of our workers was arrested once on drug charges when he carried glue to a rehearsal space to build
a set. They broke one of his teeth. During our last assessment, our organizers
from the Central district told us that they were being hunted down by the

police. So we had to tell them to stop going to areas that had become too dangerous."

Despite the increasing harassment, the Negros Theater League and Teatro Obrero continue conducting workshops, creating full-length plays, and performing skits at rallies and other public occasions. Both their networks organize regional and subregional festivals like the *Bug-os* celebration in November 1985. At this particular festival, the Negros Theater League presented *Ang Buang ang Alibang Cagang Bangkay sg Panahon* [The Mad Man, the Butterfly, and the Coffin], a play structured around the traditional practice of extemporaneously reciting poetry during a funeral wake. Like *Makiisa-II* (1984), at which the Negros Theater League was also represented, *Bug-os* did not only contain theatre. In addition to matinée performances, there were art and photo exhibits as well as music concerts.

After the elections of 1986, both the Negros Theater League and Teatro Obrero lost quite a few of their members who thought victory had already been won. But in September 1986 the Negros Theater League premiered a new play called *Negros after February '86,* which tried to show that nothing had really changed with Cory Aquino in power and that the Negros countryside continued to be as militarized and destitute as ever. Since then, the League divides its work with Teatro Obrero. Says Arbolario: "We made an agreement that Obrero works predominantly in the countryside and we in the cities. Most of our audience are middle class or urban poor. We often rehearse in the slum areas, where some of our members live." Since June 1987, the League has also branched out into educational theatre; the headmaster of La Consolacion College in Bacolod invited them to teach children's theatre as a regular part of the curriculum.

In addition to new productions and workshops, recently Teatro Obrero and the Negros Theater League have also begun to theatricalize mass demonstrations in the vein of America's Bread and Puppet Theater. "We call them cultural parades," explains Eman Carmona; "it's a new concept of street theatre, really. We have done one as part of an anti-vigilante campaign, for example. We moved down the street with murals, masks, and music. We presented the vigilantes as a heavy metal hardrock band. There also happened to be some evacuees from the countryside in Bacolod at the time. Suspected of hiding guerrillas, their village had been attacked by helicopter gunships. They participated in our parade, playing themselves. We tied a big rope around them while Cory Aquino, the military, and the vigilantes pulled them."

Despite the harassments and desertions, Joel Arbolario feels the Negros Theater League and Teatro Obrero have come a long way over the past seven years: "Some of our own members were drug addicts and criminal delinquents before. Slowly they have grown as human beings. Their newly gained awareness of the social problems that formed the original basis for their condition was the sharpest development of all."

The Mindanao Networks

Further south in Mindanao, the second largest island of the Philippines, the conditions in which the theatre of liberation has to operate are possibly even more complex than in the Visayas. The activities of right-wing death squads and the military are intense. In addition to Communist guerrillas, many competing factions of heavily armed Muslim groups are fighting for an independent Muslim state on the island. Their ideological orientation ranges from revolutionary socialism to the extreme right-wing fundamentalism of the Muslim Brotherhood. The situation is further complicated by roaming "Lost Commands," former Muslim guerrillas who have discovered that piracy, kidnapping, and armed robbery are considerably more lucrative than the revolution. Finally, indigenous tribes with traditions going back thousands of years fight an unfair battle in the mountains with an even more formidable enemy: degenerate Western culture.

Because of its strong Muslim identity, Mindanao has always considered itself very different from the rest of the Philippines. The same can be said about the theatre of liberation movement on the island. Its representatives claim that they were the first ones to introduce the workshop methodology in the Philippines. Furthermore, they proudly proclaim their workshops and theatre productions to be at least as good as those of PETA.

The sources of the Mindanao theatre of liberation must be sought in progressive circles of the Catholic Church. The first attempts to use theatre for social change in the form of workshops were made back in 1969 and therefore predate PETA's similar activities by several years. Mindanao theatre of liberation activists of the first hour like Father Dong Galenzoga and Karl Gaspar admit there was a Latin American connection; after the 1968 Medellín Bishops' Conference liberation theology also began to find its way to Mindanao's seminaries. Says Father Dong: "Of course the Latin American liberation theology influenced us. But we developed our own way of thinking. I read Freire and naturally made the connection with certain forms of creative activity."[19]

Father Dong was ordained in 1969 at the height of the First Quarter Storm when Karl Gaspar was already developing theatre for social change in Davao del Sur province and students were doing street theatre. Father Dong's first assignment was the town of Kolambugan, a mixed community of Muslims and Christians. At first he used theatre to help form Basic Christian Communities. Soon he also formed a religiously mixed dance theatre group. This group tried to project local and national issues and used the legends of the indigenous Maranao tribe as the basis for its performances. The Kolambugan Dance Theatre expanded its activities despite the armed struggle that had exploded between Christian private armies and Muslim groups in the region.[20] The group even went to perform in the Visayas and Luzon in 1974

Theatre of liberation in a Mindanao Catholic church.

and 1975. Subsequently, Father Dong left the group and went to Europe for two years. He attended the London Contemporary School of Dance for a few months, but he found the atmosphere too artsy for his taste. "I just felt stupid wearing tights and prouncing around," he grins.

After teaching for a year at a seminary in Davao City, Father Dong started a new theatre group with poor peasants in Magsaysay in the mountains of Lanao del Norte. He stayed with them for half a decade. "When I arrived there they were just in the middle of a huge conflict about land. The governor of the province wanted to take 3,500 hectares away from the peasants to make some reserve for tourist purposes. So we mobilized hundreds of peasants who wrote their own script and performed it in a huge open area." The peasants ended up making plays for Christmas, Easter, and their own village *fiestas.* "Eventually they became more politicized and formed their own study groups. Even Muslin farmers joined. Of course both Christian and Muslim peasants were being deprived of their land. That brought them together." The peasants were successful and forced the governor to drop his project. And as a clear sign of its self-sufficiency, the theatre group continued its activities even after Father Dong left Magsaysay in 1983.

For a highly religious country like the Philippines, the church forms a perfect entry point for theatre of liberation. It has a well-developed infrastructure and extensive financial resources, and, given the prestige they enjoy in the community, priests are ideal theatre animators. Says Father Larry Helar, the young and dynamic parish priest of Alicia in Zamboanga del Sur province, "I treat a church service like a performance anyway. I feel like an actor myself. There is no difference between a priest and an actor-organizer. Religion being an integral part of culture, the two are fully compatible. Actor-organizers are motivated by vocation, by social justice. So are priests."[21] Or so they should be, at least. But according to Father Dong there are also priests who opportunistically relish the material comfort and the power they hold over their flock: "They quickly say their Mass, hop in their car, and go home to watch a video while the maid serves them lunch." Naturally, such priests and their conservative allies in the upper echelons of Catholic hierarchy are not too happy with the theatre activities of their radical young brothers. To weed out the rebellion at the root, progressive students are now routinely barred or expelled from seminaries.

The first phase in the history of the Mindanao theatre of liberation happened in the early seventies when priests like Father Dong used primitive theatre workshops to raise the conscience of their parishioners and establish BCCs. Although they vaguely knew of similar activities elsewhere, most priests operated in isolation. In 1974, Karl Gaspar, a lay church activist, was working in Tagum, Davao del Norte. In that year, the church intended to launch a large Lenten campaign and had opted for theatre as its main organizational vehicle. Gaspar got involved and so did Remmy Rikken, a former Tagum resident who had moved to Manila and had become finance officer of the Philippine Educational Theater Association. Through correspondence with church friends in her former hometown, Rikken proposed the idea of a three-day interaction workshop between some PETA artists and community theatre artists from Mindanao. Lutgardo Labad, Soxy Topacio, and Frank Rivera traveled down to Tagum to share their artistic expertise with the grassroots experiences of their colleagues from the south. The workshop proved to be an eyeopener for both parties. The artists from Manila were shocked by the harsh political realities in Mindanao. Nestor Horfilla, who later became a key figure in the Mindanao theatre of liberation movement, also attended:

> I was seventeen at the time. Father Dong and Karl Gaspar provided the PETA people with extensive accounts of their experiences. Karl's group performed. Then we did lots of theatre exercises and group dynamics, which were the seeds of PETA's Basic Integrated Theater Arts Workshop and the locally developed Creative Dramatics workshops. The Tagum workshop was a small liberation for me. In the university theatre only the articulate were allowed to join. But in the PETA format anyone could participate, regardless of skill or experience. So, following the workshop, I dropped out of school and went to work with some progressive groups using the theatre skills I had learned. Until I had to leave the island for security reasons in 1975.[22]

From 1976 through 1978 the Mindanao-Sulu Pastoral Conference (MSPC), an organization affiliated with the Catholic Church, sponsored a massive

Creative Dramatics (CD) campaign. Karl Gaspar and Fe Remotigue had received funding to develop a workshop curriculum for implementation in the parishes of Mindanao. Their objective was to promote theatre performances during important events on the church calendar. For the next two years, a team composed of Gigi Impalada, Odette Chanco, Amal Tao, and George Gaspar conducted hundreds of three-day theatre workshops in virtually all important communities of the island. Most of the time, participants were recruited from church choirs or from among committed parish workers. The workshops continued until 1979 when conservative bishops, worried about leftist infiltration in the grassroots of the church, finally withdrew their financial support.

The disappearance of the Creative Dramatics desk of the MSPC was a severe blow to the Mindanao theatre of liberation movement. The church-based groups formed through the workshops were not yet strong enough to survive on their own, partly because the CD organization had failed to provide sufficient follow-up support after the initial trainings, and partly because there was no organized network in Mindanao. For the same reason, the aesthetic level of most groups was not very high. There clearly was a great need for a full-time service center that could train competent actor-organizers and maintain a network. Karl Gaspar therefore approached Kulturang Atin [Our Culture], a student theatre company at the Ateneo University in Davao City, to help him with these tasks.

At first, Kulturang Atin provided ad-hoc production assistance to community-based groups on a request basis, but in June 1980 the company decided to reorganize and become a full-fledged institution. It was renamed Kulturang Atin Foundation Incorporated, KAFI for short. It immediately established a training arm called the Mindanao Institute for Cultural Arts (MICA) and a repertory company called the Sining Malay [Art of Consciousness] Ensemble (SME), which recruited performers from among workers, housewives, and working and unemployed youth as well as professional artists. Like PETA, SME had a writers' pool, a music pool, a designers' pool, a directors' pool, and a pool of performers. Between 1980 and 1986 KAFI proved instrumental in consolidating a Mindanao-wide theatre of liberation network. During this period SME was the leading experimental theatre company in the Davao area if not in the entire island.

The first year of KAFI's existence consisted largely of in-house skills training. In 1981, SME produced a few short original laboratory plays and MICA began training activities in several communities in the Davao area. Karl Gaspar, meanwhile, had tracked down his refugee colleague Nestor Horfilla in Cebu City. When Gaspar found him, Horfilla was managing the cultural affairs program of the San Carlos University. In that function he had gained considerable experience directing theatre productions, organizing cultural festivals, and conducting community theatre workshops throughout the Visayas. Gaspar knew that Horfilla would be the ideal person to direct KAFI.

Horfilla: "After our massive summer theatre festival in Cebu we had gone to conduct workshops in some radical parishes in Negros. That's when I realized my roots were really in Mindanao and in the countryside. Besides, some conservative elements in the university had begun to point at us as agitators. I had already been in prison once. The time seemed ripe, therefore, to return to Davao and I began working with KAFI early in 1982."[23]

Horfilla's first task was to try to locate former colleagues and to take inventory of groups that had survived after the demise of the Creative Dramatics campaign. His main aim was to establish a firm network. He applied and received money for a six-week workshop from a West German funding agency and set up a summer school modeled after PETA. This big workshop took place in May 1982. Horfilla: "In retrospect it proved to be a crucial project. All the old people saw each other again. They had brought along their second-liners as well: Father Larry Helar was there. Edgarito Riconalla was there from Sining Kambayoka in Marawi City. That summer workshop created a new momentum. Although no real network was established yet, people committed themselves to staying in touch."

The workshop was followed by a conference in October 1982. Nine groups attended and reached a consensus to establish links with activists in other sectors like schools and unions. In the two years that followed, many basic grassroots workshops and trainers' training sessions were held. When Horfilla convened another island-wide conference in 1984, there were already five full-blown subregions: Davao; the prelature of Ipil; north-central Mindanao; north and south Cotabato; and Agusan/Surigao. Horfilla:

> The workshops had resulted in the formation and consolidation of many groups. Not to mention productions during mass actions and summer festivals. The whole panorama of liberation theatre in Mindanao was truly amazing. Most of the groups were very young, though; not more than two years old at most. Then we had a Mindanao-wide festival in Davao City to present samples of the kinds of dramaturgy that were evolving. In February 1985 we held a third conference in North Cotabato at which 54 delegates attended, representing as many groups. We decided it was time to launch our official network: MCTN, the Mindanao Community Theater Network. It incorporated a variety of groups, ranging from those who were only a little politicized and merely interested in performing Filipino drama material and church-based groups doing morality plays to groups that were extremely militant.

Meanwhile, the Sining Malay Ensemble (SME) was gradually developing a distinct performing style of its own. Other groups, notably Sining Kambayoka in Marawi City, were beginning to attract national attention as well. SME wanted to represent the island at *Makiisa-II* with a production full of typical Mindanao flavor. For that purpose, they dispatched two researchers to Lake Sebu in South Cotabato, in the middle of the T'boli tribal territory. After a month they returned with a wealth of material from which the SME collective created the play *Lemlunay* (1984). The show was intended to reflect the struggles of all indigenous tribes of Mindanao. The first act was an expressionistic rendering of Philippine colonial history. The second act depicted the neocolonial situation in Mindanao up to the Marcos era; its style was also expressionistic. The third act was realistic and dealt with the present-day predicament of a T'boli village that was losing ancestral lands to lowland settlers and large-scale logging corporations. Its plot centered around a T'boli girl named Lunay who is forced to marry a non-tribal landlord's son. Their troubled relationship was supposed to symbolize the irresistible infiltration of tribal territory and culture by the corrupt lowland civilization.

Lemlunay was one of the last major productions of SME. Its full-time members had become too busy conducting workshops and expanding the network. Increasingly, its part-time members, mostly university students, opted for more lucrative careers after graduation. In 1986, KAFI therefore resorted to training and organizing as its main priorities. SME continued in name but froze its repertory activities in favor of extending production assistance to community groups in Davao.

The Current Mindanao Network

At the moment, there are five institutions operating in Mindanao, servicing as many subregions. KAFI has an island-wide projection and, in addition, provides services to groups in the three Davao provinces (Davao, Davao del Sur, and Davao Oriental). Lanao Educational Arts for Development (LEAD) operates out of Iligan City and services a subregional network called ASPECT (Assembly of People's Culture and Tradition). ASPECT unites thirty-two groups spread over nine districts in the provinces Lanao del Norte, Lanao del Sur, and Bukidnon. Like KAFI, LEAD has a training arm and a repertory company. The performing group is called RANAO (Rurban and Nationalist Artists Organization) and was formed in December 1986. Like PETA's Kalinangan Ensemble and KAFI's Sining Malay Ensemble, it has collectively structured pools. It mostly creates so-called urgent plays that can be produced at short notice for performance at mass demonstrations. The group also specializes in theatricalized street parades.

RANAO's most famous play is about a Muslim chieftain named Casador who fought the Americans at the beginning of the twentieth century. *Casador* attempts to show, by historical example, that foreign infiltrators have always tried to divide the Muslim community. According to author Greg Tabañag, Mindanao Muslims reacted very positively to his play: "It was in a way reflective of the stand of the Mindanao theatre of liberation. We publicly support the Muslim right to self-determination."[24]

Educational Discipline in Culture and Arts for Development Services (ED-CADS) covers the northern provinces of Agusan and Surigao from its headquarters in Butuan City. The institution was officially founded in March 1986, but its roots go back to the Creative Dramatics campaign of the late seventies when Yolando Arban, artistic director of EDCADS, received his first theatre training. EDCADS tries to revive the former CD network through refresher courses. But Arban states that, whenever possible, his group prefers to operate independently from the church: "Our investigations revealed that the original network had not only collapsed because of militarization but also because of heavy dependency on church resources. There was a remarkable decline in theatre activities between 1980 and 1983. The reason was that priests are usually assigned for three years only. When the good ones left, their successors often were not interested in drama at all and many groups collapsed." EDCADS also has a performance group, the Dula Argus Ensemble, but like LEAD its main focus is on network development and trainer's training.

The fourth subregional network consists of fifteen groups in the Ipil prelature, Zamboanga del Sur province. Located in a diocese with a progressive bishop and coordinated by Alicia parish priest Father Larry Helar, this organization engages, not surprisingly, mostly in creative liturgy. "We do church services like theatre performances," explains Father Larry, as he pushes his motorbike back up the hill to his house. "We choreograph the offertory, for instance, and we illustrate the reading from the gospel with a realistic drama piece that contextualizes the message. Here in Alicia the group consists of thirty people, mostly youth. They meet every Sunday."[25]

Father Larry received his first exposure to theatre of liberation at the seminary of Davao City. Fascinated by the possibilities, he signed up for a five-day community theatre workshop in Cebu and subsequently attended the 1982 KAFI summer school organized by Horfilla. Father Larry: "I immediately saw the potential of its methodology for parochial work. I gained so much self-confidence from the summer school. It was incredible. We stayed up all night to write our scripts. When the school ended we were so close that we didn't want to be separated. I already dreamed of creating communities just as close as we were then."

After his ordination in 1983, Father Larry was assigned to Alicia. He immediately started implementing theatre workshops: "Theatre of liberation is very useful to activate members of Basic Christian Communities. From '83 on we received an overwhelming amount of requests to conduct workshops in neighboring parishes. Usually participants then wanted to form their own groups. So we helped them organize. We sent some of the most mature members to LEAD's summer school in Iligan. After two batches of them had gone through these trainers' training programs, we had enough people to facilitate effective workshops on a local level." In 1985, Father Larry invited representatives from eleven groups to accompany him to Horfilla's MCTN Conference in Cotabato City. Upon their return they decided to form their own subregional network in Zamboanga. Father Larry: "We formed a core group composed of representatives from each group. We still meet every two months to consult with each other and plan joint activities. We already have competent trainers in all areas of our region and have organized a regional theatre festival in Ipil."

Father Larry, who has 24,000 inhabitants in his parish, is convinced that theatre of liberation is effective: "It helps the youth to become more creative and not to think immediately of money. The theatre has definitely improved community life here." After these words, we said our goodbyes. Father Larry started his bike to travel the fifteen muddy and bumpy miles to a rural chapel where he was to conduct a church service. Waiting for my bus, I recalled what he had told me the night before by the light of an oil lamp, over a glass of coconut wine: not too long ago a sympathetic military officer had warned him not to go out by himself any longer because he thought he had seen Father Larry's name on a hit list.

Bullets were beginning to get to me a little. The day after I had arrived in Alicia from Davao City, I read in the newspaper that pirates had killed a passenger on the same dilapidated Cotabato-Agadian ferry I had traveled on only a night earlier. My next destination was Sining Kambayoka in Marawi City, in the middle of guerrilla territory controlled by the Moro National Liberation Front, or so I was told. To protect me, a Muslim member of LEAD and an officer of ASPECT would accompany me on the risky trip. The last white visitor to the city, a British Jesuit, had been kidnapped by a breakaway faction of the MNLF. They had kept him for twenty-one days and had apparently killed time by playing Russian roulette with him. At the time of my trip to Marawi there had been provincial elections that threatened to topple the corrupt governor. With the ballots still not counted, my hosts were a little worried that I, the only white foreigner for miles around, might be used as leverage in the power struggle. My companions debated for hours whether to take me in a public jeepney or in a taxi with tinted windows. They finally settled for the latter. During the entire trip from Iligan to Marawi my stomach was in a painful knot and I wished I had specialized in Renaissance Drama instead. Sining Kambayoka had better be worth it.

Sining Kambayoka derives its names from the term *Bayok*, which refers to the age-old extemporaneous story-telling tradition of the Maranao tribe that this theatre group has adapted for the stage. The company is the pride of Mindanao State University (MSU), which sponsors its frequent tours to Manila and furnishes full scholarships to its members. Kambayoka was founded in 1974 after a PETA theatre workshop conducted by Frank Rivera,[26] who subsequently accepted a permanent position at MSU. He ended up staying six years, making Kambayoka one of the best theatre companies in the southern Philippines. Under Rivera, the company developed a distinct performance style, drawing largely on Maranao cultural practices like the *Bayok*

Sining Kambayoka, Marawi City, Mindanao, performs *Ng Jaula* (The Cage).

and dances with the *malong,* brightly colored cloths worn by men and women instead of pants and skirts. Artistic excellence was the company's main concern during Rivera's tenure.

Frank Rivera returned to Manila in 1981 and Edgarito Riconalla, a former Kambayoka member, was appointed his successor. Under Riconalla's inspired leadership, new members of the company were taken on exposure trips to impoverished areas and community theatre workshops were implemented in the region. As a result, the political awareness of the Kambayoka artists grew noticeably. The direct effect of the workshop campaign was the formation of twenty cultural groups in the provinces of Cotabato, Misamis Oriental, and Misamis Occidental. In November 1984, these new groups all performed at two festivals held simultaneously in Cotabato City and Cagayan de Oro. In that same year, Riconalla also inaugurated the Kambayoka Center for Cultural Development Management, a regional service center committed to sharing Kambayoka's theatrical expertise with the member groups in their newly established subregional network. In addition, the center would dedicate itself to preserving the cultural traditions of the Maranao people and promoting understanding between Muslims and Christians.

In December 1986, Kambayoka suffered a serious blow when Edgarito Riconalla was killed by some fanatic Muslims. Riconalla had aligned himself with the new university president, who had just announced the termination of 300 jobs held by Maranao tribals. Riconalla became the first victim of a

Sining Kambayoka in a traditional *Malong* dance.

bloody reprisal that also cost the lives of five students. Eventually, Riconal-la's widow, Juanita, took over as director of the center.

By 1988, Kambayoka had virtually recovered from the loss of its charismatic leader. It had begun to reactivate the dormant network through refresher workshops. Its performance department began reviving old successes like *Halik sa Kampilan* [Kissing of the Kris], a play about landgrabbing full of Maranao ritual, music, and dance, which had even received the praise of MNLF leader Nur Misuari. During holidays and semester breaks, the company also went on a town-to-town tour around the island, performing in gymnasiums, open-air basketball courts, market places, and cockfighting arenas. Finally, noted East German director Fritz Bennewitz,[27] who had worked with the company several times before, returned to Marawi City to direct Shakespeare's *Midsummer Night's Dream*, which Kambayoka eventually also took on tour to Luzon and the capital region. In 1989, Bennewitz came back again to direct Brecht's *Caucasian Chalk Circle*.

Today, the Kambayoka Center has a performing arm composed of Sining Kambayoka, an ethno-rock combo, and a traditional music band. In 1989, the performance branch was expanded with a dance company called Sining Pananadem, which within a year developed a reputation as one of the leading ethnic dance ensembles of the Philippines. Recognition from traditional Muslim elders is considerably harder to get since they still regard women who perform in public as prostitutes. Samo Balt, one of the few female Muslim members of Kambayoka, explains: "When I joined I didn't dare tell my parents. They would behead me if they knew I performed."[28] Apart from cultural obstacles, Marawi political reality also prevents Muslims from joining the Kambayoka performing groups. Says Balt: "Our rehearsals sometimes last until two in the morning and the downtown area is under night curfew. And then there is the problem that Maranao tradition does not allow close proximity—let alone touching—of men and women."

On my way back to Davao I visited Nestor Horfilla in the town of Matalam, north Cotabato province, where he was working with Father Ely Balboa to form four roaming theatre squads of youngsters. They were preparing plays about the local histories in some of the villages in the area. After the project, a staff member of the Mindanao Community Theatre Network would stay behind in Matalam to set up a cultural institution. Back in Davao City, the Kulturang Atin Foundation was preparing a huge cultural caravan of workshops, forum discussions, visual arts exhibits, and performances. Intended as a protest against the propagandistic and commercial orientation of official Philippine culture, this campaign, entitled *Anti-Dekopyu,* wanted to present grassroots cultural alternatives in the form of a mobile festival.

Recent updates from Mindanao indicate that theatre of liberation continues to be as active as ever. The Matalam center is now a fact. New groups are sprouting up all over the interior. The summer theatre schools in Iligan and Butuan have been full for two consecutive years. The Mindanao Community

Theatre Network opened its very own office in Davao City. Contacts with indigenous Lumads are rapidly improving through some very cautiously conducted interaction workshops. To show the public in Manila and elsewhere in the north that there is more to Mindanao's progressive culture than just Sining Kambayoka and popular ethno-rocker Joey Ayala and his Bagong Lumad band, the Dula Argus Ensemble of Butuan City has also gone on tour to Luzon. Apparently they reaped rave reviews with *Lawig Balanghai,* a play about the tribal history of Butuan City written by playwright Fe Remotigue. The regional centers are all bustling with workshops, research, newsletters, and performances. But despite all these positive developments, not everything is rosy under the southern skies. Following a serious ideological dispute, the Kulturang Atin Foundation and Lanao Educational Arts for Development broke away from the Mindanao Community Theatre Network to form their own network called MCPC, the Mindanao Council for People's Culture. Luckily, the two sides are still on speaking terms. In addition, vigilantism and militarization continuously jeopardize the lives of theatre organizers, particularly in the rural areas. Says Jorge Benitez, Kulturang Atin's training director, "Some artists had to go into hiding recently after a woman in their group turned out to be an informer of the military. Several others were detained and tortured. They had their heads banged against the wall."[29] Preferring to remain anonymous, a female member of Signos, a student theatre group in Davao City, told me about her life–and–death struggle within her own family: "My father and brother are both members of the Alsa Masa vigilante group. They are convinced I am involved in Communism or something. Last night I came home late from a rehearsal and my brother threatened to have me kidnapped if I went again. I think he is serious about it."

Back in Manila, Bonifacio Ilagan, a respected playwright and one of the architects of the country's theatre of liberation network, takes a sip of his San Miguel beer in one of the city's beer gardens. Tomorrow he is flying to Mindanao for a playwriting workshop. He is in his thirties and has written some critically acclaimed plays based on stories from Philippine labor history. He agrees that in–fighting and paramilitary intimidation are the main problems facing the culture of liberation movement: "Of course we must grow but at the same time we must be very careful with those vigilantes. They're no joke; they kill for real. Consolidation must therefore be our first priority right now."[30]

Ilagan has been asked to mediate between MCPC and MCTN. "We can't afford those kinds of conflicts. Besides, their positions are not all that far apart. In fact, things in Mindanao are going quite well. The Visayan network is also functioning smoothly, given the circumstances. And in Luzon, we now have thirty-three consolidated groups in the south. The Cordillera region in the north is also beginning to take off, particularly in and around Baguio City."

Like elsewhere, the network in the Metro Manila region has also experi-

enced some setbacks in recent years. Ilagan: "In 1986 we still had eighty
active theatre groups of union-affiliated factory workers, students, and working youth. But in January 1988 there were only thirty-five of them left. I
attribute this to attempts by the radical KMU union to bring the cultural
groups of factory workers more firmly under its control. Naturally, groups
with a long-standing identity of their own didn't go for this. And many
student groups disappeared because of lack of interest from the League of
Filipino Students, the nation's largest student union. They didn't really have
a clear cultural policy."

Toward a National Network

By 1987 it was estimated that there were approximately four hundred community theatre groups operating throughout the Philippines. To streamline
communications between the groups and to coordinate their activities, the
Philippine Coordinating Council for People's Culture (BUGKOS) was established. BUGKOS is divided into regional networks of amateur and semi-profes-
sional collectives that engage in theatre, visual arts, music, dance and movement, creative writing, traditional or indigenous arts, broadcast and film,
cultural research, art and literary criticism, and training. Member groups of
BUGKOS can be found in all sectors of Philippine society, ranging from communities and schools to parishes, factories, plantations, tribes, and urban centers. The members of BUGKOS are united in their effort to build an alternative
culture opposed to government controlled culture. Geographically divided,
in Manila BUGKOS works with SINING, a federation of more than one hundred
cultural groups in the capital region. In Mindanao, BUGKOS is allied with the
Mindanao Community Theater Network and, more recently, with the Mindanao Council for People's Culture, which together represent close to one
hundred cultural groups in this southern island. In the Visayas, BUGKOS is
allied with Dungog, an alliance of cultural groups on the islands of Samar,
Leyte, Cebu, Negros, Bohol, and Panay. In the Cordillera highlands, BUGKOS
is associated with the Cordillera Cultural Coordinating Body based in Baguio City. BUGKOS also has ties with cultural workers and artists in the districts of Cagayan Valley, central Luzon, Bicol, and southern Tagalog. Various regional institutions provide the technical and artistic support for the
groups operating in the grassroots. They all provide advanced training for
cultural workers, conduct surveys and cultural research, and try to operate
high-level performing ensembles catering to multisectoral city audiences.

The performance-oriented groups fulfill several important functions. First
of all, they provide actor-organizers with a necessary outlet for their artistic
inclinations. Like first-time workshop participants, they need to continue to
nurture their own artistic growth to avoid frustration. Thus, within the various (often collectively structured) pools of the performing ensembles, they

develop playwriting, choreography, set design, music composition, and generally aim at improving the quality of performance. Second, given the community groups' priority for training and organizing, the city-based repertory companies can help them sharpen the aesthetic quality of their grassroots performances.

Most Filipino repertory companies incorporated in BUGKOS have a limited season. They perform from January until June and cater to urban popular audiences composed of students, office workers, middle class liberals, and factory workers. They also have a mobile season in which they go on tour, performing in village squares, open-air basketball courts, gymnasiums, and other publicly accessible spaces. For the rest of the year, the repertory artists conduct workshops. However, repertory companies are always on call to create "urgent" on-the-spot plays to expose burning issues like slum demolition or to encourage a community to take a stand when, for example, one of their leaders has been abducted or found murdered. The repertory companies perform these ad hoc plays in improvised venues inside the communities in question and are always available for performances during mass rallies and other political functions. But the main thrust of the repertory work within the context of the theatre of liberation movement is to elevate the aesthetics of popular theatre.

Ideologically, the groups united in the BUGKOS network would all describe themselves as "nationalist," a word that in the Philippine context should not be misread as "chauvinistic." It has everything to do with the assertion of an indigenous nationalist culture against several centuries of colonial and neo-colonial domination during which emancipatory forms of cultural expression were systematically suppressed. Likewise, the term "nationalist" is meant to be an assertion against the foreign domination of the Philippine economy and military. But the concept of nationalist culture is broad enough to contain many political differences. PETA's Alan Glinoga explains:

> After the Aquino assassination there was some confusion in political, ideological, and cultural areas. Many groups presented themselves as being THE ultimate vision of the movement. They were social democrat, nationalist democrat, popular democrat, etc. They were all doing it with a very high profile in what amounted to a public market place of ideologies. The nationalist movement had been working until then with a very low profile and found itself forced to come out into the open with its own vision for our society coming from the grassroots.
>
> Our vision of people's rights is distinct from the bourgeois concept of human rights. There is, of course, the fundamental right of the Filipino people to chart their own destiny without the interference of outside forces. That is the most basic concept of liberty in our case. Then there is also the right of the people to decide what to do themselves on economic, cultural, and political issues. More specifically, very often we run into the U.S. which is preventing us from obtaining economic, cultural, and political freedom. There is U.S.

intervention in all these fields. U.S. culture, perhaps even more importantly than its military presence and its economic exploitation, is invading almost every Filipino household.[31]

The BUGKOS network has not been able to generate the same energy as in February 1986. But the communication links have been reestablished; the infrastructure is in place; the regional and subregional institutions are providing the necessary training at whatever pace the ever-changing political circumstances allow; interesting original plays are created; and grassroots enthusiasm is high. Despite justified criticisms, the theatre of liberation workshop is still a very effective tool to generate new, self-sufficient theatre of liberation groups that are firmly rooted in their communities, although perhaps less firmly in their cultural traditions. Together, they continue to expand the ever-growing corpus of original Filipino plays, which artistically still require a great deal of work but thematically are unmatched in terms of their topicality. The aesthetic quality of many theatre of liberation performances continues to be debatable, but there are hopeful signs that new talent is emerging in provincial cities like Butuan, Davao, Bacolod, and Cebu. There is little reason, therefore, to despair of the future of the Philippine theatre of liberation. Its network itself is one of the most extensive and enduring political theatre projects ever created.

IV

RESISTANCE THEATRE IN SOUTH KOREA
ABOVE AND UNDERGROUND

The recent reunification of East and West Germany, one of the most spectacular results of the rapid thaw in the Communist block, is also beginning to have its effects on Korea, that other country forcibly divided by the Cold War. There are signs that the border between North and South, closed hermetically for almost forty years, may soon be opened to the public. The Prime Ministers of both countries have already exchanged visits. Until as recently as a year ago, attempts by South Koreans to contact relatives in the North—let alone travel there by way of Japan—were tantamount to treason and punishable by torture and life imprisonment. The replacement of former dictator Chun Doo-hwan by his handpicked successor Roh Tae Woo in December 1987 has merely resulted in cosmetic changes. The paranoia, economic woes of the peasants and industrial workers, and fundamental lack of democracy remained virtually unchanged.

Although culturally, geographically, economically, and politically speaking South Korea is very different from the Philippines, the opposition movements in both countries share some important features. They both fight a staunch group of paranoid anti–Communist military rulers who are advised by American generals, if not directly under their command. The opposition fights on many different fronts, among which the unions and the student organizations stand out. Surprisingly, in this traditionally Buddhist country, the Catholic and Protestant clergy also play an important part in the dynamics of social change on the edge of the underground. On the theatre front, a network of progressive groups has been established over the past twenty years which now has regional chapters in virtually all important provincial centers of the country. Independently of the Philippines, Korean theatre artists also discovered the empowering potential of the theatre workshop and the agitational effects of street theatre.

Big Brother Is Watching

Even before I landed in South Korea by boat from Japan in November 1986, the wholesale manipulation of my perspective began. The car ferry that plies six days a week between Shimonoseki and Pusan takes close to fourteen hours where it needs only five at most. From 1:00 until 7:30 in the morning, the ship lies anchored off the Korean shore, waiting for Customs to open. As a sleeping passenger, you may never find out. As a tourist (or as one of the 40,000 U.S. soldiers stationed in South Korea) you will be impressed by the clean high rise buildings; the comfortable and well-maintained Hyundai and Daiwoo cabs; the luxurious and punctual intercity bus services complete with cute stewardesses, air conditioning, and videos; the newly resurfaced highways connecting the major cities; the smoothly running (and graffiti-free) Seoul subway system; the apparent absence of slums; the well-organized markets; the low prices of Fila, Lacoste, and Nike sportswear, not to mention absolute rock bottom prices for leather goods; the availability of English-language newspapers and the U.S. Armed Forces television station that brings college basketball, NFL Football, and "General Hospital" right into your hotel room. Only occasionally—and then by accident—is the foreigner fortunate (or unfortunate) enough to perceive a crack in the veneer of what must have been one of the world's most efficient and cosmetic dictatorships, that of President Chun Doo-hwan.

One such crack occurred on 21 January 1987 when Secretary of the Interior Kim Chong Ho and National Police Chief Kang Min Chang were forced to resign after the death by torture of twenty-one-year-old student Park Chong Chol. President Chun spoke of an isolated incident, proclaiming that there were absolutely no political prisoners in his country. This claim is hard to believe if you have ever watched any of the always brutally dispersed student demonstrations that are occasionally featured in international news broadcasts, or, better still, if you happen to get caught in one as I was on Saturday, 29 November 1986. Next to me, a bleeding cameraman from the *Tagesschau,* the West German evening news, had his video camera knocked from his shoulder by the billy club of an overzealous policeman in riot gear while some other cops hit the poor German over the head to finish the job. The next moment, a tear gas grenade exploded at my feet and I was dragged along by a stampede of panicky people clutching wet handkerchiefs to their mouths and noses. Left and right, protesters were being pushed violently into armored vehicles.

With the lucrative Seoul Olympic Games coming up in the summer of 1988, President Chun was obviously worried about any negative publicity in the world press, hence the "accident" with the German cameraman and the general stinginess with visas for foreign journalists. Again for cosmetic reasons, the members of Chun's military junta never wear uniforms in public, only three-piece suits. The covert and overt repression of the opposition is being justified in the name of the country's stability and the continuous threat from the Communists in the North. This "red scare" strategy, with which the South Korean rulers control the minds of their people, has assumed Orwellian proportions. Throughout my six-week stay, South Korean television, radio, and newspapers—with little sense of self-irony—would almost daily announce messages like: "President Chun Doo-hwan yesterday called for beefed-up security precautions by the military against the high danger of North Korea's surprise attacks through the coastal areas and rivers in the winter season" (*Korea Herald,* 23 November 1986). Or: "Defense Minister Lee Warns '87 Most Vulnerable Year" followed by "Pyong-yang is likely to send large numbers of armed agents into the South next summer by taking advantage of the foliage season" (*Korea Herald,* 4 December 1986). The fear that the régime tries to instill in its population with such notices is further substantiated by the meticulously observed air raid drills that take place on the third Saturday of each month at 11 a.m. sharp. These are an eerie sight. Following ominous siren blasts from ubiquitous loudspeakers, hundreds of thousands of Saturday morning shoppers rush to hide in the nearest subway entrance; cars swerve to the sides of the roads and their drivers run for cover in nearby buildings or underpasses; in a matter of minutes, the streets of the bustling metropolis are as deserted as after an explosion of a neutron bomb. Then metallic voices begin to yell instructions through the loudspeakers and, after a few moments, a seemingly endless string of ambulances and police cars, lights flashing and sirens screaming, speeds through the empty streets of Seoul. Half an hour later, a couple of curt commands bring the paralyzed streets back to life as if by magic, and street vendors hawk their wares as if nothing had happened.

So tight is the government's control over all aspects of public life that any sustained form of open protest has been made impossible. On the surface, South Korea appears to be firmly in the grip of the military and a fear of the North. But the invariably dispersed student riots, the occasional torture victim who makes it to the pages of the newspapers, and the isolated spectacular cases of self-incineration are but the tip of the iceberg. Phone-tapping and twenty-four hour surveillance of suspected and actual dissidents are common practice. But South Korea's radical underground movement is beginning to find effective ways to circumvent the secret police, the dreaded Korean Central Intelligence Agency (KCIA). For example, the underground operates a nationwide communications network. Inconspicuous couriers—often old people who are called "submarines"—transport cassette editions of the Korean Free Radio News, underground newspapers, and messages. Nowadays, the activities of the underground are predominantly cultural and its leaders can be found among the clergy and artists.

I have long been fascinated by the possibilities of theatre as an effective weapon in the fight for freedom from all forms of oppression. While in the

Philippines during the overthrow of the Marcos dictatorship, I had seen the tremendous power of street theatre and the organizing capacities of grass-roots theatre workshops for illiterate farmers, fishermen, and factory work-ers. I had heard that South Korea's underground was using so-called *Madang* theatre for similar purposes. The word literally means "open square" or "meeting place" and, applied to the South Korean theatre scene, it refers to agitational street theatre based on traditional folk drama and western agit-prop. The word "agitational" should be taken quite literally here: many ma-dang performances succeed in getting the audience in such a state of ecstatic frenzy that they are spontaneously transformed from spectators into slogan-chanting political demonstrators. Many mass demonstrations are therefore initiated or animated by madang performances.

Unfortunately, two of my local contacts, activists in the Korean Ecumen-ical Youth Council, had been arrested a few days before my arrival. A third person, who had promised to serve as my interpreter, had been forced to flee the country to avoid imprisonment. Not knowing this, I sent word of my arrival to the prearranged postal address and waited ten long days for a re-sponse that never came. At long last, I decided to take the risk of a tapped phone and called the office of the Minjung People's Culture Movement. A male voice told me, in broken English, that he would see what he could do. Several days and two canceled meetings later, a frail young man finally vis-ited me in the small boarding house where I was staying. After I explained my purpose and mentioned the names of some trusted contacts he and I both knew, he agreed to help me. Over a three-week period, he took me to see madang performances in the countryside, as far as four hours away from the capital; set up meetings with other people in the underground cultural net-work in such cities as Taegu, Kwangju, and Pusan; and took me on a tour through a maze of Seoul back streets that eventually led us to an under-ground theatre collective.

Protest in the Mainstream

The contemporary mainstream theatre of South Korea, like most other me-dia in this country, is virtually unable to touch political issues in any sus-tained critical way. As a result, most professional theatre companies resort to safe productions of Western classics. The only mainstream theatre artist tak-ing any risk at all is Kim Sok-man, a New York University graduate, who is widely regarded as one of South Korea's most talented young directors. His production of *Chilsu hwa Mansu* [Chilsu and Mansu] had been running for eight months when I saw it at the end of 1986. But for Korea's real political theatre, you have to go to university campuses, Catholic community halls, or rural village squares, all of which are off limits to conspicuous for-eigners. These are the illegal venues for the exhilarating and hard-hitting madang performances and you have to know and be trusted by the organizers to be allowed to watch them.

One of South Korea's leading dissident writers, Hwang Sok-yong, works both underground and above. His immense popularity and international prestige have limited his involuntary visits to South Korea's notorious jails to relatively short periods. Others, like poet-playwright Kim Chi Ha, who spent seven years in prison and is now a physical wreck, have not been so lucky. In 1985, Hwang Sok-yong had one of his plays selected for the prestigious Annual Drama Festival of Korea. The play in question, *Han-ssi Yondaegi* [The Chronicle of Mr. Han], was directed by Kim Sok-man and produced by the Yonu Theatre Company. The play is loosely based on the life story of the playwright's uncle, who, Hwang Sok-yong told me in his brand-new home in the countryside, an hour by car from Seoul, was sent to Japan to study medicine at Kyoto Medical College. When he returned to South Korea in 1951, he became a spy for the North."[1] Hwang Sok-yong, a strong supporter of South Korea's underground theatre of liberation, sees a task for the middle-class theatre in the overall cultural movement as well. "Most mainstream theatres are afraid to do anything that might reek of anti-government criticism. But I think they respect me. . . . Kim Sok-man is a good man; he tries to create some space for criticism in the mainstream. The 1985 play we did together was about the tragedy of our divided country."[2]

Chilsu hwa Mansu, the show with which Kim Sok-man had so much success in the second half of 1986, is a Western-style, dialogue-based play about two housepainters. Mansu is a migrated peasant; Chilsu is originally from an urbanization settlement near a U.S. army base. After working all day on one of the many skyscrapers that are being erected in Seoul, they go to the top of the building and reminisce about how they came to the capital. Chilsu is loud and boisterous, a working-class playboy who has adjusted quite well to the fast, big-city life. Mansu is quiet and sentimental. He is trying to save money to send home to his mother, who is still working on the land. The play is full of flashbacks and direct interaction with the audience.

I saw the play on Sunday, 7 December, in the ultramodern, hired premises of the Yonu Theatre Company. The capacity audience of 250 was seated on bleachers that surrounded the arena stage. A brief inspection of the theatre's ceiling revealed a state-of the-art grid filled with top-quality spotlights. As the audience entered, Western disco music was played over the sophisticated hi-fi sound system.

The set was simple. One corner was taken up by a painter's scaffolding suspended with ropes and pulleys from what was obviously supposed to be the roof of a high-rise building, the wall of which was painted on a backdrop. As the lights come up and the music fades, two painters are shown working on a huge beer ad. They mime their actions and occasionally pretend to lose their balance as if a gust of wind has rocked their scaffold. Kim Sok-man had provided me with a detailed synopsis in English so that I could

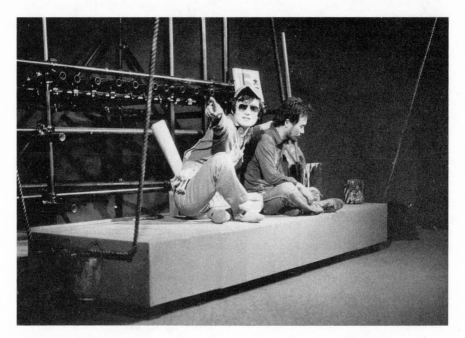

Chilsu hwa Mansu, Yonu Theatre Company, Seoul, 1986. Photo by Kim Sok-man.

comfortably follow the action as it unfolded on stage. The first dialogue of the play is between the president and the financial manager of the painting firm. Standing in front of where the painters are working, they explain that the sign Chilsu and Mansu are working on is the biggest painting job in Korean history. The two are obviously only concerned with profit and complain about what they call the unreasonable demands of the labor force. The government's slogan, duly echoed by the painting company, has been "Economic growth through hard work." "And if Koreans say 'hard work,' they mean seven days a week around the clock," explained Kim Sok-man after the show.

> Tighten your belt a bit, suffer a bit, and later you will reap the benefits. As it turned out, only a few people reaped the benefits. The greatest problem here is the distribution of wealth. So, the big building that Chilsu and Mansu are painting is a symbol of the current situation. Rapid economic growth, advertising for beer, symbol of the good life, which the painters, of course, don't feel. They work up high on scaffold. It's windy, lonely and dangerous. They have to hang on and stick together to survive and try to forget about their predicament through fantasies and hopes of a better life. The suffering, poor painters who paint a picture of the beautiful life, beer, cigarettes, jet-set life,

and gorgeous blondes, express the basic contradiction in South Korean society.[3]

As the two managers leave, the light comes up on the two painters, who are still miming their working motions. They go up and down the floors of the skyscraper, indicating their movement by pulling or releasing the ropes from which the scaffolding is suspended. At the same time, someone from backstage changes large signs with the numbers—14, 15, 16, etc.—to show the height at which Chilsu and Mansu are working. After a few minutes, Chilsu starts singing a song—his grade school anthem. Mansu tells him to shut up. Chilsu does not understand his partner's reaction: he has sung the tune many times before and Mansu never complained. The latter explains that he has just received a letter from his mother. The light on the painters fades and a single spot comes up on the mother who is tilling the land downstage. Dressed in traditional Korean farm clothes, she speaks the contents of the letter she sent her son as she works: Mansu's sister has come home pregnant. The father has disappeared, but Mansu's sister wants the child anyway. They need money and Mansu's mother asks her son to send more.

Following the mother's monologue, the action shifts back to the scaffolding. The two painters start talking about sex. Chilsu comically imitates what he saw in a porno flick a while back. "We intended to criticize the porno movie industry in Korea," commented the director. "The country is full of this trash. They suck the money from the workers and pollute their minds. It spells the total decay of popular culture. The movies don't depict real life but unattainable dreams. It's just like the advertisements they paint, but Chilsu and Mansu don't see the connection."[4] Chilsu says that after the cinema he went to the disco. The painter jumps off the scaffolding and, in another flashback, the acting space is converted into a nightclub complete with disco lights reflected from mirror balls. Chilsu goes around the audience, inviting women to dance. He tells every prospective partner that he is an artist who has come to the nightclub to find some inspiration for his next painting. Finally, he takes a fancy to a college student in the audience, a planted actress. She leaves her seat to go on stage. Chilsu follows her, telling her that he is a college student like her. She asks him the name of his school. The university he mentions does not have a fine arts program and the audience laughs. The young woman, realizing that Chilsu is a fake, tells him that she does not want anything to do with him and that by now even a dog would have understood that. Taking offense at being called a dog, the painter slaps her. The light fades and, back on the scaffolding, Chilsu explains to his partner how, following the incident, he was arrested and spent twenty days in jail.

Chilsu hwa Mansu is, then, a continuous alternation of showing and telling as the action shifts from the present on the scaffolding to flashbacks acted downstage. The next scene opens again on the scaffolding. This time, the two painters talk about why they came to Seoul. A flashback dramatizes the farewell between Mansu and his mother in the countryside. Thus it is revealed that he went to the city because there simply was not enough money to be made farming. Coming down from the scaffolding, Mansu joins his mother downstage. They are poor tenant-farmers. His mother wants him to stay, but the higher wages of the capital are too tempting. Mansu's father died many years earlier, exhausted from hard labor. Mansu and his mother realize that going to Seoul means living a lowly life, pollution, small rooms shared with two or three other migrant workers, and long workdays. In the countryside at least the air is clean, the fields are green, and new life appears in the soil every springtime, even if they do not own the land. But Mansu closes his suitcase and walks back to the scaffolding, leaving his mother behind in silence. "Our closeness to nature and to traditional lifestyles has been destroyed through industrialization," explained Kim Sok-man:

> Lots of farmers left their homes in the seventies in order to become factory workers in the cities. They were forced to leave to survive. Most of them ended up living in slums around Seoul. The kinds of slums we have here are quite different from those of, say, the South American cities. Our slums are illegally built squatter huts in the hills. People are being evicted from these slums now because the government wants to clean it all up for the Olympics. The government is building high-rise apartments, but it is only a bandage on the wound as long as the wages continue to be so low. It is like putting an animal in a cage that is a little more comfortable only to exploit it better. The South Korean social welfare system is not very good, I'm afraid.[5]

Back on the scaffolding, Chilsu explains that he is from Paju, a town two hours from Seoul and located right next to a major U.S. army base. Wherever American GI's are stationed, Koreans make a living through shady dealings, bars, and prostitution. Chilsu tells his partner that he used to get into fights all the time. Wanting to get away, he stole money from his father and went to Seoul. Chilsu wants to lead a fast life. He has no ideas or ideals; the money he earns he spends on movies, discos, and alcohol. Mansu, on the other hand, wants to save his money so he can buy the land his mother is tilling and return to his native area.

The rapid string of dialogue and flashbacks continues with a fantasy scene in which Chilsu and Mansu dream of being rich and hitting the big time. Jumping into the auditorium, they first mime robbing a bank, boisterously and playfully, like high school kids. They use the audience as kidnapped customers and the spectators seem to enjoy their antics. Then Chilsu tells about how he had always wanted to be a boxing champion. Light on his feet, he jumps around like a prize fighter and mimes the final moments of his world championship match. Boxing is a very popular sport in South Korea and many of the champs come from poor backgrounds. Their success stories inspire thousands of Korean versions of the Rocky dream.

When night falls and the workday is over, Chilsu and Mansu decide to go to the top of the skyscraper and piss on the world. With their backs to the audience, they lean over and pretend to look at the passers-by below. Gesticulating wildly, the painters shout insults from above: "Seoul and your citizens, you are all lousy motherfuckers!" They get carried away by their own antics and accidentally kick a can of paint from the roof. From this incident onwards, the play falls into a rapid succession of climactic complications.

The downstage area, previously reserved for flashbacks, now becomes the public road at the foot of the high-rise. The police and the press arrive on the scene, thinking that Chilsu and Mansu are radical students wanting to make an anti-government statement and then incinerate themselves and jump off. A police captain with megaphone wants to hear their political statement. Chilsu and Mansu answer that they don't have one. The captain does not believe them. He promises to broadcast whatever they wish to say. The two painters huddle and deliberate. They decide to ask for money and dinner because by now they are starving.

After some time, Chilsu and Mansu realize that the people below think they want to commit suicide. They are caught in a trap. The Press Man, a bespectacled figure with three cameras, headphones, and a microphone—an obvious caricatural collage of all the news media—faces an imaginary TV camera as he reports the imminent human tragedy. Chilsu and Mansu would like to climb down but they are confused and intimidated by all the uniformed authorities, the spotlights, the microphones, and the cameras. Then the manager and the president of the company return and reveal the names of the two painters. Mansu is in agony because he does not want his mother to find out that he has shamed the honor of his family. But it is too late. The Press Man has already been to his room and found his mother's letter. Downstage, he reads its contents to a national television audience. The details about his sister's pregnancy are revealed and the tone of the letter makes the mother sound really ignorant. Finally, the police captain decides to shoot tranquilizers into the painters, whose movements are becoming increasingly erratic. But the painters, thinking he is about to shoot real bullets (understandable in the light of the ruthless reputation of the South Korean armed forces), jump off the scaffolding into the backstage area. An instant blackout follows during which sirens roar and an occasional searchlight breaks through the darkness. The houselights come on and the predominantly middle-class audience files out into the dark, wintry streets of Seoul.

Chilsu hwa Mansu contains obvious criticism of the press. Kim Sok-man explains that they are always looking for sensation: "They never listen to the people. They try to manipulate opinion, particularly the government-owned Korean Broadcasting Service (KBS). All stations and newspapers are government controlled. Or at least we have strong suspicions that they are."[6]

Theatre of Liberation in the South Korean Grassroots

Kim Sok-man's play provided alternative coverage of a story that does not often get told from the workers' perspective in their own colorful slang. But radical intellectuals and artists criticized the play for merely caressing the conscience of the bourgeoisie, who laugh at Chilsu and Mansu's comedy but do not bother to do anything about their problems. Therefore, the radicals see more value in developing the grassroots activities of the people's cultural movement. Hwang Sok-yong concurred: "We need to express our ideas in the mainstream as well, but government censors make things very difficult for us. So we prefer to spend our energy on expanding the people's culture network. From that strong popular base we hope to gradually infiltrate the mainstream."[7]

The people's cultural movement of South Korea is in great need of experienced professional artists who can help improve the aesthetics and the performance techniques of the underground cultural workers. So far, the movement has not been very successful in recruiting the required professionals. "We have 5,000 years of performing arts tradition in Korea," states Hwang Sok-yong,

> Koreans love to sing, dance, and make music. The Chinese call us "players." We are very proud of our traditional culture. We are proud of our people's vitality. We also have very talented professional artists. But the current people's theatre movement was begun by amateurs at university. Later, in a prolonged and fruitful collaboration with peasants and workers, it developed to what it is today. Of course, we can learn a lot from the professional's techniques. But professionalism can be dangerous too. A lot of spontaneity gets lost in commercialism. We feel that, more than acquiring professional performing skills, we need to retain the powerful vitality of the people.[8]

Hwang Sok-yong started his grassroots activities in 1975 when he and several friends began holding theatre of liberation workshops in the factories and fields. Soon a steadily growing number of cultural workers began collaborating with progressive Catholic parishes. Culture became a weapon.

> One of the first sustained activities we started with was the People's Night School, based on Freire's Pedagogy of the Oppressed and Augusto Boal's theatre techniques. The workers loved it. Many fruitful discussions emerged from these night classes. Through them, we became more than ever convinced of the profound political nature of people's culture as it was engaged in the battle for the minds of the masses. People's cultural activities were primarily concerned with community building. We did away with specialized artists, playwrights, actors, and stars. Everyone in the night classes was equal. Farm workers had just as much creative input in the creative processes as the students and artists. Thus, we created little gems like Sweet Potato, a now legendary madang play.

At least 500 plays have already been created directly from peasant experience. We professionals only served in an advisory capacity and taught basic skills: movement based on daily working motions, "life actions," "worker's actions." In return, the workers also taught us a tremendous amount. They were passive at first, inhibited. But soon they started taking the initiative and organized people's culture festivals where they performed old traditional ceremonial plays like *Gut*.[9] They guided and we followed.[10]

Sweet Potato is a documentary of the farmers' lives, their struggles and their sadness. Sweet Potato is the name of the narrator, a man dressed in a potato sack. He asks the audience of farmers all kinds of questions about their predicament. When they respond the action starts. The play has a basic scenario upon which the farmer-actors improvise. The play opens with a group of drunken farmers in the village square who talk about the good life. Sweet Potato enters asking questions. He takes them back in time, reconstructing tragic little domestic scenes of the recent past, in order to show that it has not been all that good.

With two secret service men stationed in a car across from his home, Hwang Sok-yong told me that madang theatre is the only kind of political theatre that is able to evade censorship because it is performed underground. The South Korean news media are systematically censored and most newspapers actually have a Korean Central Intelligence agent in their editorial offices. "Everything that goes into the newspaper has to pass through his hands. Censors are everywhere. There is a so-called Cultural Officer in City Hall who controls all scenarios for theatre performances. All scripts have to be submitted to him first."[11] Madang is the public mouthpiece of the people's cultural movement and its performances are often linked with political demonstrations.

In the seventies, it was considerably easier to organize madang performances in the villages than it is nowadays. This was not because the society was any freer or more democratic than today but because the government was not so aware of the political power of culture. The Kwangju Uprising of 1980, which resulted in the massacre of two thousand citizens by South Korean soldiers, changed all that.[12] Between 1976 and 1980, many grassroots cultural groups had been organized in the Kwangju slums and in the countryside. Painters, musicians, and actors ran night classes for workers and peasants who later organized themselves into madang groups. With their performances, they spread the news about the preparations for the uprising. Community-based theatre groups thus were instrumental in the actual mobilization of the Kwangju population during the rebellion itself as madang plays were being performed throughout the city encouraging the people to persevere in their struggle. Other groups presented "Living Newspapers" as alternative news coverage or "Situation Plays," while painters painted revolutionary murals and posters. Dancers and musicians were also very active.

"What we learned from Kwangju was that it is indispensable to abolish all distinction of genres and disciplines," said Hwang Sok-yong. "All forms of artistic expression must be integrated in one culture of struggle for liberation. Many groups are dedicated to this and are operating underground throughout the entire country now. There are literally thousands of cultural workers in South Korea."[13]

Hwang Sok-yong locates the original roots of the current underground cultural movement in the Korean peasant revolts of the eighteenth and nineteenth centuries:

> The Tonghak Peasant Rebellion [1894] was a totally independent uprising devoid of any foreign ideological influence—just political anger over economic exploitation. Since its collapse Korea has been dependent on foreign powers, first Japan, then the USA. During the time of the uprising, eight days before a major battle the peasants would start playing the drums, day and night, working themselves into a powerful collective trance. It should not be forgotten that the labor forces in Korea's factories nowadays almost all migrated from the countryside. Rural traditions are still very much alive among them. The Tonghak Peasant Revolt serves as the main inspiration for the present underground cultural movement. But already during the thirty-six years of Japanese occupation in the first half of this century, it was held up as an example to the partisan forces.[14]

During the Japanese occupation (1910–1945), there was an all-out effort to impose Japanese culture. Speaking and writing Korean were outlawed. People were even forced to change their Korean names to Japanese ones.

> Koreans are traditionally nomadic horsemen, who, at the beginning of the century, still had long hair. The Japanese forced them to cut their hair and to abandon their traditional dress. The local Korean bourgeoisie was sent to Japan for training and brought back Westernized Japanese cultural forms. This influence, heavily mixed with American culture, persists to this day. That is why we must return to the roots and the forms of the Tonghak Revolt since that was the last example of unadulterated Korean popular culture that was very much alive among the rural masses. Ever since, our culture has been polluted and diluted for purposes of Western and Japanese domination.[15]

At the end of World War II, the Japanese left Korea. This was followed, in 1947, by the tragic division of the country into a Communist North and a capitalist South. But the Korean problem is far more complex than a clear-cut ideological conflict. After the Korean War (1950–1953), the South embarked on a full-scale industrialization project which completely destroyed traditional forms of communal living and popular culture. Said Hwang Sok-yong: "In the middle of the sixties, with the signing of the Normalization Treaty between Korea and Japan, people realized that Japanese culture was once again going to invade and ravage whatever was left over of ours. Some people in the government recognized this and formulated the new Korean national cultural policy. They appointed old masters of folk art as 'National Human Treasures' and assigned them to teach the younger generation."[16]

The modern development of madang was closely connected with the volatile political situation that arose in 1965 after the signing of the Japan-Korea Normalization Treaty. The treaty was widely regarded as a renewal of the economic exploitation that had taken place during the Japanese occupation, benefiting the small ruling-class élite and defying the strong anti-Japanese sentiments that still pervaded the Korean people. The Minjung cultural movement was founded in the late sixties to combat the brutal régime of President Park Chung Hee and to create a culture of liberation through the promotion of people's culture. It did not only want to revive traditional culture; it also wanted to use culture to make political statements more effectively. The madang plays were created for that explicit purpose.

Madang plays performed by community theatre groups became widespread after 1970. But the great precursor of madang was created by Kim Chi Ha in 1965 at Seoul University: a biting satire entitled *The Funeral Ceremony of National Democracy*. The title referred to the fascist ideology of the dictatorship, which the régime was fond of referring to as "national democracy." Since the early seventies, Kim Chi Ha's play has been the model for madang theatre and the form has rapidly become the most popular type of political theatre in South Korea. Its performances range from impromptu pieces composed by farmers, factory workers, and fishermen to professional shows performed by experienced actors in Seoul. Thus, since 1986, the popular film actor and singer Kim Myung Gon operates a professional madang company called the Arirang Theatre in which he also performs modernized versions of traditional *Gut* mask dramas.

Madang is very different from Western theatre. It has some resemblance to the dramatic form and treatment of space implied by the term "environmental theatre." Its basic scenario changes from venue to venue, adapting to the political particulars wherever it is performed. It may take the form of a festival of people's culture or it may be a mask ceremony. But first and foremost it is rooted in the community of the people, the *kongdong-che*. In this age of modern technology and industrialization, traditional village life and the harmony with nature have been destroyed. It has become difficult for people to express their community spirit. Madang is one attempt to overcome this block. Groups have been formed throughout South Korea even though it is very dangerous to conduct theatre of liberation workshops. Actors and students try to facilitate collective madang sessions with farmers and workers, teaching basic performance techniques and assisting the participants to create the madang plays, which they are encouraged to compose themselves. But the police and military do what they can to prevent artists and intellectuals from allying themselves with the people.

The madang theatre movement of South Korea is similar to the theatre of liberation movement in the Philippines. But the Korean military obstacles have been too formidable to allow the movement to get into heavy political organizing, although it collaborates with the farmers' and labor movements, and madang performances have precipitated many discussions and spontaneous demonstrations. There are now an estimated one hundred madang groups all over South Korea, many of which are informal theatre collectives that perform three or four times a year during harvest festivals or political rallies. Almost all of the sixty-nine universities in South Korea have their own madang groups.

Two Madang Performances

During my 1986 visit to South Korea, I observed two madang performances one in an auditorium of a Catholic college in Chonju and one in a small farmers' village an hour's bus ride further inland. All madang performances invariably start with an ecstatic drum and dance session called *Binari,* often with the audience actively participating. Drumming is still very much part of traditional Korean village culture. In the Chonju (indoor) performance, the drummers came in from outside, beating drums of all sizes, cymbals, and gongs. In the village (outdoor) performance the next day, the drummers walked through the entire community, enticing the inhabitants from their homes to follow them to the main square where the performance was to take place. Many villagers joined in the drumming and the dancing.

The madang group that performed in Chonju and in the village was composed of student actors belonging to a Catholic People's Culture group from Seoul and local Chonju factory workers with whom they had developed the play in a workshop during the previous week. After about twenty minutes of frantic drumming and dancing, the audience sat (or stood) in a circle while the actors prepared their costumes for the first scene of the play. Four or five musicians continued playing, including a narrator who played the *Book,* a traditional drum. The performers were all dressed in traditional white peasant clothes, which looked remotely like Tae-kwon-do apparel.

Following the *Binari,* one performer steps forward and starts chanting in the traditional *Pansori* style. *Pansori* is a kind of rural one-man folk opera, the origins of which date back to the beginning of the eighteenth century. It requires a very complex singing technique. The *Pansori* chants at the beginning of the madang performance list the grievances of the oppressed and their hopes for their future. This list of wishes is written on a parchment scroll, which is burned at the end of the *Binari.* The ashes rise symbolically to the sky.

One of the main purposes of madang is to celebrate the dignity of farmers' culture. It is, in essence, a showcase of traditional Korean performing arts with a very explicit contemporary political message. The first scene (or "first

Twenty minutes of drumming and dancing precede performance of madang play in Chonju. Photo by Keith Rodabaugh.

In the Chonju madang, an old woman mourns for her husband, who was killed by political and economic forces.

The ecstatic shaman tears through
the white cloth, symbolically cross-
ing the road between life and death.

madang") begins with a traditional mask dance which, together with the *Gut*
of the final madang, provide the formal structure of the performance. The
other madangs in between can vary in number, style, and content. The performances are extremely informal. Spectators get totally involved in the show,
often encouraging the performers with cries of support. All the characters
address the audience directly and spectators talk back without inhibitions.
There is a great deal of improvisation. Sometimes, if an actor forgets a line,
the narrator-drummer prompts, and the audience laughs. The performers are
purposely presented as non-superhuman. They are like the average spectator.

After the mask dance of an old peasant couple, some of the performers
dressed as farmers talk with the audience about police violence at the Konguk
University student riots the month before. Opinions are mixed and the conversation is quite animated. Their interaction is interrupted by the arrival of
another character, a conservative priest who claims that "Only faith in God
can improve the farmer's life."[17] He argues that the farmers should not get
involved in economics and politics. The audience does not like the priest's
attitude; they openly voice their disapproval.

The second madang deals with the economic problems of small farmers.
This scene is clearly pedagogical and propagandistic. The farmers are protesting the dumping of cheap cattle and agricultural produce from the USA
on the Korean market, undercutting domestic Korean products. In a scene
involving exaggerated gestures of pushing and hitting, a Korean farmer is
crushed by an ominous character in uniform and helmet who represents the

military policy and by a character personifying cheap foreign goods. This madang ends with a protest song against the importation of foreign agricultural produce. Finally, the farmer's death is reenacted. It emphasizes that he did not die of natural causes—he was killed by political and economic forces. The scene closes on his wailing widow.

The third madang features the satirical dance of the ruling class performed by an army officer, who represents the dictatorship; a rich businessman, who symbolizes monopoly capital; and a character called "USA," the symbol of militarization, imperialism, and multinationals. For a few minutes, they all jump and dance around in a circle to the beat of the drums. The three oppressors seem intoxicated. The scene subsequently turns into a boisterous farce when the spectators loudly react to the exaggerated speeches of the rulers by rooting for a peasant who is beaten up, slapstick style. The farm worker is eventually joined by several other performers dressed as farmers to support him in his struggle, "for it's the only way to achieve victory."[18]

The oppressors are presented as *kishin* or bad spirits who must be exorcised. The fourth and final madang introduces a shaman character who perform an exorcism ritual derived from the traditional *Gut,* featuring ecstatic music and dance. Progressive priests do not mind this pagan element in the show, but a considerable number of conservative clergymen strongly object to it. The actress playing the part of the shaman in the Chonju performances allows herself to be completely carried away into a seemingly unfeigned trance, which also transports the audience into a high state of frenzy. She first sings a soulful requiem that is followed by a turbulent flag dance. The climax of the ritual is the reconnection of the road between heaven and earth, symbolized by a long, white banner. By now, the actress is perspiring profusely and breathing heavily. She violently stabs a hole in the cloth, which is being held tightly at both ends by members of the cast and the audience. She pushes her head through the cloth from below and slowly tears through the white material to the other side, thus symbolically overcoming death. Many Koreans in the audience cannot control their tears. But the ritual is not over yet. The shaman dips the two separated pieces of cloth in gasoline, lights them, and starts dancing frantically in circles around the space, twirling the burning pieces. The lights are out and only the increasing pace of the fiery circles can be seen as the drums beat ever more loudly and quickly. Sometimes the shaman, who still seems to be in a trance, brings the fire dangerously close to the spectators. Then the rest of the cast returns, turning and swinging the flags they hold in their hands. The burning cloth is extinguished and the shaman shouts in the middle of all this ecstasy: "We won't pay rent! Stop the foreign imports! Let's unite our divided country! Free the political prisoners!" The audience gets up and follows the shaman, dancing behind her and repeating her words in chorus.

The awesome shouting, dancing, and drumming continue for up to half an hour after the planned performance. It was not difficult to see how madang plays often turn into spontaneous demonstrations, particularly when they are performed at universities. Their potential for inciting social unrest has by now also been recognized by the authorities. When I returned to Seoul a few days after the Chonju performance, the same frail young man who had first helped me find South Korea's underground theatre told me that the leader of the madang group whose performances I had been so fortunate to observe had been arrested and was facing a prison sentence of at least two years.

Arirang

In 1989, Kim Myung Gon of the Arirang Theatre in Seoul and Seung Jin-Jung, an exiled artist operating out of New York City, created *Arirang*, a mixture of madang and *Gut* with which they participated in the *Cry of Asia!* cultural caravan that toured Europe. The difference in performance quality from the Chonju shows was remarkable. First, Kim Myung Gon delivered the *Binari* chants with an intensity and range of voice that did justice to his reputation as one of the better *Pansori* singers of South Korea. Secondly, he introduced one of the legendary *Gut* characters, Malttugi, whom he played by placing a mask on a stick in front of his face. The first madang of *Arirang* thus became a violent exchange between a greedy landlord, also played by Kim Myung Gon, with his mask removed, and a despondent Malttugi, who is kicked off his land. But Malttugi returns with a stick to reclaim his property in a symbolic reminder of the Tonghak peasant revolt.

The character of Malttugi has been part of *Gut* mask dramas since their earliest beginnings. His name means "the rooted one" and he traditionally represents the *Minjung,* the little people. Even in the oldest *Gut* plays, Malttugi eventually always conquered the oppressive nobility with his common sense and slyness.

In the second madang, Malttugi is harassed by a Japanese colonizer, played by Seung Jin-Jung. Again he is removed from his land and manages to reclaim it by force. But this victory is not to last long. In the third madang, an American soldier, played by the masked Seung Jin-Jung, occupies the country and tears the map of Korea in two. While slides of the Kwangju massacre are projected on the white backdrop, Malttugi and the American soldier engage in a slow-motion battle. Eventually, the American's bayonet separates Malttugi's mask from the stick. Kim Myung Gon drops to the floor and sings a moving requiem over the now lifeless mask. Meanwhile, Seung Jin-Jung prepares the white banner for the play's finale. Kim Myung Gon then replaces the Malttugi mask on the stick and tears through the material. Afterwards, both performers swirl a piece of the torn banner while they dance and sing the "Arirang" folksong about the mythical mountain of the same name that symbolizes the unified Korea. The performance ends with the two actors solemnly placing the divided halves of their country back together again.[19]

The reunification of Korea seems closer now than it has been in a very long time. If negotiations between the North and the South prove successful and families can visit each other again after forty years of separation, the South Korean madang movement must be credited for keeping the hope of the reunification alive. But even with opened borders, drastic structural changes are not to be expected immediately either in the North or in the South. Too many political and economic privileges are still at stake for those in power. Malttugi, the heroic working-class clown, may have to sing, dance, and fight the illegal occupiers of his land for a long time to come.

V

THE FACTIONALIZED INDIAN THEATRE OF LIBERATION

The emerging Indian theatre of liberation operates almost clandestinely in the slums of the metropoles and in impoverished rural areas. In contrast to the Philippines and to a lesser degree South Korea, India's mainstream theatre artists, cultural administrators, and even those who consider themselves political theatre artists either ignore or dismiss it. India's modern theatre can be traced back to its colonial past. The majority of the British administrators considered the Indian traditional musical dance dramas, based on *Mahabharata* and *Ramayana* stories, to be exotic but inferior forms of art. Starved of what they considered to be "real" art, in the middle of the nineteenth century, therefore, they started bringing over some actors from the motherland to do Shakespeare in Calcutta and other major Indian cities. Subsequently, British dramatic societies sprang up in the major urban centers of India. Unavoidably, the emerging Indian middle class eventually was exposed to the new Western plays and became interested in reading and later performing them themselves. Starting around 1860, semiprofessional indigenous theatre companies produced their first plays in Calcutta and Bombay. Their repertoire was very much the product of interaction with Western drama and, in addition to Shakespeare, it came to include Shaw, Ibsen, Strindberg, and Chekhov. From its earliest beginnings, however, Western-style theatre in India tried to weave the theme of national independence into its productions. Often crushed by British censors, these first dramatic expressions of the Indian yearning to end colonialism were incidental and did not gain any sustained momentum until well into the 1940s.

From the early forties on, a great number of theatre artists began associating themselves with the Communist Party of India (CPI), organized themselves into a cultural army, and called themselves the Indian People's Theatre Association (IPTA). According to Farley Richmond, the catalyst for the formation of IPTA was a 1943 campaign by progressive artists who created a mobile performing arts festival and performed around the country to collect money for millions of victims of a widespread famine in the northern state of Bihar.[1] The nationwide political theatre movement that developed in the wake of this solidarity tour engaged primarily in street plays against social injustice and British imperialism. Often these IPTA plays made use of traditional theatre forms and injected them with a pertinent political content and a satirical tone. Not surprisingly, the British frequently served as the butts of biting satirical portraits. Eventually, branches of IPTA were established in all parts of India, including the areas now called Pakistan, Sri Lanka, and Bangladesh. IPTA stayed active until 1964, when it disintegrated, mostly because of the ideological split at the twentieth Communist Congress in Moscow.[2] Most of today's theatre personalities in India were first exposed to theatre in IPTA, which makes their dismissive attitude toward the new theatre of liberation movement all the more curious. The strategists of the current Indian theatre of liberation movement have drawn important lessons from IPTA's previous achievements. They are very impressed with the concept of the traveling theatre festival, for example, as well as with the idea of filling traditional theatre forms with new political content. Clearly, the present Indian mainstream and political fringe theatre would not have been what it is today without the Indian People's Theatre Association.

The first Indian writers to create full-length plays in the vernacular languages did not emerge until the sixties. Aesthetically, they were inspired by various twentieth century Western theatrical innovations, ranging from realism to absurdism. Talented writers like Vijay Tendulkar also started writing historical plays with contemporary relevance, sometimes using quite inventive musical theatre forms.[3] In the mid seventies, elements of rural folk theatre forms and the classical Indian theatre began to enter the experimental contemporary mainstream theatre, infused—usually by city-bred writers—with modern, social thematics.[4] By far the most successful commercial theatre enterprises in India can be found in Calcutta, where large playhouses offer a fare of romantic, sentimental melodramas. In addition, immense open-air venues present the popular *jatra* folk theatre. Boisterous and musical, these romantic epics take their audience back to the days of legends, and feature Krishna and kings and princes.[5] Utpal Dutt, film star, IPTA veteran, and stalwart of West Bengal's popular political theatre, has often used the *jatra* for his own Marxist plays.[6] Finally, to complete this cursory historical sketch of Indian mainstream theatre, over the past decade numerous Brecht plays have been successfully produced in vernacular adaptations.[7]

M. K. Raina, who divides his activities between Kashmir and Delhi, and Badal Sircar and Arun Mukherjee from Calcutta seem to be the only three established Indian political theatre makers who realize that the answer lies not with Brecht in saris, nor indeed with any of the other attempts at fitting social criticism into Western or traditional forms. Yet they find it hard to abandon their own performance orientation and to divorce themselves from the mainstream theatre in-crowd on whom they depend for their livelihood and status. Mukherjee, an accomplished actor-director, confesses: "We don't want to admit that we have compromised. But the system is so strong. We

Badal Sircar's group, Satabdi, performs *Sagina Mahato* in the library of the
Bengal Theosophical Society, Calcutta.

perform in the Academy Hall.[8] The people we really want to perform for
are not coming. If they don't come, we should go to them. We know it, but
we cannot find a practical way to implement it. Nor can Badal Sircar. A
group must go to a village, live there, find a subject, share the rice with the
peasants and develop a play with them. Maybe then, in five or six years,
something will come out of it."[9]

In a city like Delhi, close to three million people live in the slums. In
Calcutta that number is even higher and, in addition, there are more than
one million "destitutes": illegal Bangladeshi refugees who sleep in the streets
and have no official status whatsoever. In the densely populated Indian subcontinent, millions of people are starving and the majority of the population
lives well below the poverty line. They could never afford a ticket to a theatre performance, even if it cost only one rupee (which it does not). Is there
a theatre for them?

Approximately fifteen years ago, politicized drama academy students and
social activists began their first theatre of liberation experiments in the slums
of the larger Indian metropoles and rural areas of the states Tamil Nadu,
Karnataka, and Kerala, which together form the southern cone of the Indian
subcontinent. Although there is no coordinated national movement as in the
Philippines or South Korea, fully developed regional theatre of liberation networks do exist in the south. In the following pages, I will reconstruct a

journey I undertook through these informal and factionalized networks. I will first dwell on the activities of several women's theatre groups in and around the national capital territory of Delhi. Most of this chapter will deal with the work of theatre of liberation groups in southern India. In terms of artistry, workshop methodology, and network organizing, the South is considerably more advanced than the other parts of India, which will be briefly surveyed at the end of the chapter. The Indian theatre of liberation only rarely produces outstanding original plays but its social effectiveness is sometimes stunning. Likewise, the involvement of some award-winning theatre artists is encouraging for its future aesthetic development. Shashidara Adapa, a well-known designer from Karnataka state, and Jos Chiramel, a director based in the state of Kerala, are involved in full-time grassroots work. M. K. Raina, a screen actor and theatre director, serves as part-time consultant to theatre of liberation groups in New Delhi and in his native state Kashmir: "There are a lot of people working in the lower strata of society," he told me during the East-West Theatre Encounter in Bombay. "Not only with political plays but also in more direct ways. For example, we have a women's organization here in Delhi. There are a lot of problems with wife battery and bride burning. We have women doing plays about this and also helping out on the legal aspects with people's lawyers. But unfortunately that is not considered to fall within the parameters of what is called art here." [10]

Women's Theatre

The women's theatre group M. K. Raina referred to is called Theatre Union. It is the continuation of a women's collective named Stree Sangharsh [Women's Struggle] that was formed back in 1981 by Anuradha Kapoor, Maya Rao, and Rati Bartholomew. For the women's movement in India, 1979 had been a watershed year. As elsewhere in Asia, its pioneers are (upper) middle class women who were exposed to feminist ideas while studying at Western universities. That year saw the launching of *Manushi,* India's first progressive women's magazine, and in the following year, this ground-breaking publication started its daring confrontation with the past by launching a media assault on such social aberrations as bride burning for dowry. This awful practice usually involves the murder of a young bride by her in-laws following a dispute about dowry. The death is often presented to the public as a domestic accident involving fire, but everyone knows it was actually premeditated murder to liberate the bridegroom for a new, more lucrative marriage. Anuradha Kapoor, freshly returned to Delhi with a Ph.D. in theatre studies from Leeds University, decided to do a street play on this issue:

> We gathered a group of women in September and began improvising on the theme of dowry death. We took a story that had actually happened. We talked

to the parents. We developed a number of improvisations for the group which were based on this story. At the end of the day we would then sift the material that we had created. We worked on the dialogue and set up a program for the next day. It took about five weeks of devising. Apart from Maya and myself all the women were new to theatre so we also did basic acting exercises with them. It was one of the best times we had. The women enjoyed it and freely talked about their own experiences.[11]

Many of the publicized bride burning cases occurred in the northern state of Punjab, so Kapoor's group opted for a Punjabi folk form as the frame for the play, which lasted about forty minutes. It started with a brief look into a world upside down: an auction of young men, each of whom had a price tag on him. Kapoor describes the scene:

They're sold off in a very brisk and comic sort of way: "50,000 rupees for a clerk; 80,000 for a bank executive; 100,000 for an Internal Security man." We did it like a quick montage. After that we went into a Punjabi folk tune to which we had added new lyrics. It traces the life story of a young girl. Born, sent to college, married, burned. Then we move on to the neighborhood where a burning had happened. But the people there say they neither saw nor heard about it. Then we flash back to the marriage of the girl, again accompanied by a Punjabi folksong.

Since we were working out in the open, we had wanted each sequence to have one stark image that the audience could immediately grasp. We wanted the message to get across loud and clear. If the people couldn't hear, at least they could see. The central image of the first scene is the burning of the girl. We portrayed it by having two women pull two red veils off the girl and then whipping her, which could symbolize both a burning and a beating. After that we go through her life. How she is harassed by her in-laws, how she wants to go back to her own parents. But her mother and father don't want her back because it wouldn't be respectable. They force her to return to her husband. We emphasize this with an extended image of her running and running and panting, not knowing where to go. She was like a beast of burden.

In the final image of the play, the young woman is held by her in-laws. They shoot demands at her like bullets from a machine gun: "we want a fridge; we want a television." At that moment we stop and tell the audience that the girl has two options: either she dies or she gets out of the situation. We would then play both endings. In the one she dies, because her old parents can't deliver the goods. In the other one she seeks help, gets educated, and learns to stand up for her rights.

Performances of the dowry play regularly resulted in lengthy discussions with women in the audience, who often asked the performers where they should go for help.

The play premiered in one of Delhi's women's colleges in November 1981. Subsequently, the group performed in slums and villages at the invitation of local social action groups. Whenever a new case of dowry death was reported, Stree Sangharsh would go there to perform. Usually the audiences reacted positively. Anuradha Kapoor can recall only one tension-filled reaction:

> A young woman had been burned near Delhi University. We performed right in front of the house where it had happened. When we started we had a ring of children around us, which is a usual thing when you perform in the streets anywhere in India. They were very noisy. Then we had a ring of women, who were very subdued. The third ring of spectators was composed of boisterous, macho, unemployed youngsters. They tried to disturb the performance. But the women forced them to shut up, simply by being dignified and quietly watching the performance. Afterwards, tears were streaming down the women's faces. It was enough to halt any further disturbances the macho gang might have contemplated.[12]

The dowry play has been performed nearly three hundred times since 1980 and is still occasionally produced today. It is generally considered one of the first major events of India's developing women's theatre. Subsequent plays by Theatre Union, the new name of Stree Sangharsh, have dealt with themes like self-immolation by widows and rape. *Dafa 180* [Law 180], for example, was developed after a proposal for new legislation regulating the rights of women in custody was debated in Parliament. The play was intended to serve purely informational purposes in colleges, parks, and slums. Its main inspiration was the frequency with which women were raped in prison with the police rapists getting away with it by simply accusing the women of prostitution. Kapoor directed the show: "The rape scenes were the hardest to mount. We did it abstractly because there is always the question of what you are doing to the audience. Are you perhaps titillating them? We finally opted for a rape sequence which took place inside a police station. We had the woman lying on the floor and several policemen throwing a ring of bells over her head. Then she began swaying and wailing slowly to indicate that she was being raped."[13]

Dafa 180 begins with several people briefly narrating instances of rape reported in the press. Then, in a song, they list all the changes of the proposed new law and conclude sarcastically that, in future, women will have nothing to worry about anymore. But the scenes that follow clearly prove the contrary. Thus, in a heavily choreographed courtroom scene, a woman's testimony is consistently used against her while everything the cop who raped her says is accepted as truth. While they speak, the woman and her rapist move around in a circle, back to back. Another scene was about women working in the fields and the kinds of rapes that happen there. The last one dealt with cigarette factories near Bangalore, where women reputedly are often raped by their supervisors.

Apart from Theatre Union in New Delhi, apparently several women's theatre groups operate in other major cities. There are also some cultural action groups that conduct women's theatre workshops in slums and villages. But as yet there is no national women's theatre movement to speak of. Although there clearly is a great need for women's theatre in India, then, there is no efficient network to back up the performances and workshop initiatives. Says Anuradha Kapoor: "You can't do social work and theatre at once. Women only have limited free time in the afternoon and they also have to do urgent things like health education during that period. So, often there is no time to sustain a women's theatre group. I have worked with working class women on some play projects. We had five performances and then it was finished. There is no sustenance, no life afterwards. Other concerns overtake it." [14]

Kamla Bhasin and Tripurari Sharma of the cultural action unit Alarippu are less pessimistic than Anuradha Kapoor. They have received funding to conduct an extensive series of theatre of liberation workshops for women all over India with the aim of establishing a network of community women's theatre groups. Meanwhile Anuradha Kapoor, now on the faculty of the National School of Drama in New Delhi, is trying to push students toward theatre of liberation. With only five out of twenty of them being women and most of them aspiring to lucrative television and film careers, she realizes she is fighting an uphill battle: "There are so few professional repertory theatre companies in India to begin with and so limited an audience to support them financially. It would really be very hard to get a women's repertory theatre company going. What we need is small groups working in local areas with local problems. They need to get the participation of the local people and use local forms if they can find them. Local stories as the basis for theatre, only that can keep political theatre alive." Like most of her colleagues in the mainstream, however, Anuradha Kapoor is only superficially aware that quite a few such experiments have been underway in the Indian countryside for some time.

The first Indian artists to see the potential of a theatre of liberation network started their work in the southern states of Karnataka, Tamil Nadu, and Kerala around 1975. As in the Philippines, severe totalitarian repression—including widespread abuse of power, violations of human rights, and declaration of Martial Law—was the main catalyst here. Economic exploitation and extreme poverty continue to be its main driving force today.

Theatre in Karnataka during the Emergency

In 1975, a young National School of Drama graduate named R. P. Prasanna returned home to Bangalore, the capital of Karnataka state, with dreams of going beyond what the Indian People's Theatre Association (IPTA) had achieved. He recruited a group of talented young people and founded a progressive theatre company which he called Samudaya, or Community. Prasanna wanted to make high-quality politicized adaptations of Shakespeare and Brecht classics for the urban middle class. At the same time, he instinctively knew that performances alone would not be very effective. They needed to be fed by and, in turn, feed into theatre of liberation workshops at the grassroots. After first consolidating a core group of committed actors in Bangalore, Prasanna went to work for periods of three months with other interested groups of youngsters in Mysore and Mangalore, the other two major cities in Karnataka state.

Prasanna and his actors had to be careful, for this was, after all, the height of Indira Gandhi's Martial Law rule. On 12 June 1975, the High Court of Alahabad had proclaimed that Indira Gandhi had used unfair means to win the state elections of Uttar Pradesh the year before. The court ruled further that she should immediately vacate her seat in parliament and resign as Prime Minister. Gandhi refused and appealed to the Supreme Court, which, thirteen days later, overruled the Alahabad judgment. The next day, Indira Gandhi declared the State of Emergency and ordered the arrest of many of her political opponents. In the following eighteen months India turned into a virtual police state. Labor unions were outlawed and progressive political activists silenced with all kinds of legal and illegal means. The Prime Minister finally lifted the Emergency and announced parliamentary elections for 1978. She decided to run for office from Chikmagalur, an obscure constituency in Karnataka, where she was convinced her fame and rupees would assure her victory. She met with fierce opposition from unsuspected circles, however.

Spearheaded by Samudaya, progressive artists from Karnataka designed a campaign to undermine Indira Gandhi's election scheme. During the Emergency, Prasanna had managed to consolidate five theatre of liberation groups. In the middle of 1978, he mobilized these groups, developed a street show of skits mixed with political songs, sought and got the support of the political opposition, and organized a month-long mobile theatre of liberation festival in Chikmagalur district. The concept of the traveling festival had been inspired by similar projects of IPTA and became the prototype of the *jathas,* the effective political cultural caravans that developed in the eighties.

The five Samudaya units traveled from village to village by bicycle. Everywhere they went they were fed and lodged by political organizers of the opposition, who also took care of publicity. After the performances, the performers would sell postcards and books to finance the next leg of the tour. This improvised market would often turn into a spontaneous venue for political discussions. During the *jatha,* the different Samudaya units performed several hundreds of times. "It gave us tremendous confidence," Prasanna told me in New Delhi.[15] "Previously, a stationary unit could only produce two new plays per year, but by moving around in a *jatha* we could increase the impact more than a hundredfold."

At the end of the month, the Samudaya units arrived in the capital of Chikmagalur for a one-day manifestation. Indira Gandhi was solidly defeated and, for the first time since independence, the rule of the Nehru-Gandhi dynasty was broken. The Janata Party took power. It would go too far to claim that Samudaya was solely responsible for the defeat, but its creative campaign certainly made a significant contribution. Following the cultural caravan, thirty-two new Samudaya units were founded all over the state. Communication between these groups was maintained by means of a monthly magazine, meetings, and workshops. Meanwhile, the Samudaya core group in Bangalore continued its middle class proscenium activities as well. "You can't sustain a theatre movement on the street corner or on one political issue alone," explained Prasanna. "You have to work on the level of the mainstream culture as well, which is politically not necessarily very advanced yet. You have to take it as a starting point and then try to lift it up." [16]

In 1980, Samudaya organized a second, even more massive *jatha,* this time covering nineteen districts in Karnataka. But according to Prasanna many of the participating groups had become politically confused after Indira Gandhi's defeat: "you could see it in the content of their plays." After six years of full-time cultural activism, the founder of Samudaya became disillusioned and left for Delhi to work in film and television. In 1988 he became a visiting professor at the National School of Drama. After Prasanna's departure, Samudaya's network gradually broke up. For a while, the Bangalore core group kept a low profile, but there are signs that the company is beginning to regain some of its original momentum with a new young cadre.

The theatre of liberation networking and workshop activities in Karnataka did not decline along with Samudaya. Its initiatives were picked up and developed further by a new organization called Media Exploration for Social and Cultural Action, MESCA for short. Its founder, Gladius, a former mechanical and electrical engineer, had learned the value of networking and theatre while an underground student activist during the Emergency. "We tried to disseminate information about atrocities committed by the régime," he recalls. [17] "We worked inside the extensive network of the Student Christian Movement and managed to consolidate several groups in Bangalore, Mangalore, and Madras. They performed allegorical street plays about the situation. Together with the work of Samudaya, that was the beginning of political theatre in this area."

Gladius learned about Paulo Freire's methods while coordinating cultural action programs for CIEDS, the Center for Informal Education and Development Strategies in Tamil Nadu, the large state located to the east of Karnataka. While working for CIEDS from 1979 until 1982, Gladius discovered that many social workers in rural areas wanted to use cultural action but had no idea how to go about it. Therefore he set up MESCA in 1982 to cater to this growing need and to develop the necessary technology, training programs, and feedback mechanisms:

> We started training these groups, staying with them, understanding their work and their needs, trying to assimilate local cultural forms. We were concentrat-

ing on the process and on team building. They could then stay in touch with us and with other groups in the region while continuing their work. We did 10- to 15-day workshops with them. Sometimes we worked with them for as long as a month. We also set up follow-up programs for them. We traveled with them to monitor their activities, for example. Gradually we encountered a need for audiovisual aids. So we started producing our own videos and began an additional training program for video production.[18]

The MESCA workshop is quite similar in strategy to the theatre of liberation workshop model developed by the Philippines Educational Theatre Association (PETA) although the actual curriculum is worked out in less detail. MESCA works with a team of four instructors who first establish contact with social workers in a particular area. Through observation and discussion the MESCA team learns about the strategy and the objectives of the social action practiced in the target community. They also investigate the kinds of cultural forms that still exist in the area. To complete their preparation and to measure the concrete potential for cultural action, they interview community leaders. Candidates are selected from among the locals and the social workers, usually educated middle class outsiders funded by non-government organizations. MESCA makes sure at least 70 percent of the participants are indigenous to the community. The workshops proper can last from seven to fourteen days and involve accumulation of creative exercises geared toward the production of a *jatha*. Generally, at the end of the workshop, participants take the cultural caravan package they created on tour around neighboring communities.

MESCA usually feeds into existing social action groups that conduct informal education programs or organize landless farmworkers. The social workers that have set up these groups try to teach the basic structure of the economic system and show the villagers how it affects them concretely in their daily lives. If the local people become convinced that a particular unfair political system (or aspect thereof or person therein) needs to be changed, the social action team helps them organize a campaign or prepare them for negotiations. MESCA then comes in to teach how cultural action can enhance these activities. Gladius:

> When you do a workshop with the local people, you can suddenly see a certain kind of blossoming. People who are used to being passive and taking orders suddenly see themselves as active participants in a social process, which is the workshop. There is a collective recollecting of their cultural identity; they remember old traditions, for instance. Project leaders who observe the workshop suddenly realize that ours is a method that will make people participate. In regular social action work the locals usually wait for the leaders to come up with all the ideas. But cultural action gives the locals a voice to talk about their problems, whereas before they always relied on a social action leader to serve as their spokesperson. We teach them to express themselves in their own cultural forms and in their own language.[19]

The newly acquired cultural skills can also help during in-house laboratory theatre sessions in which alternative scenarios for social action can be tried out before they are actually implemented. Gladius: "All we do in our workshop is to get people to talk—in their own terms—with their neighbors about their problems, about their oppression, and how they should solve it. We try to get them to talk as realistically as possible. Thus we have even seen caste differences dissolve."

Gladius considers MESCA's theatre of liberation activities to be crucial for a genuine development of India. He believes that technological and monetary injections are insufficient. "If you want to transform structures, you have to root the change in the emotional layers of the people's minds. Rationally you can say, 'I must participate in a strike because I will get better from it economically.' But if you're not emotionally involved as well, you will give up the strike after five days. We work with the emotions of the people because all basic human desires have their roots in these emotions. You know, an argument only communicates in one direct rational way. But an artistic form communicates in many different directions all at once—including the subconscious—and it keeps on working after the initial input. It's like radiation."[20]

MESCA has ten full-time staff members. Funded by a European development agency, the organization has conducted more than 150 workshops. As a result, the state of Karnataka now has twenty self-sustaining groups that engage in street theatre. MESCA has trained about twenty-five other groups in the neighboring states of Tamil Nadu, Kerala, and Andra Pradesh as well. All of them create street theatre and cultural caravans. Four times a year, MESCA organizes statewide *jathas* for which it recruits representatives from the different groups. In this way, the community-based artists get to meet each other, learn from each other's skills and experiences, and gain confidence from the performances. They stay together, do research on a particular issue, and collectively create a complete cultural package for a caravan. After the tour, which can last up to two months, the participants return to their respective groups with new ideas, improved artistic and organizational skills, and increased confidence. Three months later, another member of the group can join in another statewide *jatha* organized and directed by MESCA. In this way, the skill level of the theatre of liberation is gradually elevated across the board.

Shashidara Adapa, MESCA's training coordinator and a former Samudaya member, favors the integration of different art forms like poster design, theatre, and puppetry in the cultural caravans. He believes that theatre of liberation should build a new popular culture from the grassroots up. He would like to see the theatre of liberation replace the former social function of the fading traditional theatre:

> In many villages traditional theatre forms are dying out and film is often taking its place. Even though the old forms were feudal and only talked about kings

and queens, the performances themselves broke through the hierarchical social structures. Landlords and tenants performed side by side. They all had a role in the production, either setting the stage or acting. I remember when I was a kid we used to make the torches for the night performances. The whole village got involved and sat under one roof. Today, there is a cinema. You buy a ticket and sit in the dark. It's commercial, the stuff you see is cheap and manipulates the emotions, and there is no social interaction. Of course it is not possible to revive the traditional forms again. It's dying and we can't stop it. But we can invigorate the old sense of community by creating new, participatory cultural forms. People should come together under one roof and not feel any differences. That's what I'm looking for: a democratic sense of community. The performance is just a pretext. What they talk about during and afterwards is much more important.[21]

One of MESCA's most successful campaigns involved an attempt to obtain new child labor legislation in 1985. At a hostel twenty kilometers outside Bangalore Adapa found a group of ten boys between nine and thirteen years old. They were all employed in a nearby brick factory. He exposed them to the MESCA workshop process and they created a play which, according to Adapa, was "developed from their own improvisations. I helped them cut some masks, but they painted them themselves." Subsequently, the boys performed their play at seminars on child labor. They also managed to penetrate Karnataka's state parliament, performing for an audience of parliamentarians and the state's prime minister. Eventually, they went to the national parliament in New Delhi to perform for the House Commission on Labor.

The child labor play opens with a direct address to the politicians: "We are small boys who haven't seen the world. Everything is dark for us. You are the people who rule this country. Listen to our story. We have never bloomed like flowers, we never see the sun. We will do a play for you."[22] Following this introduction, the boys portray two ten-minute episodes from their lives. The first scene is set in a hut in the countryside. A small boy is sick. He usually guards a herd of cows, but is too ill to go to work that day. Nonetheless, his father forces him to go. Some kids wear cow masks. The boy goes to work and is beaten by the landlord for being late.

The second scene is set in the street of a big city. Street urchins look for paper and wood to sell at second hand shops. One kid teaches a friend how to smoke a clove cigarette. He tells him about one of his buddies who got hurt the other day scavenging through garbage: he grabbed straight into a big piece of glass. As they smoke, the two boys search through a garbage can and find a picture of a beautiful child in a fashion magazine. Realizing such a life is out of their reach, they crumple the page and throw it away.

The success of MESCA's child labor play was extraordinary. It was the first time in Indian history that a volunteer group pushed for new legislation and got it passed. The thrust of the campaign had been to ban child labor in the long run, to start banning child labor in hazardous industries immediately, to regulate child labor in non-hazardous industries, and to provide working children with education and health care, paid by the employer. The government accepted all these demands except the last. Following the performance in parliament, the hostel where Adapa had recruited his child actors received a big grant from the central government to upgrade its facility.

Despite the measurable impact of some of their campaigns, Gladius and Adapa know the danger of working in isolation. They realize that long-term effects must be backed up by non-hierarchical, mutually beneficial networks. But given the widespread ideological factionalization, lack of funds, and the enormous geographical, cultural, and linguistic distances in India, this seems a well-nigh impossible task. Adapa services the regional network almost single-handedly: "I go all over the place on my motorbike. I try to build personal relations with key people who have the talent and energy to keep up local groups. I believe personal commitment is the only way to do it. I send some materials to a woman I know in a remote village, for example. It only costs me a few rupees to send it, but the effect is worth thousands of rupees. She writes back to me and describes how she used the materials to make posters. But if I don't stay in touch, she will lose interest."[23]

MESCA wants to break through the isolation by developing similar personal contacts with the various theatre of liberation groups that operate independently all over India. In 1988, Gladius attempted to bring them together for a consultation session. Gladius: "Since we have been working successfully for some time now, people are quite willing to sit down with us, share their experiences, and listen to ours. We now want to launch a bulletin and set up a festival in which all of us come together to perform."[24] But although Gladius managed to gather representative groups from all over India for his first national theatre of liberation seminar, he may well be overestimating the reputation of his institution in more radical circles. Extreme leftists consider MESCA suspect for accepting funding from the Protestant church in the West.

Cultural Caravans in Kerala

One of MESCA's main out-of-state partners is KSSP in Kerala, a state in the extreme south of India. KSSP is a statewide popular education network that organizes annual multimedia cultural caravans that include theatre of liberation components. KSSP stands for Kerala Sastra Sahitya Parishad, which, freely translated, means Kerala Forum for Science and Literature. KSSP has its headquarters in the state capital Trivandrum and has more than 1,500 affiliated chapters in villages and towns all over Kerala. Following KSSP's example, similar networks are beginning to develop in other states as well. The movement began in 1962 as an attempt by a few progressive lecturers at Kalikut University to popularize science education in the vernacular languages. Back then, English was still widely used as the main language for instructing science subjects. Eventually, the KSSP founders managed to draw high school and elementary school teachers into their movement as well. Says Krishna Kumar, the current president of the organization,

> Our idea was that science should become a tool for everyone to use to better themselves and not just a means for a few rich and powerful people to become even richer and more powerful. In India we still have a lot of feudal influences. Superstitious religious beliefs are still very strongly embedded in the minds of the people and never allow new, progressive ideas to enter. The poorest of the poor thus simply do not believe they have any problems. We want to break through that.[25]

KSSP began by publishing cheap popular science booklets, which, given the relatively high literacy rate in Kerala, proved a useful strategy to disseminate knowledge and to raise funds. By the early seventies, KSSP started backing up its publications with informal Freirian night classes in the villages. These grassroots education workshops often resulted in the formation of local popular science clubs composed of young people and school teachers, which in turn soon developed into action groups that moved from discussing local issues to tackling agricultural or ecological problems themselves. If things became too complicated, they called in a KSSP consultant.

By 1976, KSSP membership had crossed the 10,000 mark and a tight network had been established. Today, the organization counts over 40,000 members. Group leaders and network officials are elected on a rotating basis; no one is allowed to stay in a particular position for more than two years. Twenty-five groups form a region and five regions a district. All groups have a representative in KSSP's state council, which meets once a year to elect the executive committee. Says Krishna Kumar, who has taken a leave of absence from his engineering job to do his KSSP work: "It is quite common for the state president to become a grassroots unit secretary again after working in the executive office for two years. We want to avoid personality cults."[26]

KSSP started organizing cultural caravans in 1980 to expand the network, propagate particular issues, and raise funds. For this purpose, KSSP linked up with street theatre practitioners and graduates from the Kalikut University School of Drama. KSSP members are recruited from all over the state to participate in the *jathas* and travel to Trivandrum for a workshop of one month. They live together and, under the guidance of a professional theatre director, create songs and skits. Then, during the height of the dry season in October, they take to the road in three small vans and perform four times a day in village squares. Typically, the group enters a community beating the traditional Kerala *Jenda* drum. Local KSSP members join them in the parade. The performers play with bare torsos, no facial makeup, and only an occasional mask. Krishna Kumar: "Our forms have to be very simple because we have to be able to pick up and move on very quickly if we want to perform in four different places in one day." Often, the KSSP shows—which can be mov-

Kerala People's Science Forum performs a satire on the Union Carbide disaster at Bhopal. Photo courtesy Kerala People's Science Forum, Trivandrum.

ing as well as funny—are followed by discussions, workshops in local schools, and the sale of cheap reading materials. Themes of the plays have included Muslim and Hindu riots, religious fanaticism, and the damage done to the environment by industrial logging. Other plays have dealt with issues like dowry death.

The 1985 *jatha* was dedicated to the Bhopal disaster. Following an explosion in a chemical plant of the Union Carbide corporation on 3 December 1984, 30,000 tons of poisonous gas swept through the city of Bhopal in central India, leaving thousands of people dead and hundreds of thousands permanently disabled. People died in their sleep in the name of industrial development and economic progress. The fifteen-minute play that forms the centerpiece of the 1985 *jatha* begins with an image of the sleeping city of Bhopal.[27] Actors imitate the shape of a house with their arms. Cries of the dying then suddenly fill the air. Assassins disguised as the white cats from the Eveready battery labels jump into the acting area and start killing the Bhopal residents with movements derived from traditional Indian martial arts practices. This tableau is followed by a satirical behind-the-scenes cocktail party featuring Indian government officials and multinational executives wishing to build factories in India because of the cheap labor, the government corruption, the willingness of military and police to crush profit-endangering union activities, and the nonexistent safety regulations. *Bhopal* ends with a call to boycott popular Union Carbide products like Eveready batteries.

The KSSP movement shows no signs of waning. On the contrary, in 1986 it introduced a new elementary school puppetry program. Over the years, cultural groups have also spontaneously sprung up on the district level. "But we don't encourage every village to have their own theatre group," says Krishna Kumar. "If it's not done properly, the message may not get across. Some amount of performing technique is absolutely indispensable."[28]

In October and November 1987, KSSP launched its most ambitious activity yet: a nationwide cultural caravan. In 1975 and 1978 it had already held nationwide people's science and literature conventions. In 1986, twenty-six different organizations representing every state in the nation decided to cooperate with KSSP in a national *jatha*. People came from all over the country to Trivandrum for the rehearsals. Scripts were translated into the respective regional languages. Then cultural caravans started mobile performances from five different points in the country. One originated in Kashmir in the north, moving through Punjab, Haryana, Rajasthan, Delhi, and Uttar Pradesh. Another one started in the northeast and traveled through Assam southward. The eastern *jatha* went through Bihar, West Bengal, and Orissa. The western caravan covered parts of Rajasthan, Bombay, and Maharashtra. The southern one started in Kerala and went through Tamil Nadu and Karnataka. The artists traveled thousands of miles, inviting other artists to join them along the way. After a month, the five caravans had swelled to enormous proportions and merged in Bhopal for a big theatre of liberation festival with hundreds of artists from all over the country. "It was massive," says Krishna Kumar; "in Calcutta we performed for crowds of 15,000 people." But he is quick to relativize the mass impact of the event:

> It had its limitations. We in Kerala were the only ones experienced in doing this on a massive scale. We had to depend on scripts we used in Kerala. We had not much time, so sometimes translations were not all that accurate. We should have used more local colloquialisms. Although we tried to blend modern theatre with folk theatre and classical forms, our basic framework was Keralan, which may not have been all that suitable for West-Bengal, for instance. But in spite of all this, the program was a huge success. We reached a large audience and we surmounted all organizational problems. This type of theatre has now been introduced as a very useful tool all over the country. Following the *jatha,* people's science and literature forums were formed in nine other states. They have their own structures and priorities, of course. In Kerala we have a high literacy rate and we can easily sell $300,000 worth of books per year. But that doesn't work in Bihar.

Root

In Kerala there is more theatre of liberation than that of KSSP alone. Jos Chiramel, one of the state's professional theatre artists who is regularly hired to direct the performances of the KSSP *jathas,* also has a company of his own called Root. He started the group in 1983 together with some other graduates from the Kalikut University School of Drama. Their aim was to stimulate theatre activities in the grassroots by means of extended workshops in villages and professional performances of Western, Indian, and original plays. Root succeeded in consolidating several village-based theatre groups in the area near Trichur, an important regional center in northern Kerala. Their usual strategy is to first conduct a week-long workshop with village youngsters and then return to hold rehearsals for two or three days each month. With the grassroots performances that are developed in this way and with their own professional productions, Root hopes to create a counterweight to the appalling comedies that tour the countryside with increasing frequency. Jos Chiramel is adamant in his rejection of these shows: "There are at least 500 such commercial groups in Kerala. Most villages have art societies who invite them for performances once a month. The companies do it only for the money and get easy laughs with sexual innuendos. The actors, most of whom are untrained, get 75 rupees [$6] per performance. That adds up if you realize they perform an average of 100 times per year. Their manager makes a net profit of 100,000 [$8,350] rupees in a single season. With our workshops and performances we would like to purify the cultural thinking of the rural audiences."[29]

Like theatre of liberation groups elsewhere, Root also has had its share of successes. The company has several former drug addicts and small time criminals among its members. The community theatre group in the village of Katoor, founded after a Root workshop, counts an epileptic among its actors. Chiramel: "He used to be ashamed of his condition and the villagers avoided him. When we had worked there for three months he started coming to the rehearsals, just to watch. I gave him a role in the play. He gained so much confidence that after the performance he began talking to people. He is doing very well now and holds a steady job as a porter."

On Sunday, 17 April 1988, I traveled with Root to a tiny fishing village near Ernakulam. They had been invited by a local social action group to perform their adaptation of Badal Sircar's *Bhoma.* The ten actors, all male and well into their twenties, gathered in the Trichur train station around two in the afternoon. In Cochin, an hour's ride away, we took the boat for another forty-five minutes before arriving at the venue. Some local youngsters were hanging improvised lights in coconut trees around an open space when we walked in. Others were sweeping dust from the sand floor and then deposited large pieces of cloth for the audience to sit on. We shared a meal with the organizers. By five o'clock there were already a few hundred curious villagers on the scene. When the play started at seven, there were easily a couple of thousand spectators seated in the round. Jos Chiramel introduced the play by explaining that the people would get to see a new kind of theatre without makeup, without microphones, and without the elevated makeshift

Root performs Badal Sircar's *Bhoma* in a rural district of northern Kerala.

stage normally used for theatre performances. He also told them that the play would lack a continuous story line and that it was inspired by the real-life story of a simple Bengali lumberjack named Bhoma.[30] The spectators then watched silently and with intense concentration during the one-hour performance that followed.

The actors, all dressed in black, come walking through the audience and then sit down in a circle. They pretend they are meditating and gradually produce a swelling sound from which the word "Bhoma," a common family name in the northeastern state of Bengal, becomes audible. Then they get up and become office workers. They mime typing letters and signing papers. They talk about Bhoma. They have all heard about him but have no idea where he is. All they know is that he is starving. They subsequently go in search of Bhoma, not realizing they are actually walking all over him. While they are looking, they first discuss the problems of India's workers and then their own. They complain about the lack of services in the government flats they live in. They also talk about India's recent loss in the cricket test match against England. The end of the scene comes when the word "Bhoma" swells up again from their midst. He is calling for food.

In the second scene, the actors turn into middle class intellectuals. They discuss India's labor problems, but, like the office workers of the previous scene, they soon switch to their own concerns instead. They speak with pride about India's nuclear research and space program. While they boast that India is the sixth nuclear power in the world, Bhoma calls for food again, and the actors suddenly turn into deformed children to illustrate the chilling statistic that approximately two million cripples live in the proximity of India's nuclear facilities.

The third scene features a boisterous politician who claims that India is the number one nation in South Asia and that therefore it should be allowed to organize the next Olympic Games. While he shouts, the other actors all play the part of Bhoma and call for food. Almost instantly, hired goons come in to silence the multiple Bhomas by yelling: "Who is this bloody Bhoma? Who is calling for food? Don't you know the country is progressing?" Subsequently, the actors act out a communal riot in complete silence. They mime hitting, shooting, and stabbing. At the end of the commotion they emerge in a single procession, holding their fists in the air. Thus they symbolize the silent protest of the voiceless in a country where only power-hungry politicians can speak.

In the satirical scene that follows, *Bhoma* also reveals the lies broadcast by television. It features a newscaster who is continually interrupted by commercials. Thus the Prime Minister is shown handing out second-hand clothes to the needy on 15 August, India's Independence Day. Like a film montage, the actors then cut immediately to a commercial for upper-class fashion wear. Subsequently, the scene shifts to a visit of the Prime Minister to victims of the Bhopal tragedy. While stepping into his stretch limousine, he tells them to be patient and courageous. The commercial that follows advertises Eveready batteries. After this scene, the play concludes with the actors directly addressing the audience: "We are told so many things about Bhoma, but we never found him. We only heard the sound of his ax. We heard that his father starved to death." The actors then hold hands, express their solidarity with Bhoma, and walk out of the circle.

On our way back to Trichur, Jos Chiramel told me that Root also performs realistic plays of three hours in all-night theatre festivals and that the group had begun to venture into classical Sanskrit drama as well.[31] Later, while drinking tea in a small café, he started telling me about the hard-hitting performances of People's Culture Forum, the now defunct cultural arm of the Naxalite guerrilla movement.[32] People's Culture Forum started operating during the Emergency, but because of their aggressiveness and frankness about issues like bonded labor, money lending, corruption, and police brutality, they soon made a lot of enemies. In 1979, for instance, they performed a satire about corrupt doctors in front of a hospital notorious for its bribe-taking. After the show, the actors ran into the building, dragged the doctors out, and put them on public trial for refusing to treat the poor. Afterwards, the thoroughly humiliated physicians were released with the warning that next time they would not get off the hook so easily. The actors were arrested, but the incident received so much publicity that subsequently corruption in Kerala's state hospitals was drastically reduced.

From the early eighties on, the police started cracking down on the People's Culture Forum, arresting and torturing its key members. Says Chiramel, "At one point they had units of twenty-five people in every district of Kerala, but now it's all gone. I heard some of them were put in cells with water up to their knees so they couldn't sit and had to sleep standing up. Others committed suicide. Unfortunately, they were so radical that eventually they became totally alienated from the people. That's a capital mistake that genuine theatre of liberation should never make. The target groups in the grassroots should always control it themselves."[33]

The Association of the Rural Poor in Tamil Nadu

In the neighboring state of Tamil Nadu, theatre of liberation activists of the Association of the Rural Poor (ARP) practice a mixture of strategies developed by Media Exploration for Social and Cultural Action, the Kerala Forum for Science and Literature, and the People's Culture Forum. Their main target group is composed of *Harijans,* untouchable landless farmworkers.[34] ARP, founded in the early seventies by Felix Sugirtharaj, an ex-Protestant minister with a degree in community development, started doing Freirian adult education classes in a *Harijan* community one hundred kilometers from Madras.[35] These invariably resulted in short dramas in which the participants acted out their life stories. "We dramatized the tragic situations in the village themselves," Sugirtharaj told me in his Madras office.[36] "Thus they played scenes about a *Harijan* being beaten up by a money lender because he was unable to pay his debt. Or how his daughter was raped by goons of the landlord." The first ARP team stayed with its target community for nine months. By that time, the participants trusted the outsiders enough and had sufficient confidence in themselves to tackle their own problems. The boldest among them would develop scenarios in which they confronted the landlord to ask for higher wages. Every detail of the confrontation would then be minutely rehearsed, including where the spokesperson should stand in relation to the landlord or where the other members of the delegation should position themselves. Sugirtharaj:

> The next morning we would gather in the same place where we had held the performance on the previous day. We did another rehearsal and then marched to the landlord's house. There were 100 people and he was caught totally by surprise. We just stood by the roadside. The *Harijans* did all the talking themselves. Of course, the landlord refused to raise the wages, claiming he was losing money already. So we went back and decided to go on strike. That

evening and the next we went around to the neighboring villages to present
short drama pieces on the potential positive and negative effects of a strike.
The strike itself lasted one week. Then the police came and bargaining started.
We succeeded in raising the wages from six to eight rupees per day.[37]

The Association of the Rural Poor quickly expanded its team from five to
fifteen members by training youngsters from the villages to work with them.
Soon the team had covered thirty villages. In three years' time, these village-
based collectives became the backbone of a 3,000-member union called the
Rural Harijan Agricultural Laborers Association.

In 1977, ARP moved on to work with *Harijans* in other areas of Tamil
Nadu and the neighboring state of Andra Pradesh, and it has also dispatched
several of its members to Manila to learn the community theatre workshop
methodology of the Philippines Educational Theater Association. Foreign
theatre activists like the Canadian educator Ross Kidd have also conducted
advanced trainer's workshops for the ARP staff.[38] To date, the organization
has worked in more than five hundred village communities. Five different
ARP teams operate simultaneously. Each team is composed of fifteen members, most of whom were former illiterate *Harijans* themselves. They stay in
one region for two years and then move on. The teams meet once a month
to share experiences, adjust strategies, and avoid isolation. Says Mr. Brubha,
himself a native *Harijan:* "We don't just come in to perform and then leave.
The people know we are like them and that we are committed to stay with
them, participate in their struggle, and share the same risks."[39]

Sometimes the theatre activities lead directly to violence because the landlords do not want to give up their economic or caste privileges without a
fight. Mr. Murugesan, another ARP organizer, experienced this in 1978:

> I was working in the village of Kilpadur. The Hindu landlords didn't allow
> the casteless *Harijans* to take water from the public well. As a matter of fact,
> they didn't even allow them to smoke or ride a bicycle. They were treated like
> slaves, really. I worked with them mostly in the evenings, talking about caste
> and religion. After six months we staged a drama in which we dealt with
> untouchability and low wages. It was a three-hour realistic play. The landlords
> also attended. When they realized they were being criticized, they confronted
> us. We weren't afraid and told them we were only playing the truth. Angered,
> they came at us with sticks and chains and started throwing stones on the
> stage, breaking all the lights. We fixed the damage and continued our play.
> Then they switched off the main power and returned with a gang of goons
> and beat us up.
>
> As punishment, the landlords kept the *Harijans* out of work for six months.
> So we had to go to neighboring villages to plow and dig wells. Now you
> should know that, according to our tradition, *Harijans* do all the rituals, play
> drums, and carry the corpse to the funeral site whenever a caste member dies.
> After six months, an old Hindu man passed away and the landlords came to
> us to ask us to conduct the funeral rites. We refused and so did the *Harijans*

from neighboring villages. Finally the landlords were forced to promise in front of the temple that they would never treat us so unjustly anymore.[40]

Cultural Caravans in Tamil Nadu

Following the example of groups in Kerala and Karnataka, the Association of the Rural Poor also started organizing cultural caravans through Tamil Nadu in 1983. "We did it to show the people stories from elsewhere and to strengthen our own theatre skills," explains Brubha. Once every two months representatives from twenty different groups gather in Madras for a week-long workshop in which they develop new plays and songs. Then the ad hoc theatre company travels to the region of one of the representatives and performs in surrounding villages during a week. Afterwards, the participants return to their regular chores at home. The forms of these plays range from popular folk theatre to the experimental street theatre style developed by Badal Sircar. Themes include episodes from Tamil Nadu peasant history, alcoholism, and abuse of women. Says Brubha: "We talk about untouchability and the landlord's oppressions, but our *Harijan* men oppress their women also. They don't permit them to speak in public, for example."[41]

Mobile Theatre, one of the theatre of liberation groups affiliated with ARP, is based in Tiruvallur, a small town about thirty kilometers from Madras. They are still in a formative stage and are busy recruiting new members from among the village youth. The core group of nine conducts periodic ten-day *jathas* in the area and then returns to their home base to conduct children's workshops in the afternoon and evening courses for adolescents. For their *jathas* they draw on a small repertoire of plays about illiteracy, bonded labor, religious superstition, the caste structure, dowry, and alcoholism. The plays, which are characterized by a mixture of stark realism and comedy, do not have fixed dialogues. Says K. V. Madan Mohan, the group's convenor, "Only the characters and general story line are set. The rest we improvise on the basis of what people tell us about the local conditions in the village where we want to perform."[42]

Jesuit Priests as Theatre of Liberation Activists

Just as in the Philippines, progressive Catholic priests in India are using the theatre of liberation instrument for evangelization and politicization. Most of these Indian priests were first exposed to Paulo Freire and liberation theology during their studies. Unlike the Philippines, however, the Indian clerical theatre of liberation activists rarely have connections with the organized left. This mutual distrust is characteristic of the ideological and territorial factionalization within the Indian theatre of liberation movement. Thus, a purist

Actors of the Association of the
Rural Poor perform a street play
about alcohol abuse and wife
beating in a village near
Madras.

radical grassroots group operating on dogmatic Marxist principles will want nothing to do with a group or network of groups sponsored by Western development agencies, be they denominational or not. It is hardly surprising, therefore, that the leaders of Samudaya regard MESCA as decadent and that the network of Felix Sugirtharaj refuses to cooperate with the Culture and Communication network of the Jesuit province of Madurai, although in fact they do similar and equally valuable work.

Theatre of Liberation Elsewhere in India

From the preceding survey of theatre of liberation activities in the southern cone of India, a picture emerges of a large but fragmented network of potentially hundreds of groups. It covers the states of Kerala, Tamil Nadu, Karnataka, and Andra Pradesh, where there is apparently also an extensive theatre of liberation network of the rural poor propelled by an energetic theatre worker named P. V. Purnachandra Rao, who is based in the city of Secunderabad. In the central and northern states of India, the theatre of liberation is even more isolated. I have received unsubstantiated reports about a women's group and a children's theatre group operating in and around the slums of Bombay. In Rajasthan there is apparently an embryo theatre of liberation network that predominantly uses puppetry. In *Theatre in Search of Social Change* Kees Epskamp mentions the work of Lok Doot, a theatre group catering to slum dwellers in Delhi, Bombay, and Pune. Epskamp also refers to the political mime group Jagran, which seems to operate mainly in Delhi.[43] From Epskamp's account it is not clear, however, whether Lok Doot is still active. Although it seems to make aesthetically pleasing and socially pertinent shows, Jagran reputedly suffers from a high rate of turnover in its personnel and from a hierarchical structure under the dominant leadership of mime artist Aloke Roy. Apparently more concerned about their reputations than about building a national movement, neither Lok Doot nor Jagran seems to have put much energy into networking.

Punjab, the volatile Sikh state in the northwest that borders on Pakistan, has no theatre of liberation to speak of either, but IPTA veteran Gurcharan Singh creates a populist kind of political drama. Two days per month he travels around Punjab with a team of skilled actors and folksingers. They usually perform before large crowds that, in some instances, have been estimated at half a million. According to some moderate Sikh intellectuals, however, Gurcharan Singh's plays only seem to encourage communal factionalism in Punjab.

In the east, theatre of liberation initiatives are rapidly increasing in Bihar, West Bengal, and Orissa. The work of Natya Chetana, a theatre of liberation commune operating throughout Orissa from its headquarters in the capital, Bhubaneswar, looks particularly promising. Founded in 1986 by Subodh

Patnayk, a graduate from Utkal Sangeet Mahavidyalaya, Orissa's only performing arts academy, the group tours around the state by bicycle, performing folk plays based on socially relevant stories collected from common people. In collaboration with local social action workers, the collective has also
steadily expanded its grassroots theatre and puppetry workshops and is currently laying the foundations for a statewide theatre of liberation network.

The durability of the few peasant groups that operate in Bihar and West
Bengal must be doubted. They were formed after poorly prepared theatre of
liberation workshops conducted by the Calcutta-based Center for Communication and Cultural Action, which, despite its impressive sounding name,
provides little or no post-workshop support. The groups are kept alive arti-
ficially with small financial injections from the Calcutta office. Little effort is
made to train self-reliant and competent artist-organizers in the field. After
having received structural funding from abroad for several years, the Center
for Communication and Cultural Action unfortunately seems to have turned
into a small family enterprise: the salaried staff is composed of a father, a
daughter, and a son-in-law. This is all the more a pity considering the enormous wealth of theatrical talent available in Calcutta. None of these resources
is currently being tapped by the theatre of liberation. True, the established
artists resist it as well, quite contented with the respect they enjoy from the
city's intellectual and cultural élite. India's Dario Fo, the actor-playwright
Utpal Dutt, and director-playwright Badal Sircar all have their own street
theatre groups and a sizable cult following, but they increasingly prefer to
play in establishment venues to court the favor of establishment critics. It
must be noted, however, that Utpal Dutt's plays are extremely important for
the repertory of India's theatre of liberation. Many groups in the country
play his work. The same applies to Badal Sircar's aesthetic experimentations.
Over the years he has conducted a great number of workshops in other states.
Many Indian theatre of liberation artists have participated in Sircar's master
classes and have subsequently applied his techniques in their own varieties of
street theatre.[44] But Dutt and Sircar either have not taken the time to learn
what the theatre of liberation is really all about or they do not want to relin-
quish their own artistic status. The same goes for Calcutta's other politicized
and nonpoliticized theatre artists.[45]

The lack of cooperation between Calcutta's mainstream and its theatre of
liberation activists is typical for Indian political theatre in general. In terms
of networking, the aesthetic level of its original creations, and its workshop
methodology, southern India is considerably further advanced than the other
regions. Media Exploration for Social and Cultural Action (MESCA) collaborates relatively closely with the network of the Kerala Forum for Science and
Literature (KSSP) and with Felix Sugirtharaj's network of the Association of
the Rural Poor (ARP) in Tamil Nadu. But MESCA's leader Gladius is correct
when he claims that isolated groups are working in pockets all over the country without taking much interest in each other's existence. Sometimes this

isolationism is caused by suspicions that may well be justified. But more often than not they are caused by misplaced paranoia, ideological dogmatism, self-righteousness, and territorialism. Fortunately, national conferences and the KSSP all-Indian *jatha* have succeeded in breaking through some of the prejudices. Still, a smoothly operating national Indian network like the ones that exist in the Philippines and South Korea looks very remote.

VI

KILLED IN ACTION
SAFDAR HASHMI'S STREET
THEATRE IN DELHI

The sun was setting hazily on Delhi's enigmatic skyline of red brick and slums as the express train from Bangalore slowly completed the final minutes of its forty-hour journey. Dusty constructions in pale red, dilapidated multicolored vehicles, and masses of brown people pasted themselves to my weary retinas in vague orange blots. I was exhausted but somehow managed to muster the energy to search for Safdar Hashmi whom, according to friends in Pakistan, Calcutta, and Bombay, I absolutely had to meet. He was supposed to be one of India's most effective street theatre artists. After a day's search I found his modest two-room apartment tucked away in an endless row of tenement houses near Jawaharlal Nehru Stadium. He opened the door with an inviting smile. I apologized for disturbing him at home. Not at all, and would I please step in? He was lean and tall and wore slippers, a white tunic, and trousers. An unmanageable forelock of black hair hung down about his spectacles. An Indian version of Danny Kaye, I thought, with Eurocentric irreverence. "Come in," he said, "I have been expecting you." I had written to him several times without receiving a reply. Later I realized it may have been his idiosyncratic way of testing foreigners: if they really wanted to speak to him they must prove their determination by tracking him down. I had apparently passed the test, and during the ensuing five days in April 1988 Safdar Hashmi took me in rickshaws and on scooters to several performances of his legendary street theatre group, Janam, and shared with me his wealth of knowledge and his original insights into Indian politics and culture.

After I left the city I realized that dusty Delhi had become a much more pleasant place with the knowledge that friendly, smiling, gentle people like Hashmi lived there. Suddenly I was also much more hopeful about the future of India's divided theatre movement. Young, energetic, bright, and charming, Hashmi seemed to possess the qualities and the vision to pull it all together. But then, in the second week of January 1989, an ominous missive reached me from Moloyashree Hashmi, Safdar's wife.

140

In the early afternoon of 1 January 1989, Janam was performing Safdar Hashmi's latest play *Halla Bol* [Attack!] for workers in Jhandapur, an industrial town east of Delhi. The play dealt with government repression of the labor movement, and was being performed in support of CPI(M)'s local election campaign. In the middle of the show, Mukesh Sharma, a right-wing political candidate backed by the Congress (I) Party, arrived on the scene, surrounded by nearly a hundred hired goons armed with heavy bamboo sticks and guns. They ordered the actors to stop their play. When Janam refused and the audience started to protest, Sharma's gang launched a violent attack. An eyewitness saw Sharma shoot a Nepali migrant worker dead at point blank range. The crowd dispersed in a panic. Janam, including three recently recruited young women, ran for their lives to the nearby Trade Union Office where the troupe barricaded themselves behind an iron gate. "In order to give us time to escape over the back wall," wrote Moloyashree, "Safdar held the door closed as long as he could. It was inevitable that Safdar bore the entire brunt of the attack. The goons dragged his body through the streets back to the performance site and killed him there with innumerable blows to the head. It was obvious that the thugs wanted to kill—there was not a scratch on the rest of Safdar's body."[1] According to newspaper and magazine reports, Safdar Hashmi folded his hands in humble greeting when the murderers broke through the gate.[2] Despite his peaceful surrender they beat his head— the source of all his versatile creativity—to a pulp with bricks and bamboo sticks. The police never came.

The Politics of Indian Traditional Theatre

Safdar Hashmi was a respected columnist for the *Economic Times,* a Sunday paper. He also made documentaries and wrote scripts for television. But for the last fifteen years before his death his main concern was to develop a kind of political theatre that would effectively express the emotions and concerns of India's working class and peasantry. Peter Brook's *Mahabharata* and tours by Indian musicians and Kathakali ensembles have confirmed a growing Western interest in Indian performing arts, but to the committed Indian artist the traditional cultural heritage remains problematic. As Safdar Hashmi said, "We feel the need to liberate ourselves from the stranglehold of colonial and imperialist culture which has swept over our entire country and which has destroyed our traditional culture also. Of course, all of us feel the need to work in the forms which are familiar to our people and which our people have been using in expressing their own hopes for centuries. But the problem is that if you work with the traditional form, along comes the traditional content with its superstition, backwardness, obscurantism, and its promotion of feudal structures."[3]

Safdar Hashmi saw a complex collaboration between Indian upper class

Safdar Hashmi narrates in *Machine,* Thumbs Up bottling plant, New Delhi,
May 1, 1988.

bureaucrats and Western development agencies behind the upsurge in promoting traditional Indian performing arts. Despite the superficial democratic
structure, he claimed, India was still actually ruled by an alliance of capitalists
and feudal lords. One of the most potent weapons for perpetuating their
power was to keep the common people backward: "Against the backdrop of
the rising people's discontent all over the country and the growing organized
expression of this discontent in trade unions, peasant, student, youth, and
women's movements, and the people's culture movement, I think the ruling
classes have formulated their own strategy for countering it at the level of
consciousness by propagating and strengthening all that is backward, obscur-
antist, and superstitious. One of the ways they have chosen is to promote
the traditional arts in the name of promoting an 'Indianness' to our theatre."

Folk theatre continues to flourish in the countryside. The champions of
traditional theatre argue that pure Indian theatre can only achieve genuine
"Indianness" if it isolates itself from the contemporary concerns of the people. These bourgeois intellectuals, as Safdar Hashmi called them, look at theatre merely in shallow decorative terms. "They think 'Indianness' is the image of a Hindu God, the image of fire and tree worshipping, the soul dance.
Of course, looked at from an aesthetic point of view, this theatre is very

different from Western theatre. It looks 'Indian' in terms of richness of cos-
tume, dance, the rhythms. But I feel that instead of imparting a unique 'Indianness' to theatre, these things are actually imparting a unique backwardness."

Safdar Hashmi did not reject traditional performing arts outright. He and
his colleagues considered them very rich and potentially very useful for their
own kind of theatre, but they wanted to be careful not to vulgarize and
thereby exploit them. "Let us say there is a tribal hunting dance. Some dancer
becomes a bear or a lion or a buffalo and others become the hunters and they
go around and around doing their ritualistic movements until they zero in
for the kill. This dance is still reenacted although it is no longer a part of
their everyday life. Now suppose I wanted to use this form to depict, for
example, the Indian people rising up to defeat Indira Gandhi's semifascist
government in 1977. If I reduce her Congress (I) Party and all that it stands
for to that buffalo, I will be practicing mere reductionism. I will not be
enriching the understanding of the people toward the complexity of contemporary political phenomena. It is too convenient, you see. I can't just go and
sit at the feet of a Kathakali guru for six months and then come back and do
a play in the Kathakali style." Yet Hashmi believed that a different kind of
tradition lived in him and found expression in his work. Over the years he
became widely known for his songs which, he admitted, were often based
on the traditional folksongs he learned as a child. "There is a kind of song
called the *Alhay* which is still popular in the states Uttar Pradesh, Haryana,
Madhya Pradesh, and Rajasthan. It tells the story of two brothers, Ajay and
Uday, who are very brave. The narrative song has a particular rhythm. Now
the tune, the rhythm, and the narrative function are totally part of me. So
when I sit down to write a song about the history of May Day then my pen
automatically begins to move in the *Alhay* meter."

The History of Janam

Safdar Hashmi's group is called Janam, which is Sanskrit for "New Birth."
Janam is also an acronym for *Jan Natya Manch,* meaning People's Theatre
Front. Since its birth in 1973 it has performed at least 4,000 times and has
produced more than twenty plays, most of them written by Safdar Hashmi.
Eleven plays have been translated into practically every major Indian language and have been put on the repertory of hundreds of Indian theatre of
liberation groups. Janam's original plays always relate to a specific social or
political issue and therefore the troupe's curriculum vitae reads like an alternative cultural history of India's past fifteen years. Not surprisingly, it reveals
a radically different picture from the one presented by the international media
and official records: no smiling, motherly Indira, no charming, chubby Rajiv
married to an Italian hotel owner's daughter, but a ruthless dynasty of pow-

ermongers keeping their mass of 750 million starving people in a strangle-hold.

Like many other theatre of liberation activists in India and elsewhere in Asia, Safdar Hashmi first became involved in theatre during his university days. In 1971, he became a member of the Student Federation of India's cultural unit. This group performed songs from the independence movement and a short play on Vietnam at rallies. Soon the group wanted to expand its activities beyond the student movement and began calling itself IPTA after the nationwide Indian People's Theatre Association that had been active from 1943 until approximately 1958. Since then, IPTA had only been able to reorganize itself again in West-Bengal. But apart from the historical significance associated with the name, Safdar Hashmi's group had another, very pragmatic reason for calling itself IPTA. IPTA had gone into decline in Delhi as well, and from 1958 it had become a club where people gathered once a year. "They had their own office in Connaught Place, the big roundabout in the middle of Delhi's business district," Safdar told me. "In 1966 the then-Secretary of IPTA saw to it that the association became totally defunct. He captured the office and established an import-export business in it. We heard about this and went to him to tell him that we were IPTA now and that we wanted to use the office. Of course he refused but we were young and quite numerous so we physically pushed him out and threw his things down from the first floor." The reborn IPTA became a regular theatre troupe and began interacting directly with the organized left, performing full-length plays on makeshift wooden stages in working class areas. The group also operated a song squad that performed for striking workers at factory gates. Their plays were extremely popular, often attracting six to seven thousand spectators. Having little or no theatre training, the group at first performed simplistically interpreted didactic plays like Brecht's *Exception and the Rule*. "We would begin at ten o'clock in the evening and end around midnight. Then at one in the morning the second shift would come out of the factory and they would watch until 4:00 A.M."

In 1973, the new IPTA was kicked out of its Connaught Place premises as unceremoniously as it had entered them. The reason had to do with the rather complex relationship between India's two competing Communist Parties, CPI and CPI(M), which split in 1964 over the issue of whether to collaborate with Nehru's Congress Party. The CPI-Marxist faction—hence the "M"—was opposed to what they regarded as an unholy alliance with the capitalist bourgeoisie and the feudal landlords. During the State of Emergency in the mid seventies, CPI opportunistically supported Indira Gandhi's repressive régime, which cost them their mass following. Today, CPI(M) is India's largest Communist party. In West Bengal and Kerala it runs the state government and in Uttar Pradesh, Tamil Nadu, and Maharashtra it has a very strong mass base as well. Safdar Hashmi's IPTA had not yet taken sides in the early seventies and performed for the trade unions and the youth and student divisions of both parties. But in March 1973 IPTA refused to perform at a big CPI demonstration. "That's when they came and threw us out of the office," stated Hashmi laconically. "Most of our members got scared and we were unable to regroup. With four of the remaining students we then founded Janam."

Desperately needing funds, Janam decided to enter a Bengali-language version of Irwin Shaw's *Bury the Dead* in the annual *Durga Puja* festival organized by Delhi's sizable Bengali community. "During this event big circus tents are erected all over the place. Originally it was a religious festival dedicated to the goddess Durga. So on some sites you see people worshipping. But everywhere else it has become a cultural festival. In Delhi alone it is celebrated in 65 different places. Every neighborhood has its own *Durga Puja* committee which raises lots of funds for the occasion. They pay up to 1,000 rupees [US$75] for a performance. The festival lasts five days and we went racing around, performing sometimes up to three times a night." Janam's first production was received with great enthusiasm everywhere they went and quickly the group's membership grew to about fifty. Some highly respected theatre people were involved in Janam.

One very talented singer came who has now become a famous television and film star. Vinod Nagpal was his name. His wife also. She was a well-known critic and theatre director. A young playwright named Sarveshwar Dayal Saxena wrote a special play for us called *The Architect of India's Destiny*. The title is drawn from our national anthem. It was an ironic title and dealt with elections. We produced it in September. A famous music director and singer called Mohan Upreti composed the music. It was a three-hour play. It was written as a well-made play, but Kavita Nagpal, who was the director, brought in the characters of the narrator and the counter-narrator. It was a kind of Brechtian device used for comments on the action and through songs we also announced what was going to happen next.

The play became extremely popular and was very well received by the critics. We started taking it to colleges and working class areas. We also performed it in parks. In January and February 1974 we did a tour of western Uttar Pradesh during a state election campaign. In some places we had massive audiences. There is a town in western Uttar Pradesh called Amroha. We had gone there only for one show and at night we had an audience of 15,000. We weren't prepared for such a huge crowd. The stage wasn't all that high, you see. People insisted we stay one more night and perform again the next day. So we decided to stay one more day and built a higher stage. Now something very interesting happened. We advertised our play by putting a loudspeaker and a microphone in a rickshaw going around the city announcing that tonight at such and such a time and place a play would be performed. It was a town of around 100,000 and we had sent three rickshaws around. As it happened, an extreme right-wing political party had also put its rickshaws out on the streets to tell people not to go see our play because it was obscene and sponsored by Communists who had brought prostitutes from Delhi to dance. When we heard that, we told our rickshaws not to bother any more because we knew the people were going to come anyway. We ended up having about 35,000 people watching the show. It was impossible. Although we had raised the stage, people couldn't watch it from that far away. They would push from the rear trying to come to the front. Suddenly two hundred of them would be pushed onto the platform. It was an intolerable situation. At that moment something unique happened.

Vinod Nagpal, the singer, used to be quite fond of a few drinks and every night he would get slightly tipsy. We were traveling in a hired bus and the driver would buy country liquor every once in while. He would add salt to it so it would get more potent. That night, Vinod must have consumed at least half a bottle. He was totally pissed. So with all this commotion we couldn't start the play and Vinod was lying drunk in the bus. He had said that he was not in any shape to perform. He is a very tall man, about six foot two. Very handsome. Very strongly built. So I went to him and woke him up inside the bus, which was parked right behind the stage. I said, "You have to go on stage now." He entered wearing a traditional Indian dress, you know, those loose tunics and trousers. He also wore a big shawl 'round him. I told him to sing whatever he wanted to sing. He started humming something classical which usually is not appreciated by the people. He took a very heroic posture and we pressed the chords for him on the harmonium. Then, to that classical tune, he started singing lyrics by Faiz, the revolutionary poet.

There is a classical way of singing in India which requires you to just sing the notes before you come to the actual words. This is called *aalaap*. He sang those notes for about fifteen minutes. Just abstract sounds. It was as if a spell had been cast on these 35,000 people, many of them women and children. There had been total pandemonium before and now total silence. When he saw that, he couldn't stop the notes. He was an artist you know and he could sense the magic of his song. So he sang for 35 minutes standing in the middle of the stage and swaying from side to side because he was still tipsy. There was a pin-drop silence. When he finished singing the audience went on clapping for a long time. Then we started our play and it went on uninterrupted until well into the morning.

The play in question is set in a small rural constituency where two candidates representing two different parties, are pitted against each other in the election. One of them is a capitalist, the other a big landlord. They wage a cutthroat campaign. The ordinary people do not know whom to vote for because both candidates are exploiters. Eventually, they decide to enter a candidate of their own, an ordinary cobbler. He represents the untouchables. People start responding to his candidacy and flock to his meetings. This development jeopardizes the candidacy of the two others, who secretly resolve to join forces. They hire assassins who murder the cobbler. The play ends on a note of defeat, with the two narrators singing a song about how the struggle continues and how the play was intended to expose who the real enemies are.

Street Theatre during the Emergency

Janam has been punctuating landmark political events with new theatrical creations since the rigged Uttar Pradesh elections of 1974. "When Indira refused to resign," recalled Safdar Hashmi, "we got the idea to write a small skit called *Kursi, Kursi, Kursi* [Chair, Chair, Chair]. It's about this elected king who is sitting on a chair (his throne) when a new king is elected. He gets up from his chair but the chair rises with him and no matter how hard they try to separate the king from his chair, it is impossible. We had built some dialogue around this simple gag. We performed it outside on the Boat Club Lawns, which was the hub of all political activity at that time. All the political parties would hold their rallies there during lunch hour. It is the area where all government employees work, about 150,000 of them. We would go under the shade of a tree and start playing our skit. Within seconds, thousands of people would gather. The skit grew every day. We would add new things. And after the performance people would come to us and say, 'you could do this and talk about that also.' We performed it for about a week. That was our real initiation to street theatre."

During the Emergency, Janam was forced into inactivity. Safdar Hashmi left New Delhi to teach English at Kashmir University. He returned in the fall of 1978 and reactivated the troupe. But their traditional outlet, the trade unions, had been destroyed by the Emergency. They had no funds to pay for even a modest production. Lacking the confidence to write their own texts, the troupe was at a loss as to how to continue. An older leader of CPI(M) inspired the solution, explained Hashmi:

He told me about an incident that had just happened outside Delhi in an industrial town. There is a chemical factory there called Herig-India where the workers didn't have a union. They had two very ordinary demands, which you can't even call economic demands, really. Workers came from fifteen to twenty kilometers away to work. They wanted a place where they could park their bicycles and a canteen where they could get a cup of tea and heat up their food during recess. The management wasn't willing even to grant these basic demands. So the workers went on strike.

The Janata Party had just come to power and people were still very uptight about police brutality against striking workers during Emergency. So the new Janata government was not yet willing to resort to such actions, although later they proved to be just as anti-worker and anti-peasant as the Indira Gandhi government. The industrialist, unable to count on the police, hired gangs of antisocial elements from the area, gave them arms and uniforms, and made them into guards. So when the workers went on strike, the guards opened fire, killing six workers. When I heard this story I decided to write a play about it.

Machine

Hashmi and a friend sat down one night, and before they knew it a play emerged. "We created the dialogue almost naturally. Both of us had some talent in writing rhyming dialogue. Soon the image of a machine was born. We wanted to use it as a metaphor for the system. The different components of the machine would be the worker, the guard, and the owner. Each one of them would talk about their relationship to the machine. We would then show how together they made the machine work and how this collaboration was experienced differently by the worker, the guard, and the owner."

I saw *Machine* three times. The first time was at six in the morning on May Day 1988 before a large gathering of night-shift workers from a small textile mill in an industrial area of Delhi. The second time was at eleven in the morning of that same day in front of a soft drink bottling plant downtown. The third time I saw the play, at ten in the evening on 2 May, it was rudely interrupted by a well-organized gang of right-wing hooligans who created so much noise and commotion that the actors could not make themselves heard. Hashmi told me afterwards that harassments of this kind happened regularly and that they had also been violently assaulted on occasion.

The short play starts when five people dressed in black enter the circular space left open by the audience seated on the ground. The five actors represent three workers, the guard, and the owner. Together they form a machine in motion, making all kinds of hissing and peeping sounds. Then the narrator (Hashmi) comes in and addresses the audience for a few minutes. When he is finished, the sounds of the machine become audible again. Suddenly, the machine comes to a stop. The narrator says, "What has happened? The machine has stopped. This is a first-rate crisis! Why has it stopped? Can someone tell me?" One of the machine's components liberates himself and says, "I have stopped it, I could not tolerate it any longer." He is a worker. He talks about how he feels exploited by the machine. He works for the machine, for the owner, and is oppressed by the guard but gets nothing in return. After he returns to his place in the machine, the owner steps forward, and then the guard. The machine starts up again as the arms and legs begin to rotate. The narrator starts to speak but he is suddenly interrupted by an explosion in the machine. The components fall to the ground. The three workers get up and start making demands. They want a cycle stand and a canteen. They also explain that the owner has refused their simple demands and that the guard has threatened them. They decide to go on strike and shout *"Inquilab Zindabad,"* which means "Long live the revolution!" in Urdu. This time the guard fires on the workers and kills them. As they lie on the floor, the narrator pronounces a final speech: "No matter how many bullets you pump into us, the workers are not going to be defeated. They will rise again." On this cue, the workers rise and surround the terrified owner and

The factory owner explains his position in *Machine*.

Janam performs the final song in *Machine*.

guard in slow motion. The narrator continues, "The workers have always advanced. No one can stop them." The end comes with the workers, the guard, the owner, and the narrator forming a back-to-back circle, singing a revolutionary song.

Over the years *Machine* has become legendary in India's working-class circles. During the performances that I witnessed some of the workers in the audience apparently knew the text so well that they whispered along with the dialogue, adding a ritualistic dimension to the event. The 1978 premiere of the play coincided with the announcement of a new industrial relations bill allowing local governments to make preventive arrests of labor leaders during looming strikes. To coordinate the protests, on 19 November 1978 an All-India trade union meeting was held in New Delhi's Talkatora stadium and more than 7,000 trade union delegates attended. The next day a mass rally of 200,000 workers was scheduled to take place at the Boat Club. This was, of course, a golden opportunity for Janam to premier *Machine*.

> We went to the stadium early in the morning and we pleaded and pleaded with the organizers to allow us to present our play to them. But they couldn't see what a play had to do with a serious trade union session. We kept on pestering them. They didn't even know us. We stayed until evening. Finally they got sick and tired of us and told us we could perform it after the final resolutions and slogans had been passed. "We are not even going to make an announcement. If you can do it on your own you can go ahead," they said.
>
> The way the stadium was built helped us. It's an arena. There is a big basketball court in the center with seats all around. The delegates were all sitting on one side and the leaders were speaking from a rostrum on the other side. We were all wearing black tunics and blue trousers. We were five men and one woman, my wife. The moment the final slogans had died down and people were beginning to file out of the stadium, imagine these six strange people in black running to the middle of the court and quickly mounting a human machine with loud hissing, rhythmic sounds. People turned around to watch what the hell was happening. Normally we run the machine for twenty seconds at the most but since there was so much noise in the hall we kept on doing it for two minutes. We had to do it at a very high pitch so we were exhausted after that. You see, the nearest person in the audience was at least sixty feet away from us. Then they finally became silent. I gave a signal to stop the machine and started speaking.
>
> It was an incredible success. After we sang the final song, the trade union delegates jumped over the rails. The leaders were like kids. They lifted us on their shoulders. We became the heroes. People got our autographs on cigarette packs. And they invited us to come and perform during the rally the next day.

The following day Janam performed *Machine* at the Boat Club for an estimated 160,000 workers. "A month after the rally we started getting reports from all around the country that people were performing *Machine* there. Many people who had been at the rally had taken tape recordings of the play back to their people and had reconstructed it in their own languages. All the leaders of the leftist movement in Delhi were also at the rally. They saw that this was something that really inspired workers. Immediately we were flooded with invitations. We started going to the working class areas and we received a tremendous response wherever we went. The workers absolutely love this play."

Since 1979, Janam has made approximately twenty other street plays on a variety of political topics. *Gaon Se Shahar Tak* [From Village to City, 1978] deals with a small-time farmer who loses his plot of land and is forced to become an industrial worker in the city. *Hatyare* [Killers, 1979] tackles the problem of communalism, the Indian term for religiously based, violent clashes between Hindus, Muslims, and Sikhs. *DTC Ki Dhandhli* [The Strategems of DTC, 1979] was specifically designed to mobilize a mass protest against a 100-percent price hike by the Delhi Transport Corporation (DTC) in February 1979. The agitprop play succeeded in attracting large crowds which moved with the actors from one performing site to another. *Tin Crore* [30 Million, 1979] is about the ever-increasing army of the unemployed in India. *Aurat* [Woman, 1979] is one of the first Indian plays to deal openly with issues like bride burning, dowry, and wife battery. As such, it predated the Theatre Union plays on similar topics.[4]

Aurat is a collage of satirical tableaux depicting different phases in a woman's life. First she is shown as a little girl at home. Although she is fond of studying, her father cannot afford to send both the girl and her brother to school. So the boy goes. The second tableau shows the wedding ceremony. The father tells his daughter that her duty shall always lie with her husband. She should obey him and, if necessary, die for him. The third tableau is a domestic scene. The husband comes home from working in the factory and, tired and frustrated, he takes out all his anger on his wife. In the fourth scene, the woman, now in her thirties, travels by bus to a night class. On the way she is harassed by a policeman and the bus driver. In class, male students tease her. In the fifth and final scene, the woman is quite old. She works in a factory now, and is tyrannized and exploited by her boss. She eventually wins the support of the other male and female workers and in the finale of the one-hour play they all rise up and shout that they will join the union.[5]

Apharan Bhaichare Ka [Wake Up, Oh Brave, October 1986] is about the complex problem of the Punjab and Sikh extremists. Safdar Hashmi had his own historical reading of this conflict.

In 1978 there was a parliamentary by-election in Punjab. Mrs. Binder, the wife of a hated police commissioner, was the Congress (I) candidate. At that time, an unknown holy man of the Sikhs, Bhindranwale Singh, was inducted into the Congress (I) to be the election agent of Mrs. Binder. He was a nonentity in Sikh politics at that time.

The Akali Party has been dominating Punjabi politics since the 1920s. At that time they had waged a glorious struggle against the British imperialists. The party is very strongly entrenched amongst the Punjabi peasantry, which is largely Sikh. It played a healthy role during the struggle for independence. During the Emergency, it also fought very bravely against Indira Gandhi. But the party is based on religion and from the very beginning it has harbored seeds of communalism. They talk in terms of Sikh nationhood based on religious ideas, not on Punjabi cultural identity.

Congress (I) has been trying to break Akali's hold on Punjab since times immemorial. In 1978 Congress (I) started playing a very dirty trick. They built up Bhindranwale as an alternative leader of the Sikhs. They started playing the communal card. Bhindranwale took a very militant communal Sikh posture against Hindus and Akalis. He built a private army of his own. He carried arms and killed people. He even came to Delhi and moved around with armed bandits. Once he was arrested for alleged involvement in a murder but within hours he was released through intervention of the central government. Now the imperialists don't sleep, you see. They saw their chance to penetrate Bhindranwale's following and once he started receiving aid from the States via Pakistan he began to get free from Indira Gandhi. The paper tiger that Congress (I) had created started roaring for real and thus became a danger to Indira Gandhi. By this time a schism had been created in Punjab and the whole social fabric had been communalized. Indiscriminate killings of the Hindus had already started by then. And Hindu fundamentalists started retaliating down here in Delhi by first building up a hate campaign against Sikhs followed by sporadic attacks. Then came the Indira Gandhi assassination on 31 October 1984.

We see the assassination as the handiwork of the Americans. Afterwards there was organized and orchestrated violence against the Sikhs. Within three days more than 8,000 Sikhs were killed—3,000 in Delhi alone. We saw it with our own eyes. People were dragged out of buses and thrown into fires, lynched, torn apart. The police stood by and even participated in the killing, the looting, and the burning. The army was brought out in the afternoon of 1 November and for three days curfew was declared but never enforced. The army moved around and stood by, watching the killings. Rajiv Gandhi allowed all this to happen. And later, during a mass rally in Delhi, he even justified it by saying, "If a big tree falls, some of the earth will always be unsettled as well."

Operation Blue Star, the attack on Amritsar's Golden Temple complex on 5 June 1984, resulted in an enormous bloodbath in which Bhindranwale was killed along with several hundreds of his followers. But Rajiv Gandhi's Congress (I) Party did not learn from its previous mistakes, claimed Safdar Hashmi: "They're still playing the communal card and hobnobbing with the extremists. They have recently released five top extremists. At the ground level in Punjab, each of the Congress (I) leaders is involved either with a Hindu communal organization or with the Sikh extremists. They are playing lethal games with our country, you see. The extremists are very well entrenched with the people and that's why they are able to escape from the police. In many places they are running their own parallel government. They are getting arms by the thousands from across the Pakistani border, which in turn come from the Afghan Mujahidin, who get them from the United States. Now that the Afghan settlement has come, these arms are going to come in an even bigger way."

According to Safdar Hashmi, similar trouble is in store for Kashmir and other border regions. "Afghan arms are also surfacing in Darjeeling, in the Gurkhaland agitation. Through Sikkim and Nepal all these things are going on. It's a great danger to our country. Today the unity and integrity of our country is the most important problem which we have to address. The Communists are the only people in Punjab who are fighting the extremists. Many have given their lives."

Safdar Hashmi dramatized the dangers of this regional separatism in *Apharan Bhaichare Ka,* using the device of a magician's show. A boy lies down in the middle of the acting area. A black cloth is placed over his head and the magician tests the boy's ability by making him identify objects in the magician's hand. The first thing he takes is a pigeon. The boy guesses correctly and the magician continues: "Good, but what does the pigeon hold in his beak?"

BOY: A bullet-proof jacket.
MAGICIAN: Why would he be holding a bullet-proof jacket?
BOY: Well, because the government cannot protect the life and property of the ordinary people, everyone has to make his own arrangements.
MAGICIAN: So why don't you have one?
BOY: Poor people like me, our lives wouldn't be safe with bullet-proof vests. We die of hunger in any case. We need hunger-proof jackets. *(He points to the crowd.)* But what are all those people doing here anyway?
MAGICIAN: They have come to file an F.I.R.[6]
BOY: What for?
MAGICIAN: Well, you see, their Brotherhood has been abducted. Can't you go look for it?

The boy goes in search of Brotherhood and meets a person dressed half as a circus ringmaster, half as Uncle Sam. Uncle Sam introduces himself as the executive president of the World Wildlife Fund and manager of the Great American Circus. The boy asks him what he wants from India. Uncle Sam answers that he is looking for "Sam Proday Ikta," which he pronounces with a heavy American accent. The boy gets scared and responds: "I hope you don't mean *samprodayikta,*" which is the Hindi word for communalism. Uncle Sam: "I sure am, son." The boy then replies that the government has just proclaimed *samprodayikta* as India's national animal and has placed it in a sanctuary. Uncle Sam states he wants to catch it anyway in order to introduce some World Wildlife Fund measures for its protection. He leaves to get the permission of the Home Minister. As he exits, a Sikh extremist, a Muslim fundamentalist, and a Hindu communalist enter. They are spewing their poison as Brotherhood comes on stage. He wants to stop them. Brotherhood sings a song about unity but in the middle of his song the three fanatics attack him and throw him on the floor.

Meanwhile the magician has become worried about his boy and he goes looking for him. When he finds him he asks if he has found what he was looking for. The boy, thinking he is referring to Uncle Sam, answers that he has gone to see the minister. The magician gets angry and tells him, "I never told you to help the bloody Americans! Go look for Brotherhood!" So he goes off again and eventually finds the injured Brotherhood lying unconscious on the floor. He revives him and asks who he is and what has happened to him. In reply, Brotherhood yells at the boy, who becomes a symbol of the people: "I am ashamed of you. Don't you even recognize your own Brotherhood? I am the one whom you people fought for against the Britishers. You don't recognize me? Who has made you so blind?" "They have," the boy replies, pointing to the three fanatics. He wants to attack them but he is easily defeated. The three extremists capture Brotherhood instead and take him away.

As the three fanatics exit with Brotherhood through the audience, the injured boy reenters the circle. Weeping, he tells the magician that Brotherhood has been captured by the three extremists and the Great American Circus. Then the magician addresses the audience: "So, now you know where your Brotherhood is. Let us go and liberate him. Come on!" But of course the people do not move. The boy and the magician leave. During the final scene of the play, Brotherhood enters. He is held captive by the four villains and sings a song of appeal to the people: "You'd better come liberate me, otherwise this will be the end of this country." Thus the play ends on a despondent note, exhorting the people to fight for the integrity and unity of their nation.

By the time I met the group, Janam had been playing for the Indian working-class for over fifteen years. Its oldest member was 48, the others were well into their thirties. Apart from Safdar Hashmi, who made his living as a freelance writer, there were an office clerk, a printer, and a schoolteacher. But the pressure of livelihood and family were beginning to take their toll. Hashmi: "Ten years ago when we started none of us were married. Now all of us are. Many of us have children who are growing up. Our parents have retired. We have become the only earning members in the family. All these domestic pressures are there. Take Manish. He is one of our finest actors. Both his parents are over seventy-five. His wife is always ill. He has two little children. He is running a small printing press which is not doing well. He is surrounded by 1,001 problems. He wants to give time to Janam but he can't and there is this constant sense of guilt." Some of Janam's actors were among the finest in the capital. There had been offers from television and cinema. So far they had refused. But Hashmi realized that his group must become professional or perish, and he began thinking of establishing a workers' cultural centre of which Janam would become the resident repertory company.

To realize this dream many hundreds of thousands of rupees would be needed. Hashmi calculated that it would cost between 25 and 30,000 rupees just to pay minimum salaries to ten actors. He thought of writing for the cinema for a few years to save money with which to start a trust fund:

> With that trust fund, I could set up a video production business or something that could generate 40 or 50,000 rupees a month. We have built in certain safeguards, of course. The trust will be set up even before a penny comes in. No money will come in my name but only in the name of the trust. Seven people are going to have control over the money in the trust. I will become an employee of the trust and I will receive a salary of 2,500 rupees a month provided I earn at least twice as much for the trust. If I don't then I don't get anything. I come from a very poor background. If I see 200,000 rupees, I may just lose my balance. The idea is that we buy a plot of land with that money in a working-class district of Delhi and construct a simple building there without a fixed stage or anything but where we could have proscenium or theatre in the round or whatever we wanted and which could also serve as a studio so that it could go on generating money. There we could have a repertory of ten or twelve professional actors who would do nothing but theatre, training ourselves. You see, we have become rusty. We have been performing so much that we have not been able to learn. Some of us were talented ten years ago. To some extent we have been able to develop that. But theatre has advanced a great deal since then. We are feeling the need to learn so many new things.

Hashmi wanted to establish the institute and the repertory in an area with about 200,000 workers. His idea was to perform two or three nights a week in the institute, offering other things besides the agitprop theatre Janam was doing then. He dreamed of producing Shakespeare, Gorky, Chekhov, and Tolstoy for the workers to compensate for the third-rate Bombay films and television programs that constitute their regular cultural fare. But he was also aware that Janam needed to expand into some kind of people's theatre movement: "I dream of making our future institute into a training centre for groups like ours who could come to us from different parts of the country. We could arrange for their board and lodging and organize a fifteen-day workshop. During three months of the year we could also tour the country. But right now it seems a farfetched dream. To start it we would need about two million rupees. The whole thing would cost about 4 million. I don't now how we will get hold of this kind of money but we are going to try. The members of Janam have given me three years to try and raise it. If I can raise half a million rupees through work in cinema and television, even if I have to give up working in theatre for a year and a half, I will still do it. But only if I am confident the group can run without me."

But eight months after I last spoke with him, Safdar Hashmi was murdered. On January 4, three days after Hashmi was killed, Janam, including Hashmi's widow, returned to the scene of the murder to complete the performance of *Halla Bol,* its title now laden with added emotional and symbolic significance. Thousands upon thousands had come from Delhi to mourn the deaths of Safdar Hashmi and Ram Bahadur, the slain worker. On January 9, Safdar's songs and plays were performed all over India during a massive National Day of Protest, which, for the first time in recent history, united all progressive Indian artists behind one single issue. In a statement read at the opening ceremony of the Bombay International Film Festival, famous film star Shabana Azmi directly implicated Rajiv Gandhi's Congress (I) in Safdar Hashmi's murder. Artists all over the country canceled their shows and joined protest rallies. In Calcutta, film and theatre personalities like Utpal Dutt and Arun Mukherjee joined a large gathering at Chowringhee. Safdar Hashmi's violent death provides ample evidence that, despite India's claim that it is the world's largest democracy, freedom of expression continues to be a questionable right.

Even though Janam may not have been ready for Safdar Hashmi's untimely departure, the troupe has vowed to go on without him. His trust fund is firmly established now and is named SAHMAT, the Safdar Hashmi Memorial Trust. To facilitate communication among its sponsors and supporters, it has launched a quarterly magazine with information on theatre of liberation activities around the country. Thus, in addition to raising funds for its projected center for people's culture, SAHMAT is also busy setting up a national theatre of liberation network. From 13 to 15 September 1989, SAHMAT also organized a national street theatre festival that brought together groups from twelve different states who played for an audience of 40,000 people. The first anniversary of Hashmi's death was observed with street theatre festivals, cultural parades, seminars, film showings, and fine arts exhibits in hundreds of places around the country. These are clear and hopeful signs that Hashmi's death may convince progressive Indian artists to forget their differences and unite to realize Hashmi's vision—a truly people-oriented Indian theatre of liberation movement.[7]

VII

OF STAGES AND MOSQUES

THE IRRESISTIBLE RISE OF PAKISTAN'S POLITICAL THEATRE

Recent skirmishes between Pakistani and Indian soldiers high in the glaciers of the Himalayas are evidence of the continuing ill will between the two nations. Pakistani political commentators regularly fill newspaper columns with warnings of an imminent Indian navy buildup and alleged Indian nuclear missiles deployed near the border. In light of this military and political animosity, it is all the more striking (and evidence of the theatre of liberation's common sense) that regular cooperation has been established among progressive artists from India and Pakistan. In 1987 and 1988 the Indian theatre artists Badal Sircar and Safdar Hashmi held a series of workshops for Pakistani political theatre groups in Karachi and Lahore. In 1989, Musadiq Sanwal, a member of the Punjab Lok Rehas theatre company from Lahore, performed side by side with Shashidara Adapa of Media Exploration for Social and Cultural Action (MESCA) from Bangalore during the international cultural caravan through Europe called *Cry of Asia!*

A few months before his violent death, Safdar Hashmi gave the following impression of Pakistan's young political theatre movement:

> Pakistani political theatre should be seen in the context of its political situation. There has been severe repression. They have been able to start only very recently. It holds a lot of promise. But as you know this kind of theatre cannot grow in isolation. The organized left movement in Pakistan is very divided. There are very few politicians with a clear vision and a program of action. In that kind of a situation I don't see political theatre making any great headway on its own. But one is inspired by the energy of the people there. They are very brave. We are also sometimes attacked by the police but it's nothing like what they face, you see. They are in mortal danger all the time. They can't perform openly. . . . The work of Ajoka from Lahore and Dastak in Karachi I think is most important. Punjab Lok Rehas from Lahore is full of passion and energy. The people really inspire you. There are people like that in Ajoka also. The work that Punjab Lok Rehas has been doing is still crude, however. The work of Sanjh, the only group that has links with the organized left, is

157

also still very rudimentary. But what else can you expect? They have no tradition of theatre at all. Ajoka is already very advanced in that regard. They are
in touch with what's happening elsewhere in the world and they're very re-
sponsive to what's happening in the theatre in other parts of Asia. They also
have a good in-house writer in Shahid Nadeem.[1]

Pakistan as a nation is not old, a little over forty years, to be exact. Increasingly vocal radical cynics claim that it has never really existed as a homogeneous nation at all and that it is no more than a random amalgamation of
vastly different cultural and tribal minorities with perhaps a common religion
but certainly no common language, let alone a common national vision. In
its four decades of turbulent nominal independence, Pakistan has made world
headlines with such bloody and spectacular political events as the war over
East Pakistan, which resulted in the foundation of Bangladesh as a separate
state, and the public hanging of its charismatic but authoritarian Prime Minister Ali Bhutto. More recently, Pakistan's role as a conduit for U.S. arms
shipments to the Afghan Mujahidin has been highlighted in the international
press, and in August 1988 the alleged assassination of Ali Bhutto's unpopular
executioner and dictatorial successor, General Zia ul Haq, took place, in a
plane crash that also killed two high-ranking U.S. government officials. Since
then, with perfect historical irony, Benazir Bhutto, Ali's glamorous daughter, catapulted straight to the top and then was ousted. A few years prior to
Zia's death she had returned home from exile with prestigious degrees from
Oxford and Harvard. Soon after the dictator's funeral, she was installed as
Pakistan's first female Prime Minister. Her brief reign was marred by scan-
dals, mistakes, and persistent rumors of corruption on the part of her husband and other associates. In the summer of 1990 she was forcibly removed
from office by the country's conservative President, Ghulam Ishaq Khan,
undoubtedly after heavy lobbying from powerful Muslim fundamentalists
and high-ranking military officers.

Politically as well as culturally, Pakistan has always operated in the shadow
of its giant neighbor, India. In the area that is now called the Republic of
Pakistan, modern theatre in the Western sense goes back to the nineteenth
century. As in India, British colonizers were the first to introduce modern
performing arts to major urban centers like Lahore and Karachi. For several
decades, Western-style theatre was restricted to amateur productions in the
British colleges of these cities. The schools' dramatic societies mounted light
comedies and Shakespearean classics in English for the élite. With some minor
variations, then, the history of modern Indian theatre also applies to pre-
partition Pakistan. Apart from the exclusive English-language theatre, off-
shoots of the so-called *parsi* theatre, a late nineteenth century blend of Vic-
torian melodrama with elements of indigenous music and dance forms, also
made it to the northwest. *Parsi* theatre had originally started in Bombay, but
soon touring companies introduced it to mass audiences in other cities of the

subcontinent as well. It was not long before local professional companies began performing their own commercial *parsi* derivatives in the vernacular. Meanwhile, folk traditions continued to thrive in the countryside. Roaming storytellers and singers frequently performed shows based on popular legends and myths in the village squares and during *melahs,* Pakistani folk festivals often associated with the death anniversary of a popular hero or poet.

In the late thirties, the Indian People's Theatre Association (IPTA) also started branches in Karachi and Lahore, although they generally were less active than elsewhere in the colony. One of the pioneers of contemporary Pakistani theatre, Safdar Mir, therefore left Lahore in 1945 to join some friends in the Bombay branch of IPTA: "We had a show on every Sunday," he explained in a 1986 newspaper interview; "it was a composite of one-act plays, songs, dance, and sometimes mime."[2] Before returning to Lahore in 1948, Safdar Mir played the part of a madman in a show about the bloody religious riots that preceded the partition of India and Pakistan. He and his IPTA friends performed it all over Bombay in slums and on sidewalks.

After the partition, on 14 August 1947, most Hindus and Communists were forced to leave Pakistan and took most of the Pakistani political theatre with them to India, where IPTA meanwhile had become the solid foundation of a powerful modern theatre movement. Fortunately for the Pakistani theatre, Safdar Mir returned to Lahore in 1951 to accept a teaching post at Government College in Lahore. It was not long before he was able to revive the tradition of quality theatre in this academic institution. Subsequently, Government College was to become the breeding ground for the modern Pakistani theatre of the eighties.

Unbeknownst to most city people and government officials, some popular folk theatre continued to thrive meanwhile in the Pakistani countryside. Shahid Nadeem, a progressive playwright connected with Lahore's Ajoka theatre company, confesses he only learned of its existence very recently during a performance in remote Frontier Province: "After the show, some of the older spectators came up to us and told us that the 'Red Shirt Movement'—apparently a progressive grassroots movement for nationalist education and reform—had also used theatre to promote *Pokhtun* nationalism and anticolonialism. It had continued well into the forties, apparently. We had never heard of it until we went there to perform. The old folks then told us they had not seen any popular political theatre like ours since before the Partition."[3]

After the foundation of Pakistan, the tradition of English theatre continued in the élitist institutions. So did the low-brow commercial theatre, a degenerate continuation of the *parsi* tradition. Few serious original plays were written, however. In Karachi an IPTA veteran named Ali Ahmed had formed a theatre group with a left-wing orientation. But his attempts to politicize Western classics such as Beckett's *Waiting for Godot,* Camus' *Caligula,* and Molière's *Bourgeois Gentilhomme* failed to attract a large following. Now in his seventies, he heads the only part-time theatre school in the country and

still directs an occasional student production under the pretentious banner of
The National Theatre.

According to Shahid Nadeem, the departure of key Hindu and Communist intellectuals after the Partition and the establishment of an increasingly
fundamentalist Islamic republic seemed to be the chief causes of the slow
development of political theatre in Pakistan:

> The problem with Pakistani theatre is that before the partition we had all reli-
> gions: Hindus, Muslims, and Sikhs. That's why the Islamic view of theatre
> was not so influential and there could be quite a bit of theatre in Lahore, Ka-
> rachi, and other parts of the country. But after 1947 Islam became the domi-
> nant religion. As you know, it regards painting, theatre, film, and the fine arts
> as anti-Islamic and therefore they are not encouraged. Because of that attitude,
> the arts have suffered enormously. Especially now, because fundamentalism is
> on the upswing and the government is officially endorsing the reactionary views
> of the *mullahs*.[4]

By the same token, it is hardly surprising that Pakistan's municipal arts coun-
cils are, on the whole, extremely conservative. They control the few, poorly
equipped theatre venues and blatantly censor any play that reeks of social
criticism. They only encourage facile comedies.

In addition to rising Islamic fundamentalism, the banning of Communism
was another important factor in the slow development of Pakistan's modern
theatre. The Communists had been inspiring the political theatre movement
in general and the Indian People's Theatre Association in particular. But most
of the Pakistan-based Communists were Hindus and were forced to migrate
to India in 1947. The Pakistan Communist Party was officially banned in the
early fifties and its leadership arrested. For a while, therefore, not much happened on the political theatre front. In the fifties and sixties some individuals
would occasionally produce an original play or a translated Western piece at
a city arts council. But these performances were generally unexciting theat-
rically, substandard content-wise, and in any case did not occur frequently
enough to constitute a genuine movement.

Two sources eventually proved crucial to the current process of emancipation in the contemporary Pakistani theatre. One was Western and was
brought to Pakistan by highly educated returning expatriates. They had grown
fond of theatre in Britain or elsewhere in the West and wanted to create
something similar in their own country. The other source was the popular
democratic movement in the late sixties, which eventually succeeded in ousting General Yaya Khan and bringing Ali Bhutto to power. In this period,
several original Pakistani plays were written that were clearly intended to
serve progressive political causes. Major Ishaq Mohammed, an important leftist
leader, for example, wrote a play in the Punjabi language that was performed
by working class activists in popular neighborhoods. The play, *Mussali* [Muslim
Sweeper], was also performed in villages by Punjabi street sweepers them-

selves and, as such, constituted one of the first examples of theatre of liberation in Pakistan. Another trend-setting playwright of this period was Sarmad Sebhai, a young intellectual who was strongly influenced by Beckett and Brecht. With plays like *Tu Kaun, mein Kaun* [Who Are You? Who Am I?] and the award-winning *The Dark Room,* Sebhai successfully captured the rebellious spirit of middle class youth in the late sixties. But both Sebhai's and Ishaq's contributions to modern Pakistani political theatre remained incidental because they had no production outlet in the form of a competent theatre company. Shahid Nadeem recalls:

> Given the chaotic political times, people didn't need theatre as a means of expression. Political activity was high and was providing all the necessary outlets for people's desire for social change. Bhutto had only recently emerged as a leader. It was a hopeful period: through agitations, demonstrations, and party politics we thought we could change things. Culture was very much at the back. Sarmad Sebhai's *The Dark Room* and my play *The Dead Dog* were only scattered activities. Then, in 1977, Martial Law was declared and political leaders were imprisoned. When people realized that political activity was no longer possible they started looking for alternative forms of expression. That's how the present theatre movement began: as an alternative medium for political expression. The response these young pioneers received was so tremendous that they became convinced this was really an effective means of political communication.[5]

As elsewhere in Asia, then, a highly repressive political situation became the catalyst for the development of political theatre in Pakistan. It was not until the early eighties, however, that Western-educated intellectuals and home-grown talents joined forces to form the germ of a genuine national theatre movement.

Political Theatre in and around Karachi

When I visited Karachi in the second half of March 1988, this trade center and largest port city of Pakistan boasted five serious theatre companies, not counting the lowbrow commercial circuit, which playwright Shahid Nadeem sneeringly describes as a "veritable monster":

> Hundreds of thousands of rupees are involved in it, and it is now hitting the smaller towns as well. They're all cheap comedies, really, with hardly any script to speak of. It is basically ad-libbing with lots of double entendres and teasing of underdog characters. Actors will distort their faces and literally stand on their heads to get a laugh from the audience. The plots usually involve upper class drawing-room situations that are easy to relate to for the lower middle classes and the nouveau-riche emigrants who have just returned from oil-related jobs in the Arabian Gulf. There are not really any organized com-

panies, just a large pool of actors, and a few directors and producers who arrange tours. They rent a large cinema facility, pay star fees to some actors who are not necessarily all that good but have a knack for making people laugh, and the halls are solidly booked for a fortnight. It's frightening.[6]

Theatre Wallahs [Theatre People] is Karachi's only professional company. Its main aim is to provide quality drama for Pakistanis who have grown to love theatre while living abroad. The group mostly produces contemporary Broadway and West End fare, ranging from Neil Simon to David Hare and depoliticized Dario Fo. It hires experienced television actors for its productions.

Karachi also has a children's theatre company that models and even names itself after the Grips Theater from West Berlin.[7] The company is headed by a female director, Yasmin Ismail, and by Imram Aslam, a prominent local newspaper editor who also sings, acts, and writes the Pakistani adaptations of the Grips plays. The actors of Grips Theatre, a mixture of television professionals and amateurs, also regularly perform in the countryside.

In addition to Wallahs and Grips, there are three solid amateur companies that produce an average of one new play per year.[8] One of the most interesting of these is Dastak Theatre, a politically inclined company which was founded by Aslam Azhar in 1982. As a reflection of its popular political intentions, Dastak never charges more than thirty rupees per ticket, whereas the average admission price for a Theatre Wallahs show is two hundred rupees.

Educated at Cambridge, Azhar returned to Karachi in the early sixties and almost immediately became involved in theatre. One of the first productions he directed and acted in was *Hamlet*. Soon thereafter he became program director for the newly founded Pakistan Television company, where he remained a driving force until he was fired by the Bhutto régime for his progressive ideas in 1976. During his twelve-year tenure at PTV, he became a staunch promoter of quality television drama and constantly tested the limits of the government's tolerance. His forced resignation was a loss to Pakistan television and a definite gain to Pakistan's hesitantly emerging modern theatre movement.

Aslam Azhar makes no secret of his enormous admiration for Bertolt Brecht. For Dastak Theatre, he has already directed *The Exception and the Rule* (1984), *Galileo Galilei* (1985), *He Who Says Yes; He Who Says No* (1985), and *Saint Joan of the Stockyards* (1986). Says Azhar: "We do Brecht because we feel he is emotionally almost closer to the Asian mix of reason and passion than the West European mix of reason and passion. More than any other writer, Brecht explained things in terms of a human being's everyday experience."[9] Azhar is the first to admit that Dastak's fondness for Brecht and like-minded foreign political playwrights only serves to mask the absence of good homegrown playscripts. He blames this on the lack of a genuine theatre tradition in his country: "Our writers have naturally tended toward poetry and, to a lesser extent, novels. Only since the advent of television have serious writers begun to write in the language of theatre, but because they write for a state-controlled medium, their orbit of thinking has been severely restricted. Some of them who once used to be progressive have now become hack writers by overwriting for television. I don't want to go to them. And they wouldn't want to endanger their bread and butter by coming to work for us."[10] Although Azhar expects good original plays will eventually be written, he does not consider the present deficiency as a big problem. He sees the liberation of the Pakistani psyche from semifeudal attitudes as the single most important task for the modern theatre, and is convinced that this aim can be equally well achieved with adaptations of foreign texts as with locally conceived pieces.

Azhar and the fifty-nine other members of Dastak have no illusions about the difficulty of their work. In 1988, censorship was still rampant in Pakistan and all plays had to obtain a "no-objection" certificate from the police before they could be performed in public. In Lahore, theatre companies have found a loophole by performing on impromptu stages erected on lawns of sympathetic upper class families. In Karachi the political theatre resorts to metaphors instead. Furthermore, in this city police do not raise too many objections to a politically oriented play as long as ticket prices are kept above thirty rupees so that only wealthy upper middle class spectators can afford to attend. It gives the authorities an opportunity to point to Pakistan's so-called liberal policies regarding freedom of speech. "But try to do the same play in a poor neighborhood or a rural village, and you will have the authorities come down on you like a ton of bricks," warns Azhar.[11]

The word *dastak* means "to knock," and although the company does not pretend to have obtained spectacular effects, it feels that, as Pakistan's first political theatre group, it has at least succeeded in knocking away "some of the cobwebs in people's minds." Over the years, the group has also managed to forge durable links with trade unions. The unions have gradually become aware that theatre can indeed be a powerful way to get a political message across to their members. They now regularly invite Dastak to their functions. Thus, in March 1988 the group performed Brecht's *Exception and the Rule* to delegates from all over the country at the annual National Trade Union congress. Dastak now also invariably performs during election campaigns and each year on 1 May, international labor day.

The first time Dastak went out into the streets was on 1 May 1986. On that day, the group performed Brecht's *Saint Joan of the Stockyards* in three different parts of town, each time for more than 3,000 industrial workers, who, according to independent newspaper reports, were "highly attentive and involved."[12] Some of Dastak's members are factory workers themselves and live in remote slum areas. They come to the rehearsals by bicycle or bus.

Dastak represents various sectors of Pakistani society and varying levels of political consciousness. Its remaining members are university students and office workers.

Azhar considers rehearsals and production periods as veritable exercises in theatre of liberation:

> For many poorly schooled workers, being a member of Dastak is a continuous theatre of liberation workshop situation. Brecht's texts are great for political discussions. It is amazing how much comes out of these in-house debates. Then we perform the play and see the impact followed by the audience's feedback. All of that has a tremendous influence on these youngsters. Dastak thus definitely opens the windows of the minds of its members. Before joining our group, with the exception of four or five of us, no one had ever even opened a political tract. But now, more and more of them are saying, "I'm going to find out for myself."[13]

Sometimes involvement with Dastak also leads to the establishment of new groups. For example, one of Dastak's members, an actor named Yasseen, lives in a very poor part of Karachi where he had started a small community education program for high school drop-outs. After working with Dastak for a while, he began a children's theatre program in an abandoned building that used to be a hideout for heroine addicts. According to Aslam Azhar, similar spontaneous activities are beginning to spring up in other parts of Karachi as well: "Often, after performing for workers and women in the outskirts of the city, they ask us if they can have our script, and then they begin to do a little bit of theater for themselves."[14]

Aslam Azhar has learned to be careful and realistic. The painful experience with Pakistan Television is still fresh in his mind and he is cautious not to get too carried away. "We do not want to destroy Rome in one day and rebuild it the next. If we become too adventurist, we would be prevented from doing even what we have been doing so far," he knows.[15]

Political Theatre in Lahore

As in Karachi, the theatrical landscape of Lahore is dominated by commercial drawing-room comedies. In this city, the capital of Pakistani Punjab, these appalling sitcoms are generally programmed in the huge Alhamra theatre, a complex that sports three separate auditoriums of 750, 450, and 300 seats respectively, as well as an open-air theatre. Although officially intended for experimental theatre, even the smaller of these venues are inaccessible to the city's three political companies, Ajoka, Punjab Lok Rehas, and Sanjh.

Ajoka, Punjabi for Today's Theatre, is the oldest company in town. It was founded in 1984 by Madeeha Ali Gauhar, a former television actress who had made her debut in the drama serial *Suraj ko Zara Dekh* just prior to Aslam

Azhar's resignation from PTV. The former wife of a diplomat and daughter of a prominent army official, she had previously been affiliated with the Government College dramatic society, where she received her first theatre experience. The name Ajoka had been chosen by Shahid Nadeem and Sarmad Sebhai in the seventies, for a theatre company they had contemplated forming. Madeeha Gauhar adopted it for her own group, which she formed upon returning from an internship in India.

Ajoka's first play was *Jaloos,* an adaptation of Badal Sircar's *Procession.* In its original version, this play had been intended as a satire of Indian bourgeois egocentricity and its existential sense of loss. Formalistically, it was an experiment with environmental mise-en scène: it had actors performing all around the spectators, who were seated in a kind of labyrinth as if to emulate the confusions of life. Thus, the play alternated frantic body movements with brief scenes that touched upon a wide range of related themes like death as a daily occurrence in Asian metropoles, religious riots, nationalistic fanaticism, and political hypocrisy. Its mood constantly shifted between tragedy and farce.[16]

Jaloos premiered in May 1984. It generated great excitement in Lahore's theatre circles, accustomed to straightforward dialogues and realistic plays. Madeeha Gauhar recalls: "As far as technique was concerned, that play was quite innovative for us here in Pakistan. It was done in the round and stressed physical movement over dialogue. The response was tremendous. People had never seen anything like this before. We did it on the lawn of my mother's house without props. People were just sitting around us on the grass."[17]

Apart from reviving Sarmad Sebhai's *Panjawan Chiragh* [The Fifth Lamp], in the first three years of its existence Ajoka mainly adapted foreign plays. Upper class lawns remained their only possible venue. Spectators at these lawn performances typically were "invited" and afterwards the hat was passed so that the performance could legally remain a private affair that authorities would be unable to stop. Until recently, the only other venue available to Ajoka has been the terrace of the Goethe Institute, the German cultural center in Lahore, where the company has produced several adaptations of Brecht classics. In some of these, Ajoka has attempted to infuse the original text with traditional Pakistani performing art forms. In the 1985 production of *Caucasian Chalk Circle,* for example, Ajoka used local folk music and dance and a narrative form called the *bandh,* in which informal dialogues between two rural Punjabi storytellers served as Brechtian distancing devices. Thematically, Ajoka had made an effort to update the play to the contemporary Pakistani situation. Madeeha Gauhar explains: "Figures like Azdak and his judgments were extremely relevant to our own situation. In fact, when they hang the governor in the beginning of the play, you could hear the audience whisper 'Bhutto . . . Bhutto.' "[18]

Ajoka has set itself the difficult task of creating social awareness through high quality modern theatre. In the group's view, Pakistani political parties are seriously lacking in educational and cultural activities. Ajoka therefore wants to concentrate on evolving good and meaningful theatre for workers and villagers as well as for the urban middle and upper classes. Despite the risks attached to outdoor performances, the company has regularly gone out to perform in streets and factories in search of a genuine popular audience. Thus, on the death anniversary of Major Ishaq Mohammed in 1987, they performed *Jaloos* in his native village. Later, other street performances of this play followed in the interior of Sind province and in working class districts of Lahore. One of the more memorable performances in this series took place in the old walled city of Lahore with people watching from their windows in ancient red-brick five-storey tenement houses.

The most significant event in Ajoka's short history was the return from exile of playwright and television producer Shahid Nadeem at the end of 1987. He joined the company, and since then Ajoka and Nadeem have collaborated on at least two excellent original creations. While working for Amnesty International in London, Nadeem had sent Ajoka a script about women in Pakistani jails. Ajoka first produced it under the title *Barri* [The Acquittal] on 8 March 1987, International Women's Day. Subsequently, Ajoka produced Nadeem's allegorical play *Marya Hoya Kutta* [The Dead Dog] in November 1987. Originally Nadeem wrote it in the early seventies but updated it to fit the present circumstances. The new additions included references to the anti-woman clauses in some new Islamic laws and an ending which was no longer antagonistic toward the audience. Since November 1987, Ajoka has performed the play in several cities and towns outside Lahore for both working class and middle class audiences.

On the evening of 28 March 1988, I saw *The Dead Dog* performed outdoors in a working-class area of Lahore during a huge political rally organized by the progressive Awami Party. Party workers had blocked off an entire street and had put enormous mats on the cobblestones for people to sit on. A shaky stage had been erected on top of oil drums at the end of the street. It was illuminated by two light bulbs protruding from a canopy roof. Within half an hour the street was filled with people, and when the play finally started—after a poetry recital and a few political speeches—hundreds of additional spectators were also leaning from surrounding windows that formed layer upon layer of natural theatre balconies. At first, there was a lot of giggling and talking in the audience, but as the dialogue began, interested spectators soon succeeded in hushing their more restless companions.

The play is set in an old quarter of some unidentified inner city, which can be seen as a microcosm of Pakistan. This setup provides the playwright with opportunities to expose the manners of a cross-section of Pakistani society: the proprietor of a candy stall, a barber, a *mullah,* a politician, a beggar, and a street sweeper. The latter is an alcoholic. This seemingly odd phenomenon for an Islamic society is explained by the fact that since Islamization only street sweepers are allowed to purchase and consume alcohol because they traditionally are Christians. They buy their spirits at four-star tourist hotels and over the years have developed a lucrative sideline of illegal alcohol sales to Muslims.

The set is very simple. A couple of tables and a chair indicate the candy stall and the open-air barber shop. A wall full of election posters forms the backdrop. The play opens on an early morning street scene. A dead dog, represented by a crumpled bundle of black cloth, is lying in the middle of a square. The barber lights some incense sticks to get rid of the bad smell. His is merely a cosmetic remedy. A lady and a fat *mullah* shout that the black dog should be moved. The *mullah* claims he saw a similar black dog outside a mosque once before and the next thing he knew the roof of the mosque had caved in killing many praying devotees, including his spiritual teacher. But after urging the bystanders to sacrifice some food and money to Allah, he leaves the dead dog where it is.

The *mullah* is presented as a crafty dissimulator who justifies the misdeeds of the ruling class by saying it is Allah's will. By the same token, he creates a myth about the dead dog, calling it a bad omen that can only be removed with sacrifices. Thus he simultaneously profits from the incident and misleads the people about the true source of the stench, which is, after all, caused by the semifeudal structure of the country.

In addition to satirizing the behavior of Islamic religious leaders, *The Dead Dog* also analyzes the *mullah*'s position in Pakistani politics. *Mullahs* are basically instruments of the big feudal landlords, the industrialists, and the military, whose power they invest with moral authority. This incestuous relationship is depicted in a scene in which the chairman of the municipal council and the *mullah* debate about the presence of two mosques from different Muslim sects in one and the same community. Arguing, they circle around the dog, ignoring it, and act out a power struggle instead of pragmatically addressing the real issues that assail the community. In this manner, the play indirectly attacks religious and political leaders who fight only to increase their personal power while refusing to do anything significant for their country and people.

In the second scene, the dog has been removed but the smell remains. It is night, and an old man enters the square. He is unable to sleep because of the smell. "Where does that stench come from?" he mumbles to himself. "There is nothing to be seen, but it is all over the place." All the other characters come out of their houses one by one and begin to sniff. Even the *mullah* descends from his minaret, claiming the commotion has interrupted his prayers. He is joined by a policeman. The cop is not concerned about the stench of the dog or the problems of the people in the neighborhood. Instead he looks for a terrorist who does not exist. Playwright Shahid Nadeem explains:

> It is another common ploy by which the authorities inject fear and thereby control the masses through the creation of nonissues: ethnic violence is orchestrated, or fights between religious factions, or between the President and the Prime Minister. So everyone thinks that these are the main problem in our

country. But it is only intended to distract. There have been indications that the military planted a big bomb in Karachi and accused some nonexistent terrorist organization as a justification for tightening security. In *The Dead Dog* we presented this as the *mullah* conniving with the policeman.[19]

On the command of the *mullah,* the policeman disperses the people.

In the third and final scene *The Dead Dog* moves onto a surrealistic plane. By now the stench has become unbearable, but the people have not come one inch closer to discerning its source. The authorities force the citizens to look in the wrong direction all the time and, just as in communal riots in real Pakistani daily life, they eventually start accusing each other. In their search for scapegoats, the people move around in a circle and point their finger first at the alcoholic street sweeper and subsequently at the barber and the candy stall proprietor. When they run out of scapegoats, they realize that the *mullah* himself might be at the root of the problem, but before they can take action the policeman intervenes: "What about the terrorist: Let's look for him. I can smell the gun powder. He must be around somewhere." Finally they find a harmless lunatic who is arrested as a suspected terrorist. Thereupon the *mullah* distributes incense sticks to the people to diffuse the bad smell. In Pakistan, incense is used not only during religious ceremonies but also to get rid of bad odors in houses, mosques, and other public places. It also symbolically suggests that people should mind their own business and help to cover up the bad smell of others. At the end of the scene the *mullah* starts wailing: "God is patient. Now you be patient and meek too." Thus he succeeds in subduing the masses again.

In an attempt to break through the fourth wall, the actors finally jump into the audience and distribute incense sticks to the spectators, telling them: "If you want more incense you can come to the grand mosque where the *mullah* will give you as much as you want." This new conclusion of *The Dead Dog* is considerably different from the original:

> Back then it all ended in a cacophony of accusations. The mad man then rose up and started laughing at all the characters after which he jumped into the audience and started sniffing at the spectators, saying the smell came from all of them. But in the new version we went one step further. We no longer accuse them of stinking; we tell them each and everyone of them protects himself artificially from the smell and that that is no solution if the system itself stinks. You can't prosper or save yourself while upholding that kind of a system.[20]

Following *The Dead Dog,* in April 1988 the company conducted several theatre workshops at Government College and other educational institutions in and around Lahore. It also started working with factory workers. In May 1988 Ajoka premiered Brecht's *Good Woman of Setzuan,* again in coproduction with the Goethe Institute, which sponsored a young professional direc-

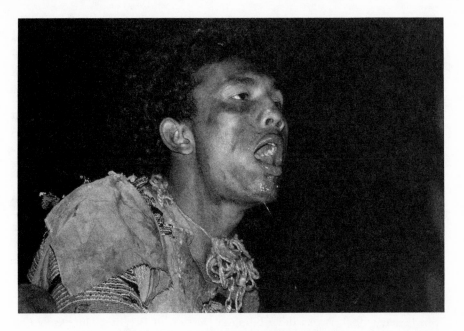

The lunatic, Ajoka, *The Dead Dog,* Lahore.

The *mullah* accused, Ajoka, *The Dead Dog*.

tor and a set designer to come over from Germany to guide the project. In July 1988, on the occasion of Nelson Mandela's birthday, Ajoka did a play called *Biko's Trial,* which it had adapted from a film documentary on Steve Biko's life. Concerned about the oppression of blacks in South Africa, Ajoka simultaneously started working on an original play about the most oppressed group in Pakistan, the Christian brickmakers. For this purpose, in the preparatory stages of the production the actors interviewed members of this minority while Shahid Nadeem processed their research into a play, calling the result *Itt* [Brick].

After two successful street performances, the Goethe Institute invited Ajoka to perform *Itt* on its lawn on 30 August 1988. Three hours before curtain time, however, Dr. Schutze, the director of the institute, received a phone call from Pakistan's Ministry of Foreign Affairs with orders to cancel the show. After all, this was a mere two weeks after Zia's death and the country's future still looked extremely unstable. Later that night, Ajoka performed *Itt* anyway on the lawn of a local human rights activist and many street performances have followed since then.

In January 1989, Ajoka did a bilingual version of Brecht's *Threepenny Opera* in Urdu and Punjabi. The show was directed by Elizabeth Lynch from England and was conceived as a contemporary satire of Pakistan's government. Thus, Polly, the daughter of beggar king Peachum, walked and talked in the same affected manner as Benazir Bhutto. Mack the Knife's gang members, who object to Polly's takeover of their lucrative affairs, were presented as a mixture of fundamentalists and upper class businessmen. To make the metaphor even more colorful and unambiguous, the play was set in Lahore's officially nonexistent red light district.

In July 1989, Ajoka came out with a new documentary play on dowry murders called *Choolah* [Stove], based on facts gathered in Lahore, where 600 women had died the previous year in so-called stove-related accidents. Later that year, the company also presented Brecht's *Caucasian Chalk Circle* at a German Play Festival in Karachi.[21] In 1990, Ajoka continued to be one of the most productive and original companies in Pakistan, although its activities slowed down slightly due to the pregnancy of Madeeha Gauhar and the temporary departure of Shahid Nadeem, who was rehired by Pakistan Television.[22]

Punjab Lok Rehas

Whereas Ajoka is predominantly performance oriented and is widely regarded as Lahore's best theatre company from an aesthetic viewpoint, Punjab Lok Rehas has the reputation of being the city's most radical troupe. Punjab Lok Rehas (the name means Punjab Popular Theatre) is also the only group in Pakistan with an outspoken theatre of liberation profile, which it has recently begun to implement in the form of grassroots workshops. The group was founded in 1985 by Muhamed Wasim and Nisar Moyud-Din, two former Ajoka actors who had left after a dispute about politics, language, and Madeeha Gauhar's alleged authoritarian attitude. The founders of Punjab Lok Rehas were interested in taking plays written in the Punjabi vernacular to the popular masses and felt that Ajoka was not doing enough of that. Moreover, they wanted to start a genuine theatre movement and began by establishing a truly democratic structure in their own group. Now they consciously avoid stardom and try to give all members an equal opportunity to act, direct, or otherwise develop their talents and explore the art of theatre.

Punjab Lok Rehas originally started with a membership of six men and one woman but has now expanded to thirty people, seven of them women. New members are selected very carefully: they first have to serve as production assistants for at least two plays before they are considered for permanent membership. Says Muhamed Wasim: "If we don't screen carefully and allow just anyone to join, they may demolish everything we have built up."[23]

Punjab Lok Rehas is closely affiliated with Lahore's visual artists, musicians, and writers, and had good contacts with students from Lahore's National College of Arts, the country's only fine arts academy. As such, the group is an integral part of the informal Punjab progressive cultural movement and benefits by having direct access to original play scripts from the Punjabi Padjar Committee, the local progressive writers' collective.

Punjab Lok Rehas is by far the most directly political of all contemporary theatre companies in Pakistan. It aims to fill the vacuum left by the splintered leftist factions, which, according to Punjab Lok Rehas, are far too dogmatic in their application to Pakistan of classical Marxist models of social change and development. Says Adnan Qadir Khan, one of Punjab Lok Rehas's three full-time theatre workers: "Only now political parties are beginning to realize the importance of culture and the significance of the nationalities question. They have not found a way of communicating with the people in their own language, with how they feel and think. It's stupid to go into a village and then start yelling Marxist slogans and that God doesn't exist. That's one sure way to get the Muslim rural folk against you."[24]

Punjab Lok Rehas is opposed to the domination of their country by a few powerful semifeudal families, the military, and the Muslim religious hierarchy. The group blends its political analysis with the cultural aim of promoting theatre in the Punjabi language, which they feel has been systematically destroyed by the rulers in the national capital Islamabad. To reach a popular audience in the cities and villages, Punjab Lok Rehas builds on whatever traditional culture is left in Punjab. "We try to make use of the old Sufi poets, for instance," explains Muhamed Wasim. "We have a very strong tradition of poetry here. We reinterpret them from a people's point of view and connect them with modern times. These classical Sufi poets were actually quite progressive and satirized the colonial British rulers, for example."[25]

Punjab Lok Rehas's popular outreach only started in the course of 1988. Before that, the group considered street performances too dangerous. Besides, not yet satisfied with the performing skills of many of its members, the company preferred to concentrate on in-house theatre training and some try-out productions for Lahore's middle class. In the first three years of its existence, the group performed only occasionally for workers. Its chief concern was to experiment with as many different theatrical forms as possible. Hence the group sports an impressive record of eight original productions from 1985 to 1988. *Andheray da Pand* [The Path of Darkness] was Punjab Lok Rehas's public debut. The play had sixteen performances. The cast invited reactions from the audience after each show and then made an effort to process the most valid of these criticisms in their next performance. In this way, *Andheray da Pand* developed from a weak melodrama into a realistic and pertinent play full of wit.

The play deals with the psychological, existential, and political problems afflicting urban middle class youngsters. A fictional Lahore café provides the dramatic setting. A whole range of characters come in to tell their life stories, including a college student, a waiter, the café owner, a political party worker, and a symbolic character named Jhalla who, sometimes poetically, sometimes humorously, spreads the message of solidarity and collective struggle.

Andheray da Pand was followed by *Dhroo* [Oppression], a play about the death of a trade union leader named Dulla and the farcical police investigation into his murder. The next production was *Zanani* [Woman], an adaptation of Safdar Hashmi's legendary Indian street play *Aurat*.[26] Other Punjab Lok Rehas productions have included *Bandiwan* [The Prisoner], a play about Ali Bhutto's final days that was coproduced with the Sanjh theatre company;[27] *Akhian* [Eyes]; and *Bujharat* [The Riddle], an experimental play about an inquisitive young woman who is thrown into a lunatic asylum because Pakistani society has no way of dealing with independently minded women. Not all of these productions were equally well received, however.

Shahid Nadeem of Ajoka finds that not enough people are criticizing the aesthetic standards of Punjab Lok Rehas: "If we criticize them it is seen as rivalry. And most of our theatre critics want to encourage new theatre, so they are not too hard on them either. But frankly I feel that they don't have good directors. They are still completely overwhelmed by the themes. They think that political theatre means the message and the analysis. They don't think carefully enough about how to package it into attractive theatre."[28]

But even Nadeem had to admit he was impressed with *Takht Lahore* [The Throne of Lahore], a historical play about emerging Punjabi nationalism in the sixteenth century and the exploitation of the Punjab region by the imperial rulers in the national capital. Despite its three-hour length and a perfor-

Andheray da Pand, Punjab Lok Rehas. Photo courtesy Punjab Lok Rehas.

"We have to write and question everything that is not logical." *Bujharat*, Punjab Lok Rehas. Photo courtesy Punjab Lok Rehas.

Takht Lahore, Punjab Lok Rehas. Photo courtesy Punjab Lok Rehas.

mance schedule that coincided with an unseasonable cold spell, *Takht Lahore*
played for ten consecutive nights in the spring of 1986 to capacity audiences.
Thanks to a generous sponsor, Punjab Lok Rehas had been able to rent lights
and costumes from a local film studio and build an elaborate set in order to
make the entourage and the upper class characters of Lahore *anno* 1586 as
convincing as possible. The play, written in 1973 by Najam Hussain Syed,
is a straightforward realistic historical drama about a rebellion by indigenous
Punjabis against the usurpation of the Mughal king, whom they regarded as
a foreign invader. The heroic uprising, led by a benevolent tribal Punjabi
chieftain named Dulla Bhatti and inspired by the humanistic philosophy of
Sufi poet Shah Hussain, was eventually crushed by the armed forces of the
central authority. The historical situation depicted in *Takht Lahore* was clearly
intended to reveal parallels with the Lahore of 1987. According to Punjab
Lok Rehas, the central government in Islamabad also regards contemporary
Punjabi nationalists as subversive rebels. Similarly, the group feels that the
corruptive power of feudal landlords and religious leaders has not changed
significantly since the sixteenth and seventeenth centuries.

   Punjab Lok Rehas intends to tour a simplified version of *Takht Lahore* to
villages in interior Punjab. This project reflects the company's desire to move
away from performances for the urban middle class and work for and with
a genuine popular audience instead. By the middle of 1988, the group had
gathered enough courage and sufficient contacts in Punjabi villages and towns

to contemplate expansion into the grassroots of the region. Links were also established with student groups at Lahore's University of Engineering and Technology. Meanwhile, two members of the group, Musadiq Sanwal and Adnan Qadir Khan, attended a theatre of liberation workshop in the Philippines, whose methods they started applying with the Punjab grassroots following their return. In that sense, Punjab Lok Rehas is breaking important new ground on the Pakistani cultural front. Unavoidably, new talent and new stories will spring from their initiatives. The first results of their grassroots outreach look promising indeed.

In 1988 Punjab Lok Rehas adopted a new strategy. The group planned to perform existing plays from its repertory in villages and towns. After the performances the actors would ask locals if they were interested in having a workshop. If the response was positive, Punjab Lok Rehas members would return to conduct a community theatre workshop with the intention to form local theatre groups. Says Nisar Moyud-Din, the chairman-elect of Punjab Lok Rehas: "They should produce their own plays for their own communities. It's not good if we try to be everywhere. Punjab Lok Rehas has never claimed that we are the only ones who can speak for the people. We realize that through our theatre we can teach the people to speak for themselves."[29]

Since 1988, the literature and arts and crafts collectives of the Lahore cultural movement have joined Punjab Lok Rehas in its new grassroots orientation. Meanwhile, the village tours are well underway and the first grassroots workshops have been held. They have already generated two new community theatre groups, one in Siraika in southern Punjab and one at the Engineering University of Lahore. Direct links with India were established after Safdar Hashmi's death, with two community theatre groups from India participating in a Safdar Hashmi memorial festival organized by Punjab Lok Rehas. In February 1990, Musadiq Sanwal, freshly returned from the *Cry of Asia!* tour, conducted a workshop with students from the Engineering University. The result was the creation of an original streetplay called *Raat* [Night], which expressed solidarity with the Muslim people in Kashmir across the border.

Sanjh

The third Lahore-based theatre company, with which both Punjab Lok Rehas and Ajoka maintain relatively good relations, is called Sanjh. Like Punjab Lok Rehas, Sanjh is an offshoot from Ajoka, but is considerably less radical and energetic. Sanjh, which means "unity," is closely associated with Benazir Bhutto's Pakistan People's Party (PPP). The office of Sanjh is located in the home of Fakhar Zaman, PPP's cultural secretary, and the group receives funding from Agha Akhter Ali Kazalbash, a wealthy PPP politician. According to Mohammed Shahid Lone, ex-convenor of Sanjh, this affiliation is not really a problem: "Some are in the group because they love theatre, others because for them it is a political activity. We work well together and all of us subscribe to the group's basic motto: to be in unity with the people and with those who struggle for freedom through theatre."[30]

Mohammed Shahid Lone was a member of Ajoka until 1985. In November of that year he left the company together with playwright-actor Rana Fawad. In 1986 Fakhar Zaman approached them to dramatize *Bandiwan* [The Prisoner], a fictional biography he had written based on the life of Ali Bhutto. Lone and Fawad formed an ad-hoc company of experienced actors and students to perform Zaman's play at the First Punjabi International Language Conference. After the production, the group decided to continue under the name Sanjh. Rana Fawad became the artistic driving force behind the group. Since 1986, the group has done a number of productions, including Brecht's *The Exception and the Rule* and Safdar Hashmi's *Machine*. Sanjh usually produces its plays at the request of PPP or other political organizations. Thus they first did *Machine* in Shaikhu Pura, a factory area outside Lahore in June 1986. The occasion was the anniversary of the death of a famous Communist leader, and a crowd estimated at 4,000 workers attended the performance.

In 1987, Sanjh also produced an original skit on women's issues for the national workshop of the Family Planning Association of Pakistan. Mohammed Shahid Lone sees the play as a long overdue tribute to women: "In it, we depicted the contribution of women to the development of men, from baby to child, through school, and how, in addition, they also work in factories, in the fields, in the office, and how men can only respond to this by raping them."[31]

Women's Theatre

The amount of women's theatre in Pakistan is amazing for such a fundamentalist Muslim country. Sanjh is not alone in lending its theatre to the promotion of women's issues. Most of the other companies in the country also annually perform women's play on International Women's Day. In this context, Ajoka, with its own female artistic director, has arguably made the most significant contribution to the growing corpus of original Pakistani women's plays.

On International Women's Day 1987, Ajoka came out with *Barri* [The Acquittal], a moving play about women prisoners in Pakistan written by Shahid Nadeem. Nadeem actually created the play while still in London. During his exile there, he had been working for the Women Prisoners of Conscience section of Amnesty International and had based his play on true stories he had collected from Pakistani women prisoners. As a student leader and, later, as a dissident television producer, Nadeem had been in Pakistani jails three times himself and thus could also draw on his own experiences for *The Acquittal*.

The play presents a realistic picture of the terrible conditions in Pakistani women's prisons. It also strongly criticizes the anti-woman bias of Islam in general. Finally, *The Acquittal* tackles the inefficiency and pretentiousness of Pakistan's drawing room, middle class–dominated women's movement. In a newspaper article that appeared in the *Frontier Post* the day after *The Acquittal*'s first performance, Shahid Nadeem suggested that if the Pakistan women's movement seemed to be running out of steam, it could hardly be for lack of issues: "Shariat courts are still sentencing women to stoning, women are still being paraded naked in Punjab villages, brides with insufficient dowry are still burned to death mysteriously due to exploding stoves. Most women are still unable to exercise whatever rights they had regarding consent in marriage, permission for second marriages, and divorce. Child custody laws still heavily favor men." [32] Nadeem concluded by urging Pakistan's women's movement to drop its untenable apolitical stance and make an all-out effort to recruit women activists from the middle and lower classes.

The Acquittal depicts the life story of four women from different social backgrounds: a middle class feminist, Zaïda; a peasant girl, Jamila; an old working class woman, Jannat; and a mystic, Mariam. The names of the characters are significant. Zaïda means "the pious one," Mariam comes from Mother Mary, Jamila means "full of life and beauty," and Jannat means "heaven." In the course of the play the four tell their life stories through conversation or by directly addressing the audience. The scenes, covering a period of several weeks, are presented as realistic vignettes of life in a women's prison.

The play was first performed at the Goethe Institute in Lahore on 8 March 1987. Despite Ajoka's limited resources, the open-air space was used inventively. The company owns two small spots and rented two additional theatre lights for this particular production. They fixed one spot high up in a tree. Its light was broken by the branches of the tree and the resulting multiple small beams created the effect of prison bars on the lawn.

The play opens when Zaïda enters through a door in the back wall of the Goethe Institute, which serves as a backdrop. She tells the audience she has been imprisoned for going on a hunger strike for women's rights: "I was taken to the women's ward of the district jail. I was subjected to a humiliating body search. I had to raise hell to get them to bring a female warden to search me. I told them their Islam was all sham: 'Islam teaches that women should be treated with respect and you're doing nothing of the sort!' " [33]

Zaïda effectively illustrates how little middle class feminists actually know of the horrendous conditions in which poor women have to live in slums and villages. She reveals she has never met any working class women before. Consequently, she considers her three cellmates to be helpless and destitute. With her patronizing behavior, Zaïda indirectly delivers a well-meant criticism to middle class women activists in Pakistan who know nothing about the real problems of the majority of the women in their country.

Jamila's story is emblematic of the predicament of many rural women. In her monologue, which follows Zaïda's, she tells the audience she is the victim of an arranged marriage. Nowadays, 95 percent of the marriages in Pakistan's countryside are still arranged by parents without consulting their children (in the cities the rate fluctuates between 60 and 70 percent). Jamila tells how, at age fourteen, she was married off to a man her father's age. Because she was still only a child she experienced her wedding like a funeral. Even her sister-in-law and her mother, who had forced her to marry, were crying. Jamila wondered whether they were crying out of compassion for her or out of self-pity because they recalled their own weddings and the sufferings that followed. In the middle of her tale Jamila recites an ancient folktale called "Hiri and Ranja," about two youngsters who fall in love. One day, Hiri is married off to another man. Before Hiri leaves her parental home, she addresses her father in a song: "You have been so kind to me as a father. You taught me to walk and sang me to sleep. But now you have forced me to marry a man I don't love. Farewell, father, farewell."

The incorporation of the popular "Hiri and Ranja" story is one of several examples in which *The Acquittal* fruitfully employs Pakistani cultural heritage. Obviously, Jamila's predicament is similar to Hiri's. Upon arriving at her new home, Jamila discovers that her old husband has a daughter her own age who, together with her father, proceeds to terrorize her. The old man is not interested in sex, while Jamila is just beginning to discover its pleasures. Before long, she becomes involved with a young man. When the old man refuses to grant Jamila a divorce, she decides to elope with her new boyfriend. Jamila: "We spent all day and all night in one room, discovering each other's bodies. It was wonderful. It was the first time I felt free." But that old man tracks them down and has them arrested. Jamila's lover manages to escape, thus becoming the third man to desert her. To punish his recalcitrant young bride, the old man ties her to a bed for fifteen days. On the first night after her release, the girl grabs an axe and walks over to where the old man is sleeping: "You said you won't divorce me, so I'll divorce you." Then she hits him three times with the axe: "Blood came gushing out of instant gashes each time my axe hit his face. The last time, the axe got stuck in his stomach. He was so surprised that he didn't even scream. Then I went to bed and fell soundly asleep."[34] The next day, Jamila was arrested and since then she has been awaiting her trial. She knows that she will probably be sentenced to death by hanging.[35]

The tale of Jannat, the old woman, is less bloody but no less tragic. She used to be a servant until one day her master found out that her son had stolen his stereo set. Since he was nowhere to be found, the police arrested the old woman instead, hoping she would reveal the whereabouts of her son.

Madeeha Gauhar of Ajoka Theatre as the young girl who kills her oppressive husband with an axe in *The Acquittal*.

Jannat, however, could not do so because, according to Pakistani custom, mothers should always sacrifice themselves for the men in their family.

Mariam, the fourth woman prisoner, is a so-called mystic devotee of Saint Shah Hussain. Mysticism in the Pakistani sense of the term refers to an enlightened variety of Islam. Its tradition goes back several centuries and from the beginning has always been quite political and opposed to the sheer limitless power of the *mullahs* and sheiks. Mystics lived with the people and, despite their devotion, were quite down to earth. The movement also produced several highly respected poets like Bulleh Shah and Shah Hussain, who lived four hundred years ago.

In her soliloquy, Mariam tells the audience that she was arrested for dancing at Shah Hussain's shrine during the celebration of his death anniversary. According to the police she had violated the fundamentalist laws of the Zia-al-Haq government, which stipulated that women were not allowed to dance in public places. Having no one to bail her out she has been in prison for almost a year. She has been raped repeatedly by the warden, the doctor, and several prison guards, and now she is pregnant.[36] Usually in such cases, prison officials force the pregnant woman to have an abortion, but Mariam wants to keep the baby, claiming that all prison officials actually were the father of her baby. Shahid Nadeem: "We were not sure how people would react, because in Pakistan you don't talk about pregnancy or rape and especially not about a woman refusing to have an abortion for her own ideological or mystical reasons."[37]

Miriam asks the audience: "My child will be illegitimate and will probably be sent to an orphanage, but I insist I am a legitimate mother. Is there any law to protect my right to be a mother?" Knowing full well there is no such law, she continues: "I have seen children killed for their illegitimacy. Once an orphaned baby was left on the steps of a mosque in Karachi. The *mullah* concluded it was an illegitimate child and ordered it to be stoned to death." Her three companions confirm Mariam's statement and proceed to list their own examples of injustice done to women. They mention wife battery and having to work excessively in fields, in factories, and in the household: "We do twice the work and then they just passed a law that says that our testimony is worth only half a man's."[38]

Jamila continues her appeal: "If I could I would kill my father, because he always favored my brothers. I would kill my brothers because they were more concerned with their own despicable honor than with my happiness. I would also kill my neighbor, who couldn't keep his dirty eyes off me. I would kill the *mullah* who forced me to marry. I would kill the policeman who beat my lover and me. And finally I would kill the judge who is going to sentence me tomorrow and those prison guards who never leave us alone." When Jamila has finished speaking, Mariam the mystic falls into a fit and relives her rape while her body contorts on the floor.

As a result of their testimonies and the recognition of their shared sufferings, the four women gradually become friends. Zaïda, once so patronizing, has been shattered by all the things she has heard and experienced. Slowly she gets up, walks to each of her cellmates, and solemnly pronounces their acquittal. To illustrate their newly found solidarity, the women sit down and delouse each other's hair. Before *The Acquittal* no one had ever dared to show this very common but intimate activity between sisters and female friends on stage in Pakistan.

The peaceful louse-picking scene precedes the turbulent finale of the play. Suddenly everything breaks down. First Jamila is called to the warden's office to hear that her hanging is scheduled for the next day. Second, Mariam is taken away by the guards to have a forced abortion. Zaïda's brother, a sensation-hungry journalist, had run a story on Mariam's case in his newspaper and the jail authorities want to get rid of the evidence in order to prevent further negative publicity. Then the old woman is informed she will be released because the authorities have found and arrested her fugitive son. But this is no real acquittal for her because now her son will be a prisoner. Nor will Jamila be freed by her execution or Mariam by her abortion. Even Zaïda's release is only partial: she will return to a domestic bourgeois prison of sorts. She will carry the burden of her recent experience and the memory of her fellow inmates. When she walks out, she is welcomed by a large group of photographers and reporters. Her relatives have installed new curtains for her at home and the middle class women's group she belongs to has prepared a glamorous reception in her honor. Fearing negative publicity, even the prison superintendent goes out of his way to apologize for any possible ill treatment she might have received. As Zaïda disappears, Mariam remains behind on the stage and quietly sings an old song written by Bulleh Shah. Then she addresses the audience: "Don't be fooled. For us women the whole country is really still one big jail."

With plays like *The Acquittal,* playwright Shahid Nadeem underlines that he finds theatre a much more powerful vehicle with which to express opinions than the press:

> Despite the fact that papers are relatively free now, most of them have lost credibility. What they print is not necessarily the truth and people know it. Moreover, newspaper coverage is very superficial. They don't go into the background of things nor add personal feelings about issues that affect the people. But through theatre you can control the reality you wish to depict. You can condense it and thereby make it more effective. In normal reality, you may not notice those things because you have never questioned them and they have existed over a long period of time. They have become invisible over time. Theatre also allows you to draw characters in such a way that the audience gets emotionally involved with them. But don't get me wrong: we do not want to give people the catharsis they crave so they can go home satisfied. On the contrary, we want to disturb them.[39]

The enormous success of *The Acquittal* emphatically demonstrates the correctness of Nadeem's view:

> We were actually surprised it was received so well. We had been worried we might get into trouble. But the time was obviously ripe for it. The response has been tremendous, especially from women's groups. They have bought the video we made of the play and have begun a micromedia project with it. They are showing the video in remote rural areas and are succeeding in generating discussions between men and women. It was also shown at a women's conference in Kuala Lumpur. And Cendit, an Indian feminist media group, has decided to make an English version of the video that they want to distribute all over Asia.[40]

Tehrik-e-Niswan: Karachi's Own Women's Theatre Company

The women's pieces created by Ajoka, Dastak, Punjab Lok Rehas, and Sanjh for the annual Women's Day celebrations do not constitute the total extent of women's theatre activities in Pakistan. Women's Action Forum (WAF), a nationwide association of middle class women activists, has been incorporating theatre in the curricula of its adult education courses since 1981. Themes of improvised theatre pieces created by WAF workshop participants include the systematic halving of women's social and legal rights and the banning of women from spectator sports. One of the funnier WAF skits involved a slap-stick hockey match with women players constantly tripping over exagger-ated layers of saris and veils and running blindfolded male umpires into the ground.

Pakistan also boasts a genuine women's theatre company based in Karachi. The group is called Tehrik-e-Niswan [Women's Movement] and is actually an offshoot from a feminist discussion club that started in 1980. The group developed from organizing seminars to cultural sessions that included read-ings of poetry and short stories. In December 1981, Tehrik-e-Niswan pre-sented its first theatre production, an adaptation of *What Have You Done for Me Lately?* Since then, the group has done an average of two new produc-tions per year.

Initially, the group had difficulty finding enough actresses. Sheema Ker-mani, a classically trained performer of traditional Indian dances and co-foun-der of Tehrik-e-Niswan, explains how hard it still is to recruit women: "Even in the middle class it is extremely difficult to find girls who have permission from their husbands, brothers, or fathers to act on stage or to go to rehears-als. It is considered dishonorable." Similarly, women performing in working class areas or in the streets simply ask for trouble: "It's not like India, where you can perform and people will either agree or disagree, but no one will get hurt. When we performed at Karachi University for International Women's Day in 1983, for example, there were fundamentalists who explicitly threat-ened to start shooting the moment a man and a woman would come on stage together. But luckily the auditorium was filled with 3,000 girls, so I think they got a bit scared."[41]

Tehrik-e-Niswan mainly specializes in adaptations of foreign plays and dramatizations of short stories about women. The list of productions in-cludes an Urdu version of Jean Anouilh's *Antigone,* Safdar Hashmi's *Aurat,* and Vijay Tendulkar's *Anji.* The feminist relevance of Anouilh's play con-sisted mainly of Antigone's rebellion to male dictatorial authority. It was first produced in 1986. *Aurat* has been in Tehrik-e-Niswan's repertory continu-ously since May 1982. The title *Anji* refers to the name of a courageous young woman. Using live music and narrators derived from roaming folk theatre traditions, the play depicts the painful process of Anji's emancipation. The group first produced Tendulkar's play in March of 1985 and has regu-larly performed it since then.

In 1983, Tehrik-e-Niswan also did a dramatization of three realistic stories by Pakistani woman writer Khadija Mastoor. Two of these deal with the plight of urban middle class working women, and the third, "Khirman," is a moving story about a young peasant girl who is sold to an elderly farmer who needs her to help him in the household because his first wife is mortally ill. Sheema Kermani: "It is a realistic vignette that shows the sadness of the girl as she tries very hard to win the man's affection. It also deals with her psychological problems when he forbids her to stay on after his first wife's death. She then has to return to her impoverished parents to whom she is only going to be an extra burden again. *Khirman* literally means "little nest." For a while she had a little nest, but in the end she is thrown out of it." [42]

Another recent Tehrik-e-Niswan production was *Birjees Qadar ka Kumba* [The House of Birjees Qadar], an Urdu adaptation of García Lorca's *House of Bernarda Alba,* which the group produced on the occasion of International Women's Day 1988. By Pakistani standards it was a big success, with seven consecutive sell-out performances. Khalid Ahmad, the male director of the play, explains why the group elected to produce the play: "Lorca's story is amazingly relevant here. It is truly surprising how well the situation of a Spanish village permeated by traditional Catholic values translates to our rural situation in Pakistan and the kind of life women lead here. We only had to change one or two things, like the serenading under the girl's window. Instead, we had the neighbor's son leap over the wall to make a pass at the girl. [43]

Birjees Qadar had a cast of eighteen women for whom the production period constituted a veritable theatre of liberation process. Eight of the women had never acted before. Khalid Ahmad: "Emotionally, they got very deeply involved in the play and as a result they formed the most disciplined group I've ever worked with. Everyone was always on time, which rarely happens in Pakistan. There was also very much an element of discovering a talent and a hidden joy in themselves." [44] To those from conservative backgrounds, the play also meant an opportunity to identify themselves with oppressed women in semifeudal Spain. On opening night several of them experienced an anxiety that went far beyond mere stagefright: they knew some of their fundamentalist male relatives were coming to watch the show and expected trouble afterwards. Explains Sheema Kermani: "It goes against their concept of female virginity and of keeping women sheltered and locked up. But somehow they took to it, maybe because of the tragedy of the situation. Apparently people tolerate more in the theatre than in real life." [45]

Naturally, Tehrik-e-Niswan is not exempt from censorship. Police administrators routinely eliminate words like "pregnancy," "uterus," "womb," and "motherhood" from their plays. Emboldened by the recent success of *Birjees Qadar,* however, the group now plans to produce Dario Fo's and Franca Rame's hard-hitting *A Woman Alone.* [46] It will very likely cause heart attacks and plenty of overtime work in Karachi's censorship office.

VIII

BEYOND THE SHADOWS
OF *WAYANG*

THEATRE OF LIBERATION
IN INDONESIA

In the West, when we think of Indonesian theatre, we are usually reminded of the various traditional forms of *wayang*—the live theatre with human actors of *wayang orang,* the wooden stick puppet theatre of *wayang golek,* or the shadow theatre of *wayang kulit,* which is created with two-dimensional leather puppets manipulated in front of a gas lamp behind a silk screen. Outside Indonesia, relatively little is known about its modern theatre. Few people know that an extensive political theatre movement was developed in the fifties but had to go underground after the bloody coup of 1965.[1] But since the early eighties a new and courageous generation of theatre artists from Yogyakarta (or Yogya) has begun to use the stage again to express increasingly vocal political criticism. Inspired by the successful workshop and networking methods of the Philippine theatre of liberation, several young Indonesian theatre artists have also started laying the foundations for a similar movement in their own country with some remarkable results.

The Fifties and After

Modern theatre in Indonesia does not have a very long history. The Dutch colonizers, unlike the British in India, never really bothered to introduce European performing arts, with the occasional exception of amateur productions of light Dutch comedy for and by the expatriate community. Modern Indonesian theatre can therefore safely be assumed to have started in or about 1950, after the violently obtained independence.

Western drama was first introduced through university literature departments.[2] Several young poets, notably in the central Javanese city of Yogyakarta, formed small amateur theatre companies and began to translate plays from the West. Artists like Putu Wijaya, Arifin C. Noor, and Rendra, who today form Indonesia's mainstream theatre élite, have their roots back in Yo-

gya in the fifties, when the most important and original theatre was undoubtedly created in LEKRA, the cultural umbrella organization of the PKI, the
Communist Party of Indonesia.

At its height, LEKRA, which is an Indonesian acronym for Lembaga Kebu-
dayaan Rakyat [League of People's Culture], was reputed to have had more
than 500,000 active members.[3] Its activities ranged from literature and music
to drama, dance, and film. In the theatre, LEKRA specialized in rural touring
performances of modernized and politicized versions of traditional theatre
forms like the *ludruk* of East Java and the *wayang orang,* with which it intended "to inspire the self-respect of the peasants and to consolidate the strength
of the peasant organizations."[4]

LEKRA's performances, which preceded political meetings, seminars, conferences, and demonstrations in the period between 1955 and 1965, were very
popular. They often depicted the actual conditions of Indonesian workers,
peasants, and fishermen, supporting their aspirations and demands for democratization and land reforms. Fred Wibowo, the current artistic director
of Teater Arena, one of Yogyakarta's oldest political theatre companies, recalls how in the early sixties virtually the entire Indonesian theater scene was
heavily politicized:

> I joined Arena in 1964 as an apprentice actor. I was seventeen at the time. All
> drama groups were affiliated with a political faction of some sort. Arena worked
> with the Catholic Party. But particularly the Nationalists and Communists
> were very strong and had many theatre companies. I remember that the Na-
> tionalists were particularly fanatical in trying to dominate the cultural move-
> ment. They tried to destroy any kind of theatre company that didn't quite
> agree with their politics. The bad thing was that they controlled all the gov-
> ernment censors who granted permission for performances. So at the end of
> 1964, many Indonesian artists came together and drafted a cultural manifesto
> which demanded that all arts be free from oppression.[5]

Not long after the publication of the manifesto, the playwright Rendra was
arrested and forced into inactivity. His harassment only formed a confusing
prelude to a wider crackdown that eventually led to the bloody events of
October 1965. These left many hundreds of thousands of alleged leftists, many
of them LEKRA artists, imprisoned, tortured, or dead.[6]

It took Yogyakarta's group theatre several years to recover from the violent repression. It gained a new impulse, however, when Rendra returned on
the scene in 1968 and founded the now legendary Bengkel Teater [Workshop
Theatre], in which he tried to fuse Western theatre forms with Javanese myths,
poetry, and music.[7] Other now prominent playwright-directors like N.
Riantiarno, Ikra Negara, Arifin C. Noor, and Putu Wijaya soon started similar experiments of their own. Lacking Rendra's charisma and, some say, his
populist opportunism, they were initially not very successful but soon found
a growing audience for their high-quality theatre among the affluent urban
middle class. In these circles, a certain measure of social criticism was al-

Indonesian rebel playwright Rendra.

lowed as a superficial sign of the régime's so-called political tolerance. Any real manifestations of dissent, however, were invariably checked by increasingly efficient government censors.

In 1978, Rendra was arrested again, this time during a performance at Gajah Mada University in Yogya, and banned from performing in public until January 1986. From that moment on, Rendra was no longer a force to be reckoned with in Indonesia's political theatre. His critics claim that after the ban was lifted he became a publicity-hungry caricature of his former self and that he had struck a deal with the military for permission to perform his theatrical poetry shows for the Jakarta bourgeoisie.

While in the late seventies Arifin C. Noor, Putu Wijaya, N. Riantiarno, and Ikra Negara left the dangerous territory of political drama and began to work either in the cinema or in Jakarta's mainstream, Teater Arena and the newly formed Teater Dinasti slowly began their search for a new and effective political theatre. Their inspirations came from Latin America, the Philippines, and their own Indonesian realities.

Teater Arena

Teater Arena was founded in 1963 by Yasso Winarto, who is now editor-in-chief of *Exekutif,* a big Jakarta-based magazine. In the sixties, Arena pro-

Fred Wibowo, artistic director of Arena Theater and Audiovisual Studio Puskat in Yogyakarta.

duced mostly adapted Western classics like *Macbeth, Hamlet,* and *Oedipus Rex.* Later it also started doing works by "moderns" like Ibsen, Shaw (*Arms and the Man,* 1968), and, in 1969, Sartre's *Putain Respectueuse.* One of the crucial moments in Arena's history occurred in 1971 when it was invited to join Studio Puskat, a professional audiovisual institute sponsored by the local Catholic seminary. Teater Arena, now under the artistic directorship of Fred Wibowo, a former classical dancer, and Studio Puskat, led by Father Rüdi Hoffmann, a progressive Swiss Jesuit priest, developed into one of the country's more effective media outfits.

At the moment, its activities range from videos advocating grassroots development, social change, and liberation theology to high-caliber original theatre shows based on meticulous grassroots research into the condition of the people. But Arena also conducts theatre of liberation workshops of the type developed by the Philippines Educational Theater Association (PETA). Throughout the seventies, Arena and Puskat read the pedagogical writings of Paulo Freire and books on liberation theology. Father Hoffmann even went to Latin America for a year and, in 1978, became involved in the formation of a Basic Christian Community in the Colombian city of Medellín.

For Fred Wibowo and Teater Arena, the definitive push toward theatre of liberation came in 1979 when PETA's Remmy Rikken visited Yogyakarta and invited him and three other members of the group to come to Manila to

participate in a six-week community theatre workshop in 1980. Wibowo remembers the experience as inspiring: "It was very exciting and convinced us
to build our theatre around a similar orientation. We had been trying to think
for a while about how to conduct cultural action for social change. But when
we finally saw its power right on our own doorstep, naturally we were very
enthusiastic."[8]

It had already become clear to the members of Teater Arena that only a
small urban minority was benefiting from whatever development took place
in Indonesia. In the countryside things were not improving. Arena therefore
was looking for a way to use theatre to alleviate the plight of the rural populace. PETA's theatre of liberation workshop model provided them with a
perfect tool.

As if by divine planning, upon Fred Wibowo's return from Manila an
invitation was waiting for him to conduct a workshop in a remote leper
colony. Here was the ideal opportunity to test the newly acquired method in
practice. So, in March 1980, Fred Wibowo, Father Rüdi Hoffmann, and three
other members of the group traveled to Lewoleba, located under the smoke
of the Illiape volcano on Lembata island, near Timor in the distant southeast
of the archipelago. They were scared and excited at the same time, affirms
Wibowo:

> We made some adjustments in the syllabus to accommodate the different con-
> ditions in Lewoleba, but we didn't prepare too strictly because we anticipated
> that the lepers would be restricted in their physical movements. Our basic
> workshop structure was the same as the PETA model: (1) integration with the
> community, group dynamics, and get-to-know you games; (2) basics of acting
> and drawing out of people's stories through structural analysis of the com-
> munity; (3) production of a collectively created original script.[9]

Fred and his group need not have worried. In six weeks' time, they created
an unprecedented level of confidence in the leper colony. The facilitators
worked with the patients for seven or eight hours per day. The evenings
were often taken up by storytelling, mask making, or music and song practice. The solidarity among the lepers grew with each rehearsal.

In the final two weeks of the workshop, the participants developed a play
called Yang Terbuang [The Outcast], which was based on their own experiences. The plan was to perform it before an audience composed of villagers
from the surrounding district. Until the last moment, some of the lepers
were afraid to act in public. "Even I was hesitant," said Wibowo, "but in
the end we decided to all plunge together."[10]

The cast and crew were astonished to see so many people gathered in front
of the leper hospital that had been designated as the performance space. Only
a few hand-painted signs had been posted around the market place the day
before. But in Lewoleba the market is held only once a week and peasants

and fishermen come to it from miles away to sell their products. The play was scheduled to start at night after the market had closed down. Many came out of curiosity. The petroleum lamps and torches used for lighting added a magical glow to the event.

Yang Terbuang draws on traditional songs and theatre forms, but the words of the songs were changed and the plot is based on the lepers' own story. The opening scene features the expressionistically rendered public lynching of an alleged witch at the hands of enraged villagers, who are all masked.[11] The witch leaves three children behind—Ola, Kopong, and Barek—who are subsequently chased from the community and rejected wherever they go until one day Ola finds a job as an office clerk. With his salary he is able to support his brother and sister, is promoted to supervisor, and becomes engaged to one of the girls in the office.

Then disaster strikes. He falls ill and the diagnosis is leprosy. Fearing contamination, his boss fires him. His uncle and aunt, in whose house he was living, kick him out, and his fiancée breaks off the engagement. He wanders around aimless and depressed, banished for the second time, until one day someone suggests he go to the leper colony in Lewoleba. But even there he is unable to come to terms with his disease until he finds a new friend in Boli, whose advanced leprosy has already cost him the loss of several fingers, but who nevertheless manages to play beautiful tunes on a traditional stringed instrument.

The simple tale of Ola, enhanced by many choral songs and performed with great integrity by the residents of the leper colony, did not fail to touch the large audience, many of whom had to wipe away tears at the play's end. After the performance, they all went up to the performers to shake their hands, completely forgetting these were the same lepers they used to avoid.

After Fred Wibowo's team departed from Lewoleba, the lepers spontaneously decided to form their own theatre company which they called Teater Padma [Flower Theatre]. They even took their play on tour around Lembata and other neighboring islands, gaining acceptance wherever they went. Often, spectators even invited the leper actors to share a meal with them at their homes.

Upon their return from the east, Teater Arena dedicated most of the next three years to the promotion of theatre of liberation through a series of workshops. From August through December 1980, the company conducted weekend workshops in the seaside resort of Parangtritis, twenty-seven kilometers south of Yogya. More than 150 youngsters participated in this extended course.

In addition to the normal workshop structure, the facilitators took the participants on exposure trips that helped them internalize the socioeconomic and political conditions of the town. The interaction resulted in three public performances of a collectively created play that dealt with issues like the detrimental effects of tourism and Western influence on local culture, inefficient police protection against crime, youth unemployment, and the control of the Parangtritis economy by a mafia of Chinese businessmen from Yogyakarta.

Stylistically, the play used a mixture of traditional drama, realism, and poetic expressionism. Fred Wibowo describes the show: "The group came up with a long poem about the problems of the community. It was accompanied by a movement composition using expressionistic masks. This was followed by a realistic slice of life based on the stories we had collected from the inhabitants. Finally, the traditional piece was derived from a local legend that related thematically to the Parangtritis social problems. We performed it in the authentic style, of course."[12] After the Parangatritis workshop, several participants joined Teater Arena. Others returned to their home towns and founded their own companies, some of which are still active today.

Most of 1981 was taken up by the consolidation of Arena's new orientation through in-house training sessions. By 1982, Arena was ready for its next big project: an eight-month workshop in the village of Tanen, near the Borobudur. Here, a pre-workshop investigation had revealed that Tanen's economy was in poor shape, that no help from the government was forthcoming, and that the village chief was incompetent, while many of Tanen's youth had migrated to the city.

The workshop facilitators this time brought along a Flexaflan, a flannel board with thin cardboard puppets and objects that could be moved around the surface to assist the villagers in analyzing the local situation by visualizing their stories. The people got very involved, heatedly arguing about placement and relationships of the various puppets to best represent the social structure in their community. In this way, many stories emerged that were later used as the basis for some locally developed theatre of liberation plays. The entire community was mobilized; at times, even residents from nearby villages attended some of the sessions.

Although the process took a long time, Fred Wibowo never despaired: "We knew it would work. We were very optimistic. The only real worry we had was that the village chief might stop us, but he didn't. When he saw how successful it was, he even asked us to come back and do it in other villages. Actually the showcase was very critical of him. It made him realize that he had made mistakes. Although the play was set in historical times, the people clearly recognized him. The name of the fictional village in which the play was set sounded more or less like Tanen."[13]

The Tanen workshop eventually resulted in two different theatre productions, one by a youth group and another by a company of twenty adults. Virtually the entire village was involved in scriptwriting, playing music, building the set, or other production-related activities.

The Tanen youth group reconstructed a traditional *wayang orang* play called *Ajisaka*. Accompanied by a full gamelan orchestra and wearing elaborate costumes, the village teenagers presented the story of a mythical king who liked to eat people. He is particularly interested in the head of a certain Ajisaka, a popular community leader. Ajisaka tells the king that he can have his head if he beats him in battle. However, if Ajisaka wins, the king must promise that he will never bother the people of the valley again. Not surprisingly, with the collective support of the people, Ajisaka beats the king.

For *Ajisaka,* Fred Wibowo, himself a master dancer, thoroughly trained the young performers in the intricacies of classical Javanese dance movements. In the process, they learned to appreciate the richness of their own traditions. In addition, they discovered how, with simple plot and character changes, the traditional theatre could be made relevant to their own times and how much fun they could have doing it.

The adult group from Tanen was similarly empowered. Using the style of *kethoprak,* a popular theatre form from Central Java,[14] and their own local dialect, the inhabitants created a play about an irresponsible *demang* or regent, a thinly veiled version of their own village chief. The daughter of the *demang* in the story is in love with the son of a poor farmer from one of the villages under the *demang's* jurisdiction. The father of the young man, meanwhile, visits the regent to request assistance: a drought has caused all the rice plants in the *sawahs* to go dry. But the *demang* can't be bothered; he is too preoccupied with his rebellious daughter. He tells the farmer to solve his own problems, and, in consultation with his wife, decides to forbid his daughter to marry the son of the poor farmer. But the girl resolves to remain true to her love and flees to the village of her fiancé.

A tragedy is in the making. In a quick succession of events, the regent's oldest son, in a bid to reclaim his sister, is repelled by the villagers. The regent thereupon assembles a task force to teach the rebels a lesson. Meanwhile, the villagers prepare for the confrontation and, in the same breath, discuss the possibility of forming an agricultural collective if they win the battle.

Finally, the *demang,* claiming he will not tolerate disturbance and dissension in his territory, attacks the community. The choreographed fight, portrayed with dance movements borrowed from traditional Javanese martial arts forms, is eventually stopped by a respected village elder who invites both parties to resolve the crisis in a debate that he offers to moderate. But, he insists, the *demang* must be willing to listen.[15]

In a striking illustration of the theatre of liberation's immediate effectiveness, the Tanen workshop showcase produced some very tangible results, Wibowo claims:

> They all got together to improve the community. Before, there was no electricity. The government had given them an old generator without the knowhow and the tools to install it. It had been gathering dust in a corner of the village chief's house for seven years. Through the collective experience of the play, however, the villagers had gained the confidence to express their needs.

So they asked some engineering students from a nearby university to help them fix the generator. They all helped to lay the cables, to build a little shack, etc. And now every home has electricity. Only twenty-five watts, mind you, but enough for light. They are now also working on an irrigation project for the rice fields. The process of making a play helped them discover their own hidden creative resources and taught them the power of collective action.

In the true spirit of theatre of liberation, the history of Teater Arena is largely contained in the birth and the development of other groups. In 1983, the company recorded ten radio dramas which had been adapted from Mario Kaplún's sociopolitical court cases that he developed for Latin American radio stations and in which the listeners were invited to act as jury. Two of these programs, both dealing with the repressive Indonesian educational system, were broadcast on a local Catholic radio station. The other eight were used in media groups around Yogya, with Arena actors facilitating the discussions.

Since 1983, Teater Arena has conducted many other theatre of liberation workshops. Early in 1984, the group was invited by Teater Padma to return to the leper colony and work with a new group of patients. The play that was created in this process bore the title *Jalan Masih Panjang* [The Road Is Still Long]. Again it is based on a true story.

This time, the play contains quite sophisticated satirical portraits of medical doctors and government health officials who continue to harbor prejudices against cured lepers although they are supposed to know that their condition is no longer contagious. The protagonist of the story is Igo, and *Jalan Masih Panjang* dramatizes his many encounters with prejudice in his attempts to reintegrate himself into society after he is cured. Unable to find a job, rejected by his own family, he finally addresses the audience directly in a song: "Why do you all run from me? This loneliness is deadly." [16]

Teater Padma's second play became even more successful than the first. Even the governor of the province heard about it and invited the company to the capital, Kupang, to perform it in a regular theatre house. After the show, in front of the entire audience the governor invited the lepers, some of them bandaged, to have dinner with him. This honor boosted the self-confidence of the leper actors enormously. It was only further consolidated when the same governor announced he would sponsor Padma's tour through the island of Timor in 1985.

Understandably, Teater Arena's theatre of liberation activities are conducted with a very low profile. Very few people in Yogyakarta know about it. In local theatre circles the company is best known for its competently produced annual shows that alternate contemporized Western classics like *Antigone* (1987) with increasingly political original plays. These new plays are usually created after intensive social investigation and during rehearsals in which the actors use some of the same processes that they apply in their theatre of liberation workshops. *Tumbal* [Victim, 1986] is typical of this process.

Tumbal attacks the government's development policies, which, it claims, are usually designed by city-bred technocrats with no knowledge of the realities of village life. "It is a very simple story," explains Fred Wibowo, who directed the play. "It is about a village youth wanting to get to the big city. But his girlfriend wants him to stay with her in the village. 'Why don't you try a few more possibilities here first?' she pleads. 'What possibilities?' he retorts. 'There are no opportunities left here.' As a favor to her, he also asks the old village physician for advice, but the doctor has to agree with him: 'I stay here because otherwise there would be no hope for the people here, but you are young. I think you should go.' "[17]

The boy leaves on foot. In order to get to the city he has to cross a dilapidated bridge that has been left in disrepair for lack of government funds. The youth falls into the gorge and is badly hurt. He is eventually found and the old doctor realizes the boy must be taken to the hospital in the nearest city if he is to survive. They are unable to call for an ambulance because the only telephone in the subdistrict is out of order, and there are only two cars in the community; one is broken down, the other has no lights. Since it is already late afternoon, they decide to postpone the trip until morning. The distance is not all that great but, due to the poor condition of the road, the bridge which has now been completely washed away, and a few other mishaps, the doctor and his young patient do not reach the hospital until the next evening.

Despite emergency surgery, the boy dies. Frustrated, the old physician realizes that, in fact, the youth has been killed by the system. He decides to file a lawsuit. Fred Wibowo reconstructed part of the preliminary court hearings of *Tumbal* as follows:

JUDGE: Who do you accuse?
DOCTOR: I don't know.
JUDGE: If there is no plaintiff, how can we have a court case?
DOCTOR: Let's start with the Minister of Development then . . .
MINISTER OF DEVELOPMENT: Hey, it's nothing to do with me. I agreed a long time
    ago to build new roads in that area. What can I do if the Ministry of Finance
    doesn't come up with the money?
FINANCE MINISTER: Money is not the problem. We give millions and millions for
    development projects. But your honor, we unfortunately do not decide where
    the money goes. That is the responsibility of the Bureau of Development Plan-
    ning.
DIRECTOR: Give me a break! I decided long ago to help this village. But my decisions
    need to be ratified by the national assembly. And as you know the parliament is
    chosen by the people.[18]

Teater Arena stops short of saying out loud that the DPR, the Indonesian caricature of a parliament, is handpicked by the President and his junta. In a politically cautious finale, the play accuses the elusive system of development instead. A civil engineer, called in as a witness, takes the doctor to the court-room windows and points to the city below: "All these high buildings and cars prevent us from seeing the village. We have roads, health care, and food in the city. You have nothing. You are the only doctor for 10,000 people; in the city we have three doctors for 5,000 people. No, the city is to blame, my friend."

Teater Arena handled the complex scene changes of *Tumbal* by performing on two levels. The play opens with the trial on the ground level, with the audience cast in the role of public observers. The story of the boy and his ill-fated trip is acted out in the form of flashbacks on an elevated platform, using mime for the travel sequences. *Tumbal* was performed seven times for a total of more than 5,000 spectators.

The Parliament of the Streets

Fred Wibowo envisions the future establishment of a national theatre of lib-eration movement in Indonesia, although it will perforce be less aggressive than the network that exists in the neighboring Philippines: "People there can speak more openly. Over here their consciousness has not been raised that much yet. In the Philippines, the theatre has really become the parlia-ment of the streets because the official parliament refuses to defend the peo-ple's interests. We would like to promote theatre in a similar vein, to help increase the people's self-reliance."

The Indonesian theatre of liberation movement is already beginning to take shape. In June 1987, some fifty social workers from all over Indonesia at-tended a two-week theatre of liberation workshop organized by Arena in the community of Baron Beach, sixty-five kilometers south of Yogya. The par-ticipants were meticulously taken through the theatre of liberation process, then returned to their communities where they set up local theatre groups of their own. In October of that same year, they joined many other cultural workers from elsewhere in the country in a national symposium held in Jak-arta at which they planned a joint strategy for the future.

Since 1987, theatre of liberation workshops have been implemented with greater frequency than before, also in the outlying islands. But there are some obstacles, says Father Rüdi Hoffmann: "The situation here is very dangerous and that is why we have to be pragmatic. The bishops are also quite con-servative and have already created difficulties for us. If necessary, we are prepared to take risks. We are not scared, but we prefer to operate cau-tiously. What's the point if the authorities stop us?"[19]

An even greater obstacle to Arena's effectiveness is, possibly, its financial and organizational link with the Catholic Church, which virtually blocks the company's access to Indonesia's overwhelming Muslim majority. That group

of Indonesians, which constitutes almost 90 percent of the country's population, forms the target of Yogya's other theatre of liberation company, Teater
Dinasti, led by the popular Muslim poet Emha Ainun Nadjib.

My visit to Yogyakarta had been announced to Emha by a mutually trusted
actress-friend from Manila who had conducted a theatre workshop in Yogya
a few weeks before my arrival. By the time we met, the poet had heard
enough about me to share many revealing insights about Indonesian culture,
politics, corruption, Islam, political theatre, and, what was perhaps most interesting to me personally, how Indonesians view the colonial past and the
Dutch. Our numerous conversations took place over a period of more than
a week; sometimes in Emha's home, a small dwelling with a black façade
and a giant red mask next to the front entrance; sometimes after midnight in
one of the many *warungs,* the typical Javanese portable snack bars spread out
on the city's sidewalks and lit with oil lamps.

Emha was born in 1952 in the village of Jumbal, East Java. His father was
a relatively well-to-do farmer and teacher. From an early age, Emha (or M.H.,
which stands for Mohammed) was known for his rebellious spirit. He had a
fist fight with his grade school teacher, for example, and at age fifteen he
was kicked out of the *pesantren,* a type of Islamic boarding school which can
be found throughout the country. He had written slogans on the blackboard,
ridiculing the school's excessive discipline. His parents had already found out
long ago that getting mad at their funny son was absolutely useless. The first
and last time they punished Emha—when he was seven—he ran away, jumped
on a train without knowing its destination, and returned only three agonizing
weeks later. On the insistence of his mother the boy eventually finished high
school in Yogyakarta. He even studied economics for a semester at Yogya's
prestigious Gajah Mada University but had to stop for financial reasons when
his father died. Afterwards, he began making a living by writing essays and
poems for local magazines and newspapers. He soon developed a reputation
as Yogya's most talented young poet. Important literary awards followed,
together with invitations to read his poetry in the capital of Jakarta and other
big cities. His fame even spread across the border: in 1984–85 he spent six
months at the Iowa International Writers Program and appeared at poetry
festivals in Rotterdam and West Berlin.

Emha enjoyed reminiscing about how he once roamed an entire night
through the streets of Amsterdam in the freezing January cold; he had lost
his keys and did not want to wake up his Dutch hosts. He chased away a
would-be mugger by coolly swallowing a razor blade, a trick he had learned
from a Javanese magician. "In Holland I had a hard time suppressing the
inclination not to pay for public buses and trains. Historically speaking I
didn't see why I should. Besides, the organizers of my tour never paid me
the full allowance for January that they had promised me."[20] Only once did
he really get mad: when the clerk at Utrecht's police headquarters refused to
extend his visa for an extra seven days. "What?" Emha yelled, "you damned

Poet/playwright Emha Ainum Nadjib, artistic director of Teater Dinasti, Yogyakarta, reciting his poetry in Malang, Java.

Dutch stayed three hundred and fifty years in my country without ever asking anyone's permission! And I fill out a form and everything in order to give one more lecture in your lousy little country and you dare to refuse my request?"

Emha is convinced that most Indonesians don't feel too bitter toward the Dutch. One night he took me on his old blue Vespa scooter to a whole bunch of bars and food places to verify this hypothesis. A corn vendor of about fifty had not found the Dutch all that bad: "They built good roads and nice-looking hotels like that one over there," he said, pointing to a stately building across the street. "Better than the Japs, at least," opined a *becah* driver.[21] Strange how four years of Japanese fascism and forced labor camps were able to virtually blot out three and a half centuries of blatant Dutch oppression and exploitation.

"The greatest crime the Dutch colonizers committed was to leave us with an immense cultural inferiority complex," explains Emha. "We still look up to foreigners. We have a chronic lack of creativity. People here are incapable of thinking in an original manner or of organizing themselves properly. The main cause for that is the postcolonial trauma from which Indonesia is still suffering today." Not surprisingly, he sees cultural action for social change as the key to a successful opposition to the present dictatorial régime of General Suharto. For more than ten years now Emha has been placing his art at

the service of the people, taking huge risks in the process. Why did he abandon a glorious and potentially profitable literary career for a quixotic battle
against a thoroughly corrupt system protected by ruthless soldiers? "It really
started back in 1980 when I spent two months in the Philippines and saw
many extremely talented artists working with the people, creating the most
amazing things together. After my return form Manila, I went to visit my
village and I suddenly realized that my award-winning poems didn't mean a
thing there. I, Emha, the celebrated poet, belonged to the élite. Since that
time, I write in the people's own language, about the humor, the persever-
ance, and the suffering of the peasants, the factory workers, and the sugar
cane workers."

It is difficult for us Westerners to grasp how popular Emha's poetry read-
ings are. In 1983, he started presenting poetry and music shows together
with a group of musicians belonging to Teater Dinasti, a progressive theatre
company for which Emha has been writing since 1979. It is not uncommon
to have five or six thousand spectators come to these shows. I could not
believe it. "Well, if you don't, why don't you come along to Malang this
Saturday?" challenged the poet.

It is eight gruelling hours by bus from Yogya to Malang, a city of half a
million inhabitants located in East Java. The poetry reading was organized
by the student council of Malang's Brawijaya State University, and the secretary of this organization had come all the way to Yogya to pick us up in a
specially chartered van. By Indonesian standards it seems to have been a
comfortable trip, but I was a broken man when I stepped out of the vehicle
at five in the morning, my brain in a severe state of concussion from the
potholes in the road and the hundred and thirty-nine near-misses with oncoming trucks and water buffaloes.

At seven-thirty the calls to prayer started coming from the loudspeakers
on the minaret. At a quarter of eight, Utung, the student council secretary,
Emha, Michael Bodden (an actor and literature scholar from Wisconsin who
proved to be an invaluable interpreter), and I walked to the mosque, protected from the steady rain by a huge umbrella. Unable to find a seat in the
giant mosque, people were spilling into the streets. Hundreds of fans came
running toward us, holding up copies of Emha's poetry collections for au-
tographs. It took us more than twenty minutes to work our way through
the crowd. Suddenly it dawned on me why the military had never dared
harass the poet. His arrest would surely have resulted in a mass revolt among
Indonesia's 140 million Muslims. Emha has a profound knowledge of the
Koran and usually illustrates his radical political ideas with lyrical religious
images. His strategy can best be compared to an Islamic variety of liberation
theology. He is fond of quoting stories with themes of social justice from the
Islamic Holy Book.

After a brief prayer, the poet begins to speak. I am told that he always
does his speeches off the top of his head. They are captivating and full of

humor. "A liberating view of Islam doesn't always look at the devotions, the fasting, or the moralistic regulations of what we should and shouldn't do to be a good Muslim. Seeing to it that the poor have enough to eat is far more important than praying five times a day in the direction of Mecca: we have to liberate Islam from within so that the fat *kyai* not only preaches that we shouldn't steal but actually goes out of the mosque himself and works to create the conditions necessary for people not to steal."[22]

Then the poems start in which Emha reveals himself to be a brilliant actor who is able to recreate the voices of peasants and street vendors who talk, in colorful Javanese vernacular mixed with Bahasa Indonesia, about the realities of trying to survive in city and countryside. The poet explains about the structural causes of the injustice: "Suharto's idea of development is to improve agricultural production but not the conditions of the peasants. Each day, more and more of them lose their land. If you go to Sulawesi, for instance, you will discover that Minister X and General Y from Jakarta own all the plantations. The government only sees figures and statistics and turns an increasing number of peasants into underpaid agricultural laborers. Also the big cities are sucking all the lifeblood from the villages. And if the government takes the trouble of building a road to a village, I can guarantee you that they do it to take stuff from the village instead of bringing things to it to improve conditions. Many small farmers are therefore forced to sell their little plots of land and go to the cities."

There are many other problems in Indonesia's countryside; the forced cultivation of lucrative cash crops (lucrative for plantation owners and government-run cooperatives, that is); the widespread use of dumped pesticides and fertilizers that have long been banned in the West; and the forced so-called *transmigrasi*, a socially and economically dubious project to relieve Java's overpopulation by subsidizing the migration of millions of Javanese to Sulawesi (former Celebes), Kalimantang (former Borneo), and the disputed territories of Irian Jaya (West Papua New Guinea) and East Timor. The indigenous populations of these islands often find themselves kicked off their land to accommodate Javanese settlers. Millions of rupiahs designated for transmigration purposes have simply disappeared in the bottomless pockets of government officials.

The excesses of Indonesian society seem to originate in the thoroughly corrupt economic system, which appears to be controlled by Chinese businessmen in league with high-ranking military officers. "There is no democracy in this country," Emha points out. "There are three legal political parties: Suharto's Golkar, the PPP [United Muslim Development Party], and the PDI [Indonesian Democratic Party]. There is virtually no difference between the three, however, since they all adhere to the official *Pancasila* state ideology [Faith in One God; Humanism; Nationalism; Representative Government; Social Justice], which sounds nicer on paper than it is in practice." For Emha there is no doubt that the present system must be dismantled. But what to replace it with? Socialism? An Islamic system? "We haven't decided on a specific alternative yet and, at the same time, I do not want to get involved in an ideological debate," says the poet. "The essential thing is that, no matter what system is decided on, the people themselves must think about it and negotiate it."

Teater Dinasti

Most of Emha's plays are produced by Teater Dinasti. The company started in the mid seventies when Fajar Suharno, a playwright, and several actors decided to leave Rendra's Bengkel Teater and continue on their own. From the beginning, the new group had a clearly sociopolitical orientation, which was emphasized by the recruitment of several street kids from the rough Kampong Tipo neighborhood on the outskirts of Yogyakarta. Some of the actors who now form the core of Teater Dinasti used to make a living as pimps, pickpockets, and drug dealers. One new recruit was even a grave-robber. Today, the company still maintains a clearly proletarian profile and its members survive from odd jobs as parking attendants and night guards. Only two or three actors come from the student ranks.

By taking the street kids into their company as apprentice actors, Teater Dinasti encouraged them to acquire new values and to contribute something to society rather than to blindly abuse themselves and others. But this social healing process was not without problems, as Emha, who gradually became involved in Dinasti at the end of the seventies, recalls: "Some of them have been in jail. Others used to gang-rape deranged street women. And even after they joined us, sometimes, when we traveled to a performance by train, they would find a woman and rape her in the toilet. So for a long time their behavior remained problematic. They continued to pee in the wrong places, in full view of hundreds of veiled women, for instance. Total lack of respect for the community they were supposed to perform alternative theatre for."

For most of the seventies and early eighties, Teater Dinasti remained largely performance oriented. In 1980, Emha and Simon Hate, another gifted poet, participated in the same international PETA workshop in Manila that Fred Wibowo attended. Unlike Wibowo, who immediately went out to apply the methodology at the grassroots, Emha and Simon Hate first thoroughly tried it out with the other Dinasti actors. Meanwhile, they continued establishing a name for themselves as a group of competent and entertaining performers that defied the censors with increasingly critical original plays directed against Indonesia's authoritarian structure.

Dinasti Mataram [The Mataram Dynasty, 1977], the company's first play, written by Fajar Suharno, was a historical piece set in sixteenth-century Yogyakarta, then the seat of the fascist Mataram kingdom. Emha explains that the roots of Indonesia's modern problems can be traced back to the Mataram period:

> I always call Suharto the second Mataram, because his order is similar: the approach to ethnic minorities, legitimizing Javanese superiority through religion. The playwright, Suharno, comes from Manirang, the area with the strongest opposition to the Mataram kingdom. Our play is about the defeat of its powerful leader who is lured into a trap when he falls in love with the king's daughter without realizing who she is. Overcome by his feelings, he is forced to visit the king, which he had always refused to do before. As soon as he folds his hands and bows in submission, the king stabs him in the nape of the neck.

Although *Dinasti Mataram* used *kethoprak* movements and costumes and gamelan instruments, its dramaturgy was distinctly modern, with dialogue in Bahasa Indonesia. In subsequent plays like *Jendral Mas Galak* [General Geluk, 1978], a historical piece about the reign of terror of Dutch General Geluk during colonial times, and *Palagan Palagan* [Field of War, 1979], the company gradually moved away from traditional Javanese theatre forms. Thematically, Teater Dinasti has worked its way through Indonesian history. After dealing with the Javanese kingdoms and the Dutch occupation, the company tackled the struggle for independence. More recently, it has begun to criticize Suharto's new order in plays like *Patung Kekasih* [Lover's Statue, 1983] and *Mas Dukun* [Mr. Witch Doctor, 1987], both written by Emha Ainun Nadjib.

Designed to expose the régime's shady dealings with multinational corporations and local Chinese businessmen, and speaking largely in symbolic terms to elude the censors, *Patung Kekasih* features the story of an old sculptor and his young apprentice. The aging artist makes beautiful images which he sells to international art dealers. But in the end his rebellious apprentice creates a fantastic new statue, surpasses his teacher, and becomes the new master sculptor. Yet instead of becoming more liberal and innovative he becomes even more conservative and cruel than his predecessor. "It was a way of symbolically commenting on the fact that many so-called heroes of the generation of 1966 who overthrew Sukarno were more fascist than the generation of 1945," comments Emha.

While *Patung Kekasih*'s political metaphors successfully eluded the censor's scrutiny, Emha knew that his next play, *Mas Dukun,* would have almost certainly been banned by the government censors had it not been selected, sight unseen, by the Yogyakarta Annual Theatre Festival Committee. Only Festival entries, performances on university campuses (which fall under the jurisdication of the university chancellor), and cultural events scheduled inside Islamic facilities are exempt from censorship. Over the past few years, Teater Dinasti has increasingly been refused permission to perform in public.

Theatre companies routinely have to submit their scripts to a special officer at the culture and education bureau of the regional military headquarters.

Two members of Teater Dynasti rehearse a scene from *Mas Dukun*.

Then they have to go to the police, both locally and on the district level. In addition, all performers need to show a letter that proves they were not involved in the coup of 1965, even if they were born after that date. In all, theatre companies have to pass through nine government stations before they receive or are denied permission to perform. Indonesian censors object particularly to obscene words, erotic scenes, demands for social and political justice, and references to President Suharto and members of his government. Not known for their aesthetic acumen, they habitually lift words and even complete verse lines from poems submitted for public readings, thus rendering them unintelligible.[23] Many groups therefore work with double scripts—a purified one for the censors and an alternative one for the real performance. Others simply improvise on the spot, depending on whether or not they have detected military informers in the audience, for directors are often interrogated after shows as well. Thus, in 1986, a student group from Gadjah Mada University had their production of Gogol's *Inspector General* banned. Even exhibitions of children's paintings are not safe, complains one artist: "They eliminate stuff without any apparent reason. Sometimes censors just do it to impress their superiors." *Mas Dukun,* which contained an overt satire of obligatory government indoctrination sessions, was not quite so innocent.

　　Mas Dukun was written in two weeks after several improvisational sessions. It does not have a straightforward linear plot in the Western sense. Borrowing from the comic *dagelan mataram* acting style, the play is basically a collage of eleven self-contained scenes.[24] "But it does have a story line of sorts," points out Michael Bodden, who also acted in the show. "The play tries to critique a society that is out of balance, using a *dukun,* a kind of Javanese witch doctor, as a vehicle to suggest certain solutions."[25]

By the vague glimmer of an oil lamp and the incessant rhythm of the midnight rain, during a late-night munching session in a *warung,* Emha explained what *dukuns* meant to him: "Java is full of magic," he explains. "Would you believe that Suharto himself has sixty-nine *dukuns* in his entourage? Central Java is the hub of *dukun* power. The country's three most powerful *dukuns* live in Yogyakarta, Solo, and Klaten. Their political influence should not be underestimated either. It goes all the way back to the Mataram kingdoms of the sixteenth century when kings derived their power from spectacular spiritual revelations."

Some of Emha's personal experiences prove that *dukun* magic is no joke. Realizing the political implications of *dukun* power, he once tried to influence one. "I was still a student and curious to know how *dukuns* operated," recalls Emha. "The first time I went, I was completely honest and open, because they surely would have sensed it if I had had ulterior motives. But the second time, a radical student accompanied me. Rather unsubtly, he immediately began to indoctrinate the *dukun.* Big mistake. He blew up. We were lucky he only abused us verbally."

A *dukun* can heal people. As a kind of clairvoyant, he can find lost objects and people. But as a voodoo priest, he can also place curses on enemies, kill people with magic from far away, or make them deaf and dumb. But the *dukun* in Emha's play is quite down to earth. He prescribes a taste of their own medicine to the representatives of the various sectors of Indonesian society that come to solicit his help. With humor and Freirian insight, he tells the patients not to rely on his magic but to use their own vast creative resources to improve their predicament.

In the play's final scene, the *dukun* announces his departure from the community, to which his shocked assistant responds: "But master, don't you want to heal the world anymore?" Undisturbed, the *dukun* tells him: "You kiddin'? Healing the world is everyone's job and I don't want to deprive other people of their work. There is already enough unemployment as it is. I am not a prophet or a holy man; I only ridicule people and by doing that I tempt them into looking at themselves and the conditions that surround them."[26]

At this point, the orchestra breaks into a song that is constantly interrupted by former *dukun* patients who come rushing in to tell him they are cured. First in line is a young female student who had dropped out of college to the great despair of her father, who had pinned all his hopes on her. One of her professors had been sexually harassing her, but he had apologized and now she was willing to go back to school. Her father is next. He had been complaining about his uncontrollable offspring who refuse to embark on profitable and respectable careers despite their obvious talent and intelligence. Unbeknownst to the father, however, the children have applied for a subsidy from a non-government funding agency to study the influence of *dukuns* on Indonesian society. They surprise both the *dukun* and their father as they come in to break the good news: "Wow, 75,000 rupiahs a month!" exclaims the *dukun*. "How much are you going to set aside for me?"

In the end, the only person not allowed to celebrate in the *dukun*'s going-away party is the father's nephew, a high-ranking bureaucrat who learns that he must face serious charges of corruption related to his alleged misappropriation of development funds. He was also the authoritarian teacher of the obligatory indoctrination session in an earlier scene. These lessons in the official *Pancasila* state ideology are compulsory for all employees in offices, universities, and other government institutions. This indoctrination scene was presented in an almost surreal manner, with adults dressed in shorts and red socks and acting like children. All have to repeat the principles of *Pancasila* in a loud voice. One of the "pupils" protests: "But how on earth can you say rich and poor are the same?" He is immediately scolded by the other "pupils" who turn to him and shout: "Communist! Subject him to special training, Sir!"[27]

Encouraging a Grassroots Theatre

Mas Dukun, which was performed in street clothes on a bare stage with minimal lighting (light bulbs fitted in empty tin cans), contained many jibes at the political establishment and the bourgeois intelligentsia, most of whom Emha regards as puppets of the régime. Citing the dangers of harassment and the small audiences that regularly attend the theatre performance as main factors, Emha and Dinasti harbor few illusions about the effectiveness of their performances. They now seek to expand the impact of their activities through theatre of liberation workshops.

Simon Hate had already reached that conclusion at the end of 1984. Following a near-fatal ideological split in Teater Dinasti in 1985, he left the company to dedicate himself fully to theatre of liberation in the grassroots:

> The middle class spectators at urban performances nod in agreement but refrain from doing anything. Even agitprop doesn't work in the long run. It is like an aspirin; it numbs the pain but it doesn't remove the disease. With Teater Dinasti we also sometimes conducted workshops in the communities, but we came as artists, as superiors in a sense. I've changed my attitude. I now go as a friend. The villagers accept us now more easily. They know we come from the city, but we joke with them, we eat with them, we sleep where they sleep. They realize we are university-educated, but we show them we can live like them, and they, in turn, feel we make their lives less boring.[28]

In 1985 and 1986, Simon Hate and several associates targeted twelve communities in central Java that they hoped would form the nucleus of an emerging grassroots theatre of liberation network. They were sponsored by a nongovernment funding agency for rural development. Hate and his team used the same strategy and methodology as Teater Arena, but instead of a Flexaflan they gave the participants simple "instamatic" cameras loaded with slide film. After the integration period, the villagers were instructed to photograph the things they considered to be the most important landmarks of their community. The public slide show that followed produced a flow of stories that were later used as the basis for scenarios.

When I met him at the end of 1987, Simon Hate was no longer working with the embryo central Javanese theatre of liberation network. After a dispute with the coordinator over the pace of the project—Hate felt they were rushing things—he joined another non-government organization and was based for four months in the village of Pedan, forty kilometers north of Yogyakarta. He was in the process of organizing a children's theatre group and, through nonhierarchical group dynamics exercises, teaching landless peasants how collective planting and harvesting was much more efficient than their previous individual efforts:

> We are working much more slowly now. You must understand that, unlike Fred Wibowo, we have no institution to protect us. So whenever the stories generated by the workshop become too radical we either stop for the time being or proceed very, very cautiously. We don't want them to label us as troublemakers. Besides, at the current pace we learn a lot more about how the peasants really think. Here in Indonesia less than twenty percent owns more than eighty percent of the tillable land. More than one third of the rural population has no land at all. Through theatre arts we introduce group working skills and efficient ways of organizing the community.[29]

Simon Hate is optimistic. An increasing number of officially tolerated nongovernment organizations (NGOs) are starting to see the potential of theatre of liberation workshop methods. The great problem, as he perceives it, is the chronic lack of qualified facilitators, something which he hopes to remedy through the foundation of a professional theatre of liberation institute, modeled after PETA in Manila. Simon Hate brushes away accusations by the likes of Emha Ainun Nadjib that NGOs have compromised with the government and that some of his colleagues have used funds to enrich themselves. In *Mas Dukun,* Teater Dinasti savagely satirized some of these "NGO project brokers," who have become specialists in designing attractive grassroots development projects with which they hope to secure their own salaries rather than help the poor.

If it decides to dedicate itself full time to the development of theatre of liberation, Teater Dinasti may well have the best chances of success, considering the enormous respect Emha enjoys in Indonesia's powerful Islamic community.[30] Aware of their potential, Emha is planning a whole series of workshops in *pesantren,* the typical Indonesian Islamic boarding schools that he himself attended and that provide the bulk of the country's secondary education. Emha argues that "Islam must be liberated from within" and that "anyone trying to do theatre of liberation in Indonesia by ignoring the Islamic institutions is doomed to failure." If he had his way, Emha would eventually like to see Indonesia's mosques converted into full-fledged cultural centers.

Emha's other big project for 1988 was an alternative *wayang* show he intended to present with Teater Dinasti in rural towns and villages of central Java. His reinterpretation of the *wayang* was based on an alternative analysis of the power structure in the *Mahabharata* and the *Ramayana.* In the hierarchy of these originally Indian epics, which provide the basic scenarios for all *wayang* plays, the *Dewa,* or divine authority, stands on top, followed by the *Priyayi,* the kings and bureaucrats. The *Priyayi* in turn control the army. Apart from an occasional servant, the lower classes have no role to speak of in traditional *wayang.* But, basing his convincing theory on the language modes used in *wayang,* Emha argues that the powerful clown Semar is really the representative of the people: "As you know, there are three different modes of expressing respect in Javanese. The common people have to speak *Kromo Inggil* to all those above them in the hierarchy. Kings, however, always speak *Ngoko* to their subjects but they must use *Kromo Inggil* when addressing the *Dewa.* Now, the curious thing is that Semar the clown speaks *Ngoko* to the *Dewa* and the *Priyayi* whereas they speak in *Kromo Inggil* to him!" In other words, he is treated with respect by the royalty as well as by the gods. Teater Dinasti's *wayang* therefore capitalizes on popular figures like Semar.

Bima, although technically a member of the *priyayi,* is another key figure in this emancipated *wayang.* "He is an arch rebel," explains Emha. "He defiantly speaks *Ngoko* to Krishna and Dova and he refuses to sit down or bow in the presence of gods or kings. And Bima also has two very strong and anarchic sons who are never permitted to fight in the *Mahabharata* wars because they would defeat everyone. In our *wayang,* Bima and his sons challenge the *Dewa* for the right to participate in the war. Semar the clown follows their example and wants to join in too. That's crucial because he embodies the aspirations of the common people. In traditional *wayang* he is always portrayed as a wimp. My Semar will be aggressive and progressive. Believe me, the only way to wake up the Javanese is through *wayang.* It's useless to try and get to them with lectures and intellectual ideas. You have to hit them in the guts because that's where Semar lives."

With 13,000 islands and approximately 160 million inhabitants, Indonesia presents its concerned theatre artists with a formidable task. Recent crackdowns on dissidents in nearby Singapore and Malaysia, which have landed several theatre of liberation workers in prison, are an ominous reminder of the dangers involved in this most committed form of theatre practice. Suharto's régime remains as unpredictable as ever. After first executing a former union leader in December 1989, it released dissident politician Hartono Rekso Dharsono in September 1990. Other reports indicate that a modest democratic movement is gaining some momentum.

On the theatre front, Teater Dinasti and Simon Hate seem to have reconciled some of their differences. They recently conducted a number of workshops together and Dinasti reportedly also collaborated with other groups from Yogyakarta in some joint performances that apparently attracted more than 5,000 spectators. Meanwhile, other theatre of liberation groups are becoming more active as well. Gapit, a Javanese language group based in Solo (Surakarta), is performing plays about the political aspects of daily life in villages. And Gusti Putu Alit Aryani, an award-winning Balinese dancer studying in Solo, has initiated a theatre of liberation workshop process with women from all walks of life after returning home from Europe, where she participated in the *Cry of Asia!* caravan.

IX

THEATRE OF LIBERATION
EXPERIMENTS IN THAILAND

Thailand is one of the few Asian countries that was never colonized. On the surface, this important fact would seem to set it apart from the others discussed in this book. Undoubtedly this land of palm-lined beaches, lush tropical forests, air-conditioned bargain malls, smiling people, and golden triangles of all sorts is considerably more peaceful and prosperous than, say, the Philippines or India. But the absence of a Western-instigated colonial history does not mean that the country has been free of European and American cultural and economic influences nor indeed of violent political repression. During the Vietnam War, Bangkok became the favorite place for U.S. military personnel to momentarily escape from the horrors of the battlefield. Fast food, movies, discos, and other Americana soon followed. When the American soldiers left in the mid seventies, the city's sex industry had to look elsewhere for customers and began tapping the European market. Soon, mainstream tourism also began to take off to attract wealthier Westerners yearning for a touch of the orient with Costa del Sol luxury. To them, having to stand during the national anthem, then sit through a brief documentary on the king's good works before getting to see *Robocop* in an air-conditioned Thai cinema is nothing but a charming touch of *couleur locale*. To the locals it is considerably more.

Touching scenes of a benevolent king helping peasants to dig a hole for a new well donated by the government fit perfectly with the fairytale image Thailand likes to portray in its glossy tourist brochures. But the four million foreigners who visit the country annually do not know that the king was actually born in Cambridge, Massachusetts, raised in Switzerland, and holds a Swiss passport and an ample Swiss bank account. They do not know that thousands of Thai women and children from ages six to sixteen are forced to work as prostitutes in the capital to avoid starvation in the countryside; that three million children suffer from malnutrition; that 200,000 children are addicted to narcotics; and that there is widespread use of child labor, allegedly involving eleven million children. They do not know that illiteracy rates continue to be high and that the per capita annual income is $900. Nor do they know that more than one million Bangkok residents live in slums and that all major thoroughfares of Bangkok are routinely closed off to traffic whenever the king or a member of his family pass. On these occasions, vendors are unceremoniously kicked off the pedestrian bridges over the royal itinerary because no mortal is, after all, allowed to stand higher than the semidivine king. Not surprisingly, lese majesty—defamation of the royal family—is considered the most heinous criminal act in Thailand and theoretically punishable by execution.[1]

Feudal mentality is still deeply entrenched in this staunchly Buddhist country. As the February 1991 coup demonstrates, the political power remains firmly in the hands of the king and a few hand-picked military generals disguised as civilian ministers. They share the control of the rapidly growing economy with a handful of wealthy businessmen. The Communist guerrillas, who were very active in the Thai countryside during the seventies, are no longer a factor to speak of. As a result, in the course of the eighties Thailand's rulers have gradually allowed the space of civic liberty to grow, although the country still does not have an elected prime minister. In the midst of these slow but encouraging developments of which the middle and upper middle classes are the chief beneficiaries, a small but increasingly critical homegrown modern theatre movement is beginning to assert itself.

A Concise History of Modern Theatre in Thailand

Modern, Western-oriented theatre was introduced to Thailand by American-educated teachers of the English departments at Chulalongkorn and Thammasart universities in Bangkok. They directed student productions of plays by O'Neill, Tennessee Williams, and Arthur Miller, and catered predominantly to a small academic élite and a few middle class outsiders. Later on in the sixties, two full-fledged drama departments split off from these English departments and began training students for employment in the country's emerging television and film industry. For several years, Beckett, Ionesco, and Brecht figured prominently in their repertoires. Only a few original Thai plays were ever produced. Apparently, survival of the recently published *Chant Ti Jedh* [Seventh Floor], written by Suchart Sawadsri in 1971, is due to some mild satirical portraits of a politician and a Buddhist priest and a poor imitation of a Beckettian absurdist stalemate ending ("The lift doors are open but no one moves").[2] Otherwise, it is a mediocre play at best.

Despite its obvious immaturity, *Chant Ti Jedh* contained some daring overt references to American soldiers massacring hundreds of thousands of innocent peasants in neighboring Vietnam, reflecting the growing politicization of Thai intellectuals in the early seventies. Following a successful coup in November 1971, Marshall Thanom Kittikachorn had placed the country under military control. But, encouraged by news of student movements in the

West and elsewhere in Asia, Thai students began to protest. On 6 October 1973, thirteen of them were arrested for publicly exposing the dictatorial nature of the Thanom régime. Outraged students and workers staged a mass rebellion involving close to one million people. After several days of protest they succeeded in ousting Thanom and his cronies, who fled the country. A three-year period of liberalization ensued in which a new political theatre movement came to fruition under the generic name of Art for Life's Sake Theatre.[3]

The chief instigator of this political theatre initiative was Kamron Kunadilok. While studying psychology at Thammasart University he had become involved in the writers' collective Pharajan Siew [Crescent Moon] to which Suchart Sawadsri had also belonged.[4] Kunadilok received his first theatre training from an American university teacher who cast him as Biff in *Death of a Salesman*. Upon graduating in 1970, Kunadilok went north to set up an experimental school in a tribal community. This first-hand exposure to the tribes' daily struggle for survival proved to be an eye-opener: "I was shocked to see all their problems. It started me thinking, but before I could do anything, the anti-Communist brigades kicked me out, accusing me of subversive activities."[5]

After leaving the tribal area, Kamron Kunadilok was hired to teach a course on mass communication at Chieng Mai University. During the next four years, he developed a series of plays based on true stories recorded by his students in nearby peasant communities. The first play in the sequence dealt with the problems of an illiterate rice farmer who is blatantly robbed of his land by a Chinese loan shark when he is unable to pay the exorbitant interest of 100 percent. "We first performed it at university," recalls the director. "People were very impressed. Then we went to the villages. We entered with a big torch in front. Then we sat down in the round. We had a narrator to provide the transition between scenes. Whenever an actor needed to get 'on' he or she simply stepped into the circle."[6]

Encouraged by the positive reactions of the villagers, Kamron Kunadilok's group subsequently performed the play in many other rural communities in the north. In 1973, they created a sequel highlighting the effects of the Green Revolution and consumerism on the village. It featured another small farmer who became even more dependent on borrowed capital, this time to finance imported fertilizers, a cassette player, and a motor bike for his son.

After working in the Chieng Mai area for two years, Kamron Kunadilok got word of the looming unrest in Bangkok and he and his group decided to travel to the capital to perform at Thammasart and Chulalongkorn universities. Their shows caused a sensation. Kamron Kunadilok: "The students were amazed. They had never seen anything like it before. It was so radical. So new. Many of the activists wanted to follow our example and form their own theatre groups and asked us to teach them our methods."[7]

The ensuing years saw a proliferation of newly formed student theatre collectives performing at strikes and rallies. According to Rassami Phao Luangthong, a Yale School of Drama graduate, their plays were never longer than an hour. "They often were realistic reenactments of things that had happened in factories or political events taken from the news. And of course there was a considerable influence from Chinese socialist realism."[8]

Kamron Kunadilok and his twelve young actors and actresses returned to perform in the countryside, collecting money after shows in the towns and eating and sleeping with the farmers. At the height of their popularity they did an average of forty-eight performances per month. Upon their return from Bangkok, they decided to develop a new play about the link between industrial and agricultural workers. Kunadilok: "We now wanted to make a kind of theatre with which we could educate the farmers." After defaulting on his loan and losing his land, the small farmer of the previous play in the series has no choice but to migrate with his family to the city and take an underpaid job in a factory. After a while, he and his fellow workers decide to protest against the unbearable working conditions. They form a union and go on strike. But the strike is broken by the factory's security guards. The farmer quits his job and returns to his village. Wiser from his experiences in the city, he starts organizing the farmers back home.

By 1974 the reputation of Kamron Kunadilok's theatre commune had spread from the villages to university circles. In 1975, the group was asked to conduct a national workshop for student theatre groups that wanted to do similar work. Following the workshop, several new groups were formed that committed themselves to participating in a progressive cultural front. As further confirmation of their reputation, the Goethe Institute of Bangkok, the West German cultural center, invited Kunadilok's group to collaborate with Brecht director Norbert Maier on a fourth village play. Kunadilok: "Maier had worked in other Asian countries before and was very impressed with our improvisational skills. To us that was hardly surprising. We had been working for three years full time with different village audiences. Once they had told us their problems we could improvise on the spot."[9]

Kunadilok and his group moved back to Bangkok in 1976. After neighboring countries like Laos, Cambodia and Vietnam turned Communist, right-wing forces in Thailand began to reassert their power. So-called civil home defense forces were installed in the villages and many progressive leaders were abducted. Kunadilok:

> We noticed the deterioration of the student movement. There were slander campaigns against it. So we decided to try and regain the urban middle class with a new play entitled *Before the Dawn*. We performed it at the National Theatre. It was a full-length play about life in the slums. The mother is a street vendor, the father a low-ranking policeman. Their oldest son is a mercenary fighting the Communists in Laos. He returns shell-shocked and deaf. His younger brother is a student activist, but not really a radical. Just a democrat. Our play realistically depicted this family's problems and interactions. The youngest son

is eventually killed when the riot police throw a grenade at a group of peaceful demonstrators.

The play was a huge success. The unions came in droves to watch it. But it was too little too late. The right-wing forces were already too strong and the left was divided and too dogmatic. The Communist political advisor had even wanted to tell us what to do. He wanted us to study Mao's speech at Yenan. But we countered: "Yenan happened when the revolution was finished. We're right in the middle of it. We want to be compassionate, Brechtian." No, we didn't want to compromise with these people.[10]

For several months, Kunadilok's group performed *Before the Dawn* and short satirical skits at mass rallies that were organized with increasing frequency after Marshall Thanom returned unexpectedly from exile in August 1976. Emotionally, Kunadilok recalls the events of 6 October:

The National Student Union had organized a mass meeting in the Thammasart University soccer stadium. Our group performed at about four in the morning when the place was already surrounded by the military. They began shooting the first rockets during our show. Then they attacked with machine guns and bazookas. Two hundred students were killed in the attack. Hundreds of others were arrested, including half of our members. One of us was shot in the hip. That evening, a military dictatorship was installed and we were finished. I went into hiding and managed to escape to France after one month.[11]

Kunadilok, who had been the undisputed leader of Thailand's political theatre movement, now settled in Paris with his French wife and joined the Théâtre du Mondragord, an experimental troupe under the direction of Wolfgang Mehring. Back in Bangkok, meanwhile, the stages remained empty while the streets were filled with heavily armed soldiers. Hundreds of intellectuals were arrested, so-called radical books were burned, and thousands of students and union activists fled to the countryside to join the armed resistance of the Communist Party of Thailand (CPT).

Another coup staged in October 1977 heralded a slightly more liberal government under the leadership of General Kriangsak Chamanan. He released many political prisoners and offered amnesty to activists who had fled to the jungle. In this more relaxed climate, the theatre could come out of hiding. The first performances were nonpolitical public poetry recitals on university campuses and in the small auditoriums of the Goethe Institute and the British Council. Some theatre groups started up again in the course of 1978 but they were unable to sustain their activities in a professional way until well into the eighties.

The Current Mainstream

Despite the somewhat farfetched claim by Thai drama critic Chetana Naga-vajara that a variation on the Broadway musical is the most suitable idiom for the future theatre of his country, contemporary Thai theatre remains a marginal enterprise at best.[12] There are only three more or less permanent troupes, and none of the actors full-time professionals. Although the capital's three university drama departments occasionally put up productions, there is no modern theatre outside Bangkok. The audience for theatre remains largely restricted to the university population and the repertoire to the Western canon. There are only a few original Thai scripts. Traditional drama forms like variations on Malaysian-inspired *wayang* forms in the south and the *ligay* folk theatre are gradually dying out in the countryside.[13] Indian-inspired dance drama forms are only preserved as tourist attractions by the colorful but soulless Thai National Dance Troupe, which also occasionally tours the West as part of the "Visit Thailand" campaign sponsored by the government's department of tourism and Thai Airways International. In the midst of such a dismal theatre landscape, the only glimmer of hope for a meaningful contemporary professional theatre lies with a new company with the curious name of 28 Group, and with Kamron Kunadilok, who returned from exile in 1986.

The name 28 Group refers to the year 2528 on the Buddhist calendar, anno domini 1984, when it was founded by Rassami Phao Luangthong after her graduation from the Yale School of Drama. "I started it with some friends who had studied drama but had no opportunity to use it," she explains. "They worked mostly in film and advertising. There were fifteen of us to start out with. We wanted to make a theatre that was thought-provoking and socially committed but not overtly political, because in the current climate that would only turn people off."[14]

The 28 Group does one new production per year. Thus far they have done plays by Brecht, Frisch, and Dürrenmatt, and one successful big-budget musical, *Man of la Mancha,* that attracted 18,000 people in sixteen performances. According to Phao Luangthong, 28 Group selected this musical to expand the audience base for modern theatre. "I estimate that, generally speaking, there are between six and ten thousand people in Bangkok who are interested in theatre. With our musical we succeeded in making 8,000 additional spectators see that theatre can be interesting. That is our foremost task right now, to create an audience for theatre. Only then can you start an exchange of ideas with them. You can only introduce social and political issues very slowly."[15]

Phao Luangthong regrets the absence of good Thai scripts. She and her group contemplate setting up a playwrighting workshop. They also organize discussions with the audience and occasionally tour outside the capital. At some point, they would like to get villagers and slum dwellers involved. Says Phao Luangthong: "Youngsters have so much energy. It would be great to direct that toward theatre instead of to fighting and using drugs. Better than anyone else, we know that theatre can change you a lot."[16]

The role of the Innkeeper in the 1987 production of *Man of la Mancha* was played by Kamron Kunadilok. He hated the venue: "It was held in the National Theatre. The acoustics were terrible. The place is simply too big: we had to use wireless microphones to be heard." Since then, Kunadilok has revived Crescent Moon and dreams of continuing where he left off in 1976:

> In Thailand we must develop our own homegrown ideas of revolution and liberation. We've had the Marxist-Leninists, the Stalinists, the Maoists. None of them work. We're lacking research and knowledge on the influence of Buddhism on society. Liberation should be more than forty-hour working weeks and one-month vacations with pay. It should be more like working half days and writing poems the other half. Usually people only think of the economic side of things. They forget about the world of ideas and human development. Liberation means that you're not a slave to the social and economic structure. Theatre can be a perfect tool in this liberation process. It is harmony between the physical and the mental sphere of the human being.[17]

Since his return from exile, Kamron Kunadilok has only sporadically produced plays. He is one of the few theatre directors who works with original scripts. His 1987 play *The Revolutionary* was praised as "the beginning of a theatrical renaissance in Thailand" although it only drew a few spectators.[18] On 12 March 1988 he directed a large-scale production at Thammasart University to celebrate the unveiling of a statue of Dr. Puay, president of the university during the student uprising of October 1976 and one of the country's leading progressive economists. Following the massacre, Dr. Puay was forced into exile and took up residence in Cambridge, England. The nighttime production in his honor took place on the lawn in front of the university's administration building. Impressive fifteen-foot puppets, representing the protagonist, the military, and the students, illustrated the life story of Dr. Puay. It was narrated by Kamron Kunadilok himself through an imperfect sound system.

Kunadilok has ambitious plans, the feasibility of which remains to be seen. He wants to raise funds by working in television and simultaneously establish two student groups, one in Bangkok and one in Chieng Mai. Echoing some of the theatre of liberation ideas from elsewhere in Asia, Kunadilok explains that he is more interested in the theatre process than in the cultural product: "We want to work together, exchange ideas, study the problems of Thailand, change ourselves first and then help others. We feel that, right now, all art and culture are concentrated in the capital and in the royal court. The villager has lost his sense of expression. We want to go to the villages to stimulate them to do their own performances and to make them feel proud again of their traditional forms of cultural expressions. We have the technique, the farmers have the stories. Together we can make exciting performances."[19] Unbeknownst to academic drama critics and the few mainstream artists in Bangkok, however, two youth-oriented theatre-in-education groups have already been working since 1981 along lines similar to Kunadilok's plans.

Although they respect the legendary director, these young groups are not ready to accept his commitment at face value or to simply yield to his authority. Having been in exile for over a decade, they feel Kunadilok has to prove himself again and first go back to the grassroots.[20]

Theatre of Liberation at the Grassroots: Ma-kham-pom and Maya

There is healthy sense of rivalry between Ma-kham-pom and Maya, Thailand's two theatre of liberation groups. Ma-kham-pom derives its name from a fruit found in northeastern Thailand; it tastes sour at first but develops a sweet flavor after you drink some water. Pradit Prasarttong, the training coordinator of the group, explains that they perceive their theatre similarly: "We are very young and come as strangers to a village. But after we perform and interact with the villagers, they love us."[21]

Ma-kham-pom was founded in 1981 after an ad-hoc group of teachers, journalists, actors, and dancers got together to write and produce a children's play called *Mali and Mala*. The play was received so enthusiastically in Bangkok that the group decided to request funding from the Coordinating Group of Religion in Society (CGRS) to tour the play in the countryside. Pradit: "Bangkok is so full of media, but the villages have nothing. We wanted to set up a permanent theatre group that could serve as a micromedium for the village people. We fortunately got the grant, started research on problems in the countryside, and made plays about it."[22]

Ma-kham-pom toured with their first production for six months. Afterward they contacted village committees to get permission to conduct theatre workshops for village youth. Pradit: "We taught them how to do research, how to make a script, and how to produce their play. It was something totally new. But a few months after we left, electricity came to the village. The televisions and radios destroyed our initiative."[23]

In 1982, Ma-kham-pom first created some simple children's plays based on folk tales. The shows dealt with health problems and were educational in orientation. They have become the basis of the group's activity since then. The group usually performs its plays in schools; if teachers express interest, Ma-kham-pom returns later to conduct workshops for them or their pupils. According to Pradit Prasarttong, Ma-kham-pom has been able to consolidate theatre of liberation activities in the rural areas around the towns of Nakorn Rajsima and Buriram, northeast of Bangkok. The company returns to these areas once a year, and apparently some school teachers have begun to conduct echo workshops of their own.

Several members of Ma-kham-pom attended extended community theatre workshops of the Philippines Educational Theater Association in Manila in 1983. Upon their return, they began implementing the theatre of liberation methodology in their own workshops. Says Prasarttong: "It was extremely useful. Their ideas and ours are quite similar. We are both interested in developing the creativity and self-reliance of people at the grassroots. Only their exercises are quite different. We have adapted some of them for our workshops."[24]

Ma-kham-pom conducts an average of ten five-day workshops per year with a maximum of fifty participants each. The group has two full-time workshop instructors and five other salaried staff members. In addition, there are approximately twenty volunteer interns who are taken to the slums and into the countryside. In January and February of each year, the volunteers must complete an obligatory drama course. Subsequently they must observe several workshops. During their one-year training period, the volunteers also participate in the company's theatre productions.

Ma-kham-pom has also started a tradition of performing relevant plays during the annual commemoration ceremonies of the 14 October massacre. Following a march for democracy in the mornings, the company usually performs at Thammasart University in the afternoon. Their plays generally deal with the theme of democracy in Thailand. Typical of these shows is *The Tree of Hope,* which Ma-kham-pom first performed on 14 October 1987 and which was also inserted as an intermezzo in the Dr. Puay memorial celebration I witnessed on 12 March 1988.

The Tree of Hope is an allegorical musical play set in an imaginary country easily recognizable as Thailand. It opens at a posh ball where rich people in glittering costumes dance as they brag about their profits from the tourist boom. Reminders of another reality now intrude upon this self-satisfied milieu. A young prostitute enters first, offering her services for a mere ten Baht (US\$ 0.40). A customer offers her twenty, but she refuses: "Please, only ten, otherwise I have to pay income tax."[25] As she exits stage left, a blind vendor of lottery tickets enters on the right.

In the second scene, a teenage boy wants to plant a tree of hope—an obvious symbol of democracy. His friends do not want to wait for the tree to grow. They are impatient; they want to fight for democracy instead. The boy, however, convinces them to give it a try. The lower middle class youths are then joined by a rich old lady who seeks their friendship, symbolizing that an alliance between the various classes is indispensable in order for democracy to succeed. The old lady offers her help, but is summoned back into her mansion by her son, a government official, who was napping and has been awakened by the noise. Yawning, he tells his mother she should not mingle with "those street kids," and chases them away. The two then engage in an argument about the tree of hope. "Why waste time growing it?" says the son. He maintains that it would be simpler to import a fully grown one from America, failing to realize that an old tree from abroad will not necessarily grow in Thai soil.

Despite the official's skepticism, the youngsters decide to plant seeds for their tree in front of his house, which symbolizes the national parliament. In this third scene the hopeful period of 1973 through 14 October 1976 is evoked. The tree grows well. Everyone—including the prostitute, the blind vendor, and the rich old lady—helps to water it. But suddenly her son and some military officers arrive on the scene, announcing, "Tomorrow, we'll plant a big tree from abroad right here!" The youngsters protest. "But look! Ours is already growing. We're on our way!" A fight ensues, one of the girls is knocked down, and the tree is crushed. But the old lady secretly tells the boys and girls she is going to take one of the seeds from the tree and try to grow it again—in a flower pot this time, since no land is available. "I will make it bloom," she says, "and then we can all have one in our own homes," thus arguing in allegorical terms for grassroots democracy without government approval.

In the fourth scene, the big tree planted by the official is dying because no one ever waters it. One of the military guards notices this, and wakes up his boss. But the government official is not very concerned: "Never mind, never mind. Everyone has forgotten about it already." And he goes back to sleep. This implies that his interest in democracy was never sincere to begin with.

In a romanticized musical finale, the youngsters, the blind vendor, the prostitute, a crowd of poor people, and the rich old lady all enter, each carrying a flower pot containing a tree of hope in full bloom. There is singing and dancing to celebrate the fruition of these trees of hope, planted and nurtured without government interference. Just before the curtain falls, the official's voice is heard from inside the mansion: "Can't you stop that noise! I'm trying to sleep."

Only a few miles from Ma-kham-pom's office lie the headquarters of Maya, Bangkok's other theatre of liberation company. Although its name means "illusion," the company, which like Ma-kham-pom caters predominantly to children and adolescents, aims to give its audiences and workshop participants a better grasp of reality. Both as performers and as workshop trainers, Maya enjoys considerably more respect in Thailand than its Ma-kham-pom colleagues across town. Many of the volunteers in Ma-kham-pom regard their internships as stepping stones to glamorous careers in film and television. Busaba Baratacharya of the Henry Durance Foundation for Education prefers to work with Maya for exactly that reason: "Their level of commitment is much higher and their workshop methodology much better thought out. The difference is that Ma-kham-pom was founded because the money for a project was already there. Maya started, however, because they genuinely love children and wanted to make theatre for them. A significant yardstick to measure commitments is, I think, membership turnover rates, which in Ma-kham-pom's case is very high—one of its founding members is now an important movie star—whereas the original founders of Maya are still working with the group."[26]

Maya was founded in February 1981 by a student named Santi Chitra-

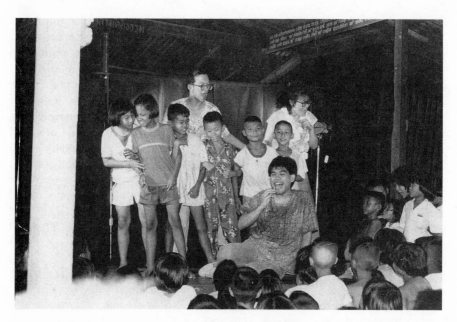

Maya believes in audience participation and making use of children's spontaneity.

chinda, who, as he says, "wanted to make a contribution to child and youth development since these population groups embody the future. We've had relatively happy childhoods ourselves and firmly believe that it is a basic human right of every child to be happy and develop its potential to become a well-rounded human being."[27] Chitrachinda had seen some foreign theatre productions and Thai adaptations of Western classics but had received no formal theatre training. All his knowledge comes from books and watching live theatre. "I had read some of the neohumanist psychologists and Paulo Freire's work and, combining their approach with what I had seen on stage, I immediately grasped [theatre's] enormous potential to make people realize important things about their lives, mankind, and the world," Chitrachinda explains. "It also had something to do with the Thai educational system being too limited for my personal development, I suppose. It doesn't allow students to think creatively and independently. So to the dismay of my parents I quit school and signed up for an arts education, which would leave me plenty of time to do theatre."

Chitrachinda and some friends taught themselves how to make and manipulate puppets, created a fifteen-minute comic puppet play on the nutritional benefits of soybean milk, and, in December 1981, went into Bangkok's slums to perform it. If they found that children did not respond to particular scenes, characters, or puppet techniques, the young puppeteers would go back to improve their show. At first, Maya performed in one particular slum area only, but when it was demolished they decided to work all over Bangkok, cooperating closely with social workers of non-government organizations to find suitable venues.

It took Maya until the end of 1982 to explore different puppet theatre forms and techniques and to develop an effective style of its own. Together with Orn-anong Vong-asavathepchai, a young visual artist, and Somsak Kanha, a dancer who had worked in traditional theatre, Santi Chitrachinda designed a light system and many puppets. By January 1983, Maya was ready to go on an extended tour around the countryside. With some funding and contacts from the Coordinating Group of Religion in Society, the same group that had subsidized Ma-kham-pom, Maya performed forty shows in four months' time. The three performers traveled by bus, carrying their stage, lights, and puppets with them. "It was very exciting for us to travel around Thailand like that," Chitrachinda reminisces:

> We learned so much from interacting with all these diverse audiences. It is street theatre and, like television drama, you have to introduce lots of climaxes to keep the children interested. We also added some *ligay* traditional verse drama elements. The show itself was composed of several different modules. One was based on one of Aesop's fables, "The Flock in Search of a Leader." It tried to show the community not always to rely on outsiders for advice and help, but to be self-reliant. One of the other modules was about a mouse who was looking for a bridegroom for his daughter. He asks the sun, then the cloud, then the wind, and finally he asks the wall. At last he realizes that the little mouse is the most powerful creature in the world. In terms of child psychology we wanted the children to understand that they are also people and that, even though they are small, they also have some value in themselves.

Already at this early stage, then, Maya wanted to use its puppet theatre to empower the oppressed by showing them they had the means within themselves to take control of their lives. Developing this innate creativity through grassroots workshops was the next logical step.

During the first nationwide tour, elementary school teachers invited Maya to come to their institutions to conduct workshops. By this time, the group was already beginning to see the limitations of performances. Chitrachinda: "We only worked with the children for a few hours at most and then we left again. We recognized the importance of giving the teachers some tools to continue our input and to help them set up local education committees." Since May 1983, Maya has been working steadily to develop a nationwide network of community children's theatre. The group collaborates closely with Busaba Baratacharya of the Henry Durance Foundation for Education, which provides funds, venues, and participants.

The main vehicle for the expansion of Maya's cultural movement is the six-day live-in puppet theatre workshop at which the three staff members can train a maximum of sixty-five participants. Like the Basic Integrated Theatre Arts Workshop (BITAW) of the Philippines Educational Theatre Association, the Maya workshop opens with a get-to-know-you phase and ice-breaking activities. The Thai approach seems more formal than the Philippine theatre of liberation workshop and less game-like. Says Chitrachinda, "Maybe it's my personal taste. I feel games sometimes work like a dictatorship: you are commanded to have fun and be happy." The Maya workshop is more instructional at first. The three puppetteers show the participants all the possibilities of puppet theatre. They delve a little into the history and theory of puppetry and subsequently present a short performance in which they create a hand puppet, a shadow puppet, and a stick puppet with a simple bamboo rod and a piece of paper. In the second phase of the workshop, the participants start making their own puppets and, under the guidance of the three instructors, they develop characters. Also in this second phase, participants are exposed to storytelling techniques and plot strategies for which the Maya puppeteers make use of a Flexaflan. Choreography, movement in space, and music are only some of the other subjects on the curriculum. If time allows, the instructors also introduce the production of low-cost media like rudimentary printing techniques using homemade cornstarch ink. The third phase of the Maya workshop is composed of rehearsals that ultimately culminate in a puppetry performance.

Maya likes to have its workshops result in cultural campaigns. Thus, the first workshop for teachers in May 1983 was geared toward the promotion of reading in the community. All the exercises were especially designed for this particular purpose and at the end of the workshop the participants went out into the community to perform. But the results of these campaigns have been considerably less encouraging than in countries like India. No firm network of community-based theatre groups has been established as yet and most groups fold a short time after the Maya workshop. According to Chitrachinda, this weakness must be attributed to the absence of well-organized grassroots people's organizations in Thailand. "We have no unions, cooperatives, or community organizations that we can feed into. We conceive of ourselves as a technical assistance group although we do give some advice on what can be done after the workshop. But what can we do if the objectives of the participants aren't clear? We cannot force them."

Despite the lack of consolidated follow-up activities, Maya remains optimistic about the possibilities of organizing a cultural movement in Thailand. Given the economic and political situation in the country, however, Chitrachinda believes it will be more humanistically inclined than radically political:

> Thailand is very different from the Philippines. We still live in a culture of silence. People don't believe in themselves. They're oppressed by the dominant mass culture. Theatre can be an extremely useful tool to break through that culture of silence. We need to do many, many workshops and create many

teams, many Mayas. We have tried to link up with the student movement, but they only talk politics in abstract terms. Even their strikes and demonstrations have no sense of media. They just gather a bunch of people and yell slogans. They regard culture as a very low priority.

Busaba Baratacharya agrees with Chitrachinda's assessment. She also dreams of a cultural movement in Thailand, which, she feels, is indispensable "to disseminate the crucial issues in our society and to make people more aware." But like Chitrachinda she realizes that the process of developing such a movement must be much slower and must be carried out with greater caution than in countries like the Philippines: "Like them we are involved in empowering people by developing their innate creativity. But here you cannot be aggressive in doing that. We prefer to start with letting children be themselves, for example. The Thai people have a much lower political consciousness because of their deceptive level of material comfort."[28]

Busaba Baratacharya knows from her own experience that the Philippine workshop methodology cannot be simply duplicated in Thai culture. As early as 1981 three Philippines Educational Theatre Association (PETA) facilitators tried unsuccessfully to introduce their community theatre workshop method at a teachers' training college in Song Khla, southern Thailand. Because the participants lacked a profound political commitment and PETA could not provide the necessary support from overseas, no permanent community theatre groups were established following the training sessions. Even after one of the Song Khla teachers and some members of Ma-kham-pom were exposed to the methodology once again during the 1983 Asian Theatre Forum workshop in Tokyo and more extensively during a six-week summer course in Manila, they were unable to get sustained theatre of liberation activities off the ground in their own country.

In 1985, PETA made another effort to export its theatre of liberation method to Thailand and sent Lutgardo Labad to Bangkok. He spoke with Busaba Baratacharya and Santi Chitrachinda to explore the possibilities for another international workshop. Baratacharya traveled to the Philippines in 1986 and finally managed to organize three five-day workshops in 1987. One of these took place again in Song Khla's teachers' training college; the second one, also for teachers, took place in Surin province in the northeast; and the third one, for social workers from non-government organizations, took place in Bangkok. Following the workshops, Baratacharya clearly had reservations about foreign input of this sort in general and PETA's methods in particular: "It was so difficult to communicate with PETA. First they said they would come; then they claimed they were too busy with their own work back home and with their international tours." The workshops themselves did have some impact, she thinks: "But only in the sense that Thai participants found out more regarding their own position in society, what social problems need to be tackled, and how to go about it in a creative manner. But follow-up was difficult because all of them returned to different organizations and working environments."[29]

Santi Chitrachinda found some of the PETA techniques useful, particularly the group dynamics exercises and its methods of conducting structural analysis of the target community, but in general he found that the PETA workshops in Thailand only confirmed the effectiveness of Maya's own methodology. "In the Philippines you either do it or die," Chitrachinda explains. "Here everything is relatively calm, although there are considerable social problems, of course. But we do not view the government as our enemy. We cooperate with the National Housing Authority on some projects, for example. There are still some good people inside who give us some room to maneuver. And, unlike PETA, our basic philosophy is not left wing but humanist. Besides, as far as children's theatre is concerned, we believe we have much more experience than they have."

Since its inception, Maya has been working steadily to nurture its own concept of a cultural movement. It has now conducted well over 500 workshops for 16,500 teachers and high school and elementary school students. It has performed more than 275 free puppet theatre shows in slums and villages, attracting over 100,000 spectators. Recently, the group also ventured into regular theatre with a children's play entitled *Fifty Ways of Torturing Children*. In addition, Maya serves as consultant for designing educational campaigns. Since 1983, the group has also produced 150 so-called puppet bags, kits of puppets and scripts that children can borrow to create their own puppet plays. Chitrachinda: "We develop tools to encourage teachers and children to do things on their own. If they can't come to a workshop, they can experiment with the medium themselves by borrowing puppet bags. We circulate them like a lending library."

Over the years, Maya has become a tightly knit family. The five full-time staff members and the ten carefully selected volunteers share vegetarian meals, jog together, and generally operate as a well-disciplined team. After almost a decade of very hard work, spirits remain high. "Other theatre artist drink the night away and do drugs," explains Chitrachinda. "That's their business, of course, but we prefer our own healthy way of life. We even do yoga together during our actor's training session."

The strong team spirit even helped Maya overcome a car crash that nearly killed Santi Chitrachinda in 1984. "One of our volunteers was driving a pickup truck we had borrowed for a tour. We were high up in the mountains of the north. The road was muddy after some heavy rainfall. Suddenly the truck slipped and turned over. The people in the back got thrown out. I was one of them. I was in a coma for two months and needed brain surgery." The ordeal brought the group closer together. It also forced them to become more efficient and design a lightweight stage and a compact light and sound system.

Maya performs throughout the country for four months out of the year.

A Maya do-it-yourself puppet
theatre kit.

A Maya member tells jokes to attract slum children to a puppet show,
Bangkok.

The rest of the time is taken up by workshops of all sorts. The group organizes youth and children's camps, for example, in which participants are taken on exposure around their communities and create their own shows on issues like pollution, corruption, malnutrition, and drug abuse. Maya has also worked with tribal minority children near Chieng Rai in the Golden Triangle. "We taught them how to make puppets from fruit," Chitrachinda recalls. "They created a story abut a cow and a tiger and during their performance we ate the puppets together."

A Maya Performance

On 4 March 1988 I traveled with Busaba Baratacharya and the five Maya staff members in a small Japanese van to the urban poor community of Pra-san Salaban. Local organizers had already alerted the children that Maya was to perform. After some television appearances, the group has become quite popular around Bangkok. While four of the members set up the equipment, Somsak Kanha plugged in the portable sound system and started telling jokes into the microphone. In no time, fifty children had gathered on the site. The black-draped puppetry box and the lights were set up within thirty minutes. The entire cast began to sing some popular songs to which new lyrics had been added. The crowd had now grown to several hundred. The night slowly descended as the battery-powered halogen spots were switched on. The five Maya artists took turns warming up their youthful audience. Busaba Baratacharya, who served as my interpreter, explained that they wanted to get rid of the children's excess energy so they would be able to concentrate better during the actual show.

The show, entitled *Forest of Dreams,* begins with a traditional Thai finger dance in which the performers don long shiny fake nails and use them to create a stunning variety of different shapes. After this brief prelude, the puppeteers step forward and introduce themselves. Suddenly a wolf appears and chases them around the stage. The children become all excited. A spontaneous dialogue between performers and audience ensues, which is clearly an attempt to break through the fourth wall. Then the actual storytelling begins.

All the scenes are quite short and work toward quick climaxes. The colorful puppets are cleverly designed by Orn-anong Vong-asavathepchai. The set changes are quick because they are simply projected onto a white backdrop by means of an overhead projector set up behind the stage. In the first story an old man is introduced who lives in a castle and speaks a funny language. He does not use the word "water," for example, but a long poetic phrase instead. He tries to teach this strange language to his maid. One night, a fire breaks out in the castle and the maid tries to call for help but forgets the words her master had taught her and has to ask the children in the audience

Maya uses many different forms of puppet theatre. This is a traditional Thai "Golden Swan" finger dance.

A Maya performance in the Bangkok slums.

Children as participants in Maya's *Forest of Dreams*.

Forest of Dreams.

for assistance. The children shout all kinds of strange words until the old man finally emerges to extinguish the fire.

The next story further explores the possibility of audience participation. An old peasant couple mime planting a sweet potato, which quickly grows even higher than their house. The old folks are unable to pull the invisible yam out of the ground. The puppeteers ask if there is perhaps a grandson and a granddaughter of the old peasants among the spectators who care to help. Several kids join the fantasy but they fail to pull the yam out as well. Then the puppeteers asks for a dog and a cat. Several more kids join in, making the required animal noises. Soon a long string of children is pulling at the plant together with the puppeteers. Slowly it begins to move. It will take only one more small child to pull the yam out, the puppeteers say, and finally, with the help of one more participant, they are able to remove the plant, thus proving that even the smallest creatures are indispensable for a collective effort to be successful.

The other five stories in *Forest of Dreams* are equally pedagogical. Thus, "The Snakedance" is a variation on a Thai folk game called "The Snake Bites Its Own Tail." In Maya's version of the game ten little hand–puppet snakes form two teams and fight each other. Each team tries to catch a member of the other team so it will become bigger and stronger. A captured snake is added to the team that caught it. A wild game ensues during which the puppeteers introduce the different biological varieties of poisonous and non-poisonous snakes the children might encounter in the slums or in the forest.

Maya tries to use as many different styles of puppetry as possible in their shows. By lowering a transparent white curtain in the front and using the overhead projector, they can quickly convert their portable puppet theatre into a *wayang kulit* stage. This type of two-dimensional shadow puppetry is still found in some parts of southern Thailand, where the influence of Malay culture has been the strongest. Maya's shadow puppetry piece is based on an old Thai folk tale about a poor old peasant couple. One day, they are visited by a monk and, as Buddhist tradition requires, they have to feed him the best food they have. They only possess a hen, a rooster, and a couple of young chicks. They decide to kill the hen, who loves the old peasants so much that she does not run away. In the morning the gentle old folks cook her over a slow fire. The chicks adore their mother so much that they spontaneously jump into the fire with her. As they burn, sparks rise up to the sky and the hen and her children are converted into a new constellation. In a brief discussion that follows the presentation, in which spectacular effects were created with different gels and colored liquids on the overhead projector, most children in the audience say they believe the monk is to blame.

In the next tale, Maya tackles arrogance by introducing a self-righteous mother bull-frog who, when she is proved wrong, becomes so angry that she inflates her chest until it finally explodes. The puppeteers achieved this spectacular effect with a green balloon and a hand pump. The final story,

"The Old Lady Who Swallowed a Fly," simultaneously tackles another human flaw—greed—and the importance of hygiene. In a variation on an old English nursery rhyme about an old lady who swallowed a horse, the Maya puppeteers introduce a life-size torso of a funny-looking old woman who hungrily gulps down all kinds of things. First she swallows a fly and the puppeteers comment that flies can cause all kinds of children's diseases like the potentially fatal diarrhea. "And," the puppeteers continue, "if you begin with flies, who knows what you will end up swallowing next? A spider? A bird?" As the story progresses, the objects the old lady swallows become crazier and crazier, and the imaginations of the children in the audience are stimulated to the utmost. The end of the story comes when the old lady explodes after swallowing a real living puppy that the puppeteers have borrowed from a local family.

The ninety-fourth performance of *Forest of Dreams* in three months' time is finished. The artists step forward to receive the ovation, thank the local organizers and the children for being such wonderful hosts, and invite the audience to come forward to have a look at the puppets. After half an hour, the stage and the equipment are packed in handy crates and the Maya artists share a meal with the organizing committee. By 10 P.M., the small van departs from Prasan Salaban and drops off puppeteers along the way. Unable to afford their own apartments, most of them still live in a room in their parental homes. The van drops me off at my hostel on Phayathai Road. I see hundreds of young Thai couples in fancy Western clothes and permed hair, lining up for Kubrick's *Full Metal Jacket* in the cinema across the street. Santi Chitrachinda, Orn-anong Vong-asavathepchai, and Somsak Kanha, the three Maya veterans, disappear with their van in the busy evening traffic of *took-took* scooter taxis, blue buses, and Japanese cars. They need to get a good night's rest. Tomorrow is their ninety-fifth performance of *Forest of Dreams*. With each show, they plant a new tree of hope in an increasing Thai cultural wasteland that is also rapidly expanding into the decimated rain forests. Quixotic? Perhaps, but certainly not more so than producing a Thai version of *Man of la Mancha* in Bangkok.

X

CONCLUSION

The Asian theatre of liberation constitutes an important and widespread sociocultural phenomenon whose dynamic growth shows no signs of waning. From the preceding discussions of its development in half a dozen Asian countries, several general characteristics can be distilled that also apply to the theatre of liberation now emerging in several other countries in the region.

Invariably, excesses of repressive political measures like the declaration of martial law (Philippines, India) or coup-instigated installations of military dictatorships (Pakistan, South Korea, Thailand, and Indonesia) served as the main catalysts for the inception of the theatre of liberation. Most often, middle class artists from the city were the chief agents for its development. Politicized by fascistic political developments, human rights abuses, and censorship in their countries, they gradually became dissatisfied either with the smug and pretentious mainstream or with the moribund traditional theatre. In its early stages, therefore, theatre of liberation, commonly had an element of protest and mainly flourished underground in the form of hit-and-run street plays and invisible workshops.

Theatre of liberation is most effectively disseminated through all levels of society when the urban middle class initiators train talented young people who are native to the target grassroots communities and commit themselves to returning home to work as community-based artist-organizers. The best results have been obtained when this type of training was structured into a transparent, easily duplicatable workshop format and consistently implemented over a long period of time in as many grassroots target communities as possible. Ideally, the initial theatre of liberation input should be backed up by a smoothly operating network that can include other art disciplines as well and that provides follow-up care consisting of monitoring, refresher courses, advanced leadership training, organization of festivals and conferences, setting up communication channels in the form of newsletters and magazines, coproductions, exchanges of artists, and research in traditional theatre forms. Only then, and in close collaboration with other organizations of like-minded concerned citizens, can the theatre of liberation blossom into a veritable democratic and self-sustaining, long-lasting cultural movement. In its most advanced manifestations, particularly in the Philippines and South Korea, the

228

theatre of liberation had and continues to have a profound impact on the grassroots emancipation processes through workshop inputs and artistic outputs that reveal varying levels of aesthetic competence and political commitment and that function in virtually all layers of society.

It is a misconception to think that all theatre of liberation activists are by definition leftist. On the contrary, the vast majority oscillate between humanist liberalism and varieties of democratic socialism. Only a small, albeit vocal, minority subscribe to ideals of the extreme left. Although the theatre of liberation is definitely bipartisan in nature, then, its practitioners are emphatically united in their anti-fascist, anti-imperialist stance and conceive of themselves as generating an alternative, people-controlled culture through small-scale media to provide a healthy, democratizing counterweight to the often manipulative, doctrinaire, and mind-narrowing culture disseminated by the official and commercial media in their countries.

As I hope the preceding chapters have illustrated, the levels of development of the theatre of liberation differ considerably from country to country. Even within one nation, it can be more advanced in one region than in another, depending on external factors like political repression and internal factors like the commitment, courage, energy, and creativity of the individuals involved. Thus, in Thailand, arguably the least advanced of the countries discussed in this book, a national theatre of liberation movement is still remote, although individual groups like Maya do excellent work in terms of both performance and grassroots training. Most of its disseminators continue to be from the middle class.

Much the same can be said of Pakistan. Most if not all theatre of liberation practitioners there come from the middle and upper classes. The performing level of some groups in Karachi and Lahore is rapidly improving, but there is a lack of good original scripts and, with the exception of Shahid Nadeem, of committed writers.[1] But several recent festivals indicate that a Pakistani national theatre movement may not be too far off, and there is at least a sincere willingness to cooperate. Although the theatre of liberation workshop methodology has by now also been introduced to Pakistan, given the repressive authoritarian conditions and the continuing expansion of Islamic fundamentalism, its implementation on the grassroots level remains problematic.

The Indonesian theatre of liberation is already quite balanced in terms of repertory building, workshop implementation, and grassroots participation. Even though the small network is still predominantly concentrated in central Java, workshops have reaped impressive results in some of the outlying islands as well. In addition, there are encouraging signs that social workers and accomplished artists are on the verge of expanding their activities to a national level, as the government's control over daily life and political dissent seems to be relaxing slightly.

India's theatre of liberation presents us with a very complex picture indeed. On the one hand, there certainly is no lack of ideas, good plays, talented actors, and committed groups that can already boast some extraordinary results. In particular, southern states like Kerala, Karnataka, Tamil Nadu, and Andra Pradesh are quite advanced in building regional theatre of liberation networks. But India is a vast country in more ways than one and nowhere do geography, religion, ideology, language, pride, ambition, and greed throw up higher barriers than here. It does not seem likely that the huge differences will soon be resolved, although the untimely death of the charismatic playwright-actor Safdar Hashmi succeeded in momentarily uniting India's divided progressive artists. Despite the differences, there is no doubt that India's theatre of liberation represents a sorely needed positive force in a country that is currently in the middle of an explosion of potentially fatal religious fanaticism.

The South Korean theatre of liberation is operating very smoothly and full of discipline under the aegis of a national steering committee, the Council for the National Theater Movement, a continuation of the *Minjung* People's Culture Organization. Communications are maintained by means of an "underground railroad" of sorts. Workshops are steadily implemented throughout the country in villages, urban communities, and university circles, often with the help of committed teachers and priests. The most common output is the madang performance, a very effective mixture of traditional theatre and contemporary agitprop that has the double function of expressing a community's grievances and mobilizing the masses. The movement has also succeeded in forging durable links with some of the country's best performers and writers.

In the Philippines, arguably the most advanced country in Asia, the theatre of liberation has been steadily expanding over a twenty-year period and now boasts an impressive network of an estimated four hundred theatre groups that represent all social sectors. Over the years, the Philippine theatre of liberation has produced a remarkable corpus of new plays and has recently even succeeded in infiltrating the broadcast media with its own pertinent television drama series. Its greatest achievement, however, remains the creation of a particularly effective and sophisticated theatre workshop and network strategy, the methodology and tactics of which are continuously updated to stay ahead of the ever-changing political developments in this volatile country.

On the negative side, the Philippine theatre of liberation workshop has come under increasing criticism from the grassroots. It is claimed that the method is still fundamentally middle class and creates too much dependence on a few skilled artist-organizers. Once they leave a community, the theatre of liberation activities often decline and ultimately disappear, despite the theory that the method generates self-reliant theatre groups. Moreover, due to a lack of advanced training, many Philippine workshop instructors are still unable to generate quality scripts and a variety of theatre styles. The majority of the Philippine artist-trainers continue to come from the urban middle class and are unable to genuinely communicate with and stimulate target groups in rural or tribal communities, partly because investigation of local conditions and integration with people in the grassroots are also often insufficient. Training more artist-organizers from the grassroots is an obvious necessity, but here the claim that the theatre of liberation workshop structure is transparent enough for anyone to be able to duplicate it in so-called echo workshops proves to be an exaggeration. Says Joel Arbolario from Negros: "We have discovered that many people do not understand the overall importance of particular exercises, for example. They merely echo without knowing very well what they are doing."[2]

Theatre of liberation activists from the grassroots also object to the centralization practiced by colleague artists in the capital. Several First Quarter Storm veterans seem to suffer from "Manilitis," a condition distinguished by arrogance and forms of megalomania found often if not exclusively among (upper) middle class artists from the capital who are either flattered by their increasing international recognition or confused by their own grandiose visions that cause them to see humans as mere pawns in an abstract political game and themselves as prophets. Manilitis has already caused conflicts between artists from the capital and theatre of liberation practitioners from the provinces, who, like everywhere else in Asia, receive less recognition and are therefore less likely to be eligible for development money, although they usually have to work under much more difficult (and dangerous) circumstances.

Undoubtedly finances play a crucial role in the theatre of liberation. Like everybody else, theatre of liberation activists have to survive somehow. In particular, artists based in the capitals divide their time between work at the grassroots and economic employment on the stages and in the film and television studios of the mainstream. As the example of radical people's theatre in the West has shown, however, this unholy alliance with money and glamour is often eventually self-defeating, for as age progresses and family obligations increase the temptations of greater material comfort and artistic recognition become more and more difficult to resist.

Other sources of income are increasingly provided by Western development agencies, which discovered the potential of the theatre of liberation—or "theatre for social change" as they prefer to call it—in the mid seventies. But since their objectives and criteria do not necessarily always coincide with those of their Asian partners, this relationship can be problematic as well. In some cases, theatre of liberation groups, tempted by the prospect of regular salaries for their staff members, turn into "project brokers": experts in drafting attractive theatre of liberation grassroots projects on paper, but only halfhearted in implementing them. A more radical category of activists court development agencies with a mask of smiles and impressive proposals with which they hide their fundamental contempt for all Westerners, who, in their vision, will always remain representatives of the very imperialist cultures that created colonies in the first place and continue to benefit from neocolonialism now. These groups try to raise Western development funds under the motto: "Their grants are essentially surplus profit made by neocolonial multinational capitalism and the money is therefore better in our hands than in theirs."

Craving success stories to satisfy their own governments, churches, and private donors, representatives from development agencies, flown in for quick consultations and often unfamiliar with the genuine dynamics and complexity of the theatre of liberation, are unable to separate the chaff from the wheat. In the final analysis, the influence of Western development agencies can therefore be just as detrimental as government subsidies were to radical people's theatre in the West. Sooner or later, the artists become economically dependent on them and when the external financial incentives disappear, as eventually they all must, their commitment, and subsequently their activity, dies. Trust funds established by foreign or local donations and fed by the sale of books, music tapes, and arts and crafts in combination with rotating leadership of the kind practiced by the Kerala Forum for Science and Literature (KSSP) or as proposed by the late Safdar Hashmi in India may be considerably more cooptation-proof. Genuine theatre of liberation can never provide more than subsistence wages. It requires a lifetime commitment and a willingness to shed star complexes as well as high material expectations. Its only payoffs are moral, social, and cultural, never monetary.

Geographically speaking, the theatre of liberation is now beginning to spread into other Asian and Pacific countries as well, although activities in Nepal, Burma, and Vietnam remain extremely limited at best. Some theatre of liberation activities have been reported in refugee camps on the Thai-Cambodian border.[3]

Theatre of liberation has existed in Bangladesh since 1971, when the university group Aranyak began its activities in and around the capital city of Dacca. Over the years this group developed its own workshop methodology to introduce the theatre of liberation process in the countryside. In 1976 they were joined in their effort by Proshika, a social action group working predominantly with landless farmworkers and using community theatre as an organizing device. In March 1980 and again in February 1983, Proshika organized international conferences on theatre for social change which united many theatre of liberation practitioners from other developing countries in Koitta. They were crucial for the establishment of an informal international theatre of liberation network. According to several sources, Aranyak and Proshika continue to be actively involved in grassroots theatre workshops, but have not yet been too successful in establishing an extensive network in their impoverished country.[4]

The same applies to Sri Lanka, although the situation in that country is further complicated by the ravages of a brutal civil war between various militant factions of the Tamil minority, radical Communists, different factions of the Singhalese majority, and government forces. I have received unsubstantiated reports of theatre of liberation activities stimulated by the Jaffna

School of Drama in the Tamil-dominated northern part of the country. In addition, in the capital, Colombo, a theatre company named The Open Arts Circle is apparently using the theatre of liberation process to set up a network of women's theatre groups.

Malaysia's modern theatre history reveals a tripartite development similar to most of the other Asian countries examined in this book.[5] Modern urban theatre developed after World War II amidst a dying traditional theatre, fed in this case by a Malay heritage similar to that of Indonesia. In addition, British colonial history has led to the creation of a still growing corpus of Malaysian plays in the English language. Modern Malaysian theatre in *Bahasa Malaysia* maintains close ties with Indonesia's mainstream, thanks largely to the linguistic and cultural bonds between the two countries. But Malaysia's contemporary mainstream theatre is considerably less developed than the Indonesian.[6] It is fighting a losing battle for audiences with cinema and television, which has by now penetrated into virtually every Malaysian household. Despite a great deal of formalistic experimentation, theatre practitioners have not been able to create new forms that appeal to the urban and rural masses. Modern Malaysian theatre therefore remains a marginal affair at best, restricted to small intellectual circles in the large cities. Politically speaking, Malaysia's mainstream theatre has been insignificant as well, having to maneuver cautiously between a repressive authoritarian government on the one hand and growing Islam fundamentalism on the other. The rapid expansion of the fundamentalist power base, which started at the end of the seventies, has apparently been particularly devastating to the modern Malaysian theatre. It also curtailed whatever theatre of liberation activities existed in the slums of Kuala Lumpur and Penang and in the rural areas. The first Malaysian theatre of liberation workshops were held in the early eighties, but the Penang-based social action center that was its most fervent practitioner and disseminator was forced out of business in 1987 following a nationwide crackdown on what the government perceived as a subversive grassroots conspiracy. During this campaign, several theatre of liberation activists were arrested and tortured.

In the same year, a similarly brutal act of government repression virtually destroyed the small, peaceful theatre of liberation movement of Singapore, spearheaded by the Third Stage amateur theatre company. In its five-year existence, Third Stage had been steadily expanding its lower middle class popular audience base with such socially critical musical comedies as *Cora-bella,* which satirized a new government policy that allowed university-educated women to have more children than others; *Oh Singapore!,* a satire on the tendency of the Singapore government to regulate all aspects of civilian life, from heavy fines for jaywalking to all kinds of restrictions on intellectual activity; and *Esperanza,* a play about the exploitation of Filipina maids in Singapore. Several Third Stage members participated in PETA's summer courses and returned home to implement their newly acquired workshop skills in some Catholic parishes and labor organizations. The Third Stage ideal of wishing to create theatre and theatre-related activities that deal with people's daily lives and that would provoke people to reflect on their conditions certainly did not warrant the paranoid reaction of the Singaporian authorities, who arrested and subsequently tortured several Third Stage actresses and actors on charges of a "Marxist conspiracy to overthrow the government." This reprehensible act meant the instantaneous removal of the only concerned element in Singapore's contemporary theatre, which is otherwise characterized by a strong Western identity with Malay, Mandarin, and some Tamil ethnic accents. With the demise of Third Stage, the development of a meaningful Singaporean theatre is back to square one. Its only hope now lies with stalwarts like director Max Le Blond and former dissident playwright-director Kuo Pao Kun, both of whom have already produced pertinent plays.[7]

Kuo Pao Kun is known to maintain close ties with theatre companies in mainland China, Taiwan, and Hong Kong, but activities in these places fall beyond the scope of the theatre of liberation and, therefore, of this book. Only PETA regularly performs in Hong Kong and has conducted workshops there for the sizable community of Filipino migrant workers and for Christian social action groups.

PETA has been largely responsible for exporting the theatre of liberation methodology across Asia and into the Pacific. This Manila-based company has also made significant contributions to the establishment of an international theatre of liberation network by organizing conferences, international summer courses, foreign workshops, and performance tours. In addition to training theatre artists from Indonesia, Thailand, Japan, Pakistan, India, and Bangladesh in its annual summer theatre school, the company has also sent teams of workshop trainers to Papua New Guinea, Aotearoa (New Zealand), and Australia.

Apart from the interesting blend of indigenous elements with Western dramaturgy practiced by the Raun-Raun Theatre, which has even performed in Europe, little else is known of additional grassroots theatre of liberation activities of the Papuans.[8] A series of nine theatre of liberation workshops in urban and rural Maori communities, conducted by three Filipino actors in 1987, resulted in the establishment of a Maori community theatre network in Aotearoa (New Zealand) that apparently is still expanding today. In this country, the workshop process has even caught on with progressive *pakeha* actors, particularly women's theatre activists. The same has happened in Australia, where the theatre of liberation process was originally introduced to enhance the emerging Aboriginal arts movement, but has also rubbed off on white community theatre activists, university drama programs like the one at Flinders in Adelaide, and politicized mainstream artists like Madeleine Blackwell, who makes a living in the movies and the professional theatre but who has also started a theatre of liberation project for female drug and alcohol addicts in Sydney.

Although the Philippine initiative to introduce the theatre of liberation workshop methodology in other Asia-Pacific countries is generally praiseworthy, it has also met with occasional resistance. By the same token, the optimism with which organizations like PETA and the more opportunistic Manila-based Asian Council for People's Culture (ACPC) talk about the establishment of a pan-Asia-Pacific network must be seriously questioned. Even on a regional and national level—where the theatre of liberation has the advantage of operating under relatively homogeneous social, political, economic, and cultural conditions—ideological factionalization and cultural resistance, especially from the tribal minorities, have hampered the harmonious development of networks. These difficulties are compounded when national borders are crossed. Pride in one's own indigenous culture and achievements has already caused some international conflicts when hosts were not always prepared to yield authority to more experienced guest artists from abroad. All too often it is forgotten that unfeigned humility and cultural sensitivity are even more important when operating internationally than locally, as when a middle class artist enters a backward rural community a mere hundred miles from his city home, where the maid is doing the laundry.

Nowhere did this become more clear than during the 1989 *Cry of Asia!* campaign, which tried to unite fifteen theatre of liberation artists from ten Asia-Pacific countries to tour Europe in the form of a cultural caravan. Apart from a haphazard financial structure, the project suffered from underestimation of aesthetic expectations and logistical difficulties in both Asia and Europe, careless casting (including some unpoliticized artists), and a lack of respect for foreign partners. Overestimating his own organizing and artistic abilities and the Philippine vanguard position in the embryo Asian theatre of liberation movement, Al Santos, the Filipino organizer of the tour, wanted to do too much too quickly. *Cry of Asia!* was his brainchild, instead of a collaborative project of an international artistic movement. As a result, many participating artists felt frustrated because they did not get sufficient opportunity to assert their own talents and equally valid achievements. Although brilliant in concept, *Cry of Asia!* thus unfortunately gave Europe an imperfect picture of the true artistic and sociopolitical potential of the theatre of liberation.

This is not to say that Asian theatre of liberation would have no place in the West. There is still a considerable lack of information here about the realities of day-to-day life and culture of the developing world. International tours by government-sponsored dance troupes, short news items, and the *Mahabharata* simply do not do the trick. The live presence of passionate actors recreating the very plays they developed with their people back home potentially can. But if most of the artists are selected from the urban middle class, some of the passion gets lost then and there. Western television cameras and computerized spots in prestigious theatre halls will do the rest. Short of bringing along a partisan Asian audience of landless farmworkers or radi-

Orn-Anong Vong-Asavathepchai from Thailand in a scene from
Cry of Asia! Photo © Michael Kooren.

Hemi Rurawhe, a Maori musician
from Aotearoa (New Zealand), as
Minokawa, the diabolical monster
in *Cry of Asia!* Photo ©
Michael Kooren.

Kim Myung Gon from South Korea as Nuno sa Punso, the benevolent magician in *Cry of Asia!* Photo © Michael Kooren.

Vitidnan Rojanaparnich from Thailand in a scene from *Cry of Asia!* Photo © Michael Kooren.

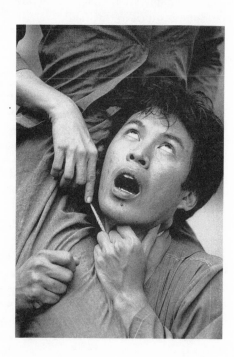

cal university students, the performances need to be contextualized much more than they were in past attempts. Purely on their intrinsic aesthetic merits, the theatre of liberation plays simply do not hold up in the West.

Undoubtedly, the West needs to be exposed to theatre of liberation. But if some of the best theatre of liberation artists are taken from their crucial duties at home for an entire year to reap dubious ovations on Western stages, then it seems justified to ask whether the potential costs and losses are not higher than the benefits. Recent Broadway and West End successes of Black South African theatre productions have raised similar doubts. Artist-organizers at the grassroots question the right of ad-hoc urban-based theatre companies to represent the cultural struggle for liberation with slick performances in the West, harvesting glory and money in the process. The difficulty of returning to dirty and dangerous chores at the grassroots after these glamorous tours often presents an additional problem—not to mention jealousy about or delight in a new status constructed from Western newspaper reviews and video excerpts of television appearances.[9]

Very likely theatre of liberation practitioners in Asia-Pacific can benefit from occasionally exchanging methods and strategies with their colleagues from other countries in the region (or beyond) in some kind of informal network. Annual international consultation and workshop sessions are useful in this regard. But rotating leadership and representation are an absolute necessity at all network levels. In addition, a professionally edited Asia-Pacific theatre of liberation magazine would answer a clear need for international communications in this field.[10]

Recent experiences have shown that the forced pace of an institutionalized Asia-Pacific network can work counterproductively, certainly as long as huge artistic and political differences persist and the control of such an organization remains concentrated in the hands of a few ambitious individuals who regard themselves as visionaries. Many countries are simply still struggling too hard activating their own grassroots to spare the energy required to launch and sustain an international network of which the benefits are doubtful and the expenses in terms of human and financial resources disproportionately high.[11] The danger of creating a privileged in-crowd doing all the traveling and fundraising and that is theoretically and practically light years ahead of the committed small-time peasant artist in the jungle is far from imaginary. The main strength of Asia's theatre of liberation lies in its grassroots workshops. A great deal of work still remains to be done to make these more effective. Undoubtedly that is where the main creativity, energy, and the limited resources of Asia's theatre of liberation should be directed.

The importance of the theatre of liberation to the other geographical areas that comprise the developing world is obvious, although it is far from fully explored. And to the West, the Asian theatre of liberation has considerably more to offer then the rather limited impact of *Cry of Asia!* and the PETA tour through North American and Europe. Its positive effects on theatre practitioners in countries like New Zealand and Australia have begun to inspire speculations about its potential to invigorate the increasingly depoliticized Western theatre in general. The workshop methodologies developed in the Philippines, India, South Korea, and Thailand can be fruitfully combined with Boal's, Spolin's, and other Western methods to promote meaningful community theatre activities. Increasingly marginalized groups of migrant workers, minorities, and indigenous inhabitants can benefit from it, as can the homeless, the unemployed, and other alienated groups working toward their emancipation in Western societies.[12] Pretty much undiluted, the Philippine process has already proved to be effective with Western target groups like women, migrants, and third world solidarity groups. No doubt theatre-in-education can benefit from the process as well. Several people have already started experimenting with theatre of liberation for psychosocial therapeutic purposes like treatment of drug and alcohol addicts and rehabilitation of prisoners.[13] Emerging movements like the European Black Arts Network, the Etats Généraux de la Culture, feminist theatre alliances, and ethnic minority theatre organizations can learn a great deal both from the theatre of liberation process and from its networking strategies.

The relationship between the West and the developing world remains complex, not only in terms of politics and economics but also in cultural terms. Prejudices continue to exist at both ends. As far as the theatre of liberation is concerned, the West has a tremendous amount to learn from the orient. In terms of traditional aesthetics these lessons may be limited. Mnouchkine, Brook, Schechner, and Barba have already deconstructed and reappropriated most Asian theatre symbols, (e)motions, rhythms, and shapes. But the sheer passion and courage of the Asian theatre activist could still inspire the dormant generosity of the egocentric, precious, glamorous, and career-oriented Western repertory actor and his equally complacent middle class audience.

The West has more to offer in return than the television serials, adventure movies, and porn flicks that are flooding the Asian cultural market at the moment. It also has more to give than the subsidies of development agencies, the purposes, distribution models, and structures of which should be carefully reconsidered in any case. German and British cultural centers in Asian cities have made some important contributions over the years by funding theatre professionals from their countries to work with Asian companies, although they have tended to favor established urban middle class groups. One could think instead of mutually beneficial but Western funded partnerships between Asian theatre of liberation groups and Western people's theatre companies like the San Francisco Mime Troupe and the Bread and Puppet Theatre, both of which have already worked under makeshift conditions in Latin America. In exchange for their exposure to grassroots workshops and a journey through the network, which is bound to be inspiring to any committed Western artist, the Mime Troupe could offer sorely needed training in acting and scriptwriting. In light of the growing popularity of cultural parades and mobile political theatre festivals in India, Thailand, and the Philippines, the very thought of Bread and Puppet's giant sculptures wandering through Asia calls up all kinds of exciting visions. If complete tours prove to be too costly or too disruptive of the company's own regular activities, one could think of simply exchanging one or two artists. But in that case sufficient precautions should be taken to prevent culture shock or undesirable top-down behavior.[14]

Partnerships between Asian theatre of liberation groups and Western theatre academies offer additional possibilities for future cooperation. Informal student exchange programs already exist between the Utrecht Theatre Academy in the Netherlands and the Filipino Negros Theater League in Bacolod City and MESCA in Bangalore, India. Similarly, students of the drama department of the Flinders University of South Australia in Adelaide have started exposure tours through the Asian theatre of liberation network. Now in its second phase, the Flinders project, directed by Julie Holledge, aims to facilitate creative interaction between grassroots theatre of liberation groups from the Philippines, South Korea, and Japan and multicultural target groups in the Adelaide area. From this international collaboration, Holledge hopes to distill a community theatre workshop model tailor-made for the South Australian grassroots and create an embryo theatre of liberation network.

It would certainly not be a luxury to include the theatre of liberation workshop process as an obligatory course in the curricula of Western theatre academies. It is a powerful cultural first-aid instrument that should be in any actor's tool box. As a vehicle for launching cultural resistance movements against fascist violation of human rights, abuse of power, and manipulation of the media, its strength has already been sufficiently demonstrated. After all, despite the recent thawing of the Cold War, all is not yet well in the West. Racist and neofascist political parties are stealthily expanding their electoral base from New Orleans to Orléans and into the former Eastern block. Anyone with a historical perspective reaching beyond a half century knows that we can never really rest on our laurels, put our souvenir piece of the Berlin wall on the mantelpiece, pop open a bottle of beer, kick back, and switch on the tube to watch a game or a soap. The rapid growth of the television entertainment industry and the mind-narrowing escapist products it continuously dumps on us and our children is a worrying form of cultural pollution that is ironically much less mediagenic than acid rain, exhaust fumes, and holes in ozone layers. In addition to reading, writing, arithmetic, and environmental education, it is high time we designed courses for our elementary schools in critical television viewing.

The theatre of liberation can be a tremendous resource to tackle all these problems and more. By developing its methods under the most difficult of circumstances, Asian artists have made a major contribution to humanity at large and world drama in particular. Their plays, parades, and workshops pay glorious tribute to theatre's essential vitality and ultimate indomitability. Even tanks, electronic rods, machetes, boots, and bullets have not been able to silence it. That should be a comforting thought to all of us.

NOTES

Preface

1. I am referring, of course, to Barba's ongoing experiments with the Odin Tea-
tret and the International School for Theatre Anthropology in the Danish city of
Holstebrø, Brook's (and Jean-Claude Carrière's) version of *Mahabharata,* and
Mnouchkine's *Sihanouk,* among others.

2. James. R. Brandon, *Theatre in Southeast Asia* (Cambridge, Mass.: Harvard University Press, 1967). See also his recent retrospective article "A New World: Asian
Theatre in the West Today," *The Drama Review* 33. No. 2 (Summer 1989), pp. 25–
50.

3. Kees P. Epskamp, *Theatre in Search of Social Change* (The Hague: CESO, 1989).

1. Revolution, Freedom and Theatre

1. Susan George, *How the Other Half Dies: The Real Reasons for World Hunger*
(London: Penguin, 1986), p. 113. All further quotations from this book refer to this
edition and are indicated parenthetically in the text.

2. President Suharto of Indonesia and President Aquino of the Philippines are two
of the better-known examples of megalandowner politicians in Asia.

3. The term "synthetic culture" comes from Filipino historian and cultural com-
mentator Renato Constantino, who provides sharp insight into third world consumer
patterns and media manipulations in his book *Synthetic Culture and Development* (Quezon City: Foundation for Nationalist Studies, 1985). Two other books worth reading
on the subject of mass media, multinational corporations, and the manipulating influence of government-controlled culture are Armand Mattelart's *Multinational Corporations and the Control of Culture: The Ideological Apparatus of Imperialism* (Brighton, Sussex: Harvester Press, 1979) and its sequel *Mass Media, Ideologies, and the Revolutionary
Movement* (Brighton, Sussex: Harvester Press, 1980).

4. See for instance W. F. Wertheim, "Europees Revolutiemodel en Aziatische
Werkelijkheid," in A. J. Rasker, ed. *Revolutie en Contrarevolutie* (Alphen aan den Rijn:
N. Samson, 1968); V. G. Kiernan, *Marxism and Imperialism* (London: Edward Arnold,
1974); Gérard Chaliand, *Revolution in the Third World: Myths and Prospects* (Hassocks,
Sussex: Harvester Press, 1977); and the following books by Noam Chomsky: *Ameri-
can Power and the New Mandarins* (New York: Pantheon Books, 1969); *At War with
Asia* (New York: Random House, 1970); *The Washington Connection and Third World
Fascism* (Nottingham: Spokesman, 1979); and *After the Cataclysm: Postwar Indochina
and the Reconstruction of Imperial Ideology* (Nottingham: Spokesman, 1980). Chomsky
cowrote the last two with Edward S. Herman.

5. See Chaliand (note 4) for more details about revolutionary movements in Asia.

6. Gustavo Gutierrez, *A Theology of Liberation: History, Politics, and Salvation*
(Maryknoll, N.Y.: Orbis Books, 1973), p. 36. All further quotations from this book
refer to this edition and are indicated parenthetically in the text.

7. Erich Fromm, *The Heart of Man,* quoted by Paulo Freire in *Pedagogy of the
Oppressed* (New York: Continuum, 1983), pp. 52–53.

8. Erich Fromm, *Fear of Freedom* (London: Routledge and Kegan Paul, 1960), p.
119. All further quotations from this book refer to this edition and are indicated
parenthetically in the text.

9. Erich Fromm, *Beyond the Chains of Illusion* (London: ABACUS-Sphere Books, 1980), p. 132.

10. Fromm, *Fear of Freedom*, pp. 118–119.

11. See Renato Constantino's *Synthetic Culture* for a similar view on public opinion and private thought (note 3).

12. Frantz Fanon, *The Wretched of the Earth* (New York: Grove Press, 1968), p. 47. All further quotations from this book refer to this edition and are indicated parenthetically in the text.

13. Hussein Abdilahi Bulhan, *Frantz Fanon and the Psychology of Oppression* (New York and London: Plenum Press, 1985), p. 257. All further quotations from this book refer to this edition and are indicated parenthetically in the text.

14. Norman K. Gottwald, ed., *The Bible and Liberation* (Maryknoll, N.Y.: Orbis Books, 1983), provides a useful introduction to liberation theology.

15. Clodovis Boff, "The Nature of Basic Christian Communities," *Concilium* 144 (1981), pp. 53–54. Further quotations from this article are indicated parenthetically in the text.

16. From the early seventies on, the Mindanao-Sulu Pastoral Conference sponsored a series of so-called creative dramatics workshops throughout the island of Mindanao. These workshops included structural analysis of the local community, basic theater exercises, and community organizing. As a result of these workshops, local theatre groups were organized. They functioned like Basic Christian Communities and presented liturgical plays which focused on the need of Christians to be involved in the struggle of the poor. See chapter 3 for a detailed description of the creative dramatics campaign.

17. Paulo Freire, *Pedagogy of the Oppressed*, p. 54. All further quotations from this book refer to this edition and are indicated parenthetically in the text.

18. Paulo Freire, *Cultural Action for Freedom* (Harmondsworth: Penguin, 1972), p. 27.

19. Ross Kidd and Krishna Kumar, "Co-opting Freire: A Critical Analysis of Pseudo-Freirian Adult Education," *Economic and Political Weekly* XVI Nos. 1–2 (Bombay), 3–10 January, 1981, pp. 27–36. See also Ross Kidd and Martin Byram's unpublished "Demystifying Pseudo-Freirian Non-Formal Education: A Case Description and Analysis of Laedza Batanani."

20. Indonesian playwright-poet Emha Ainun Nadjib sneeringly refers to such coopted development workers as "project brokers." See chapter 9.

21. John McGrath, *A Good Night Out* (London: Methuen, 1981), pp. 21–22.

22. Paulo Freire, *Pedagogy of the Oppressed*, pp. 177–178.

23. Augusto Boal, *Theatre of the Oppressed* (London: Pluto Press, 1979), pp. 120–156.

24. Boal: "After '68, I started developing the newspaper theatre and we became more clandestine. The repression was so violent that I was arrested. Two of my assistants were killed. I escaped, but they did not. And many other people in the theatre were killed also. But my group was only twenty people. Ten percent of our group was killed. It was horrible; it was very difficult to go on working there. When I got out of jail in '71 they told me, 'Well, that's the last time we arrest you, the next time we are not going to interrogate you, we are going to kill you. So you get the hell out of here.' It was the only advice I accepted from them." From: "To Dynamize the Audience," an interview with Augusto Boal transcribed by Robert Enright, *Canadian Theatre Review* No. 47 (Summer 1986), pp. 43–44.

25. Ibid, p. 48.

26. Boal, *Theatre of the Oppressed*, p. 126.

27. For detailed information on the Living Newspapers of the Federal Theater Project see chapters 3 and 7 of Sam Smiley's *The Drama of Attack: Didactic Plays of the Amer-*

ican Depression (Columbia: University of Missouri Press, 1972) and Jane de Hart Matthews, *The Federal Theatre, 1935–1939* (Princeton, N.J.: Princeton University Press, 1967).

28. For detailed descriptions of these other types of theatre of the oppressed, see Boal, *Theatre of the Oppressed,* pp. 149–155.

29. A. K. Pickering, "Village Drama in Ghana," *Fundamental and Adult Education* (UNESCO), Vol. 9, No. 4, 1957.

30. Ross Kidd and Mamunur Rashid, "Theatre by the People, for the People and of the People: People's Theatre and Landless Organizing in Bangladesh," *Bulletin of Concerned Asian Scholars* Vol. 16, No. 1 (1984), p. 35.

31. In 1984 two PETA members participated in a theatre of the oppressed workshop conducted by Boal in Paris.

32. In "Liberation or Domestication: Popular Theatre and Non-Formal Education in Africa," *Educational Broadcasting International* Vol. 12, No. 1 (March 1979), pp. 3–9, Ross Kidd cites some examples of how theatre of liberation methods have been used to "domesticate" rural populations in various African countries by attempting to change their behavior only to serve better as unquestioning elements in Western imposed development schemes.

33. Personal interview with Lutgardo Labad, Manila, 15 February 1986.

34. Ibid.

35. Lutgardo Labad, "Towards a Curriculum of People's Theater," PETA *Theater Studies* No. 3 (1983), p. 22.

36. Picket-line workshops, organized in collaboration with progressive labor unions, have had similar effects. In many ways, strikes are perfect occasions for such activities because the participants have time to spare and are in desperate need of finding a voice to express their grievances—or their grief over deaths of striking comrades who have been killed by military bullets. Joy Barrios, one of the driving forces behind Peryante, a theatre of liberation group composed of students from the University of the Philippines at Diliman, near Manila, told me how in December 1985 her group went to work for two weeks with the striking workers of the Artex rubber factory just outside Manila. Every day, after classes, the actors traveled to the plant by jeepney to conduct theatre workshops with the workers on the picket line. Together they created a play in which the police killing of a striking worker was reenacted. Thus, the theatre activities served a multiple purpose: it helped the workers occupy their free time on the picket line in a meaningful way; it channeled anger and grief over the comrade's death into positive action; the play was performed for friends and relatives and around town, thereby disseminating the facts about the strike and inviting contributions for the strikers' relief fund.

37. Script annotated from a reconstruction by Nestor Horfilla, Chris Millado, and Dessa Quesada.

2. Building Stages of People Power

1. Laban was formed after Ferdinand Marcos announced presidential elections in December 1985. It comprises the liberal political forces associated with Corazon Aquino and the more conservative, pro-American Unido [United] party headed by former Marcos ally Salvador Laurel. Bayan [People] combines the progressive democratic forces in the Philippines, ranging from radical union members on the far left to moderate social democrats.

2. Makati is Manila's fashionable business district and residential suburb for the rich.

3. See Isagani R. Cruz, ed., *A Short History of Theatre in the Philippines* (Manila: De La Salle University Press, 1971); Doreen G. Fernandez, *The Iloilo Zarzuela* (Que-

zon City: Ateneo de Manila University Press, 1978); Nicanor Tiongson, *Kasayayan at Estetika ng Sinakulo at Ibang Dulang Panrelihiyon sa Malolos* (Quezon City: Ateneo de Manila University Press, 1979) and *Kasaysayan ng Komedya sa Pilipinas* (Manila: De La Salle University Press, 1982).

4. For a useful and readable introduction to traditional and contemporary forms of Filipino theatre, see Nicanor Tiongson's "What Is Philippine Drama?" PETA *Theatre Studies* No. 1, 1984.

5. With the possible exception of Nick Joaquin's *Portrait of the Filipino as an Artist* (1952).

6. Cecilia Reyes Guidote, "A Prospectus for the National Theatre of the Philippines" (M.A. Thesis, Trinity University, Dallas, Texas, February 1967), p. 88.

7. Claro M. Recto was a progressive intellectual active in the 1950s. José-Maria Sisson is one of the leading ideologues of the Communist Party of the Philippines. He was released from prison in March 1986 and now lives in exile in the Netherlands. Renato Constantino is a widely respected historian whose books have strongly influenced the current Philippine cultural movement.

8. Personal interview with Nicanor Tiongson, Manila, 5 March 1986.

9. A version of *Pagsambang Bayan* was published in a special issue of the Japanese magazine *Ampo* XI, Nos. 2–3 (1979), pp. 48–65. It lists a certain Reverend J. Elias as the author instead of Bonifacio Ilagan.

10. Personal interview with Behn Cervantes, 4 March 1986.

11. This was only the first in a series of detentions which Cervantes, as one of the most outspoken Filipino dissidents, had to suffer.

12. Personal interview with Lutgardo Labad, Manila, 4 March 1986.

13. Brenda V. Fajardo, "The Aesthetics of Poverty: A Rationale in Designing for Philippine Theater," PETA *Theater Studies*, No. 5 (1985), p. 3.

14. Ibid, p. 2.

15. Malou L. Jacob, *Juan Tamban* (Quezon City: PETA Publications, 1984), p. 16.

16. Ibid,. p. 10.

17. Fajardo, p. 18.

18. Jacob, p. 42.

19. Nicanor Tiongson, *Pilipinas Circa 1907* (Quezon City: PETA Publications, 1985), p. 198. All further quotations from this play refer to this edition and are indicated parenthetically in the text.

20. Labad interview.

21. Nicanor Tiongson, "General Introduction," in *The Politics of Culture: The Philippine Experience*, ed. Nicanor Tiongson (Manila: PETA Publications, 1984), p. 5.

22. Ibid., pp. 4–5.

23. U.P.-Peryante, which stands for University of the Philippines Carnival Players, was founded by Chris Millado and Joy Barrios in 1981 in an attempt to get student theatre away from the repetitive and ineffectual red-banner and clenched-fist plays that were the fashion of the day.

24. Personal interview with Chris Millado, Manila, 12 February 1986.

25. U.P.-Peryante, *Ilocula, Part II*, in *Politics of Culture*, pp. 204–210.

26. Imelda Marcos was widely ridiculed for her desire to be an acclaimed singer. She often performed romantic songs on television, although her talents were hardly considered impressive. The daughter of the King of Thailand seems to suffer from the same affliction.

27. *Ilocula*, p. 209.

28. Ibid., p. 204.

29. René Villanueva is a professor of literature at the University of the Philippines. He also wrote *One Hundred Dreams*, a controversial play lampooning the First Lady's extravagance.

30. The Chico River Dam is a hydroelectric project in Kalinanga province in the northern Cordillera of the island of Luzon. The project involves the flooding of the sacred ancestral lands, burial grounds, and traditional dwellings of thousands of tribal people. The Chico River Dam project, financed by the IMF–World Bank, is still under construction but several houses have already been destroyed and the mountain people are forced to leave their homes for government housing made of concrete walls and sheet iron roofs.

31. The quotations from *Sigwa* are taken from the simultaneous translation provided by PETA staff member Joaquin Yabut during the performances at Dulaang Raha Sulayman, Fort Santiago, Intramuros, Manila, on the evenings of 13, 14, and 16 February 1986.

32. Behn Cervantes is considered a stalwart of the Philippine professional theatre. In the Philippines, he is best known for his productions of large-scale musicals like *Jesus Christ Superstar, Godspell,* and *Evita,* and for the highly political plays he used to direct at the University of the Philippines in the seventies. He is currently chairman of its Drama and Speech Department and hosts a television talk show. Lino Brocka is now an internationally renowned film director who is best known for his films *Angela Markada*—which won the Grand Prize in the Festival of the Three Continents in France—and *Kapit sa Patalim,* selected Best Film at the London Film Festival. As recently as 1989 his latest film, *Macho Dancer,* was selected as an official entry for the Cannes Film Festival. Brocka founded the Concerned Artists of the Philippines in July 1983. Both he and Cervantes have been imprisoned several times for their outspoken criticism of the Marcos régime.

33. The first public buildings the rebel soldiers occupied were the radio and television stations, thus clearly indicating how important control of culture and the media had become in the Philippine liberation struggle.

34. From a pamphlet provided to me by Behn Cervantes.

35. The quotations from *Nukleyar* are taken from a simultaneous translation provided by PETA staff member Jojo Sanchez during the performance at Gregorio Araneta University, Manila, 27 February 1986.

36. Personal interview with Al Santos, Manila, 27 February 1986.

37. PETA writers' pool, *Panata sa Kalayaan,* unpublished playscript.

38. Personal interview with Alan Glinoga, Las Piñas, 27 December 1987.

39. Ibid.

40. Ibid.

41. Reconstructed by Phil Noble during a personal interview, Manila, 26 February 1988.

42. Glinoga interview, 1987.

43. Ibid.

44. PETA has four different collectively structured departments. The first occupies itself full time with research and training; its output is the workshop. The production department comes next; its output is the television program, the film, or the stage performance. The third department manages the company's documentation, its library, and its publications. The fourth and last department, called "Support, Organizing, and Linkages," or SOL, coordinates PETA's networking activities. It provides the workshop teams with indispensable information before entering an area. Similarly, it also arranges the follow-up activities. One of SOL's most effective components is the so-called PETA extension desk service it has installed in different regions. In the 1987 interview, Alan Glinoga, SOL's former program director, described its function as follows: "We distinguish three classifications in our regional work: (1) there are areas like Mindanao where we are phasing out because the groups and institutions there are so developed that we no longer have a role to play; (2) areas where we are only beginning to phase in to lay the foundations for a full-blown program.

An example of that would be southern Tagalog, the Quezon provinces, Batangas, Laguna, Cavite, Mindoro, Palawan; (3) the established extension desks like Cordillera and the Visayan islands." A PETA extension officer has different tasks depending on the region where he or she operates. In Cordillera, for example, the extension officer carries out basic cultural research that will eventually lead to a comprehensive knowledge of the region. She takes inventory of cultural activities and local traditions and formulates a cultural action program based on that information. Extension officers do not provide training themselves but they allocate resources. They first identify the needs and then identify the resources best suited to meet those needs. In fact, the extension desks serve as advance teams: they survey a province or a community before the training unit comes in. PETA does not only rely on its own criteria when selecting target groups for workshops. It has good contacts with other people's organizations like neighborhood committees, progressive trade unions, teachers, and women's groups. These contacts also ensure that the workshop is not conducted in a vacuum but in a larger organizational structure that is already well established and can ensure future continuity of the process.

45. Glinoga interview, 1987.
46. Ibid.

3. Inside the Philippine Theatre of Liberation Network

1. Personal interview with Mimi Villareal, Cebu City, 4 January 1988.
2. Ibid. The archetypal *Dula Tula* is "The Incredible Adventures of Juan Peryodista," written by José F. ("Pete") Lacaba. It is a narrative poem about a day in the life of a young reporter who is not allowed by his editor to write the truth about all the artrocities he encountered walking around Manila. It was first performed by PETA and was published in Nicanor Tiongson, ed., *The Politics of Culture: The Philippine Experience* (Manila: PETA Publications, 1984), pp. 145–151.
3. Villareal interview.
4. Personal interview with Beth Mondragon, Cebu City, 5 January 1988.
5. Personal interview with Angela de la Cruz, 5 January 1988.
6. Personal interview with Sylvia van Raaij, the Dutch director of the "Prayer" show, Cebu City, 17 February 1988.
7. Personal interview with Teresita Palang, Mandaue, 9 January 1988.
8. Personal interview with Sally Minoza, Mandaue, 9 January 1988.
9. Personal interview with Toto Cuhit, Cebu City, 11 January 1988.
10. Personal interview with Julian Jagudilla, Cebu City, 11 January 1988.
11. Personal interview with Dolor Mercadez, Cebu City, 11 January 1988.
12. Ibid.
13. Personal interview with Babie Delmoro, Cebu City, 11 January 1988.
14. Ibid.
15. Personal interview with Joel Arbolario, Bacolod City, 22 January 1988.
16. Personal interview with Bundo Dedma, Bacolod City, 21 January 1988.
17. Arbolario interview.
18. Personal interview with Eman Carmona, 19 January 1988.
19. Personal interview with Fr. Dong Galenzoga, Marawi City, 10 February 1988.
20. This was the time that the Muslims created their own private army, called the Barracudas, to defend themselves against illegal landgrabbing by the Ilagas, the private army of the Christians. A bloody war was fought between these two armies from 1971 until 1973, when the Moro National Liberation Front (MNLF) was formed.
21. Personal interview with Fr. Larry Helar, Alicia, 6 February 1988.
22. Personal interview with Nestor Horfilla, Davao City, 15 February 1988. After his escape from Mindanao, Horfilla went to Cebu City where he conducted the first DKR workshop, in which Angela de la Cruz also participated (see note 5).

23. Ibid.
24. Personal interview with Greg Tabañag, Iligan City, 9 February 1988.
25. Helar interview.
26. Frank Rivera was a member of the PETA team that had participated in the Tagum workshop earlier that same year.
27. Fritz Bennewitz, director of the (former) DDR National Theatre in Weimar, has been involved in Asian theatre for twenty years. He has directed (mostly Brecht) productions for Indian theatre companies and PETA.
28. Personal interview with Samo Balt, Marawi City, 10 February 1988.
29. Personal interview with Jorge Benitez, Davao City, 3 February 1988.
30. Personal interview with Bonifacio Ilagan, Manila, 23 February 1988.
31. Personal interview with Alan Glinoga, Las Piñas, 26 December 1987.

4. Resistance Theatre in South Korea

1. Personal interview with Hwang Sok-yong, Kwangju, 4 and 5 December, 1986.
2. Ibid.
3. Personal interview with Kim Sok-man, Seoul, 14 December, 1986.
4. Ibid.
5. Ibid.
6. Ibid.
7. Hwang Sok-yong interview.
8. Ibid.
9. *Gut* or *Kut* (as it is also spelled sometimes) is the Korean term for a shamanistic ritual, referring particularly to the portion where the shaman, in trance, establishes contacts with the spirits through music, chanting, and dance. Over the generations, the dance and drama of the *Gut* seemed to have gained considerably in importance. The final segment of all madang plays is, essentially, a *Gut*.
10. Hwang Sok-yong interview.
11. Ibid.
12. Conflicting reports exist about the number of casualties of the Kwangju massacre, partly because of the total news blackout. Following the assassination of dictator Park Chung-hee on 26 October 1979, a mass movement for democratization was quickly mobilized. But on 17 May 1980, General Chun Doo-hwan took power and declared Martial Law. This resulted in mass demonstrations, particularly in the rebellious southern city of Kwangju. The military sent in a batallion of marines, who proceeded to murder some students from the local Chonnam University with bayonets. This brutal attempt at repression resulted in a mass revolt involving most of the population of this city of 800,000. Organized in civil brigades and arming themselves with truncheons and guns, they forced the army to withdraw. Meanwhile, Kwangju was sealed off from the outside world. A group of citizen representatives negotiated a settlement with the army commander: they would surrender all weapons on condition that the rebels would not be charged with sedition. Despite the agreement, the marines attacked the next day killing 2,000 people and wounding 3,000. Government officials claim there were not more than 286 dead.
13. Hwang Sok-yong interview.
14. Ibid.
15. Ibid.
16. Ibid.
17. Both performances were translated simultaneously by my guide from the *Minjung* movement who requested that he remain anonymous.
18. Ibid.
19. Reconstructed from the video registration of the *Arirang* performance at Kikker Theatre, Utrecht, Netherlands, 22 October 1989.

5. The Factionalized Indian Theatre of Liberation

1. Farley Richmond, "The Political Role of Theatre in India," *Educational Theatre Journal* 25, No. 3 (1973), pp. 318–334.

2. See Sudhi Pradhan, ed., *Marxist Cultural Movement in India* (Calcutta: National Book Agency, 1985) for a detailed survey in three volumes of IPTA and Communist-inspired art movements in India.

3. Vijay Tendulkar's most famous play is *Ghasiram Kotwal* (Calcutta: Seagull Press, 1984). It depicts the decadence of the Brahmins in 18th-century Poona.

4. The most successful exponent of this type is Habib Tanvir's *Charan das Chor,* a play performed by uneducated tribals and based on Chattisghari folk theatre and Sanskrit drama.

5. For a detailed account of *jatra* folk theatre and political theatre in West Bengal, see Rustom Bharucha, *Rehearsals of Revolution* (Calcutta: Seagull Press, 1983).

6. See Bharucha, *Rehearsals of Revolution,* chapter 2.

7. Fritz Bennewitz, director of the (former) East German National Theater in Weimar, has been directing Brecht plays in India since 1970.

8. The Academy Hall is one of Calcutta's more prestigious theatre venues.

9. Personal interview with Arun Mukherjee, Calcutta, 25 January 1986.

10. Personal interview with M. K. Raina, Bombay, 16 January 1986.

11. Personal interview with Anuradha Kapoor, New Delhi, 3 May 1988.

12. Ibid.

13. Ibid.

14. Ibid.

15. Personal interview with Prasanna, New Delhi, 1 May 1988.

16. Ibid.

17. Personal interview with Gladius, Bangalore, 25 April 1988.

18. Ibid.

19. Ibid.

20. Ibid.

21. Personal interview with Shashidara Adapa, Bangalore, 25 April 1988.

22. Reconstructed from a video registration, translated simultaneously by Shashidara Adapa.

23. Adapa interview.

24. Gladius interview.

25. Personal interview with Krishna Kumar, Trivandrum, 20 April 1988.

26. Ibid.

27. Reconstructed from a MESCA video documentary on KSSP.

28. Krishna Kumar interview.

29. Personal interview with Jos Chiramel, Trichur, 18 April 1988.

30. The Root play I witnessed is based on a Badal Sircar script by the same title which was published in his *Three Plays* (Calcutta: Seagull Press, 1985).

31. The Sanskrit play in question is called *Mudra Rakshasa.*

32. The ultra-leftist Naxalite movement started in the late sixties. After some initial success, the movement splintered in the mid seventies and has lost considerable momentum since then. Small Naxalite terrorist cells occasionally still shock the country with some violent actions.

33. Chiramel interview.

34. There are an estimated 200 million *Harijans* in India.

35. For a description of this workshop see Kees Epskamp, *Theatre in Search of Social Change* (The Hague: CESO, 1989), pp. 148–150.

36. Personal interview with Felix Sugirtharaj, Madras, 15 April 1988.

37. Ibid.

38. Ross Kidd is actually one of the pioneers of the theatre of liberation workshop methodology. He worked with Karl Gaspar in the Philippines and also helped to introduce the theatre of liberation to several African countries.

39. Personal interview with Mr. Brubha, Madras, 15 April 1988.

40. Personal interview with Mr. Murugesan, Madras, 15 April 1988.

41. Brubha interview.

42. Personal interview with K. V. Madan Mohan, Tiruvallur, 16 April 1988.

43. For more information about Lok Doot, see Epskamp, *Theatre in Search of Social Change,* pp. 150–152. On pp. 152–154 of this book, Epskamp also discusses the work of Jagran. See also Parminder Kaur Bakshi, "Jagran: Theatre for Education and Development," *New Theatre Quarterly* V, No. 18 (May 1989), pp. 124–139.

44. Jos Chiramel of Root in Trichur and MESCA's Shashidara Adapa have both participated in Sircar's workshops.

45. For a description of these other theatre artists from Calcutta see Bharucha, *Rehearsals of Revolution.*

6. Killed in Action

1. Personal letter from Moloyashree Hashmi, 4 January 1989.

2. The weekly newsmagazine *India Today* reported this in its issue of the second week of January 1989.

3. All quotes attributed to Safdar Hashmi are from interviews with the author conducted in New Delhi on 29 April and 3 May 1988.

4. See the beginning of chapter 5 for a detailed discussion of Theatre Union's women's plays.

5. Distilled from a description of *Aurat* given by Pakistani director Mohammed Shahid Lone, Lahore, 23 March 1988.

6. "F.I.R." stands for First Instance Report. When a crime is committed in India the victim files an F.I.R. at the police station.

7. I wish to thank Mr. Sudipto Chatterjee for correcting some of the misspellings in the earlier version of this chapter which appeared in *The Drama Review* 33, No. 4 (Summer 1989), pp. 32–47.

7. Of Stages and Mosques

1. Personal interview with Safdar Hashmi, New Delhi, 3 May 1988.

2. Ahmed Salim, "A Curtain-Raiser on Theatre," *The Star,* 27 March 1986, p. iv. Ahmed Salim is a respected Pakistani intellectual and poet whose newspaper articles on theatre have been a factor of note for the self-confidence of the current modern theatre movement in Pakistan.

3. Personal interview with Shahid Nadeem, Lahore, 19 March 1988.

4. Ibid.

5. Ibid.

6. Ibid.

7. For a detailed discussion of the Grips Theater see my *Radical People's Theatre* (Bloomington: Indiana University Press, 1988), pp. 109–124.

8. One of these groups, Tehrik-e-Niswan will be discussed in the section "Women's Theatre" below.

9. Personal interview with Aslam Azhar, Karachi, 27 March 1988.

10. Ibid.

11. Ibid.

12. Ifrain Husain, *The Star,* 2 May 1986.

13. Aslam Azhar interview.

14. Ibid.

15. Ibid.

16. *Procession* was published in Badal Sircar's *Three Plays* (Calcutta: Seagull Books, 1985).

17. Personal interview with Madeeha Gaudar, Lahore, 19 March 1988.

18. Ibid.

19. Personal interview with Shahid Nadeem, Lahore, 19 March 1988.

20. Ibid.

21. This festival was held in the first week of December 1989. Apart from Ajoka, Dastak participated with *Galileo* and *Exception and the Rule*. Grips Theatre also performed one of its children's plays and a new puppet group from Karachi called Peerzada presented an adaptation of *Faust*. Finally, a theatre group from Kuetta, a city near the Iranian border, also participated in the event, which took place in various private venues around the city.

22. In 1989, Nadeem wrote and directed several carefully researched television documentaries on folk culture in rural Pakistan and won a national award for a thirteen-part drama series based on his play *Barri,* which featured Madeeha Gauhar in the lead role.

23. Personal interview with Muhamed Wasim, Lahore, 22 March 1988.

24. Personal interview with Adnan Qadir Khan, Lahore, 22 March 1988.

25. Wasim interview.

26. See the previous chapter for a description of Hashmi's *Aurat.*

27. See the section on Sanjh Theatre Company below.

28. Nadeem interview.

29. Personal interview with Nisar Moyudin, Lahore, 22 March 1988.

30. Personal interview with Mohammed Shahid Lone, Lahore, 23 March 1988.

31. Ibid.

32. Shahid Nadeem, "Women's Movement Running Out of Steam," *Frontier Post,* 19 March 1988, p. 4.

33. All quotations from *The Acquittal* are from a video presentation in Lahore on 19 March 1988. Shahid Nadeem and Sohail Akbarwarrich provided the simultaneous translations.

34. According to a conservative interpretation of Islam, one can divorce a marital partner by saying the words "I divorce thee" three times. It is widely practiced in Pakistan.

35. Hers was a serious crime: premeditated murder preceded by adultery. Each year there are between six and seven hundred executions in Pakistan. Thirty-five of these are women.

36. Women prisoners in Pakistan are often raped.

37. Nadeem interview.

38. Such a law was actually passed in Pakistan in 1986. It stipulated that in order to prove rape, four male witnesses were required. Furthermore it declared a woman's testimony invalid for severe crimes like murder and worth only half a man's for any other cases.

39. Nadeem interview.

40. Ibid. Cendit stands for Centre for the Development of Instructional Technology.

41. Personal interview with Sheema Kermani, Karachi, 28 March 1988.

42. Ibid.

43. Personal interview with Kahlid Ahmad, Karachi, 28 March 1988.

44. Ibid.

45. Kermani interview.

46. I discuss this play in my *Radical People's Theatre,* p. 142.

8. Beyond the Shadows of *Wayang*

1. Correcting the earlier version of this chapter that appeared in *New Theatre Quarterly* 5, No. 17 (February 1989), pp. 36–52, Indonesia expert Michael Bodden writes: "Who engineered the coup is still a matter of debate. Some say the PKI (this is the official Indonesian government version and one that is generally accepted by most Western scholars for the obvious and usual reasons); some contend that it was simply a group of lower officers from the Central Javanese Diponegoro Division who objected to the decadent lifestyle of the chiefs of staff in Jakarta whom they also suspected of planning a coup against Sukarno, to whom the Diponegoro officers were quite loyal. Some rumors persist, and there is interesting evidence that does not allow these rumors to be completely put to rest, that Suharto himself organized the coup, or at least manipulated the events for his own ends once he knew things were afoot." Bodden recommends the following books for more detailed information: Julie Southwood and Patrick Flanagan, *Indonesia: Law, Propaganda, and Terror* (Boston: ZED, 1983); Benedict R. Anderson and Ruth McVey, *A Preliminary Analysis of the October 1 1965 Coup in Indonesia* (Ithaca, N.Y.: Cornell University Press, 1971); Peter Dale Scott, "Exporting Military-Economic Development" in Malcolm Caldwell, ed. *Ten Year's Military Terror in Indonesia* (Nottingham: Spokesman Books, 1975); and W. F. Wertheim, "Whose Plot? New Light on the 1965 Events," *Journal of Contemporary Asia* 9, No. 2 (1979).

2. Michael Bodden suggests that Western-type theatre may actually have started on a minor scale as early as the Japanese occupation in the forties.

3. According to Agam Wispi in his unpublished paper, "The Ups and Downs of Popular Theatre in Indonesia."

4. Ibid., p. 2.

5. Interview with Fred Wibowo, Yogyakarta, 14 November 1987.

6. Ibid.

7. During his absence of four years, Rendra also studied for a while at New York's Academy of Dramatic Arts.

8. Wibowo interview.

9. Ibid.

10. Ibid.

11. Annotated from the Studio Puskat video production *Der Verstossene*, 1987.

12. Wibowo interview.

13. Ibid.

14. *Kethoprak* is a central Javanese form of dance drama with plots derived from local histories and legends. Its rhythms allegedly originate in the songs peasant women sang while stamping rice in hollow logs. According to James R. Brandon, the Yogyakarta variety of *kethoprak*, which emphasizes spoken dialogue over dance and *gamelan* over Western instruments, came to be dominant after the 1920s. See James R. Brandon, *Theatre in Southeast Asia* (Cambridge, Mass.: Harvard University Press, 1967), pp. 47–48.

15. Annotated from the Studio Puskat video registration of the Tanen workshop. I am grateful to Michael Bodden for translating the commentary from Bahasa Indonesia into English.

16. From the Studio Puskat video production *Der Weg ist noch weit*.

17. Wibowo interview.

18. Ibid.

19. Personal interview with Father Rüdi Hoffmann, Yogyakarta, 14 November 1987.

20. Personal interview with Emha Ainun Nadjib, Yogyakarta, 19 November 1987. All further quotes attributed to Emha Ainun Nadjib are from this interview.

21. A *becah* is the Indonesian version of what Indians call a *rickshaw,* or bicycle taxi.

22. *Kyai* is the Indonesian term for Islamic spiritual community leader.

23. Earlier in 1987, Emha Ainun Nadjib discovered to his dismay, minutes before he was due to give a poetry reading in Jakarta, that his poems had mysteriously disappeared from the stage where he had placed them.

24. *Dagelan mataram* is a type of coarse peasant farce that has domestic quarrels as its main theme. The qualifier *mataram* indicates that this type of play was mainly performed and developed in the territory of the old Javanese Mataram kingdom, present-day central Java. The term *dagelan* is also used to indicate the clown figures in *kethoprak.*

25. Interview with Michael Bodden, Yogyakarta, 20 November 1987. All quotes from *Mas Dukun* were reconstructed by Michael Bodden in this interview.

26. Ibid.

27. Ibid.

28. Personal interview with Simon Hate, Yogyakarta, 16 March 1986.

29. Interview with Hate, Yogyakarta, 19 November 1987.

30. Generally speaking, Indonesian Islam is less fundamentalist in nature than, say, Islam in Pakistan, Malaysia, or the Islamic countries of Asia Minor. Nevertheless, certain Islamic traditions, not necessarily written down in the *Koran,* hinder the development of theatre as performing art. Conservative Islamic priests wage active campaigns against all kinds of artistic expression that promote secularism. More specifically, Islam in Indonesia and elsewhere discourages the presence of women in the theatre, both on the stage and in the auditorium. Particularly in the big cities, however, a gradual change is noticeable among the educated middle class, where female participation in theatre activities has become more widely acceptable.

9. Theatre of Liberation Experiments in Thailand

1. These statistics are based on information from the Thai Union of Civil Liberties.

2. An English translation of the play was recently published under the title "Seventh Floor" in *Tenggara* 23 (1989), pp. 115–124.

3. This term comes from Rassami Phao Luangthong. See note 8 below.

4. The name Crescent Moon refers to a similarly named group of Chinese writers in the Sun Yat Sen period of the Chinese Revolution. A crescent moon is also widely regarded as a symbol of continuous search for spiritual growth.

5. Personal interview with Kamron Kunadilok, Bangkok, 14 March 1988.

6. Ibid.

7. Ibid.

8. Personal interview with Rassami Phao Luangthong, Bangkok, 9 March 1988.

9. Kunadilok interview.

10. Ibid.

11. Ibid.

12. Chetana Nagavajara, "A Persistence of Music Drama: Reflections on Modern Thai Theatre," *Tenggara* 23 (1989), pp. 106–115.

13. *Ligay* is a type of Thai folk theatre that is related to similar forms found in Malay culture. Performers improvise the verse dialogues as well as the hand movements. Characters, mostly representing royalty and the upper class, wear elaborate and colorful costumes. *Ligays* also feature epic narrators who present the gist of the plot in the play's prelude.

14. Phao Luangthong interview.

15. Ibid.

16. Ibid.

17. Kunadilok interview.
18. Nagavajara, p. 113.
19. Kunadilok interview.
20. According to information I received in November 1990, Kunadilok still has not returned to the grassroots. Apparently he is currently employed by the Thai government as a media consultant.
21. Personal interview with Pradit Prasarttong, Bangkok, 11 March 1988.
22. Ibid.
23. Ibid.
24. Ibid.
25. I reconstructed the quotations from *Tree of Hope* with the help of Pradit Prasarttong.
26. Personal interview with Busaba Baratacharya, Bangkok, 4 March 1988.
27. Personal interviews with Santi Chitrachinda, Bangkok, 10 and 11 March 1988. All further quotes attributed to Chitrachinda come from these interviews.
28. Baratacharya interview.
29. Ibid.

10. Conclusion

1. The lack of good scripts and good writers is a problem not restricted to the theatre of liberation of Pakistan alone. One of the great weaknesses of Asian theatre of liberation in general is the failure to recruit the support of accomplished literary artists.
2. Personal interview with Joel Arbolario, Bacolod City, 22 January 1988.
3. See for instance Paul Früh, "Le droit international humanitaire porté à la scène," *Diffusion* 5 (August 1986), pp. 10–11; and "Humanity Amidst the Horrors of War," *National Geographic* (November 1986), pp. 665–666. Both articles describe theatre activities sponsored by the Red Cross in Khmer refugee camps on the Thai border.
4. See Kees Epskamp, *Theatre in Search of Social Change* The Hague: CESO, 1989), pp. 154–158; and Ross Kidd and Mamunur Rashid, "From Outside In to Inside Out: People's Theatre and Landless Organizing in Bangladesh," *Theater Work* 3, No. 2 (1983), pp. 29–40.
5. See Krishen Jit, "Contemporary Malaysian Theatre, *Tenggara* 23 (1989), pp. 179–187.
6. See Krishen Jit, "A Survey of Modern Southeast Asian Drama," *Tenggara* 23 (1989), pp. 1–26; and Mary Zurbuchen, "The *Cockroach Opera:* Image of Culture and National Development in Indonesia," *Tenggara* 23 (1989), pp. 125–150.
7. See Krishen Jit, "Modern Theatre in Singapore—A Preliminary Study," *Tenggara* 23 (1989), pp. 210–226.
8. Papua exiles in Holland have reported theatre activities among refugees from West Papua (the disputed territory of Indonesian Irian Jaya) in the mountainous border zones with Papua Niugini (Papua New Guinea). See also G. Murphy, *Raun Raun Theatre, 1979–1981* (Goroka: Raun Raun Theatre, 1981).
9. This controversy in South Africa's Black theatre of liberation movement came to light during a recent symposium at the University of Utrecht, 3 October 1990. The debate on the dubious benefits of Western tours started after the commercial success of *Wozza Albert* and *Bhopa!* and intensified after the acclaim of the Broadway production of the children's musical *Sarafina*.
10. Two such magazines have been launched in the past four years. One is edited by the Philippines Educational Theater Association (PETA) and is called *Makiisa*. The other one, *Mandala*, is more emphatically international in scope but appears irregularly and is editorially controlled by Filipino artists.

11. The inefficient drain on resources is only compounded by the parallel existence of several organizations claiming to be Asian networks of progressive artists. The organizations in question—Asian Theater Forum (ATF), Asian Cultural Forum on Development (ACFOD), Asian Council for People's Culture (ACPC), and the Solidarity-Outreach-Linkages (SOL) department of the Philippines Educational Theater Association (PETA)—all have their own separate offices, networks, financial partners from the West, and cadres with a disproportionately large presence of artists from Manila.

12. One of the sensations of the 1990 Edinburgh Fringe Festival was a play about the life of the homeless in Glasgow which was created and performed by the homeless themselves and directed by a professional theatre artist. See also Linda Frye Burnham, "Hands Across Skid Row: John Malpede's Performance Workshop for the Homeless of L.A.," *The Drama Review* 32, No. 2 (summer 1987), pp. 126–150.

13. I have already mentioned Madeleine Blackwell's involvement with Sydney's Detox theatre. During the 1987 New Zealand tour of three theatre of liberation artists from the Philippines, they also conducted a workshop in a women's prison near Wellington.

14. There have been some negative experiences when prejudiced Western theatre professionals went to work with Asian artists and turned out to be mentally unprepared for cultural differences, primitive circumstances, and the sensitivity of their target groups.

BIBLIOGRAPHY

General

Bappa, S., and M. Etherton. "Third World Popular Theatre: Voices of the Oppressed." *Commonwealth* 25, No. 4 (1983): 126–130.

Barba, Eugenio. "Theatre Anthropology." *The Drama Review* 26, No. 2 (Summer 1982): 5–32.

———. *Beyond the Floating Islands*. New York: Performing Arts Journal Publications, 1985.

———. *The Dilated Body*. Rome: Zeami Libri, 1985.

———. "Eurasian Theatre." *The Drama Review* 32, No. 3 (Fall 1988): 126–130.

Barrett, M., et al., eds. *Ideology and Cultural Production*. London: Croom Helm, 1979.

Benegal, Som. *Puppet Theatre Around the World*. New Delhi: Bhartiya Natya Sangh, 1961.

Berger, P. L. *Pyramids of Sacrifice: Political Ethics and Social Change*. Harmondsworth: Pelican Books, 1977.

Bhasin, Kamla. *Towards Empowerment*. New Delhi: FAO-India, 1985.

Boal, Augusto. *Técnicas lationamericanas de teatro popular: una revolución copernica al revés*. Buenos Aires: Corregidor, 1975.

———. *Theatre of the Oppressed*. London: Pluto Press, 1979.

———. *Jeux pour acteurs et non acteurs*. Paris: La Decouverte, 1985.

———, et al. "Special Section on Boal in the Late Eighties: Belgium, New York University, in Women's Theatre, and a Bibliography." *The Drama Review* 34, No. 3 (Fall 1990): 24–87.

Boff, Clodovis, "The Nature of Basic Christian Communities." *Concilium* 144 (1981): 53–58.

Brandon, James R. "The Social Role of Popular Theatre in Southeast Asia." *Modern Drama* 9 (1967): 396–403.

———. *Theatre in Southeast Asia*. Cambridge, Mass.: Harvard University Press, 1967.

———, ed. *The Performing Arts in Asia*. Paris: UNESCO, 1971.

———. *Traditional Asian Plays*. New York: Hill and Wang, 1972.

———. *Brandon's Guide to Theatre in Asia*. Honolulu: University Press of Hawaii, 1976.

———. *Asian Theatre: A Study Guide and Annotated Bibliography*. Washington, D.C.: University and College Theater Association of the American Theater Association, 1980.

———, "A New World: Asian Theatre in the West Today." *The Drama Review* 122, No. 2 (Summer 1989): 25–50.

Brown, Tom. "U.S. Think Tank in Panama Formulates Counterinsurgency." *Korean Herald* (13 November 1986): 12.

Brunet, Jacques. *Les Spectacles traditionnels et les moyens de communication de masse en Asie du Sud-Est*. Tehran: Asian Cultural Documentation Centre for UNESCO, 1979.

——— "Masks of Southeast Asia." *The Drama Review* 26, No. 4 (Winter 1982): 66–69.

Bruyn, Louise. "Theatre for the Living Revolution." *Theater Work* 1, No. 1 (1980): 3, 10–11; 18–20.

Bulhan, Hussein Abdilahi. *Frantz Fanon and the Psychology of Oppression.* New York and London: Plenum Press, 1985.

Buruma, I. "Political Propaganda and the Power of the Puppets." *The Far Eastern Economic Review* (9 August 1984): 34–36.

Cabral, A. "The Role of Culture in the Liberation Struggle." In: *Political Education in Africa.* Toronto: Latin American Research Unit, 1977.

Canclini, N. G. *Arte Popular y Sociedad en América Latina; Teorías Estéticas y Ensayos de Transformación.* Mexico: Editorial Grijalbo, 1977.

Chaliand, Gérard. *Revolution in the Third World.* Hassocks, Sussex: Harvester Press, 1977.

Chomsky, Noam. *American Power and the New Mandarins.* New York: Pantheon Books, 1969.

———. *At War with Asia.* New York: Random House, 1970.

———. *Problems of Knowledge and Freedom.* London: Narrie and Jenkins, 1972.

———and Edward S. Herman. *The Washington Connection and Third World Fascism.* Nottingham: Spokesman, 1979.

———and Edward S. Herman. *After the Cataclysm: Postwar Indochina and the Reconstruction of Imperial Ideology.* Nottingham: Spokesman, 1980.

Chu, C. G. *Moving a Mountain: Cultural Change in Asia.* Honolulu: University Press of Hawaii, 1979.

Courtney, Richard. *Play, Drama, and Thought: The Intellectual Background to Drama in Education.* London: Cassell, 1968.

DAGA, ed. *Migrant Labor for Sale.* Hong Kong: DAGA, 1985.

Epskamp, Kees P. "Getting Popular Culture Internationally Organised." *Sonolux Information* 11 (December 1983): 19–21.

———. "Going 'Popular' with Culture: Theatre as a Small-Scale Medium in Developing Countries." *Development and Change* 15 (1984): 43–64.

———, ed. *Education and the Development of Cultural Identity: Groping in the Dark.* The Hague: CESO, 1984.

———. "Avant-garde en volkstheater: een schreeuw uit Azië." In Kees Epskamp and Rogier van 't Rood, eds. *Populaire Cultuur op de planken: Theater, Communicatie en de Derde Wereld.* The Hague: CESO, 1989.

———. *Theatre in Search of Social Change.* The Hague: CESO, 1989.

van Erven, Eugène. "Theatre and Liberation: Political Theatre That Works (For a Change)." *Illusions* 3 (Spring 1986): 6–12.

———. *Radical People's Theatre.* Bloomington: Indiana University Press, 1988.

———. "The Theatre of Liberation of India, Indonesia, and the Philippines." *Australasian Drama Studies* 10 (April 1987): 5–21.

———. "Aziatische Karavaan trekt door Nederland." *Onze Wereld* 10 (October 1989): 41–44.

Eschenback, J. *The Role of Broadcasting in Rural Communication.* Bonn: Friedrich Ebert Stiftung, 1979.

Fanon, Frantz. *The Wretched of the Earth.* New York: Grove Press, 1968.

———. *Peau noire, masques blancs.* Paris: Editions du Seuil, 1952.

Frank, M. "The Real Cultural Revolution." *Development and Cooperation* 1 (1982): 16–18.

Freire, Paulo. *Cultural Action for Freedom.* Harmondsworth: Penguin, 1972.

———. *Pedagogy of the Oppressed.* New York: Continuum, 1983.

Fromm, Erich. *Fear of Freedom.* London: Routledge and Kegan Paul, 1960.

———. *Beyond the Chains of Illusion: My Encounter with Marx and Freud.* London: ABACUS-Sphere Books, 1980.

George, Susan. *How the Other Half Dies: The Real Reasons for World Hunger.* London: Penguin, 1986.

Gottwald, Norman K. ed. *The Bible and Liberation: Political and Social Hermeneutics.* Maryknoll, N.Y.: Orbis Books, 1983.

Gough, K., and H. P. Sharma, eds. *Imperialism and Revolution in South Asia.* New York: Monthly Review Press, 1973.

Guma, Greg. "Liberation Theology and Art: The Basic Connection." In: *Bread and Puppet: Stories of Struggle and Faith from Central America.* Burlington, Vt.: Green Valley Film and Art, 1985.

Gutierrez, Gustavo. *A Theology of Liberation: History, Politics, and Salvation.* Maryknoll, N.Y.: Orbis Books, 1973.

Hecht, Werner, Karl-Claus Hahn, and Elifius Paffrath, eds. *Brecht in Afrika, Asien und Lateinamerika.* Berlin: Henschelverlag, 1980.

Hyland, Peter, ed. *Discharging the Canon: Cross-Cultural Readings in Literature.* Singapore: Singapore University Press, 1986.

Illich, I. *Tools for Conviviality.* Glasgow: Fontana-Collins, 1979.

Jit, Krishen, ed. "Special Issue on Contemporary Theatre in Southeast Asia." *Tenggara* 23 (1989).

———. "A Survey of Modern Southeast Asian Drama." *Tenggara* 23 (1989): 179–187.

Kaplún, Mario, and J. O'Sullivan-Ryan. *Communication Methods to Promote Grassroots Participation.* Paris: UNESCO, 1979.

Kapoor, Anuradha and Sushma. *Women and Media in Development.* New Delhi: Cendit, 1986.

Katz, Elihu. "Can Authentic Cultures Survive New Media?" *Journal of Communication* 27, No. 2 (1977): 113–121.

———, and George Wedell. *Broadcasting in the Third World: Promise and Performance.* Cambridge, Mass.: Harvard University Press, 1977.

Khaznadar, Chérif. "Tendencies and Prospects for Third World Theatre." *The Drama Review* 17, No. 4 (1973): 33–35.

———, Françoise Chatal, and John Donne. "Masks in Tiber, India, Bhutan, and Sri Lanka." *The Drama Review* 26, No. 4 (Winter 1982): 73–78.

Kidd, Ross. "Liberation or Domestication: Popular Theatre and Non-Formal Education in Africa." *Educational Broadcasting International* 12, No. 1 (March 1979): 3–9.

———. "People's Theatre, Conscientization, and Struggle." *Media Development* 27, No. 3 (1980): 10–14.

———. *The Popular Performing Arts, Non-Formal Education, and Social Change in the Third World: A Bibliography and Review Essay.* The Hague: CESO, 1982.

———. "Reclaiming Culture." *Fuse* 6, No. 5 (January–February 1983): 264–275.

———. *From People's Theatre for Revolution to Popular Theatre for Reconstruction: Diary of a Zimbabwean Workshop.* The Hague: CESO, 1984.

———, and N. J. Colletta, eds. *Tradition for Development: Indigenous Structures and Folk Media in Non-Formal Education.* Berlin: German Foundation for International Development, 1980.

———, and Krishna Kumar. "Co-opting Freire: A Critical Analysis of Pseudo-Freirean Adult Education." *Economic and Political Weekly* XVI, Nos. 1–2 (3–10 January 1981): 27–36.

———, Lutgardo Labad, and Raul A. Leis. *Popular Theater = People's Theatre.* Calcutta: CCCA, 1985.

Kiernan, V. G. *Marxism and Imperialism.* London: Edward Arnold, 1974.

Kim, Eui-kyung, ed. *Four Prize-Winning Original Plays.* Seoul: Korean Centre of the ITI, 1984.

Lambert, Pru. "Popular Theatre: One Road to Self-Determined Development Action." *Community Development Journal* 17, No. 3 (1982): 242–249.

Lappé, Frances Moore and Joseph Collins. *World Hunger: Twelve Myths.* New York: Grove Press, 1986.

Lent, John A. *Topics in Third World Mass Communications: Rural and Developmental Journalism, Cultural Imperialism, Research, and Education.* Hong Kong: Asian Research Service, 1979.

———. "Grassroots Renaissance: The Increasing Importance of Folk Media in Third World Nations." *Folklore* 9, No. 1 (1979): 78–91.

Lerner, D., and W. Schramm, eds. *Communication and Change: The Last Ten Years and the Next.* Honolulu: University Press of Hawaii, 1976.

Lewis, George. H. "The Sociology of Popular Culture." *Current Sociology* 26, No. 3 (1978): 6–17.

———. "Mass, Popular, Folk, and Elite Cultures." *Media Asia* 6, No. 1 (1979): 41–42.

Malik Baljit, ed. "Special Issue on Asian Rural Drama." *Asian Action* 7 (1977).

Mattelart, Armand. *Multinational Corporations and the Control of Culture: The Ideological Apparatus of Imperialism.* Brighton, Sussex: Harvester Press, 1979.

———. *Mass Media, Ideologies, and the Revolutionary Movement.* Brighton, Sussex: Harvester Press, 1980.

———, and Seth Seigelaub. *Communication and Class Struggle.* Bagnolet, France: International Mass Media Research Centre, 1979.

McCann, Dennis P. *Christian Realism and Liberation Theology.* Maryknoll, N.Y.: Orbis Books, 1981.

McGrath, John. *A Good Night Out.* London: Methuen, 1981.

Moreno, J. L. *Psychodrama.* New York: Beacon House, 1946.

Mydral, Jan. *Confessions of a Disloyal European.* New York: Pantheon Books, 1968.

O'Brien, Conor Cruise. "God and Man in Nicaragua." *The Atlantic Monthly* (August 1986): 50–72.

Orr, I. C. "Puppet Theatre in Asia." *Asian Folklore Studies* 33 (1974): 69–84.

Pacific-Asia Resources Center. *Theater as Struggle: Asian People's Drama.* Special issue of *Ampo* 11, Nos. 2–3 (1979).

Prosser, M. H. *The Cultural Dialogue: An Introduction to Intercultural Communication.* Boston, 1978.

Rasker, A. J., ed. *Revolutie en Contrarevolutie.* Alphen aan de Rijn: N. Samson, 1968.

Richmond, Farley. "Asian Theatre Materials: A Selected Bibliography." *The Drama Review* 15, No. 3 (1971): 312–323.

Said, Edward W. *Orientalism.* New York: Pantheon, 1978.

San Juan, E. "Art against Imperialism, for the National Liberation Struggle of Third World Peoples." *Journal of Contemporary Asia* 4, No. 3 (1974): 297–307.

Santiago, Jesús Manuel. "The Emerging Culture of Resistance in Asia-Pacific." *Mandala* 1, No. 2 (1987): 1–3.

Schechner, Richard. *Essays on Performance Theory, 1970–1976.* New York: Drama Books, 1977.

———. *Performative Circumstances from the Avant Garde to Ramlila.* Calcutta: Seagull Books, 1983.

———. *Between Theater and Anthropology.* Philadelphia: University of Pennsylvania Press, 1985.

———, ed. "Special Issue on Theatre and Social Action." *The Drama Review* 21, No. 1 (March 1977).

Schiller, Herbert. *Communication and Cultural Domination.* White Plains, N.Y.: International Arts and Sciences Press, 1976.

Schipper-de Leeuw, Mineke. *Toneel en Maatschappij in Afrika.* Amsterdam: van Gorcum Assen, 1977.

Scott, A. C. *The Theatre in Asia.* New York: Macmillan, 1973.

Serkkola, A., and C. Mann, eds. *The Cultural Dimension of Development.* Helsinki: Publications of the Finnish National Commission for UNESCO, No. 33, 1986.

Southern, Richard. *The Seven Ages of the Theatre.* London: Faber and Faber, 1962.

Spolin, Viola. *Improvisations for the Theater.* Evanston, Ill. Northwestern University Press, 1983.

Sternhell, Seev, et al. *Naissance de l'idéologie fasciste.* Paris: Fayard, 1989.

Sticks and Stones. *Neighbourhood Action Recipes for Change.* Sudbury, Ontario: Neighbourhood Action, 1985.

Taylor, Debbie. "Living Images: The Politics of Culture." *New Internationalist* 98 (1981): 7–9.

———. "All the World's a Stage: Popular Theatre in the Third World." *New Internationalist* 100 (1981): 20–22.

Tham, Seong Chee, ed. *Essays on Literature and Society in Southeast Asia.* Singapore: Singapore University Press, 1981.

Trussler, Simon, and Clive Barker, eds. "Special Issue on Theatre for Social Change." *Theatre Quarterly* II, No. 8 (October–December 1972).

Usmani, Renate. "To Rehearse the Revolution." *Canadian Theatre Review* 47 (Summer 1986): 38–55.

Villalba, Noel. *Dialog-Asia.* Hong Kong: Christian Conference of Asia, 1986.

Wang, Georgette. *Annotated Bibliography on Folk Media for Development Communication.* Honolulu: East-West Communication Institute, 1981.

Wardle, I. "Rituals in the Desert: The Shiraz Festival." *Gambit* 5, Nos. 18–19 (1971): 144–158.

Wilson, Dick. *Asia Awakes: A Continent in Transition.* New York: New American Library, 1971.

Yabes, Leopoldo Y., ed. *Asian Writers on Literature and Justice.* Manila: Philippine Center of P.E.N., 1982.

Zarrilli, Phillip, "For Whom Is the 'Visible' Not Visible?" *The Drama Review* 32, No. 1 (Spring 1988): 95–106.

Australasia

Campbell, Russell, and Jeremy Royal. "Hakas and Jasmine: The Filipino Workshop Tour and the Maori Theatre Network." *Illusions* (New Zealand) 6 (1987): 9–15.

Dizon, C., and C. Johnson. "Theatre, Politics, and the Australian Aboriginal." *Canadian Theatre Review* 29 (1981): 33–36.

"Doing It Like the Dua Dua." *New Nation* (Papua New Guinea) 3, No. 8 (1979): 8–9.

van Erven, Eugène. "Philippine People's Theatre Down Under." *New Theatre Australia* 2 (December 1987): 33–38.

Kennedy, Kathy. "What Is Drama, Man?" *New Nation* (Papua New Guinea) 2, No. 2 (1978): 4–5.

Murphy, Greg. "Kainantu Farces and Raun-Raun Theatre." *Gigibori* 4, No. 1 (1978).

———. The Concept of a National theatre in Papua New Guinea." *Culture* 3 (1980): 9–11.

———. *Raun Raun Theatre, 1979–1981.* Goroka: Raun Raun Theatre, 1981.

Oxford, Gilian. "The Purple Everlasting: The Aboriginal Cultural Heritage in Australia." *Theatre Quarterly* 7, No. 26 (1977): 88–97.

Quesada, Dessa. *"Kia Ora!* Filipino Cultural Workers in Aotearoa." *Makiisa* 1, No. 1 (1988): 14–15; 40.

Ross, Margaret Clunies. "The Aesthetics and Politics of an Arnhem Land Ritual." *The Drama Review* 33, No. 4 (Winter 1989): 107–127.

Royal Commission on Social Policy. *The Treaty of Waitangi and Social Policy*. Auckland, Wellington, and Christchurch: Office of the Race Relations Conciliator, 1988.

Bangladesh

Bangladesh People's Solidarity Centre. *The Peasant Movement and the Future of Bangladesh*. Amsterdam: B.P.S.C., 1988.
Epskamp, Kees. P. "Popular Theatre and development in Bangladesh: Some Notes on the 'Popular Theatre Dialogue' in Koitta/Dhaka, 4–16 February 1983." The Hague: CESO Occasional Papers, 1983.
Haque, A. S. Z. "The Use of Folklore in Nationalist Movements and Liberation Struggles: A Case Study of Bangladesh." *Journal of the Folklore Institute* 12, Nos. 2–3 (1975): 211–240.
Jasimuddin. "The Drama of the People: East-Pakistan's Soul in Action." *Pakistan Quarterly* 9 (1959): 36–39.
Kidd, Ross, and Mamunur Rashid. " From Outside In to Inside Out: People's Theatre and Landless Organizing in Bangladesh." *Theatre Work* 3, No. 2 (1983): 29–40.
Roy, Rati Ranjan. "Folk Poetry in Bangladesh: Updating Traditional Forms to Carry Timely Messages." *Development Communication Report* 34 (1981): 84.

Burma

Becker, A. L. "Journey through the Night: Notes on Burmese Traditional Theatre." *The Drama Review* 15, No. 3 (1971): 83–87.
"Burmese Theatre: Outlet for Dissent." *New York Times* (13 November 1977).
Sein, Kenneth, and Joseph Withey. *The Great Po Sein: A Chronicle of the Burmese Theatre*. Bloomington: Indiana University Press, 1966.

Cambodia

Bharucha, Rustom. "Cambodia and Theatre." *Theater* 11 (1980): 92–95.
"Cambodia Is Putting Propaganda to Music." *New York Times* (13 November 1977).

China

Chu, C. G., ed. *Popular Media in China: Shaping the New Cultural Patterns*. Honolulu: University Press of Hawaii, 1979.
Committee of Concerned Asian Scholars. *China! Inside the People's Republic*. New York: Bantam Books, 1972.
Howard, Roger. "People's Theatre in China since 1907." *Theatre Quarterly* 1, No. 4 (1971): 67–82.
———. "Agitation and Anaesthesia: Aspects of Chinese Theatre Today." *Theatre Research International* 11 (1976): 53–64.
———. *Contemporary Chinese Theatre*. London: Heinemann, 1978.
MacKerras, Collin, *Amateur Theatre in China, 1949–1966*. Canberra: Australian National University Press, 1973.
———. *The Chinese Theatre in Modern Times: From 1840 to the Present Day*. London: Thames and Hudson, 1975.
———. "The Taming of the Shrew: Chinese Theatre and Social Change since Mao." *Australian Journal of Chinese Affairs* 1 (1979): 1–16.
McDougall, Bonnie S. *Mao Zedong's "Talks at the Yan'An Conference on Literature and Art": A Translation of the 1943 Text with Commentary*. Ann Arbor: Center for Chinese Studies, University of Michigan, 1980.

Meserve, W. J. and R. I. Meserve. "Theatre for Assimilation: China's National Minorities." *Journal of Asian History* 13, No. 2: 95–120.

Rea, Kenneth. "New Theatre in China." *The Drama Review* 21, No. 1 (March 1977): 18–26.

Zheng, Wang, et al. "Speaking about China's Spoken Drama." *The Drama Review* 33, No. 2 (Summer 1989): 87–103.

India

Abrams, Tevia. "Folk Theatre in Maharashtran Social Development Programmes." *Educational Theatre Journal* 27, No. 1 (1975): 395–407.

Ahmed, Huma. "Protest Movements by Women." *Indian Journal of Youth Affairs* 2, No. 2 (1980): 15–26.

Ashley, W. "From Ritual to Theatre in Kerala." *The Drama Review* 26, No. 2 (Summer 1982): 59–72.

Awasthi, Suresh. "The Scenography of the Traditional Theatre of India." *The Drama Review* 18, No. 4 (December 1974): 36–46.

———. "Theatre of Roots': Encounter with Tradition." *The Drama Review* 33, No. 4 (Winter 1989): 48–69.

———. "Retrospective of Modern Indian Theatre." *The Drama Review* 34, No. 3 (Fall 1990): 183–189.

Bakshi, Parminder Kaur. "Jagran: Theatre for Education and Development." *New Theatre Quarterly* V, No. 18 (May 1989): 124–139.

Bandyopadhyay, Samik. "Badal Sircar: Middle-Class Responsibilities." *Sangeet Natak* 22 (October–December 1971).

Banu, Georges. "Talking with the Playwright, the Musician, and the Designer." *The Drama Review* 30, No. 1 (Spring 1986): 72–81.

Barreto, Duarte. *India's Search for Development and Social Justice.* Bangalore: Centre for Social Action, 1984.

Bartholomew, Rati. "Samudaya: Searching for a People's Culture." *Alternative News and Features* 4 (1980): 3–5.

———, ed. "People's Theatre." Special Issue of *How* 6, No. 1–2 (January–February 1983).

Benegal, Som. *A Panorama of Theatre in India.* New Delhi: Indian Council for Cultural Relations, 1968.

Bharucha, Rustom. *Rehearsals of Revolution.* Calcutta: Seagull Press, 1983.

Bhattacharya, Ashutosh. "Jatra of Bengal." *Sangeet Natak* 12 (1969): 20–39.

Bhattacharya, Malini and Mihir. "An Armoured Car on the Road to Proletarian Revolution: Interview with Utpal Dutt." *Journal of Arts and Ideas* (July–September 1984): 25–42.

Communist Party of India (Marxist). *Political Resolution.* New Delhi: Hari Singh Kang, 1986.

———. *Role of Stalin as the CPI (M) Views It.* New Delhi: National Book Centre, 1987.

———. *CPI (M) in Punjab: The Martyrs of the Struggle for National Unity.* New Delhi: Hari Singh Kang, 1987.

"Cultural Jatha." *Deccan Herald* (Bangalore) (13 October 1978).

Das, Kajal Kumar. *Burrakatha of Andrah Pradesh.* New Delhi: Indian Institute of Mass Communication, 1980.

Desai, A. R., ed. *Peasant Struggle in India.* Bombay: Oxford University Press, 1979.

Desrochers, John. *Education for Social Change.* Bangalore: Centre for Social Action, 1987.

Dutt, Utpal. *Invincible Vietnam.* Calcutta: People's Little Theatre, 1976.

————. *Towards a Revolutionary Theatre*. Calcutta: Sarkar and Sons, 1982.

Emigh, John and Ulrike. "Hajari Bhand of Rajasthan: A Joker in the Deck." *The Drama Review* 30, No. 1 (Spring 1986): 101–130.

van Erven, Eugène. "Tragedy Shocks New Delhi's Theatre Movement." *New Theatre Australia* 10 (May–June 1989): 40–44.

————. "Plays, Applause, and Bullets: Safdar Hashmi's Street Theatre." *The Drama Review* 33, No. 4 (Winter 1989): 32–47.

————. "Theater, Applaus und Kugels." *IKA* 38 (January 1990): 16–18, 27.

————, and S. Chatterjee. "Postcolonial Imperialism?" *The Drama Review* 34, No. 3 (Fall 1990): 16–19.

Fernandez, A. "Jagran: Theatre of the People." *Seva Vani* (India) 6, No. 1 (1976): 6–9.

Gargi, Balwant. *Folk Theatre of India*. Seattle: University of Washington Press, 1966.

Gunawardana, A. J. "Revolution: Calcutta; Theatre as Weapon: An Interview with Utpal Dutt." *The Drama Review* 15, No. 3 (Spring 1971): 226–237.

————. "Problems and Directions: Calcutta's New Theatre." *The Drama Review* 15, No. 3 (Spring 1971): 241–245.

Gupta, Bhabani Sen. *Communism in Indian Politics*. New York: Columbia University Press, 1972.

Hashmi, Safdar. "The Theatre of Dynamism: An Interview with Peter Brook." *Student Struggle* II, No. 9 (March 1982): 18–21.

————. "The Enchanted Arch." *Student Struggle* III, No. 10 (April 1983): 14–17.

————. "Hindustani Theatre: Hiding behind Forms." *The Economic Times* (16 June 1985): 6–7.

————. "Inner Wilderness of 'Aranya'." *The Economic Times* (18 August 1985): 3.

————. "What Is Secular Theatre?" *The Economic Times* (29 September, 1985): 3.

————. "Face to Face with Mythology." *The Economic Times* (6 October 1985): 3, 6.

————. "A Disturbing Scenario." *The Economic Times* (13 October 1985): 3.

————. "Cleanse Thy Soul." *The Economic Times* (20 October 1985): 3, 6.

————. "The Tradition of Street Theatre." *The Economic Times* (6 April 1986): 4–5.

————. "Anti-Colonialism and Religion." *The Economic Times* (3 August 1986): 4.

Jain, Nemi Chandra, ed. "Special Issue: Traditional Idiom in Contemporary Theatre." *Sangeet Natak* Nos. 77–78. (July–December 1985).

Kapur, Jyotsna. "Update: Safdar Hashmi." *The Drama Review* 34, No. 1 (Spring 1990): 16.

Kosambi, D. D. *Science, Society, and Peace*. Pune: Academy of Political and Social Studies, 1986.

Krishnan, P. "Jagran: Theatre of the People." *Voluntary Action* 21, No. 12 (1979): 4–7.

K.S.S.P. *In Praise of Learning*. Trivandrum: KSSP, 1985.

Lèvi, Sylvain. *The Theatre of India*. Calcutta: Writers Workshop Books, 1978 (2 volumes).

Malik, S. C., ed. *Dissent, Protest, and Reform in Indian Civilization*. Simla: Indian Institute of Advanced Studies, 1977.

Mathur, J. C. *Drama in Rural India*. Bombay: Asia Publishing House, 1964.

————. "Theatre as a Vehicle for Adult Education." *Indian Journal of Adult Education* 38, No. 1 (1977): 1–2.

Mehra, Rekha. *Jagran Evaluation: An Attitudinal Evaluation of the Impact of Pantomime*. New Delhi: CASA, 1978.

Millon, Martine. "Talking with Three Actors." *The Drama Review* 30, No. 1 (Spring 1986): 82–91.

Mukhopadhyay, Durgadas. *Lesser Known Forms of Performing Arts in India*. New Delhi: Sterling Publishers, 1978.

Pani, Narendar. *Staging A Change*. Bangalore: Samudaya Prajashana, 1979.
———. "Calcutta Jathas on 4,000 km. March through Rural Areas of Karnataka." *How* 4, No. 1 (1981): 15.
Patnayk, Subodh. *Beyond the Psycho Theatre*. Bhubaneswar: Natyachetana, 1990.
Paul, Seema. "All Work and All Play." *The Telegraph* (9 April 1988): 13.
Pereira, M. J. "Using Puppets to Teach Ideas: Khel Dori Ka: An Audiovisual with Puppets from Bombay." *Development Communication Report* 40 (1982): 3–4.
Pradhan, Sudhi, ed. *Marxist Cultural Movement in India: Chronicles and Documents (1936–1947)*. Calcutta: National Book Agency, 1985.
Prem Chandran, John. "Why Popular Theatre?" *Dialogue* 3, No. 1 (April 1986): 1.
Raha, Kironmoy. *Bengali Theatre*. New Delhi: National Book Trust, 1978.
Rangacharya, Adya. *The Indian Theatre*. New Delhi: National Book Trust, 1971.
Rao, Purna Chandra. "In Search of an Alternative Theatre of the Rural Poor." *Mandala*. 1, No. 2 (1987): 4–5.
Rea, Kenneth. "Theatre in India: The Old and the New, Part III." *Theatre Quarterly* 8, No. 32 (1979): 47–66.
Richmond, Farley. "The Political Role of Theatre in India." *Educational Theatre Journal* 25, No. 3 (1973): 318–334.
"Samudaya Project." *Deccan Herald* (23 September 1979).
Sangeet Natak. "Special Issue on Contemporary Relevance of Traditional Theatre." *Sangeet Natak* 21 (1971).
Schechner, Richard, et al. "The *Mahabharata:* Talking with Peter Brook." *The Drama Review* 30, No. 1 (Spring 1986): 52–71.
Singh Surjeet, Harkishan. *On CPI(M)-CPI Differences*. New Delhi: National Book Centre, 1985.
Sircar, Badal. *There's No End*. Delhi: Enact Publications, 1971.
———. *Evam Indrajit*. Calcutta: Oxford University Press, 1977.
———. *The Third Theatre*. Calcutta: Badal Sircar, 1978.
———. "A Letter from Badal Sircar." *The Drama Review* 26, No. 2 (Summer 1982): 51–58.
———. *Three Plays*. Calcutta: Seagull Press, 1985.
Srivasta, S. N. *Rural Drama*. New Delhi: Indian Adult Education Association, 1961.
"Street Corner Plays on Delhi Transit Corporation Fare Hike." *National Herald* (New Delhi) (20 February 1979).
Surgirtharaj, Felix. "Organising Harijan Action. *Voluntary Action* 21, No. 1 (1979): 14–15.
———. "The Role of Popular Theatre in Rural Development and People's Movement." *Dialogue* 3, No. 1 (April 1986): 3–14.
Swaminathan, M. "Communicating with Adults through Drama in Mobile Creches." *Indian Journal of Adult Education* 40, No. 12 (1979): 7–12.
Tanvir, Habib. "The Indian Experiment in Theatre." *International Theatre Information* (Summer 1976): 2–9.
———. "Tribal Development through Performing Arts." *How* (India) 1, No. 1 (1978): 21–22.
Tendulkar, Vijay. *Ghashiram Kotwal*. Calcutta: Seagull Press, 1984.
Varapande, M. L. *Traditions of Indian Theatre*. New Delhi: Shakti Malik, 1967.
Vatsyayan, Kapila. *Classical Indian Dance in Literature and the Arts*. New Delhi: Sangeet Natak Academy, 1968.
———. *Multiple Streams: Traditional Indian Theatre*. New Delhi: National Book Trust, 1980.
Waltz, M. L. "The Indian People's Theatre Association: Its Development and Influences." *Journal of South Asian Literature* 13, Nos. 1–4 (1977–1978): 31–37.

Zarrilli, Phillip. B. *The Kathakali Complex: Actor, Performance and Structure.* New Delhi: Abhinav, 1984.

——. "The Aftermath: When Peter Brook Came to India." *The Drama Review* 30, No. 1 (1986): 92–99.

——, and Richard Schechner. "Collaborating on Odissi." *The Drama Review* 32, No. 1 (Spring 1988): 128–138.

——, et al. "More Aftermath after Peter Brook." *The Drama Review* 32, No. 2 (Summer 1988): 14–19.

Indonesia

Agassi, Judith B. *Mass Media in Indonesia.* Cambridge, Mass.: M.I.T. Center for International Studies, 1969.

Anderson, Benedict, R. *Mythology and Tolerance of the Javanese.* Ithaca, N.Y.: Cornell University Press, 1965.

——, and Ruth McVey. *A Preliminary Analysis of the October 1 1965 Coup in Indonesia.* Ithaca, N.Y.: Cornell University Press, 1971.

Belo, Jane, comp. *Traditional Balinese Culture.* New York: Columbia University Press, 1970.

Buurman, Peter. *Wayang Golek: The Entrancing World of Javanese Puppet Theatre.* Oxford: Oxford University Press, 1988.

Colletta, N. J. "The Use of Indigenous Culture as a Medium for Development: The Indonesian Case." *Prisma* (Indonesia) 1, No. 2 (1975): 60–73.

van Erven, Eugène. "Beyond the Shadows of Wayang: Liberation Theatre in Indonesia." *New Theatre Quarterly* 5, No. 17 (February 1989): 36–52.

——. "Encounter in Yogya." *Minnesota Review* 32 (Spring 1989): 18–27.

——. "Workshop auf dem Dorf." *IKA* 38 (January 1990): 5–9.

"Indonesia's Iconoclastic Elite." *Asiaweek* 6, No. 42 (24 October 1980): 44–45.

"Indonesia Today," *Times on Sunday* (Australia): 7–10.

Foley, Kathy. "Drama for Development: Sundanese Wayang Golek Purwa: An Indonesian Case Study." *East-West Culture Learning Institute Report* 6, No. 1 (1979): 1–6.

——. "My Bodies: The Performer in West Java." *The Drama Review* 34, No. 2 (Summer 1990): 62–80.

Hatley, Barbara. "Ludruk and Wayang: Polarities in Java." *The Drama Review* 15, No. 3 (1971): 88–101.

——. "Ludruk and Kethoprak: Popular Theatre and Society in Java." *Review of Indonesian and Malaysian Affairs* 7, No. 1 (1973): 38–58.

Jenkins, Ron. "Topeng: Balinese Dance Drama." *Performing Arts Journal* 3, No. 2 (1978): 39–52.

——. "The Holy Humour of Bali's Clowns." *Asia* 3, No. 2 (1980): 28–35.

Kaye, Lincoln. "The Early Dawning of a Jakarta Spring." *Far Eastern Economic Review* (23 January 1986): 41–43.

Long, Roger. *Javanese Shadow Theatre: Movement and Characterization in Ngayogyakarta Wayang Kulit.* Ann Arbor, Mich.: UMI Research Press, 1982.

Mubyarto, ed. *Growth and Equity in Indonesian Agricultural Development.* Jakarta: Yayasan Agro Ekonomika. 1983.

Muncie, P. C. *Doctors and Dukuns, Puppets and Pills: A Look at Indonesia's Family Planning Program.* Washington, D.C.: World Bank, 1972.

Mylius, N. "Die Funktion des javanischen Wayang in der Gegenwart." *Anthropos* 57 (1962): 591–603.

——. "Wayang Suluh und Wayang Wahju." *Archiv für Völkerkunde* 16 (1961): 94–104.

Nadjib, Emha Ainun. *Isra Mira Yang Asyik.* Yogyakarta: Kerja Sama Delegasi-Dinasti, 1986.
Peacock, J. L. *Rites of Modernization: Symbolic and Social Aspects of Indonesian Proletarian Drama.* Chicago: University of Chicago Press, 1976.
Polomka, P. *Indonesia since Sukarno.* Harmondsworth: Penguin Books, 1971.
Rass, J. J. "The Historical Development of the Javanese Shadow Theatre." *Review of Indonesian and Malay Affairs* 10, No. 2 (1976): 50–76.
Revel-MacDonald, Nicole, "Dayak and Kalimantan Masks." *The Drama Review* 26, No. 4 (Winter 1982): 70–72.
Schechner, Richard. "Wayang Kulit in the Colonial Margin." *The Drama Review* 34, No. 2 (Summer 1990): 25–61.
Scott, Peter Dale. "Exporting Military-Economic Development." In Malcolm Caldwell, ed. *Ten Years' Military Terror in Indonesia.* Nottingham: Spokesman Books, 1975.
Sears, Laurie Lobell. "Aesthetic Displacement in Javanese Shadow Theatre: Three Contemporary Performing Styles." *The Drama Review* 33, No. 3 (Fall, 1989): 113–121.
Sievers, A. M. *The Mystical World of Indonesia: Culture and Economic Development in Conflict.* Baltimore: The Johns Hopkins University Press, 1974.
Southwood, Julie, and Patrick Flanagan. *Indonesia: Law, Propaganda, and Terror.* Boston: ZED, 1983.
Suryadi, Linus. "Beyond Borobudur." Paper presented at the second Southeast Asian Writers Conference, Toya Bungkah, Bali, Indonesia (15–23 September 1985).
Vanickova, E. *The Indonesian Theatre in the Changes of the Nationalist Movement.* Prague: Oriental Institute, 1967.
Wertheim, W. R. "Whose Plot? New Light on the 1965 Events," *Journal of Contemporary Asia* 9, No. 2 (1979).
Yatim, Debra H. "A Batavian Interpretation of Bertolt Brecht." *The Jakarta Post* (5 August 1985).
Zarrilli, Phillip. "Structure and Subjunctivity: Putu Wijaya's Theatre of Surprise." *The Drama Review* 31, No. 3 (Fall 1987): 126–159.
de Zoete, Beryl, and Walter Spies. *Dance and Drama in Bali.* London: Faber and Faber, 1938.
Zurbuchen, Mary. "The *Cockroach Opera:* Image of Culture and National Development in Indonesia." *Tenggara* 23 (1989): 125–150.

Malaysia

Gunawardana, A. J. "Theatre in Malaysia: An Interview with Mustapha Kamil Yassin." *The Drama Review* 15 No. 3. (1971): 48–62.
Jit, Krishen. "Towards an Islamic Theatre for Malaysia: Noordin Hassan and *Don't Kill the Butterflies." Asian Theatre Journal* 1, No. 2 (Fall 1984): 127–147.
———. "Contemporary Malaysian Theatre." *Tenggara* 23 (1989): 179–187.
Manaff, Abdullah. "Modern Malaysian Theatre." *Asian and Pacific Quarterly of Cultural and Social Affairs* 6, No. 4 (1975): 64–67.

Pakistan

Azhar, Aslam. *The Arts in Pakistani Society.* Berlin: O.P.P., 1987.
Choldin, H. M. "Pakistan: Shopkeeper Sales and Local Entertainment." *Studies in Family Planning* 13 (1966): 8–9.
Joyo, Mohammed Ibrahim. *Pakistan: What Becomes of It?* Hyderabad, Sindh: Sindh Friends' Circle, 1987.
Salim, Ahmed. *Amrita Sher-Gil: A Personal View.* Karachi: Ista'arah Publications, 1987.

Sarwar, Beena. "Chadar Aur Chardewari." *The Star* (10 March 1988): 4.
Syed, Najm Hosain. *Recurrent Patterns in Punjabi Poetry*. Lahore: Punjab Adbi Markaz, 1986.
Von Euler, Roland. *The Mass Communication Experiment in Pakistan*. Lahore: Swedish-Pakistan Family Welfare Project, 1970.
Zaman, Hameed, "Karachi Causerie." *Pakistan Quarterly* 13, No. 1 (1965): 70–79.

Philippines

Amnesty International. *Philippines: Unlawful Killings by Military and Paramilitary Forces*. London: Amnesty International Publications, 1988.
Ang, Gertrude R. "Three Cebuano Playwrights: Case Studies in Emergent Nationalism." *Philippine Quarterly of Culture and Society* 1, No. 2 (1973): 80–85.
Bain, D. H. *Sitting in Darkness: Americans in the Philippines*. Boston, 1984.
Balasoto, Lorenzo T., et al. *Manual on Development Theater*. Manila: U.P. Institute of Mass Communication, 1979.
Barrios, Joy. "There's a Theatre in the Streets." M. A. Thesis. Diliman, Quezon City: University of Philippines, 1985.
Buenviaje, Homero. "Interview: José Ma Sisson." *Midweek* III, No. 12 (27 January 1988): 3–6; 35–36.
Carpio, Rustica C. "The Plight of the Philippine Theatre." *Solidarity* 2 (1967): 9–14.
Constantino, Letizia. R. "Low Intensity Conflict." *Education Forum TAP* VII, Nos. 120–121 (September 1987).
Constantino, Renato. *The Philippines: A Past Revisited*. Manila: Tala, 1975.
———. *Insight and Foresight*. Quezon City: Foundation for Nationalist Studies, 1977.
———. *The Philippines: The Continuing Past*. Quezon City: Foundation for Nationalist Studies, 1978.
———. *Synthetic Culture and Development*. Quezon City: Foundation for Nationalist Studies, 1985.
———. *The Aquino Watch*. Quezon City: Karrel, Inc., 1987.
———. *The National Alternative*. Quezon City: Foundation for Nationalist Studies, 1987.
———. "Civil Liberties and the Aquino Rhetoric." *Midweek* III, No. 12 (27 January 1988): 19–22.
Cruz, Isagani R. *A Short History of Theatre in the Philippines*. Manila: De La Salle University Press, 1971.
de la Cruz, Enrique, et al. *Death Squads in the Philippines*. Davao City: Alliance for Philippine Concerns, 1987.
van Erven, Eugène. "Theatre of Liberation in Action: The People's Theatre Network of the Philippines." *New Theatre Quarterly* III, No. 10 (May 1987): 131–149.
———. "Philippine Political Theatre and the Fall of Ferdinand Marcos." *The Drama Review* 31, No. 2 (Summer 1987): 57–78.
———. "BUGKOS: The Boldest Step." *Makiisa* 2 (April 1988): 9–11.
———. "Stages of People Power: The Philippines Educational Theater Association." *CESO Verhandelingen No. 43* (1989).
———. "PETA coördineert theater training bji onderwijs aan volwassenen: een case study." In Kees Epskamp and Rogier van 't Rood, eds. *Populaire Cultuur op de Planken: Theater en Communicatie in de Derde Wereld*. The Hague: CESO, 1989.
Evans, D. "Training Popular Theatre Workers in the Philippines." *Convergence* 18, Nos. 3–4. (1985): 140–142.
Fajardo, Brenda. "The Philippines Educational Theatre Association." *Sonolux Information* 6 (September 1982): 6–10.
———. "On the Quest for a New Pedagogy." *Sonolux Information* 6 (September), p. 25.

————. "The Aesthetics of Poverty: A Rationale in Designing for Philippine Theater." PETA *Theater Studies* No. 5 (1984).

————, and Socrates Topacio. *BITAW*. Quezon City: PETA, 1989.

Fajardo, Mary Joan, and Ernie Cloma. *Children's Theater Teacher's Manual*. Quezon City: PETA, 1984.

Fernandez, Doreen G. *The Iloilo Zarzuela*. Quezon City: Ateneo de Manila University Press, 1978.

Gaspar, Karl. "Passion Play, Philippines, 1984." *New Theatre Quarterly* II, No. 5 (February 1986): 12–16.

————, Jehovenh Honculado, Wilfredo Rodriguez, Victorino Carillo, Jackie Schramm, and Fe Remotigue. *Creative Dramatics: Trainers Manual*. Hong Kong: Plough Publications, 1981.

Grossman, Zoltan. "Inside the Philippine Resistance." *Race and Class* XXVIII, No. 2 (1986): 1–29.

Guidote, Cecilia Reyes. "A Prospectus for the National Theatre of the Philippines." M. A. Thesis. Dallas, Tex.: Trinity University, 1967.

Guillermo, Alice. "U.S. Intervention in Philippine Culture." *Mandala* 1, No. 3 (1987): 1–6.

Guillermo, Gelacio. "Cultural Work and Mass Movement in the Philippines." *Mandala* 1, No. 2 (1987): 78.

Hernandez, Thomas C. "The Emergence of Modern Drama in the Philippines (1898–1912) and Its Social, Political, Cultural, Dramatic and Theatrical Background." Ph.D. Dissertation, Honolulu: University of Hawaii, 1975.

Jacob, Malou L. *Juan Tamban*. Quezon City: PETA Publications, 1984.

Joaquin, Nick. "Popcorn and Gaslight." *Philippine Quarterly* (September 1953).

KAFI Editorial Committee. *Community Theater: The Mindanao Experience*. Davao: Kulturang Atin Foundation Inc., 1983.

Labad, Lutgardo, et al. "An Invitation to Growth" and "Towards a Curriculum for People's Theater." PETA *Theater Studies* No. 3 (1983).

Lapena-Bonifacio, A. *The "Seditious" Tagalog Playwrights: Early American Occupation*. Manila: Zarzuela Foundation of the Philippines, 1972.

Leon, Voltaire de. "Interview with Lino Brocka." *Fuse*. (May–June 1986): 34–37.

Liu, Melinda. "With the Rebels." *Newsweek* (4 April 1988): 10–16.

Lowe, Kathy. "Setting the Stage for Social Change." In: *Operating Eyes and Ears*. Geneva: World Council of Churches, 1983.

Maglipon, Jo-Ann. *A Smouldering Land*. Quezon City: National Council of Churches, 1987.

Manuud, A. G., ed. *Brown Heritage: Essays on Philippine Cultural Traditions and Literature*. Quezon City: Ateneo de Manila University, 1967.

Millado, Chris. *Panata Sa Kalayaan*. Unpublished revised playscript.

Montana, Jason. *Clearing: Poems of People's Struggle in Northern Luzon*. Manila: ARMAS, CNL, NDF, 1987.

Morante, Melchior. "Theatre of the Small People: Experiments in Community Theatre in the Philippines." *Asian Action* 7 (1977): 42–43.

Neumann, Lin. "The Art of Being Artists under Marcos' Martial Law." *One World* (October 1979): 14–15.

Pimentel, Jr., Benjamin. "Lorie by Laulhati, Dessa and Malou." *Midweek* 5 April, 1989: 28–29.

Rikken, Remmy. "The Community as an Art Form." *International Foundation for Development Alternatives Dossier* 16 (1980): 127–129.

Robinson, Cedric J. "The American Press and the Repairing of the Philippines." *Race and Class* XXVIII, No. 2 (1986): 31–44.

Russell, George. "A Test for Democracy." *Time* (3 February 1986): 4–11.

Sison, José-Maria. *Philippine Crisis and Revolution*. Quezon City: University Of the Philippines Asian Center, 1986.

Smith, Alex. "PETA: Theatre of Conscience; an Interview with Gardy Labad." *Theatre Work* 3, No. 3 (1983): 55–59.

Sträter, Bas. "Brieven over theaterwerk op de Filippijnen." *Speltribune* 5 (September–October 1988): 18–20.

Tiongson, Nicanor. *Kasaysayan at Estetika ng Sinakulo at Ibang Dulang Panrelihiyon sa Malolos*. Quezon City: Ateneo de Manila University Press, 1979.

———. *Kasaysayan ng Komedya sa Pilipinas*. Manila: De la Salle University Press, 1981.

———. "What Is Philippine Drama?" *PETA Theatre Studies* No. 1 (1984).

———, ed. *The Politics of Culture: The Philippine Experience*. Manila: PETA Publications, 1984.

———. *Pilipinas Circa 1907*. Quezon City: PETA Publications, 1985.

de la Torre, Edicio. *Touching Ground, Taking Root: Theological and Political Reflections on the Philippine Struggle*. Manila: Socio-Pastoral Institute, 1986.

Singapore

Clammer, John. *Singapore: Ideology, Society, Culture*. Singapore: Chopmen Publishers, 1985.

Fernandez, George, comp. *Poets of Singapore*. Singapore: Society of Singapore Writers, 1983.

Jit, Krishen. "Modern Theatre in Singapore—A Preliminary Study," *Tenggara* 23 (1989): 210–226.

South Korea

Cho, Oh-kon, *Korean Puppet Theatre: Koktu Kasi*. East Lansing: Michigan State University Asian Studies Center, 1979.

———. "Yangyu Pyolsandae: A Theatre of Traditional Korean Mask-Dance Drama." *Korea Journal* 21, No. 4 (1981): 27–34.

van Erven, Eugène. "Resistance Theatre in South Korea: Above and Underground." *The Drama Review* 32, No. 3 (Fall 1988): 156–173.

"Eyewitness." *Asiaweek* (2 November 1986): 33–49.

Han, Sang-chul, et al. *The Korean Theatre, 1977–1979*. Seoul: Korean Center of the ITI, 1979.

He Sok-yang. *The Korean Theatre '84*. Seoul: Korean Center of the ITI, 1984.

Khaznadar, Chérif. "Korea's Masked Dances." *The Drama Review* 26, No. 4 (Winter 1982): 64–65.

Kim, Chi-ha. *Cry of the People and Other Poems*. Hayama, Kanagawa-ken, Japan: Autumn Press, 1974.

Kim, Moon-hwan. "Folk Drama and its Tradition." *Korea Journal* 10, No. 5 (1970): 37–41.

Korean National Commission for UNESCO. *Korean Dance, Theater, and Cinema*. Seoul: Si-sa-yong-o-sa Publishers, 1983.

———. *Wedding Day and Other Korean Plays*. Seoul: Si-sa-yong-o-sa Publishers, 1983.

Lee Tae-ju, et al. *The Korean Theatre in 1983*. Seoul: Korean Center of the ITI, 1983.

———. *The Korean Theatre in '85*. Seoul: Korean Center of the ITI

Lim, Chung-Hi, and Andreas Jung, eds. *Malttugi*. Heidelberg: Koreagruppe der ESG, 1986.

Qdong, Zeong, *The Korean Theatre, 1973–1975*. Seoul: Korean Center of the ITI, 1975.

———. *The Korean Theatre, 1975–1977*. Seoul: Korean Center of the ITI, 1977.

Yoo, Min-jung. *Theater Areas in Asia: With Emphasis on the Korean Theater*. Seoul: Korean Society for Theater Research, 1977.

Sri Lanka

Da Silva, M. A., and R. Siriwardena. *Communication Policies in Sri Lanka*. Paris: UNESCO, 1977.
Devananda, Yohan, "Theatre and Conscientization in Sri Lanka." *Asian Action* 7 (1977): 45–47.
Goonatilleka, M. H. *The Rural Theatre and Social Satire of Sri Lanka*. Colombo: Ceylon Tourist Board, 1976.
Gunawardana, A. J. *Theatre in Sri Lanka*. Colombo: Department of Cultural Affairs, 1976.
Sarachchandra, E. R. *The Folk Drama of Ceylon*. Colombo: Department of Cultural Affairs, 1966.

Thailand

Anderson, Benjamin, and Ruchira Mendones. *In the Mirror: Literature and Politics in Thailand during the American Era*. Bangkok: Duang Kamol, 1985.
Conquergood, Dwight, "Health Theatre in Hmong Refugee Camp: Performance, Communication, and Culture." *The Drama Review* 32, No. 3 (Fall 1988): 174–208.
Continuing Education Center, Chulalongkorn University. *A Survey of Thai Arts and Architectural Attractions*. Bangkok: Chulalongkorn University, 1987.
Früh, Paul. "Le droit international humanitaire porté à la scène." *Diffusion* 5 (August 1986): 10–11.
———. "Humanity Amidst the Horrors of War." *National Geographic* (November 1986): 665–666.
Miller, T. E., and J. Chonpairot. "Shadow Puppet Theatre in Northeast Thailand," *Theatre Journal* 31 (1979): 293–311.
Nagavajara, Chetana. "A Persistence of Music Drama: Reflections on Modern Thai Theatre." *Tenggara* 23 (1989): 106–115.
Nopakun, Oonta. *Thai Concept of Khit-Pen for Adult and Non-Formal Education*. Bangkok: Asian and South Pacific Bureau of Adult Education, 1985.
Phongphit, Seri, ed. *Back to the Roots: Village and Self-Reliance in a Thai Context*. Bangkok: Rural Development Documentation Centre, 1986.
Smithies, Michael. "Likay: A Note on the Origin, Form and Future of Siamese Folk Opera." *Journal of the Siam Society* 59, No. 1 (1971): 33–63.
Vella, Walther F. *Chaiyo! King Vajiravudh and the Development of Thai Nationalism*. Honolulu: University Press of Hawaii, 1983.
Wibha, Senanan. *The Genesis of the Novel in Thailand*. Bangkok: Thai Watana Panich, 1975.

Vietnam

Karl, Terry, et al. *Children of the Dragon: A Story of the People of Vietnam*. San Francisco: People's Press, 1974.
Khôi, Lê Thành. "Literacy Training and Revolution: The Vietnamese Experience." In *A Turning Point for Literacy*. Oxford: Pergamon Press, 1976.
Song-Ban. *The Vietnamese Theatre*. Hanoi: Foreign Languages Publishing House, 1960.
Van, Tran Dinh. "Artistic and Literary Life in the Liberated Zones of South Vietnam." *Vietnamese Studies* (Hanoi) 14 (1967): 11–23.
"Vietnam." *The Drama Review* 13, No. 4 (1969): 146–153.

Weiss, Peter. *Notes on the Cultural Life of the Democratic Republic of Vietnam.* London: Calder and Boyars, 1971.

This bibliography is far from complete. Many additional articles pertaining to Asian politics and culture can be found in *Theater Work* (Minnesota, U.S.A.), *Asian Theater Journal* (University of Hawaii) *Frauensolidarität* (Berlin, Germany), *The Diliman Review* (University of the Philippines), *Mandala* (ACFOD, Philippines), *Makiisa* (PETA, Philippines), *Gi-Os* (Negros, Philippines), *Kalasikas* (Mindanao, Philippines), *Balangay* (Mindanao, Philippines), *Bangkaw* (Mindanao, Philippines), *Minda Now* (Mindanao, Philippines), *Sulog* (Mindanao, Philippines), *Tenggara* (Universiti Kebangsan Malaysia), *Citra Yogya* (Yogykarta, Indonesia), *India Nieuwsbrief* (Netherlands), *Onze Wereld* (Netherlands), *New Theatre Australia* (Sydney, Australia), *Australasian Drama Studies* (Brisbane, Australia), *The Rural Poor* (Madras, India), *Sangeet Natak* (Delhi, India), *Journal of Arts and Idea* (India), *Sahmat* (New Delhi, India), *Korea Report* (Washington, D.C., U.S.A.), *Korea Newsletter* (Tokyo, Japan), *BTT Newsletter* (Tokyo, Japan), *Concerned Theatre Japan* (Tokyo, Japan), *Voices of Women* (Sri Lanka).

INDEX

Abadesco, Father Alan, 76, 77
Aboriginals, 234
Absurdism, 115, 159, 208
Adapa, Shashidara, xvi, 117, 124–25, 126, 157
Adult education, 13, 14, 104–5, 123, 133, 151, 182, 239
Advertising, 2, 3, 99, 101, 132, 212
Aesthetics, 37–38, 57, 83, 230
—of poverty, 92, 93, 94, 104, 115, 117, 137, 138, 142, 170, 172, 201, 229, 233, 235, 238, 239, 240
Afghanistan, 153, 158
Africa, xii, 2, 14, 19, 245n32
Agit-prop, 29, 53–55, 59, 66, 95, 98, 151, 154, 155, 203, 230, 246n23
Agusan-Surigao (Philippines), 84, 85, 86, 91, 94
Ahmad, Khalid, 183
Ahmed, Ali, 159
Ajoka, x, 157, 158, 159, 164–70, 171, 172, 175, 176, 179, 181; The Dead Dog, x, 161, 166–69; The Acquittal, x, 166, 176–81, 252n22
Alarippu, 120
Alcohol abuse: as dramatic theme, 135, 136, 166–67, 168, 234, 239
Alderete, Peter, 78
Alit Aryani, Gusti Putu, 206
Allegory, 36, 45, 122, 147, 166, 170, 174, 200, 215–16, 218. See also Metaphor
Alorro, Bubu, 67
Alviola, Hanzel, 69, 70
Amnesty International, 166, 176
Andra Pradesh (India), 124, 134, 137, 229
Anouilh, Jean: Antigone, 182, 192
Aotearoa (New Zealand), ix, xv, 16, 22, 234, 236, 239, 256n13
Apartheid, xii, 170, 235, 255n9
Aquino, Benigno ("Ninoy"), 44, 46, 54, 56, 93
Aquino, Corazon (widow of Benigno), 29, 45, 48, 50, 51, 53, 55, 56, 57, 68, 73, 79, 243n2, 245n1
Aranyak, 232
Arban, Yolando, xvi, 86
Arbolario, Joel, xvi, 76, 77, 79, 231
Arellano, Glecy, 59
Arena, Teatro (Sao Paulo, Brazil), 15
Arena, Teater (Yogyakarta, Indonesia), x, 185, 186–94; Tumbal, 193–94
Arirang, Theatre, 107, 112–13
Aristotle, 15

Artists: as liberation activists, 8, 52, 97, 104, 228, 230, 239, 240; as dramatic characters, 47, 51, 200
Art: multidisciplinary, 65, 66, 70, 79, 83, 90, 92, 105, 124, 160, 171, 175, 228, 230
Artist-Teacher-Organizer-Researcher (ATOR), 33, 63, 74, 82, 83, 92, 138, 204, 220, 228, 229, 230, 238; defined, 21; in action, 22–28, 69–72, 77, 188, 230, 234; criticized, 63, 220–21, 230–31, 235. See also Cultural worker
Asian Council for People's Culture (ACPC), 235, 256n11
Asian Theatre Forum, 220, 256n11
ASPECT, 85, 87
Association of the Rural Poor (ARP), ix, xvi, 133–35, 136, 138
Audience: response of, 15–16, 20, 57, 102, 110, 111, 118, 119, 131, 141, 145–46, 148, 150, 164, 165, 166, 172, 189, 203, 212, 226, 227, 233, 239
—participation, 15–16, 59, 73, 98, 99, 100, 101, 110, 150, 168, 194, 217, 223, 225–26. See also Farm workers; Fishermen; Middle class; Upper class; Workers; Women; Children; Youth
Australia, xvi, 22, 234, 239, 240
Authoritarian, 12, 16, 19, 28, 51, 97, 103, 112, 120, 165, 167, 171, 182, 193, 194, 196, 199, 203, 229, 233, 234, 235. See also Fascism; Dictatorship
Ayala, Joey, 53, 91; Nukleyar, 53–55
Azhar, Aslam, xvi, 162–63, 164, 165

Bacolod City (Philippines), 76, 77, 94, 240
Balboa, Father Eli, xvi, 90–1
Balt, Samo, xvi, 90
Banaag, 65–66
Bangalore (India), xvi, 119, 120–21, 122, 125, 140, 240
Bangkok (Thailand), x, 4, 207–18, 220, 222–27
Bangladesh, 12, 22, 115, 116, 158, 232, 234
Baratacharya, Busaba, xvi, 216, 218, 220, 223
Barba, Eugenio, xii, xiii, 239, 242n1
Barrios, Joy, 245n36, 246n23
Bartholomew, Rati, 117
Basic Christian Communities (BCC): defined, 12; and theatre of liberation, 13, 15, 80, 82, 86, 244n16; in Philippines, 80, 82, 86, 244n16; in Indonesia, 187
Bayan Party, 29, 50, 51, 53, 74, 245n1

273

EUGENE VAN ERVEN is Lecturer in the American Studies program at the University of Utrecht and author of *Radical People's Theatre*.